KAREN NEUBURGER®

Comfortable living
begins with good food,
friends and family.

We hope you enjoy this
special edition cookbook and
many memorable occasions.

The KN Karen Neuburger® brand
invites you to celebrate
the real joys of life
with comfort-inspired apparel
and everyday essentials
for family and home.

www.karenneuburger.com

THE SILVER PALATE COOKBOOK

25 years
ANNIVERSARY EDITION
FULL COLOR

JULEE ROSSO & SHEILA LUKINS

WITH MICHAEL McLAUGHLIN

PHOTOGRAPHS BY PATRICK TREGENZA AND SUSAN GOLDMAN

ILLUSTRATIONS BY SHEILA LUKINS

WORKMAN PUBLISHING | NEW YORK

Library of Congress Cataloging-in-Publication Data is available.
ISBN-13: 978-0-7611-5238-5
(KN Edition)

Cover design by Paul Hanson with Patrick Borelli
Front cover photograph by Arnold Katz
Author photograph by Gwendolen Cates
Cover food photograph by Patrick Tregenza
Book design by Paul Hanson and Lisa Hollander with David Riedy

Workman books are available at special discounts when purchased in bulk for premiums and sales promotions as well as for fund-raising or educational use. Special editions or book excerpts also can be created to specification. For details, contact the Special Sales Director at the address below.

Workman Publishing Company, Inc.
225 Varick Street
New York, NY 10014-4381
www.workman.com

Manufactured in the United States of America
First printing March 2007
10 9 8 7 6 5 4 3 2 1

CONTENTS

THE STORY OF THE SILVER PALATE

"There are three types of creatures that seem to be coming when they are going and going when they are coming—diplomats, crabs, and women."

—JOHN M. HAY, SECRETARY OF STATE, 1898–1905

In truth, crabs go sideways, they sort of zigzag their way along. No doubt that's how we must have looked in 1982 when this cookbook was first published. We were immersed in our little gourmet takeout shop on Columbus Avenue in New York City. One minute cooking, the next catering. Our friends thought we were crazy: If we gave away our secret recipes, we'd be out of business. But little did any of us know the joy that writing a cookbook would bring to our lives. Now here we are twenty-five years later, celebrating with a brand new edition that highlights our recipes with beautiful color photographs. They add an exciting new dimension to a cookbook that has been beloved for two and a half decades.

Looking back, it doesn't seem so long ago that we opened our shop. It was the summer of 1977: Jimmy Carter was in the White House, there were endless lines for *Star Wars*, Elvis had left the building, and we were all dancing to the Bee Gees at a "Saturday Night Fever" pitch. Julee, "a gal from Kalamazoo," was working at her dream job in the fashion industry, doing marketing, publicity, and advertising. Along the way, she taught herself how to cook by cooking, from start to finish, through Julia Child's *The French Chef.* Sheila, married and the mother of two very young daughters, Annabel and Molly, had long enjoyed cooking and entertaining. Sheila had graduated from Le Cordon Bleu school in London, and had become increasingly intrigued by food during the family's time living in Paris. Back in New York, she created The Other Woman Catering Company, with the motto "so discreet, so delicious, and I deliver." Her business was directed primarily toward bachelors, who struggled to entertain without a "little woman" in the kitchen. One of those bachelors was Julee's on again, off again beau, who needed a cook when Julee was "off again." So we finally met: Julee, the advertising director, needed Sheila, the caterer, to help host a press breakfast for a major fashion designer. The press arrived at the designer's lavish apartment (resplendent with nine-foot-tall suits of armor) and waxed ecstatic as we served them fresh figs wrapped with prosciutto, Baked Ham with Apricots, warm croissants, cappuccino, and jewel-like bowls of lemon, blackberry, and raspberry mousses. The designer was lauded, but it was the food that got the real raves. That morning, a fantasy food partnership was born.

At the time, we confided to each other that we both felt overwhelmed trying to juggle work, family, and the various hobbies, interests, and obligations that occupied our time. It was all too much. And we each admitted, with some dismay, that with so much going on, our shared passions of cooking and entertaining seemed to be getting the short end of the deal. It occurred to us that if we "good cooks" needed help . . . well, we just couldn't be alone.

That's when Julee had the idea for a food shop where people could pick up great food on a whim, for one or for many, to take home and graciously serve as their own. The concept was simple: a tiny gem of a shop featuring the best of our home cooking repertoire—no pretense, just good, simple food with the bold flavors we both loved. We'd make it easy for working people to have a picnic in the park, take a break from restaurants, or serendipitously invite friends home for a bite.

We were excited about the idea and set the wheels in motion, but had difficulty describing it as simply as we had envisioned it. About a month before opening, Florence Fabricant, writing an article for *New York* magazine on the renaissance of Columbus Avenue, made it easy. She tasted our food and said, instantly, "Call it the Silver Palate." Perfect. When we said, "Print it, we'll go national," we had no idea where we were headed.

When we finally opened our doors at 4:00 P.M., on July 15, 1977, the block had already been abuzz. It was two days after the infamous New York City blackout, and despite the insistent 103°F heat, by 4:15 we were jammed. We had stocked the store to the brim and our food looked glorious. Little did we know that the Philharmonic was playing in Central Park that evening—customers flooded the shop wanting picnics, picnics, and more picnics. Our air conditioner promptly broke. Then we realized our little antique French scale and longhand computing weren't going to cut it when someone wanted a medium-size container of Tarragon Chicken Salad, which was priced by the pound. Yikes! We sold out long before closing, and collapsed, having learned some lessons that we'd apply the next day, and the day after that.

We cooked as we did at home, with fresh, seasonal ingredients, no shortcuts ever. Every day our menu included great breads and cheeses, and an array of foods that were cooked in Sheila's kitchen and carried down the street to the store: Salmon Mousse, Cheese Straws, Saucisson en Croûte, Pâté Maison, Chicken Marbella, Ratatouille, Torta Rustica, Moussaka, Nutted Wild Rice, Blanquette de Veau, Lemon Squares, Giant Chocolate Chip Cookies, Blackberry Mousse, and on and on. Sheila's mother made carrot cake in Connecticut and drove it down to the shop. Julee made gravlax at home in the early morning hours, then picked up warm fresh croissants and cheeses in a taxi before heading across the park. We were never short of ideas.

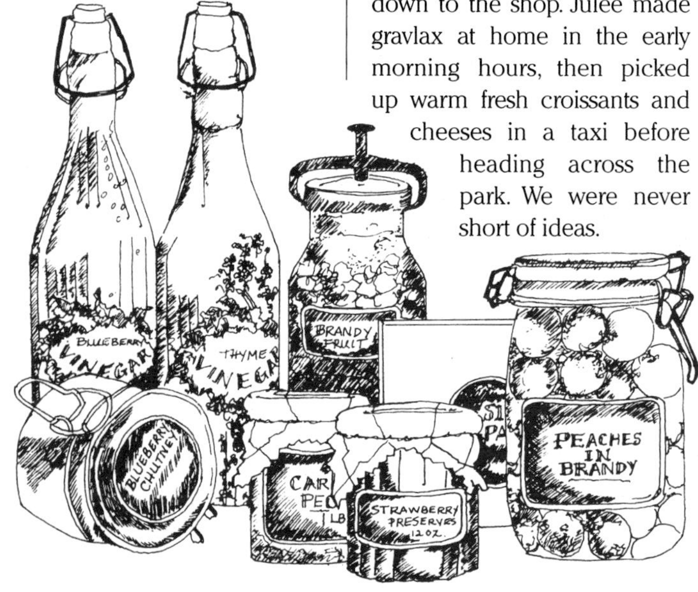

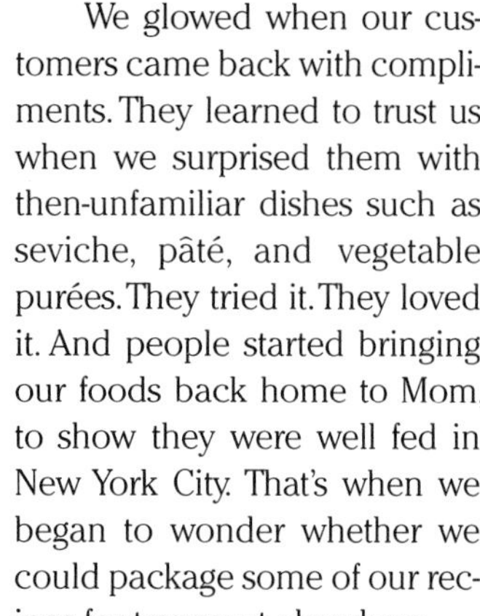

We glowed when our customers came back with compliments. They learned to trust us when we surprised them with then-unfamiliar dishes such as seviche, pâté, and vegetable purées. They tried it. They loved it. And people started bringing our foods back home to Mom, to show they were well fed in New York City. That's when we began to wonder whether we could package some of our recipes for transport elsewhere.

The summer of 1978 found us up to our elbows in our "Canning Kitchen." We wanted to present our wonderful food in beautiful jars and bottles. So

during yet another heat wave we found ourselves making Vegetable Mosaic, Damson Plums in Brandy, Blueberry Vinegar, Winter Fruit Compote, Fudge Sauce, Lady Apples in Wine, and Sweet and Rough Mustard. We tied bows on bottles, put fabric atop jars, and doilies everywhere. We had more tenacity than shelves. Within days both the president of Saks Fifth Avenue and the founder of Crate and Barrel appeared in our shop, asking to sell our products in their stores that Christmas. We were over the moon—and quickly back in the Canning Kitchen. We wanted both stores to sell out at Christmas, so we convinced them to let us hold tastings—we knew no better way to sell Blueberry Chutney than to let people sample it for themselves. It worked. One taste of our Caramel Pecan Sauce (made with real butter, sugar, cream, and toasted pecan halves) and people

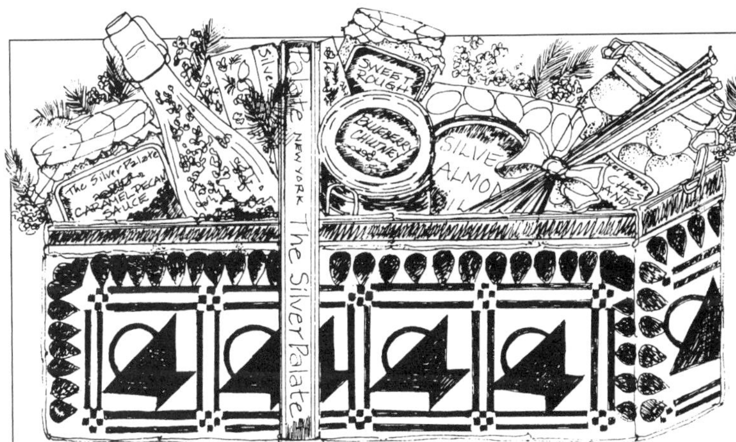

swooned. It was a very good Christmas! We were on our way. Soon the Williams Sonoma catalog found us, Pat Wells of *The New York Times* wrote a story, and *New York* magazine's Gael Greene described our Blueberry Vinegar as "blueberries sailing like stars in a midnight sky in vinegar more precious than vintage wine." What fun! Imagine our delight when we saw our products on shelves in stores across the country, and then overseas.

As awareness of our business grew, awards arrived. We were invited to speak on entrepreneurship at business schools and food and wine symposiums. We cooked on *Today* and *Good Morning America,* and at Mondavi's Great Chefs Cooking School. Mike Wallace even interviewed us for a *60 Minutes* segment. It was all beyond our wildest fantasies—we were having a ball.

Then, in the spring of 1981, an editor from Workman Publishing suggested we write a book. "Send me the outline," she said. Book?! Outline?! Who knew? We figured she'd forget. She didn't. Three weeks later found us at Sheila's with a bottle of Scotch and a legal pad. We outlined the kind of cookbook we envisioned—Sheila would illustrate it, Julee would write it, and we would use the recipes from our shop. It would be the cookbook of our dreams.

A modest number of copies were published for Mother's Day 1982 and we celebrated with a book party at Saks. Later that summer, the mother of one of our colleagues called from Lake Tahoe, California, to say that food from our cookbook was being served at every dinner party she attended. Soon we saw our cookbook published in French, Japanese, and Dutch, and we were making friends around the world. We were included in the James Beard Who's Who of American Food, and this book was inducted into the Cookbook Hall of Fame. Who would have thought that following our passion would lead to all this? We literally danced in the street on Columbus Avenue.

Though we sold our business in 1988, today we "girls" are as passionate about good food as ever. Over the past few months we've spent wonderful times reflecting on the journey we've taken together, both through our shop and this cookbook. When we first wrote this book, in many places it was difficult to find fresh herbs and excellent produce, meat, and seafood. Now, with the new emphasis on seasonal, local, artisanal, and organic foods at farmer's markets, and increasingly, at supermarkets, the culinary climate mirrors our beginnings in that tiny shop on the Upper West Side.

Barely a day goes by that we don't bump into someone or get a letter telling us of a recipe of ours they've made, or how much they've enjoyed our book. It's always such a nice surprise. When we meet someone with a food-spattered *Silver Palate* cookbook held together by a rubber band, we've found an old friend. We speak the same language, we've cooked together for years, and we've laughed together along the way.

The publication of this exciting new edition with its zillions of color photographs gives us an opportunity to make even more new cooking pals. Thank you for enjoying our book, and for making our journey so fulfilling. We hope we meet you again, or for the first time, as we come and go along our way.

—Julee Rosso,
Saugatuck, Michigan

—Sheila Lukins,
New York, New York

ACKNOWLEDGMENTS

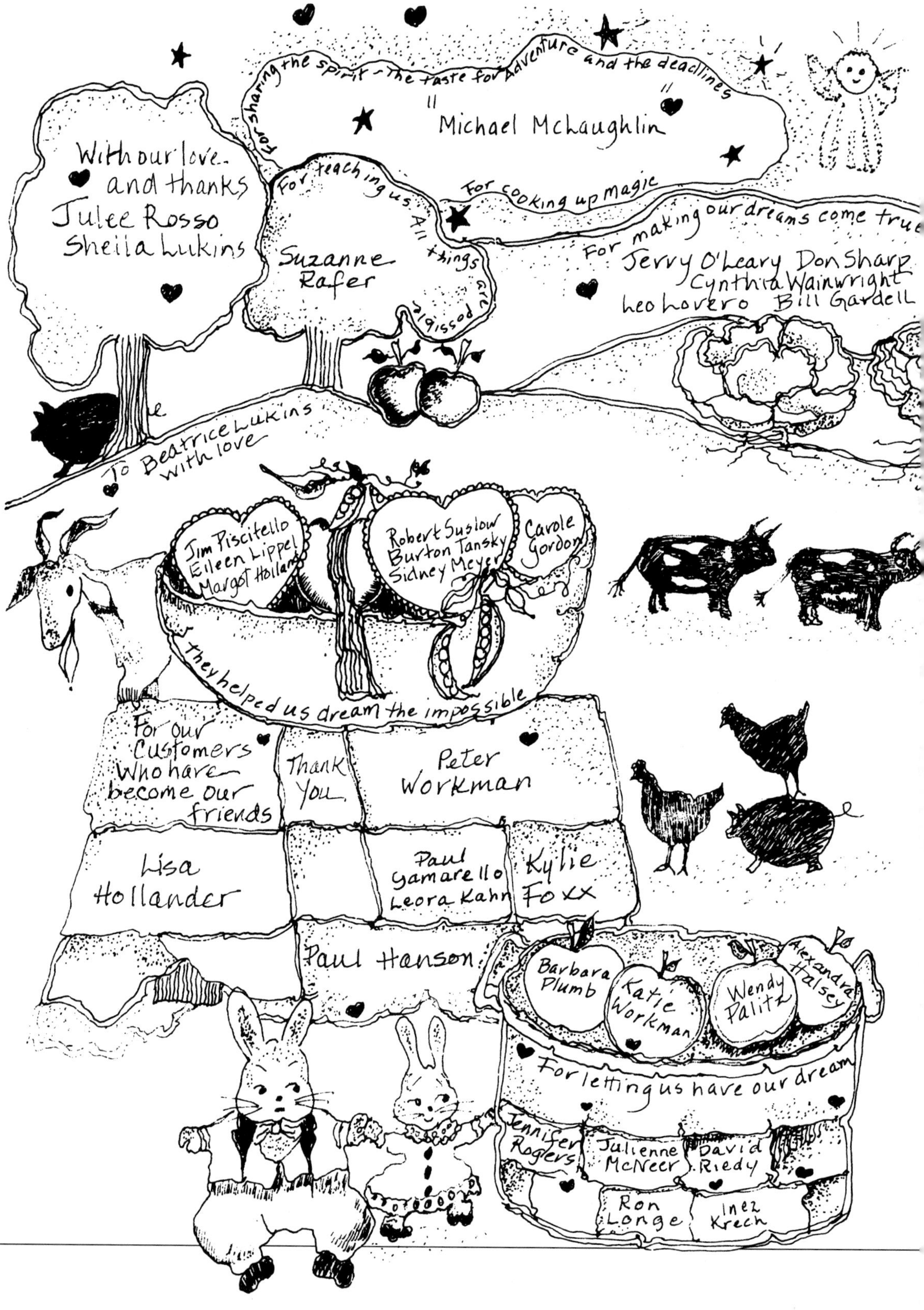

For sharing the spirit – The taste for Adventure and the deadlines
"Michael McLaughlin"

With our love and thanks
Julee Rosso
Sheila Lukins

For teaching us All things are possible
Suzanne Rafer

For cooking up magic

For making our dreams come true
Jerry O'Leary Don Sharp
Cynthia Wainwright
Leo Lovero Bill Gardell

To Beatrice Lukins with love

Jim Piscitello
Eileen Lippel
Margot Hollan

Robert Suslow
Burton Tansky
Sidney Meyer

Carole Gordon

They helped us dream the impossible

For our Customers Who have become our friends

Thank You

Peter Workman

Lisa Hollander

Paul Gamarello
Leora Kahn

Kylie Foxx

Paul Hanson

Barbara Plumb

Katie Workman

Wendy Palitz

Alexandra Halsey

For letting us have our dream

Jennifer Rogers

Julienne McNeer

David Riedy

Ron Longe

Inez Krech

For her touch—She created sweet dreams to devour
Ellen Bartlett
For helping us soar
Arthur and Joy
For Constant Love
Berta & Mike Olderman
Saul
Stanley
Mort
Gene
For having faith in us
For Always Understanding—George, John, Louie
For Knowing what we wanted before we did—Lance Brown
Thad
Susan
George
Judy
Amy
PS
Bill
Greg
Diana
Ellen
Liz
Joe
Francine
David
For Always being there—Supporting Us! No matter how difficult!
Wrighty
Greeny
Tom
Tim
Laurie
Pam
Beth
Elaine
Don
Harvey
For not forgetting the hours we laboured together no matter
Sharon
John
Megan
Claire
Judith
Deirdre
Molly and Johnny

TO BEGIN A
GREAT
EVENING

The opening of the evening is ideal for mingling your favorite interesting friends. The transition period between day and night is also a good time for mixing a tennis partner, the chairman of the board, your favorite aunt, your college roommate who just opened to rave reviews on Broadway, a princess or two, an industrial giant, the bass player in the string quartet, and your next-door neighbor. For all of them, you'll want your menu to be very special.

Herewith a collection of our favorite hors d'oeuvres. Many are "finger food," easily eaten while standing—perfect at a cocktail party. Others are more elaborate, requiring a small plate and a fork. These are the sturdier foods we serve as part of a cocktail buffet. Finally, we've also presented more elegant and involved appetizers, best suited as sit-down openers to a dinner party.

from

THE SILVER PALATE NOTEBOOK

♥ Grand and unusual flowers, soft lighting, and music—all can set the scene for a shining memory. If the mood is lovely, no one will notice the crack in the hallway mirror.

♥ The most successful hosts are those who welcome their guests by making them feel special; be sure that everyone is properly introduced.

♥ A small informal group becomes a party more quickly when there is no official bartender. A serve-yourself bar makes people comfortable and promotes friendly interaction.

♥ Arrange each hors d'oeuvre on a separate plate or tray. Your guests will be better able to identify the offering without interrupting a lively discussion.

♥ Trays should be beautifully but naturally garnished with fruits, vegetables, flowers, and bouquets of fresh herbs.

♥ Finger food should, obviously, be just that. Awkward, soggy, or drippy food has no place at a stand-up party.

♥ Beautiful glasses are like candlelight—they make the drink and the person holding it look much better. Invest in a dozen or so; it's a small price to pay for a very special effect.

♥ Schedule just enough time to relax with a quiet drink before the party begins; this will help you catch your breath. Welcome the first players to your scene with a confident smile and enjoy your own party!

FANCY FINGER FOOD

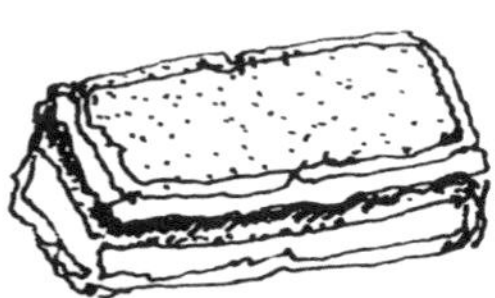

Finger food complements easy conversation during cocktail time. It is the most difficult kind of food to create: interesting and attractive but not messy. We find that a little bit of pastry wrapped around or filled with something is one solution. Others include such edible "containers" as mushrooms, figs, or grape leaves.

SESAME, HAM, AND CHEESE BITES

Accompany these tiny sandwiches with an assortment of your favorite mustards.

8 slices of boiled ham (about 7 x 5 inches, ⅛ inch thick)
4 slices of prosciutto cut in half crosswise
8 slices of Gruyère cheese (about ⅛ inch thick), to fit across ham slices
5 teaspoons corn oil
5 eggs
Freshly ground black pepper, to taste
Dash of cayenne pepper
1½ cups sesame seeds
2 cups unseasoned dry bread crumbs
½ cup chopped fresh Italian (flat-leaf) parsley
1 cup unbleached, all-purpose flour
¾ cup (1½ sticks) unsalted butter, melted

1. Lay out 8 slices of boiled ham. Cover each with a slice of prosciutto and a slice of Gruyère, and top with a second slice of boiled ham. Cut each into 6 squares.

CURED HAMS

Imported European hams enliven our menus year round, especially during cocktail time and as a first course. *Prosciutto crudo* is Italian raw cured ham that has been seasoned, cured with sea salt, and air dried for 9 to 18 months. Prosciutto should be firm but chewy, and rosy colored with a slight gloss—never greasy. It has a salty-sweet flavor, with a hint of pepper and a subtle nuttiness.

The two most famous types of prosciutto crudo are Prosciutto di Parma from Emilia-Romagna and Prosciutto di San Daniele from the Friuli-Venezia Giulia region. The pigs raised for Prosciutto di Parma consume a diet enriched by whey from Parmigiano-Reggiano cheese, which lends the ham a slightly nuttier flavor than its Friulian cousin. Prosciutto di San Daniele is prized for its delicate pink meat and velvety texture, which comes from lengthy massaging during the curing process. The finest prosciutti are aged for 16 to 18 months. They are definitely worth watching for.

Heading west a ways we encounter delicious cured hams from Spain. Authentic Spanish Serrano ham is so full-flavored that a little goes a long way. Unlike prosciutto, which is cured with its outer layer of fat intact, Serrano ham is cured with its meaty face exposed. This allows much of the ham's natural moisture to evaporate during the 12- to 15-month curing process, resulting in a more intensely flavored meat.

Jamón Iberico, Spain's legendary fatty cured pork, is also now available in the U.S. Iberico ham is made from a special breed of black-hoofed Iberian hog, and is imported as whole hams and as *lomo,* the meat of the loin. Jamón that is labeled *bellota loma* comes from Iberico hogs that are raised in specially maintained oak forests, where they roam freely and consume acorns almost exclusively. The hogs' diet and lifestyle contribute directly to the quality of the ham, which is soft, savory, nutty, and beautifully marbled.

Cured hams are best served sliced paper-thin with a ribbon of the hams' delicate white fat, which is sweet and tender. Serve it with the season's best melon, figs, peaches, or plums; atop arugula with shaved Parmigiano-Reggiano cheese and cracked black pepper; or gently draped across crostini or a creamy cheese. A crisp white wine or a light fruity red are ideal accompaniments.

2. Beat the oil, eggs, pepper, and cayenne together in a shallow bowl. In another bowl toss the sesame seeds, bread crumbs, and parsley together.

3. Preheat the oven to 400°F.

4. Dip each square first into the flour, next into the egg mixture, last into the sesame seed mixture.

5. Put the squares on a buttered baking sheet and drizzle the melted butter on top. Bake until the sandwiches are golden and the cheese is melted, 10 to 13 minutes.

6. Drain on a paper towel for 1 minute; serve immediately.

48 sandwiches

MINIATURE CHEVRE TARTS

Double recipe of Pâte Brisée (see page 408)
1½ pounds Montrachet or other soft mild chèvre cheese
4 tablespoons (½ stick) unsalted butter, at room temperature
⅓ cup whipping cream
4 eggs
Salt and freshly ground white pepper, to taste
Pinch of cayenne pepper
⅓ cup chopped well-rinsed scallions (green onions)

1. Preheat the oven to 375°F.

2. Working with one fourth of the dough at a time, roll each portion out to ⅛ inch thick and large enough to fit six 2-inch tart pans. Line the dough in the tart pans with aluminum foil and fill with uncooked rice or beans. Bake until lightly browned, 15 minutes. Cool the tart shells and remove the foil and weights. Slip the shells from the pans and cool completely. Leave the oven on.

3. Combine the Montrachet, butter, cream, and eggs in a food processor and process until completely smooth. Shut off the motor. Season the filling with salt, pepper, and cayenne; chèvre can be quite salty and peppery and may not need additional seasoning. Stir in the scallions.

4. Arrange the cooled shells on a baking sheet and spoon in the filling. Slide the sheet onto the center rack of the oven and bake until the tarts are puffed and brown, 15 to 20 minutes. Serve immediately.

Approximately twenty-four 2-inch tarts

FRESH FIGS

Ripe fresh purple figs with rosy centers and luscious fresh green figs can make perfect cocktail fare. Allow 1 fig, quartered, for each guest. For each fig, cut 2 thin slices of prosciutto lengthwise into halves. Wrap a half slice around each fig quarter so that it looks like a rose. To serve, sprinkle with fresh lime juice and freshly ground black pepper. Garnish with fresh mint sprigs.

Another of our favorites: Slice each fig lengthwise in half, 1 fig per person. Into each half, spoon 1 teaspoon of Pecan Cream Cheese (page 421). Sprinkle with finely chopped pecans.

"A good cook works by the fire of imagination not merely by the fire in the stove."

—ROBERT P. TRISTRAM COFFIN

A trio of finger foods: Miniature Quiches with smoked salmon and fresh dill, Cheese Straws, and crostini topped with Peppers Provençal.

MINIATURE QUICHES

Buttery miniature quiche shells filled with custardy surprises are always a cocktail favorite. Use our Pâte Brisée recipe (page 408) for the crust and bake the tiny quiches in 2- or 3-inch tart molds (available at better houseware stores).

One recipe of Pâte Brisée will produce about sixteen 2-inch tarts. One recipe of Basic Quiche Custard (recipe follows) will fill a similar number of tarts. Yield will vary slightly depending on the size of the tart molds used.

1. Preheat the oven to 375°F.

2. Prebake the tart shells for 10 minutes. Cool slightly, unmold, set on baking sheets, and place a spoonful of your chosen filling in each shell (our list of favorites follows). Spoon in basic quiche custard to cover the filling and come just below the edge of the tart shell.

3. Bake until the filling is puffed and lightly browned, 10 to 15 minutes. Serve immediately.

BASIC QUICHE CUSTARD

1½ cups heavy cream
3 large eggs
Salt and freshly ground black pepper, to taste
Pinch of grated nutmeg

Whisk the cream and eggs together thoroughly. Add the salt, pepper, and nutmeg. Refrigerate, covered, until baking time.

1½ cups custard, enough for one 10-inch quiche or sixteen 2-inch tarts

SOME FAVORITE QUICHE FILLINGS

(About 1 tablespoon per 2-inch tart)

- ♥ Crumbled imported Roquefort cheese and diced unpeeled apple in equal amounts
- ♥ Finely minced smoked salmon with chopped fresh dill to taste
- ♥ Equal parts of chopped ham and grated Gruyère; whisk Dijon mustard to taste into the basic custard
- ♥ Equal parts of flaked crabmeat and butter-sautéed scallions
- ♥ Mushrooms sautéed in unsalted butter
- ♥ Equal parts of red and green bell pepper, sautéed in unsalted butter until tender

PEPPERS PROVENCAL

These peppers add a vibrant accent of color when served on little toasts as an hors d'oeuvre. You can also fill a quiche shell with this mixture, or fill your own little tarts. We also love it as a vegetable side dish, served warm or at room temperature.

¼ cup best-quality imported olive oil
2 tablespoons unsalted butter
2 cups thinly sliced yellow onions
2 red bell peppers, stemmed, seeded, and sliced into very thin strips
½ teaspoon herbes de Provence
Salt and freshly ground black pepper, to taste
2 garlic cloves, finely minced
½ cup finely shredded fresh basil leaves

1. Heat the oil and butter in a heavy skillet or saucepan over medium heat until the butter is melted. Add the onions and peppers; season with herbes de Provence and salt and pepper. Simmer, stirring frequently, until the vegetables are limp, tender, and lightly browned, about 45 minutes. The peppers should have a marmalade-like appearance.

2. Add the garlic and basil and cook for another 5 minutes. Remove the vegetables from the skillet and let cool to room temperature. Drain any excess oil. The peppers are now ready to use.

2 cups

CHEESE STRAWS

These crisp and mildly spicy twists of puff pastry have been a favorite "nosh" for years. Arrange a basketful on the bar and watch them disappear!

1 pound Puff Pastry (page 409)
¾ cup grated Parmigiano-Reggiano cheese

1. Preheat the oven to 350°F.

2. Roll out the puff pastry dough into a rectangle 20 x 24 inches. Sprinkle half of the cheese evenly over the dough and gently press the cheese into the dough with the rolling pin.

3. Fold the dough in half crosswise, roll it out again to 20 x 24 inches, and sprinkle on the remaining cheese.

4. Using a sharp thin knife, cut the dough into ⅓-inch-wide strips. Take each strip by its ends and twist until evenly corkscrewed. Lay the twists of dough on an ungreased baking sheet, arranged so they are just touching each other; this will prevent untwisting.

5. Set the baking sheet on the center rack of the oven and bake until the straws are crisp, puffed, and brown, 15 to 20 minutes.

OLIVES

We love bowls of olives as part of a "to begin" table. Their saltiness is perfect with drinks, and their earthy colors complement a variety of other foods. Olives have been a dietary staple around the Mediterranean for more than 4,000 years; they are still prepared today as they have been for centuries.

"The olive tree is the richest gift of heaven."

—THOMAS JEFFERSON

The ripeness of olives when picked and the curing process they undergo before packing contribute to the taste of the finished product. Traditionally, imported olives had more flavor, while the domestically produced olive was fairly bland. Tastes are changing, we're glad to see, and the domestic product is acquiring more flavor. In either case, offer your guests a choice of at least two kinds of olives. Some of our favorite choices are these:

- ♥ Alfonso: These South American olives are black-purple, meaty, and large, with a delicious, fruity flavor.
- ♥ Amfissa: Soft and sweet, these purple-black olives from Delphi, Greece, seem to melt in your mouth. They are familiar to many as the pungent Greek olives sold in bulk.
- ♥ Arbequina: Uniquely nutty, small, round, and brown, these olives are grown in Spain's Catalonia region.
- ♥ Calabrese or Cerignola: A mellow olive, dull bronze-green in color, that is grown in Southeastern Italy.

- Elites: Deep in color, quite sweet, and exceedingly tender, these are Crete's tiniest olives. They're difficult to find in the U.S., but worth seeking out.
- Gaeta: These small, Italian olives are black and wrinkly when dry cured and packed in oil and herbs, smooth and deep purple when cured in brine.
- Hondroelia: Known in Greece as "heroes," these enormous hand-picked brown olives are almost two inches long and are often eaten with a knife and fork. They're grown in Acadia on the Peloponnesian peninsula and are traditionally cured in salt brine for an entire year. Great fun to serve.
- Kalamata: This large, almond-shaped Greek olive—often considered to be the best of all olives—is purple-black, cracked, and cured in red wine vinegar, which gives it a very full, tangy-salty flavor. Kalamatas are grown in the Valley of Messenia on the Peloponnesian peninsula. The very best are hand-picked—once you've tasted them, you'll know the difference.
- Manzanilla: These round "little apples" are crisp, nutty, cracked, and brownish green. They are Spain's best olive.
- Moroccan: Dry-cured black olives with a meaty texture and full, rich flavor. They're excellent marinated in cumin and hot chiles.
- Nafplion: Cracked green Peloponnesian olives with a nutty, slightly smoky flavor.
- Niçoise: This tiny, tender, black French olive is cured in brine and packed in oil, frequently with provençal herbs. It is often used in making olive oil.
- Nyons: These pleasantly bitter oil-cured olives are small, round, and reddish brown.
- Picholine: Green olives from France—crisp, tender, delicate, and mild.
- Queen Olives: Or "gorda," meaning fat, Spain's largest green olives are meaty and firm, often flavored with cumin, garlic, thyme, and sherry vinegar.
- Royal or Victoria: Very large, black Greek olives that are cured in olive oil.
- Sicilian: Traditionally spiced with red pepper and oregano, these green Italian olives are small, oval, cracked, and cured in salt brine.
- Taggiasca: Very meaty small black olives that are picked later than most, from Liguria on the Italian Riviera.

Offer a selection of hors d'oeuvres, grouped together to suggest abundance.

6. Remove the straws from the oven, cool for 5 minutes, then cut them apart with a sharp knife. Finish cooling the straws on a rack, then store them in an airtight tin or plastic bag until serving time. They will stay fresh for about 1 week.

About 20 straws

PHYLLO TRIANGLES

1 pound phyllo dough (24 sheets)
Filling of choice (recipes follow)

1. Uncover the dough and remove a sheet. Brush well with melted butter. Sixty triangles will use about ½ pound of butter. Stack a second sheet on top and butter again. Be sure to cover the unused phyllo with the damp towel each time.

2. Cut the buttered phyllo sheets into fifths the short way with a sharp knife.

3. Place a teaspoon of filling in the center of the first strip, about 1 inch from the top. Fold a corner against the filling and then continue to fold, as if you are folding a flag, until the strip is all folded; the filling will expand as it cooks, so do not wrap the triangle too tight. Tuck any excess under.

4. Place the triangle on a buttered baking sheet. Brush the top of the triangle with butter. Continue until you have the desired number of triangles. Filled, unbaked triangles can be refrigerated, covered, for up to 24 hours before baking.

5. Preheat the oven to 350°F.

6. Bake in the upper third of the oven until the triangles are well browned and the filling is bubbling and hot, about 25 minutes. Serve immediately.

7. Completed triangles freeze beautifully and are ready in minutes when you need a quick appetizer. Prepare as above, but place the triangles on an unbuttered baking sheet and omit the final brushing with butter. Freeze them overnight on the baking sheet and then wrap them tightly in clear plastic wrap or in a plastic bag until needed. *Do not defrost;* they get soggy. Put the frozen triangles on a buttered baking sheet, brush with butter, and bake at 350°F until well browned and hot (test one to be sure), about 45 minutes. Serve immediately.

Makes about 60 triangles

THREE FILLINGS FOR PHYLLO TRIANGLES

ROQUEFORT AND PISTACHIO FILLING

¼ pound imported Roquefort cheese
¼ pound cream cheese
1 egg
½ cup coarsely chopped shelled pistachios (or substitute walnuts or pecans)
Pinch of grated nutmeg
Freshly ground black pepper, to taste

1. Bring the Roquefort and cream cheese to room temperature and mash them together thoroughly in a small bowl.

2. Stir in the egg, combine well, and stir in the pistachios.

3. Season with the nutmeg and pepper. The Roquefort is usually so salty that no additional salt is needed.

Enough filling for approximately 60 triangles

SPINACH-FETA FILLING

10 ounces frozen chopped spinach
½ cup finely chopped yellow onion
3 tablespoons olive oil
Pinch of grated nutmeg
Salt and freshly ground black pepper, to taste
½ cup finely chopped fresh dill or fresh mint
⅓ cup ricotta cheese
¼ cup feta cheese

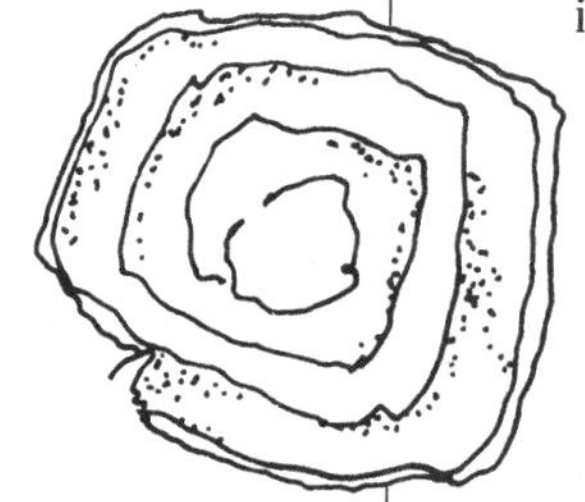

WORKING WITH PHYLLO (FILO)

One of the most versatile, delicious, and widely available aids to the party-giver is phyllo, the tissue-paper–thin dough commonly used in Greece and other Middle Eastern countries. While those of us in large cities may have access to an ethnic pastry shop that makes its own fresh phyllo daily, the frozen variety is available in nearly all large supermarkets and specialty food shops. Best of all, this ready-when-you-are frozen phyllo is virtually interchangeable with the fresh variety. The dough usually comes in 1-pound packages, each of which contains 24 or more sheets.

Let the phyllo defrost in its original wrapper in your refrigerator for at least 2 days. (When well wrapped and still sealed in its original package, defrosted phyllo will keep in the refrigerator for up to a month. This is preferable to refreezing, which can make the dough crumbly.)

Be sure the phyllo is completely defrosted before beginning to work with it. Have a damp (not wet) towel handy. Unwrap the dough, unroll it, and cover it immediately with the towel. Let stand for 15 minutes; moisture makes phyllo easier to handle.

from THE SILVER PALATE NOTEBOOK

You can never plan and organize too much; the larger the party, the more you must prepare. Planning ahead will leave extra time for you to enjoy the marketing, preparation, and presentation of the meal to your guests.

Working from checklists can be an invaluable aid. You may prefer index cards or some other system. Don't try to plan a large gathering in your head.

COCKTAIL PUFFS

Any number of soft, savory mixtures can be used to fill a tiny cocktail puff. For the puffs, use Pâte à Choux. Elsewhere in this book you will find recipes for Tapenade, Pâté Maison, Taramasalata, Salmon Mousse, and Peasant Caviar (see the Index for page numbers). We have tried them all in puffs at one time or another with great success.

1. Defrost the frozen spinach. Drain it, then squeeze out as much remaining moisture as possible with your hands.

2. Sauté the onion in the olive oil over low heat until tender and golden, about 20 minutes. Add the spinach and cook, stirring constantly, until mixture is dry, 10 to 15 minutes. Season with the nutmeg and salt and pepper, and transfer to a bowl. Cool to room temperature.

3. Stir in the dill or mint, the ricotta, and finally the feta, crumbled into small pieces. Taste and correct the seasoning.

Enough filling for approximately 60 triangles

ROSEMARY AND PROSCIUTTO FILLING

2 egg yolks
1 cup ricotta cheese
¼ pound prosciutto, finely chopped
¼ cup grated Parmigiano-Reggiano cheese
1½ teaspoons crumbled dried rosemary
Salt and freshly ground black pepper, to taste

Beat the egg yolks into the ricotta. Stir in the prosciutto, cheese, and rosemary. Season with salt and pepper.

Enough filling for approximately 60 triangles

GOUGERES

Gougère, the splendid hot cheese pastry from the Burgundy region of France, makes a spectacularly easy cocktail snack. Of course it is delicious with a glass of red wine, but we also love to serve it with the best vintage Port we can muster. Traditionally it is baked into a large, wreathlike ring, but it is easier to handle at cocktail time if formed into tiny individual puffs.

1 cup milk
8 tablespoons (1 stick) unsalted butter
1 teaspoon salt
1 cup sifted unbleached all-purpose flour
5 eggs
1½ cups grated Parmigiano-Reggiano cheese (or half Parmigiano-Reggiano, half Gruyère), plus an additional (optional) ½ cup grated Parmigiano-Reggiano to top puffs

1. Preheat the oven to 375°F. Lightly butter a baking sheet.

2. Combine the milk, butter, and salt in a small saucepan and bring to a boil over medium heat. Remove the pan from the heat and add the flour all at once. Whisk vigorously for a few moments, then return the pan to medium heat and cook, stirring constantly, until the batter has thickened and is pulling away from the sides and bottom of the pan, 5 minutes or less.

3. Again remove the pan from the heat and stir in 4 eggs, one at a time, making certain the first egg is completely incorporated before adding the second. Then stir in the cheese or cheeses.

4. Drop the batter by tablespoons onto the prepared baking sheet, spacing the puffs at least 1 inch apart.

5. Beat the remaining egg in a small bowl. Brush the tops of the puffs with the beaten egg, and sprinkle with additional Parmigiano-Reggiano if desired.

6. Set the baking sheet on the center rack of the oven, reduce the heat to 350°F, and bake until the gougères are puffed and well browned, 15 to 20 minutes. Serve immediately.

About 20 puffs

STUFFED GRAPE LEAVES

Stuffed grape leaves, or *dolmades,* originated in ancient Mesopotamia and were a popular dish of the Ottoman Empire. Its exact origin remains unknown, though a slew of countries take credit for creating the dish. Variations can be found throughout Greece, Turkey, Armenia, the Middle East, the Balkans, and central Asia, and its ingredients tend to change with each region. When stuffed with meat, dolmades are typically served warm, though we like them just as much cold. A long-lasting staple of Middle Eastern *meze* (an appetizer assortment), they are a wonderful hors d'oeuvre for dinners and cocktail parties.

50 medium-size preserved grape leaves (about 1½ pounds)
1 pound ground very lean lamb
16 ounces canned Italian plum tomatoes, crushed
1 cup raw long-grain rice
1 cup best-quality olive oil
2 bunches of scallions (green onions), well rinsed and chopped
3 cups loosely packed fresh mint leaves, chopped
Juice of 2 lemons
Plain yogurt seasoned with lemon juice and coarse salt to taste, for serving

1. Drain the grape leaves, separate them, and rinse them under running water, being careful not to tear them. Reserve.

2. Combine the lamb, crushed tomatoes and their liquid, rice, olive oil, scallions, and mint in a bowl.

3. Lay a grape leaf, vein side up, stem toward you, on your work surface. Place 1 tablespoon of filling at the base of the leaf and roll it up, tucking in any excess leaf at the sides to make a tiny bundle. Repeat with the remaining filling and leaves, packing each bundle seam side down into a small saucepan.

4. Squeeze lemon juice over the leaf bundles, and add water nearly to cover. Weight with 1 or 2 small plates or saucers. Cover, bring to a boil, reduce the heat, and simmer until rice in stuffing is completely cooked, 1 hour.

5. Serve hot or cool, cover, and refrigerate the leaves in their cooking liquid. Offer the yogurt mixture as a dip or sauce.

Approximately 50 grape leaves

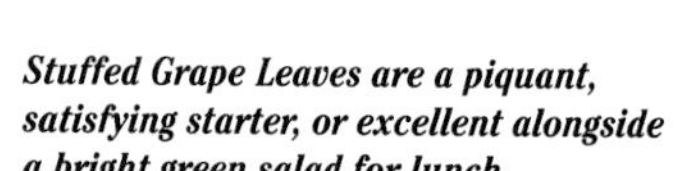

Stuffed Grape Leaves are a piquant, satisfying starter, or excellent alongside a bright green salad for lunch.

"Ask . . . any Greek for the origin of dolmades and you will in all likelihood be told that they were served atop Mount Olympus."

—FRED FERRETTI

MUSHROOMS STUFFED WITH WALNUTS & CHEESE

12 medium-size mushroom caps
1 tablespoon olive oil
1 tablespoon unsalted butter
½ cup finely chopped yellow onion
2 tablespoons coarsely chopped walnuts
1 garlic clove, peeled and minced
5 ounces frozen chopped spinach, thoroughly defrosted and squeezed dry
1 ounce feta cheese, crumbled
1 ounce Gruyère cheese, crumbled
2 tablespoons minced fresh dill
Salt and freshly ground black pepper, to taste

1. Remove the mushroom stems and save for another use. Wipe the mushroom caps with a damp paper towel and set aside.

2. Heat the olive oil and butter together in a small skillet, over medium heat. Add the onion and cook, covered, until tender and lightly colored, about 25 minutes.

3. Preheat the oven to 400°F.

4. Add the walnuts and garlic to the onion and cook for another minute. Add the spinach and cook for another 5 minutes, stirring constantly. Remove from the heat and cool slightly. Stir in the cheeses, dill, salt, and pepper.

5. Arrange the mushrooms, cavity side up, in a baking dish. Divide the spinach mixture evenly among the mushroom caps.

6. Set the baking dish on a rack in the upper third of the oven. Bake, until the filling is browned and the mushrooms are thoroughly heated, 8 to 10 minutes. Serve immediately.

12 mushrooms, 3 or 4 portions

STUFFED MUSHROOMS

Easterners like them whiter than white, while Westerners prefer them a bit beige, but in any case the widely cultivated American button mushroom must always be at its freshest for the cocktail hour. It is terrific raw, marinated, or cooked. When stuffed, it becomes a perfect finger food. It is quiet, attractive, and completely self-contained.

SAUSAGE-STUFFED MUSHROOMS

2 Italian sweet sausages (about ⅓ pound)
¼ teaspoon fennel seeds
Pinch of crushed red pepper flakes (optional)
¼ cup finely minced yellow onion
1 garlic clove, peeled and minced
Olive oil, as needed
¼ cup chopped fresh parsley
¼ cup chopped black olives, preferably imported
⅓ cup thick Béchamel Sauce (page 415)
Salt and freshly ground black pepper, to taste
12 large white mushrooms
Grated Parmigiano-Reggiano cheese, to taste

STICKING WITH SKEWERS

A simple bamboo skewer about 6 inches long, available at Asian food stores, can make a dazzling cocktail display. Spear an assortment of complementary bites onto a single skewer, or stand them like a forest at the edge of a bowl of marinated shrimp, dilled meatballs, or other foods too messy for fingers. Smaller skewers can also be useful for single-bite hors d'oeuvres, and nearly anything edible is a little easier to handle when speared in this fashion.

FAVORITE SKEWER COMBINATIONS

- ♥ Shrimp and green grapes
- ♥ Melon and prosciutto with smoked turkey
- ♥ Apple chunks and ham
- ♥ Lime-marinated sea scallops and avocado chunks
- ♥ Cherry tomatoes and vinaigrette-marinated cubes of roast beef
- ♥ Swiss cheese cubes, ham cubes, and watermelon pickle

1. Preheat the oven to 450°F.

2. Remove the sausage meat from the casings and crumble into a small skillet. Sauté over low heat, stirring often, until the meat is thoroughly done. Season with the fennel seeds and, if desired, the red pepper flakes. With a slotted spoon, remove the sausage to a bowl, leaving the rendered fat in the skillet.

3. Sauté the onion and garlic in the rendered fat over low heat, adding a little olive oil if necessary, until tender and golden, about 25 minutes. Stir in the chopped parsley, then add to the reserved sausage meat.

4. Stir the olives and béchamel into the sausage mixture; combine thoroughly. Taste the mixture, and season with salt and pepper if necessary.

5. Remove the mushroom stems and save for another use. Wipe the mushroom caps with a damp cloth and season lightly with salt and pepper.

6. Fill each cap generously with the stuffing. Arrange the caps stuffed side up in a lightly oiled baking dish. Sprinkle the tops of the stuffing with the cheese.

7. Bake, until bubbling and well browned, about 15 minutes. Let settle for 5 minutes before serving.

12 mushrooms, 3 or 4 portions

MINIATURE LAMB KEBABS

These little kebabs liven up any party, whether an informal get-together or something more upscale. The marinade makes the lamb deliciously fragrant, savory, and tender.

Cubed lamb (¼ pound per person)
Marinade for Lamb (recipe follows)
Cherry tomatoes
Green bell pepper, stemmed, seeded, and cut into 1-inch squares
Small white onions, peeled

1. Cut the lamb into ½-inch cubes and marinate overnight, covered and refrigerated.

2. Preheat the broiler.

3. Remove the lamb from the marinade and drain on paper towels. Slide the cubes onto skewers (either metal skewers or wooden ones that have been soaked in water), alternating with 2 cherry tomatoes, a square of green pepper, and a small white onion.

4. Broil until done, about 10 minutes. Serve immediately.

MARINADE FOR LAMB

¼ cup red wine vinegar
1 teaspoon mixed dried herbs (for example, half rosemary, half thyme)
2 garlic cloves, peeled and slightly crushed
¼ cup olive oil
1 tablespoon soy sauce
1 tablespoon dry sherry

In a large bowl, combine all the ingredients. Stir briskly.

About ¾ cup marinade, enough for 1½ pounds lamb cubes (to serve 6)

THE BARBECUED BITS

We love to serve tiny, tiny spareribs and chicken wings at cocktail time. They're messy finger food, but no one seems to care. If yours is a black-tie affair, then these really aren't quite appropriate, but on other occasions they tend to get nibbled up very quickly. The leftover bones somehow manage to disappear as well, though it's a good idea to think ahead and arrange for their disposal with a few strategically placed bowls.

COCKTAIL RIBLETS

Our butcher supplies us with what he calls "cocktail ribs," regular spareribs that are cut apart and then chopped crosswise into 2-inch lengths, perfect for eating with fingers. If your butcher won't, you can accomplish this task yourself with a sharp knife and a cleaver. Alternatively, just cut the ribs apart and serve them full-size. Depending on your menu, allow ¼ to ½ pound of ribs per person. Spread them in one layer in a shallow baking pan or on a broiler pan with a slotted insert, if you have one. Salt and pepper to taste. Bake at 400°F for about 40 minutes. Turn ribs once at the halfway point.

Drain any accumulated fat and brush the riblets generously with Mustard Glaze (page 18). Bake for another 10 minutes, then repeat the glazing and baking process one more time. Serve hot or at room temperature. One cup of Mustard Glaze will glaze about 2 pounds of riblets.

COCKTAIL CHICKEN WINGS

Depending on your menu, allow 2 to 4 chicken wings per person. Remove the tips and place the chicken wings in a dish just large enough to hold them; pour in Barbecue Sauce (page 18), and marinate, covered, in the refrigerator for 2 hours. Preheat the oven

from THE SILVER PALATE NOTEBOOK

Time cocktails to last no more than an hour before dinner is served; an endless cocktail hour can result in bored guests or guests who have drunk so much they ignore the food or cause other problems.

After your one good drink before the guests arrive, confine yourself to sipping.

Always remember to have sparkling water, fruit juices, and unsweetened soft drinks on hand for nondrinkers.

to 400°F. Lift the wings from the marinade and arrange them in a single layer in a broilerproof baking dish. Season to taste with salt and pepper and bake for 20 minutes. Baste the wings at the halfway point with more sauce.

When the wings have baked for 20 minutes and are nearly done, slide the dish under the broiler until the wings are browned, cooked through, and bubbly, another 5 to 7 minutes. Serve immediately or at room temperature. One cup of Barbecue Sauce is sufficient for 6 or more chicken wings.

MUSTARD GLAZE

½ cup Dijon mustard
½ cup orange marmalade
⅓ cup honey
3 tablespoons fresh orange juice
2 tablespoons cider vinegar
1 teaspoon ground ginger
½ teaspoon grated nutmeg
Salt and freshly ground black pepper, to taste

1. Combine all of the ingredients in a small, nonreactive heavy saucepan. Cook over low heat to melt the marmalade.

2. Raise the heat to medium and simmer, whisking occasionally, until the sauce thickens slightly, 5 minutes.

3. Cool, cover, and refrigerate until ready to use. Refrigerated, the glaze keeps for up to 3 weeks.

Makes 1½ cups

BARBECUE SAUCE

2 cups ketchup
½ cup cider vinegar
½ cup water
Juice from 1 lemon
2 tablespoons Worcestershire sauce
2 tablespoons Tabasco sauce
2 tablespoons unsulfured molasses
2 tablespoons Dijon mustard
¼ cup (packed) dark brown sugar
2 tablespoons chili powder
2 teaspoons finely minced garlic
2 teaspoons smoked paprika
Salt and freshly ground black pepper, to taste

Combine all the ingredients in a heavy nonreactive saucepan. Cook over medium-low heat, stirring, to heat through and to blend the flavors, 10 to 12 minutes. Do not boil. Strain the sauce to remove the garlic. Cool to room temperature. Use immediately or refrigerate, covered, for up to 2 weeks.

Makes about 3 cups

from THE SILVER PALATE NOTEBOOK

We like to serve a wide variety of foods to our guests so they can taste, graze, and sample many different flavors.

The trick is to serve these foods with style and pizzazz! Small serving trays mounded with a single type of hors d'oeuvre and garnished lavishly with herbs make a dramatic presentation. A large platter with heaping mounds of a variety of salads looks spectacular. A giant clam shell overflowing with shellfish is dramatic. Numerous small bowls piled with condiments look terrific, much more appealing than larger bowls that look half empty.

Then, once the buffet is spread, take a moment to cluster the food even closer together so that it makes yet a stronger statement. You get the picture. The buffet now looks lush and abundant and each dish cries out, "I'm delicious, try me first!"

"One cannot have too large a party."

—JANE AUSTEN

FRESH FROM THE SEA

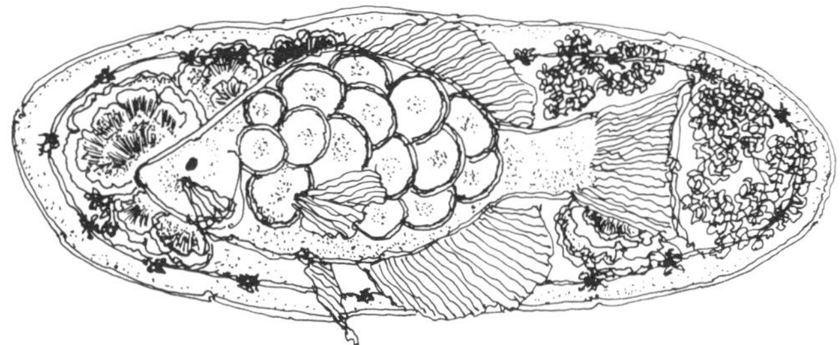

Today as never before, there is a wider and more interesting variety of wild and farmed seafood available and Americans are eating more seafood than ever. Not only are the calorie-conscious regularly eating seafood, but it's become a popular choice when company's coming, as well. So, remember when serving seafood, be sure to make plenty. It will be the star of any cocktail buffet!

SPICY SHRIMP

Serve these shrimp as a first course or on the ends of long bamboo skewers as an appetizer.

2 tablespoons unsalted butter
1 tablespoon olive oil
1 tablespoon finely minced garlic
2 tablespoons finely minced shallots
1¾ pounds large raw shrimp, peeled and deveined
Salt and freshly ground black pepper, to taste
2 tablespoons fresh lemon juice, or more to taste
2 tablespoons finely chopped fresh dill

1. In a large skillet over low heat, heat the butter and olive oil. Add the garlic and shallots and sauté for 2 minutes without browning.

2. Add the shrimp, increase the heat slightly, and cook until the shrimp are just done, about 4 minutes. Add salt and pepper and toss well. Transfer to a bowl, scraping in all the sauce.

3. Add the lemon juice and dill; toss together well. Cover and refrigerate 3 to 4 hours before serving. Adjust the seasonings and serve.

10 portions as an hors d'oeuvre; 4 to 6 as an appetizer

SHRIMP AND SNOW PEAS

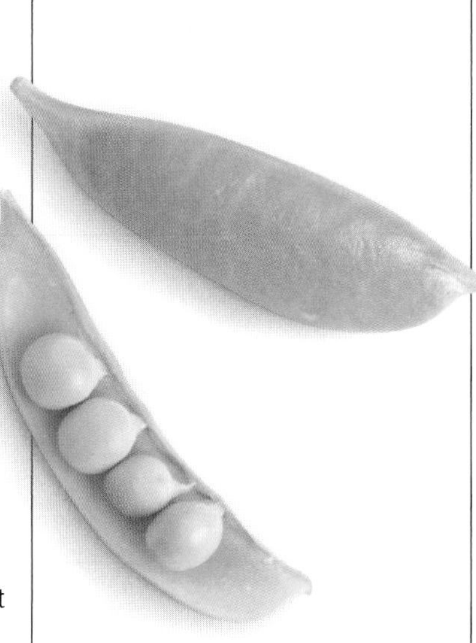

2 tablespoons peanut oil
1 pound (about 18) raw large shrimp, peeled and deveined
1 cup Sherry Vinaigrette (page 283)
18 snow peas (about ½ pound)
Salt, to taste

1. Heat half the peanut oil in a small skillet over medium heat. Sauté half of the shrimp, stirring and tossing frequently, until done, about 4 minutes; the shrimp will turn pink and become firm. Do not overcook.

2. Lift the cooked shrimp from the skillet with a slotted spoon and transfer them to a small deep bowl just large enough to hold them. Repeat with the remaining shrimp.

3. Pour ¼ cup sherry vinaigrette over the warm shrimp and let stand for 1 hour.

4. Meanwhile, trim the snow peas and drop them into a pot of salted boiling water. Let them cook for about 2 minutes; the water need not even return to the boil. Drain immediately and plunge them into a bowl of ice water; this will stop the cooking process and set the brilliant green color.

5. When the snow peas are completely cool, drain them and pat dry. Split them along their seams, leaving the halves joined at one end.

6. Remove the shrimp from the vinaigrette, one at a time, and close a snow pea around each shrimp. Skewer into place with a cocktail pick and arrange on a platter. Cover the platter and refrigerate until serving time.

7. Drizzle some of the remaining vinaigrette over the shrimp just before serving, if desired.

6 portions

FIRST DAY OF SPRING BUFFET

CHEESE STRAWS

AMERICAN GOLDEN CAVIAR ON TOASTS, WITH SOUR CREAM AND MINCED RED ONION

ASPARAGUS WITH PROSCIUTTO

HERB CHEESE

FRESH SUGAR SNAP PEAS

SESAME MAYONNAISE

TARAMASALATA

We've seen this wonderful appetizer increase in popularity over the years. No longer just a Greek taste, but one that brings a tart fish flavor to a buffet without the expense of caviar. Serve with pita bread triangles, little toasts, or as a dip with fresh vegetables.

1 pound smoked whole cod roe, casing removed
1 pound cream cheese, at room temperature
1 garlic clove, peeled and pounded
Juice of ½ lemon
¼ teaspoon freshly ground black pepper
¼ cup olive oil
¼ cup heavy cream

1. In a food processor combine the cod roe, cream cheese, garlic, lemon juice, and black pepper. Process just until smooth.

2. With the motor running, pour the olive oil and heavy cream through the feed tube until just blended. Transfer to a bowl, cover, and refrigerate until serving.

4 cups

GRAVLAX

Gravlax is a Scandinavian preparation in which raw salmon is cured with salt, sugar, and spices. The marinating action "cooks" and tenderizes the fish. The result, sliced paper-thin, is one of the best appetizers we know. Serve with ice-cold vodka, aquavit, or dry white wine.

1 piece (3 pounds) fresh salmon, center-cut from the fish, halved lengthwise and thoroughly boned
2 large bunches of fresh dill
¼ cup coarse salt
¼ cup sugar
2 tablespoons crushed white peppercorns
Thinly sliced pumpernickel, for serving
Lemon wedges, for garnish
Freshly ground black pepper, for garnish
Dill Mustard Sauce, for serving (recipe follows)

1. Place half of the fish, skin side down, in a deep glass dish. Spread the dill over the fish. Sprinkle the salt, sugar, and peppercorns over the dill. Top with the other half of the fish, skin side up.

2. Cover with aluminum foil and weight with a board and a 5-pound weight. Refrigerate for 48 to 72 hours, turning the salmon and basting every 12 hours with accumulated juices.

3. To serve, remove the fish from the marinade, scrape away the dill and spices, and pat dry. Slice the salmon thinly on the diagonal and serve on small plates or squares of pumpernickel. Garnish with lemon wedges and black pepper and accompany with dill mustard sauce.

8 to 10 portions

DILL MUSTARD SAUCE

Use this sweetly pungent dill sauce on gravlax, or as a dip for shrimp and other shellfish.

1 cup sweet mustard (see page 283)
1 cup sour cream
½ cup chopped fresh dill

Mix all the ingredients together. Cover and refrigerate until ready to use. The sauce will keep for up to 3 days if refrigerated.

2 cups

"To invite a person into your house is to take charge of his happiness for as long as he is under your roof."

—JEAN ANTHELME BRILLAT-SAVARIN

SMOKED SALMON

Smoked salmon should be sliced paper-thin, on the diagonal, as close to serving time as possible. We like to serve it as simply as we can.

- ♥ Remove the salmon from the refrigerator 30 minutes before serving.
- ♥ A squirt of fresh lemon juice is delicious; offer generous lemon wedges.
- ♥ Pass a peppermill; fresh black pepper is a must.
- ♥ Danish pumpernickel is a natural accompaniment.
- ♥ Other embellishments include a dab of caviar, a dollop of sour cream, or a sprinkling of chopped fresh dill.
- ♥ Champagne or chilled vodka, neat, are the approved libations.

SALMON MOUSSE

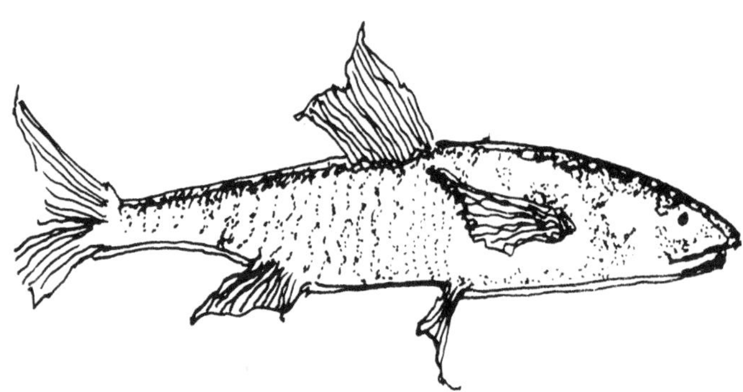

This is a *Silver Palate Cookbook* classic and continues to taste just as fresh and new to us each time we make it. It was with us the first day we opened the store and the only time it wasn't available was when we'd sold out. It's light and pretty, and one of those foods you'll just enjoy time after time.

1 envelope unflavored gelatin
¼ cup cold water
½ cup boiling water
½ cup mayonnaise, preferably Hellmann's
1 tablespoon fresh lemon juice
1 tablespoon finely grated onion
Dash of Tabasco
¼ teaspoon sweet paprika
1 teaspoon salt
2 tablespoons finely chopped fresh dill
2 cups finely flaked poached fresh salmon or canned salmon, skin and bones removed
1 cup heavy cream
Watercress, for garnish
Toast, pumpernickel, or crackers, for serving

1. Soften the gelatin in the cold water in a large mixing bowl. Stir in the boiling water and whisk the mixture slowly until the gelatin dissolves. Cool to room temperature.

2. Whisk in the mayonnaise, lemon juice, grated onion, Tabasco, paprika, salt, and dill. Stir to blend completely and refrigerate until the mixture begins to thicken slightly, about 20 minutes.

3. Fold in the finely flaked salmon. In a separate bowl, whip the cream until it is thickened to soft peaks and fluffy. Fold gently into the salmon mixture.

4. Transfer the mixture to a 6- to 8-cup bowl or decorative mold. Cover and refrigerate for at least 4 hours.

5. Garnish with watercress, and serve with toasts, pumpernickel, or crackers.

At least 12 portions

CONCERT IN THE PARK PICNIC

SALMON MOUSSE
WITH
PUMPERNICKEL TOASTS

VEAL ROLL

ASPARAGUS WITH BLUEBERRY VINAIGRETTE

SPICY SESAME NOODLES

ASSORTED CHEESES, FRESH FRUIT

CHOCOLATE MOUSSE
AND COOKIES

"No restaurants? The means of consoling oneself: reading cookbooks."

—BAUDELAIRE

WHITE WINE

Extra-dry, extra-cold white wine can provide the basis for a dazzling array of "cocktails" that make for light and interesting party fare.

- ♥ Add a spoonful of Framboise, Mirabelle, or Poire Williams to a glass of chilled white wine and garnish with the appropriate fruit.
- ♥ Fresh fruit makes a glass of white wine prettier and adds flavor of its own as well.
- ♥ Try adding a dash of peach or berry purée, a few grapes, a slice of mango, or a few balls of fresh melon to make this classic more festive.
- ♥ A sprig of mint is beautiful and tasty, too. Crush it lightly in the bottom of the glass and pour in the chilled white wine.
- ♥ Peel and slice a kiwi and freeze the slices. Float 1 or 2 frozen slices in a glass of chilled white wine. Frozen strawberries and black cherries are nice, too.
- ♥ Stir a spoonful of fresh orange juice and a splash of soda or seltzer into the white wine. Serve iced or straight up.
- ♥ Don't forget the trusty lemon. Something as simple as a freshly cut lemon section or a twist of lemon peel dropped into a glass of white wine, iced or not, is a refreshing touch.

SPICY CRAB CLAWS

For this recipe, buy crab fingers from the fish market. If they are frozen, let them defrost and wash and drain them well before using.

3 pounds cooked crab claw meat
1 cup minced well-rinsed scallions (green onions)
½ cup chopped fresh Italian (flat-leaf) parsley
2 celery ribs, chopped
3 garlic cloves, crushed
1 cup olive oil
½ cup tarragon vinegar
3 tablespoons fresh lemon juice
1 tablespoon Worcestershire sauce
Dash of Tabasco
Salt and freshly ground black pepper, to taste
Buttered pumpernickel, for serving

1. Place all the ingredients except the crab, salt, and pepper in a saucepan and heat to blend over low heat. Add salt and pepper. Pour the sauce over the crab. Cover and refrigerate overnight.

2. Remove from the refrigerator 1 hour before serving. Drain off the sauce. Serve the crab claws with buttered pumpernickel. Super as cocktail fare.

6 portions as a first course or 24 portions for cocktail buffet

SEVICHE

Our version of a Latin American favorite is another of the world's great marinated raw seafood dishes. With the growing awareness that much seafood is sadly overcooked, this method of preserving the texture and flavor of fresh fish without subjecting it to heat seems beautifully simple and logical.

2 pounds bay scallops
1 fresh hot red pepper, stemmed, seeded, and cut into julienne
1 small red bell pepper, stemmed, seeded, and cut into julienne
½ small red onion, cut into julienne
2 ripe tomatoes, seeded and cut into ¼-inch cubes
1 garlic clove, finely minced
2 teaspoons light brown sugar
2 tablespoons chopped fresh cilantro
2 tablespoons chopped fresh Italian (flat-leaf) parsley
Salt and freshly ground black pepper, to taste
2 cups fresh lime juice
½ cup fresh lemon juice
2 avocados, peeled and cut into 16 slices, brushed with lemon juice, for garnish
Chopped parsley, for garnish

1. In a large glass bowl combine all the ingredients except the avocados and parsley for garnish. Toss gently but thoroughly, being certain the scallops are well coated with citrus juice.

2. Cover and refrigerate until the scallops lose their translucent appearance, at least 5 hours. Stir them occasionally during the marination.

3. Serve in individual bowls garnished with avocado slices and additional chopped parsley.

8 portions as a first course

Seviche is bright and flavorful—the ideal start for a light meal.

THE CRUDITES CONNECTION

We find the crunch of fresh vegetables welcome at parties year round. And, the available varieties of exotic, baby, heirloom, imported, and organic vegetables have never been more exciting. Crudités just never seem to go out of style!

We like crudités to look bright and abundant, as if they're just picked from the garden. Use only the crispest and freshest vegetables and arrange them to resemble a plentiful garden at its peak. Vary colors, textures, shapes, and sizes; it will increase the impact. Or, mass single vegetables in individual baskets and arrange them in a dramatic design. Nestle dips in vegetable "containers" amidst your display.

THE PRESENTATION

We like to offer our dips in hollowed-out vegetables: a purple cabbage; a red, yellow, orange, or green bell pepper; an interesting heirloom tomato; a fat scooped-out zucchini or cucumber half, or a giant portobello mushroom. Be sure to contrast the vessel with the color of the dip. Then garnish with edible flowers, fresh herbs, or tall scallions sprouting out of your display.

ROQUEFORT DIP

¾ cup heavy cream
¼ cup Crème Fraîche (page 414)
1 teaspoon Worcestershire sauce
¼ teaspoon salt
½ teaspoon freshly ground white pepper
1 cup imported Roquefort cheese (see Note)

1. Combine the cream, crème fraîche, Worcestershire sauce, salt, and pepper in a food processor and process briefly.

2. Add the Roquefort and process again to blend. Do not over-process; the dip should remain chunky.

3. Transfer the dip to a bowl, cover, and refrigerate until ready to use.

About 2 cups

Note: You can substitute an equal amount of Stilton or Gorgonzola for the Roquefort.

AVOCADO DIP

1 clove garlic, peeled and chopped
2 tablespoons chopped fresh Italian (flat-leaf) parsley
1 tablespoon tarragon vinegar
½ teaspoon dried tarragon
6 anchovy fillets
¼ cup tarragon shallot mustard
1 cup Homemade Mayonnaise (page 413)
1 very ripe avocado, peeled, seeded, and roughly mashed
3 tablespoons half-and-half
Salt and freshly ground white pepper, to taste

1. Combine all the ingredients in a food processor and blend, scraping down the sides of the processor bowl with a rubber spatula as necessary. Add salt and pepper, and blend again.

2. Transfer the dip to a bowl, cover, and refrigerate until needed.

About 2 cups

GREEN PEPPERCORN MUSTARD DIP

1 cup Homemade Mayonnaise (page 413)
¼ cup Dijon mustard, or more if needed
1 small garlic clove, peeled and chopped, or more if needed
1 teaspoon water-packed green peppercorns, drained, plus additional peppercorns, to taste

1. Combine all the ingredients in a food processor and purée until smooth.

2. Taste, and add more mustard or garlic, if needed. Stir in additional whole green peppercorns. Do not process further.

3. Transfer to a bowl, cover, and refrigerate until serving.

About 1 cup

FAVORITE CRUDITE COMBINATIONS

ALL-GREEN:
- ♥ Artichokes
- ♥ Asparagus
- ♥ Baby fennel
- ♥ Broccoli/broccolini
- ♥ Chinese long beans
- ♥ English cucumber
- ♥ Green beans
- ♥ Green bell pepper
- ♥ Kohlrabi
- ♥ Scallions
- ♥ Snow peas
- ♥ Sugar snap peas
- ♥ Zucchini

GREEN AND PURPLE:
- ♥ Baby beets
- ♥ Baby eggplant
- ♥ Eggplant spears
- ♥ Purple cabbage
- ♥ Purple string beans
- ♥ Tiny new redskin potatoes

RED/WHITE/GREEN:
- ♥ Cauliflower
- ♥ Mushrooms
- ♥ Onions, Maui or Cippolini
- ♥ Radishes, red or white
- ♥ Red bell pepper
- ♥ Tomatoes: cherry or grape
- ♥ Turnip spears

ORANGE/YELLOW/RED:
- ♥ Baby carrots
- ♥ Baby corn
- ♥ Baby squash
- ♥ Red radishes
- ♥ Red, yellow, orange bell peppers
- ♥ Summer squash spears
- ♥ Tomatoes: cherry, grape, currant

Compose crudités and dips as an artist's palette, assembling a variety of colors, flavors, and textures.

“The greatest dishes are very simple dishes.”

—AUGUSTE ESCOFFIER

TAPENADE DIP

This dark and lusty sauce speaks to us with all the accents of Provence. It seems barely tamed by civilization and still full of secrets. Do we make too much of it? Try it for yourself and see. Stuff it into sun-ripened tomatoes, hard-cooked eggs, or grilled baby eggplants. Thin it slightly and offer it as a dip for crudités, or toss it with cold pasta. In the heat of summer its flavor seems only logical; in winter it stirs memories of summer warmth.

½ cup imported black olives, such as alfonso or kalamata, pitted
¼ cup imported green olives, such as Sicilian, pitted
4 anchovy fillets
1 garlic clove
2 tablespoons capers, thoroughly drained
2 tablespoons oil-packed tuna, drained
1 tablespoon fresh lemon juice
1 cup fresh basil leaves, rinsed and patted dry, or more to taste (see Note)
¼ cup best-quality olive oil
¼ cup Homemade Mayonnaise (page 413; optional)

1. Combine the black and green olives, anchovy fillets, garlic, capers, tuna, lemon juice, and basil in a food processor. Process until smooth.

2. With the motor still running, dribble in the oil to make a thick, fluffy sauce. For a lighter sauce, ideal for raw vegetables, blend in the mayonnaise.

3. Taste, and correct the seasoning. Scrape the dip into a bowl and cover. Refrigerate until ready to serve. Tapenade will keep, refrigerated, for 1 week.

About 1½ cups

Note: If fresh basil is not available, substitute 1 cup fresh parsley leaves and 2 teaspoons dried basil.

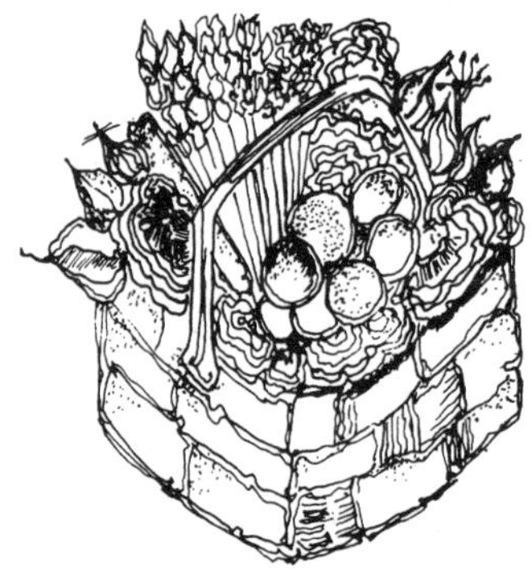

THE ENDIVE SCOOP

Individual leaves of Belgian endive make natural edible scoops for some of the thicker mixtures we serve as finger food. Past successful combinations include Salmon Mousse, Green Herb Dipping Sauce, and Taramasalata (see Index for recipes). We prefer the milder, more tender inner leaves, and love to surround a small bowl of our chosen dip with a pale green sunburst of endive.

THE CHARCUTERIE BOARD

Originally the *charcuterie* in France was the only store licensed to sell pork products. Although these restrictions have been relaxed, the charcuterie is still a great French tradition, dispensing pâtés and sausages made on the premises, and often supplying quiches, breads, cheeses, wine, and other picnic food and drink.

The charcuterie board is becoming an American favorite as well, and we think it makes a fine gastronomic accompaniment to a wine tasting. Really taste the wines while your palate is clear before starting in with the spicier food.

The traditional charcuterie accompaniments are mustards, the tiny pickles called cornichons, cherries in tart brine, olives, country breads, cheeses, chutneys, and an assortment of hearty salads or roasted vegetables. Group the wines at one end of the table, spread with a checked cloth, if you like, and arrange the bread in baskets. Display the pâtés, sausages, and cheeses on heavy cutting boards, and arrange the condiments in simple bowls and crocks. Your finished table should look like a rustic picnic, the image of a rural cornucopia.

STEAK TARTARE

Steak Tartare is wonderful fare for a cocktail buffet or early before-theater supper. Since the meat is served uncooked, it is most important that you purchase it on the day you intend to use it, and that the dish be prepared just before you serve it. Have your butcher prepare his freshest top-quality organic meat for you, and purchase the freshest organic eggs you can find (since the eggs will remain raw as well).

STEAK

2 pounds best-quality organic top sirloin or top round, finely ground
1 medium-size yellow onion, finely minced
¼ cup chopped fresh Italian (flat-leaf) parsley
3 tablespoons Dijon mustard
2 uncooked egg yolks
2 teaspoons salt
Freshly ground black pepper, to taste
1 teaspoon caraway seeds

Combine all the ingredients in a large bowl and blend thoroughly but gently. The egg yolks will help to bind the meat with the seasonings. Refrigerate until serving time.

GARNISH

1 head of Ruby Red lettuce or Bibb lettuce
¾ cup fine-snipped fresh chives, plus a few whole
2 cups pitted black niçoise olives
2 hard-cooked eggs, chopped fine
1 red onion, cut into fine dice
1 cup tiny capers, drained
2 pints cherry tomatoes, cut into ⅛-inch-thick slices
80 thin slices of cocktail rye and pumpernickel bread
2 or 3 crocks of unsalted butter

TO ARRANGE

1. Choose a large round decorative tray or platter. Arrange the lettuce leaves in the center.

2. Mold the meat into a ring on top of the lettuce. Sprinkle fresh chives over the steak and place the niçoise olives in the center of the ring.

3. Arrange the eggs, onions, capers, and tomatoes in an attractive pattern around the meat so that everyone can choose what he or she wants.

4. If your platter is large enough, place the bread slices in alternating colors in a ring around the garnish. Place the whole chives attractively poking out from different places. Have the crocks of butter nearby to spread on the bread.

5. To eat, lightly butter the bread, scoop on a portion of steak, sprinkle with your choices of garnish, and enjoy.

Enough for 75 to 80 pieces of bread, 38 portions, 2 pieces per person

"A good salami leaves the mouth clean."

—ITALIAN PROVERB

SAUSAGES

Sausage has been a part of our culinary heritage as long as there has been pork. Within every country, every region seems to have its own technique for the preparation. When serving a sausage board, let people carve for themselves. Provide good boards and sharp knives, and offer a selection of breads, mustards, horseradish, and pickles.

Artisanal sausage making—long a tradition in Europe—is experiencing a renaissance in the U.S. At Salumi in Seattle, Armandino Batali is now handcrafting extraordinary spicy and smoky soppressata, fennel and green peppercorn-flavored salumi, chorizo, lardo, prosciutto, culatello, spicy boar sausage, coppa, and lamb prosciutto. At Paul Bertolli's Fra' Mani, in Berkeley, California, a fabulous full range of salami has been introduced, and the line will continue to expand. The more widely distributed Ticino brand, made with Niman Ranch pork, is still authentically crafted and worth searching out. Handcrafted salami and sausage making very much remains an art, and one that discriminating palates appreciate.

ABRUZZI: Dry Italian sausage, made from fresh pork and spices, cured and air-dried. Spicy and nice for antipasto plates, hors d'oeuvres, or just munching.

ALLESANDRI: Italian-style; hard, dry, and spicy.

ALPINO: Made from an old Alpine recipe; hard and spicy.

ARLES: French-style; lots of garlic and red pepper.

BEEF LOG: Dry, smoked beef salami.

BLUTWURST OR BLOOD SAUSAGE: German delicacy; highly seasoned, very salty, and totally cooked.

BROCKWURST: Mildly seasoned; usually made with veal, pork, milk, chives, eggs, and parsley.

BRATWURST: A German classic. Pork and veal seasoned with sage and lemon juice.

FRESH BRAUNSCHWEIGER: Pork and beef liver mixture, cooked but not smoked.

BRAUNSCHWEIGER: The smoked version.

BÜNDNERFLEISCH: Swiss, one of our favorites; this is salty and spicy air-dried beef.

CACCIATORE: Italian-style sausage in very small sizes.

CALABRESE: Coarse salami with hot peppers.

CAPOCOLLO: Pork butt seasoned with red peppers, cured, and air-dried. Spicy and hot.

CERVELAT: Dried German sausages that are thick, peppery, and smoked.

CHORIZO: A dry-cured spicy sausage made with garlic and the smoky Spanish paprika, pimenton. Many are made in the U.S. and Mexico, but the best comes from Spain.

COPPA VENEZIANA: An Italian sausage with Italian ham in the middle.

DANISH SALAMI: Smoked, small little sticks, like cervelat.

FELINO: A dry, slowly aged Italian pork sausage. Although not imported, a satisfactory American-made variety is available.

FILSETTE: Mild, Italian Genoa-style salami.

FINOCCHIONA: Salami from Firenze with large pieces of coarse pork scented with sweet fennel seeds.

GELBWURST: Looks like liverwurst, but actually a bland, spongy pork and veal sausage.

GENOA PICCOLO: Pork and beef plus beef hearts, garlic, and pepper. Dried up to 5 months, which makes it very hard.

ITALIAN SALAMI: Chopped pork and beef, mixed with red wine or grape juice, and flavored with garlic and spices.

LACHSSCHINKEN: Lightly smoked pork loin, no seasonings. Dry. Eat it with a squeeze of lemon and a grind of black pepper.

LIVERWURST: Pork liver and meat trimmings, ground with onions and spices, cooked and/or smoked. Smooth, creamy texture; mild, livery taste; is available fresh. Either you love it or you don't.

MILANO: Finely ground mixed meats.

MORTADELLA: The true bologna, to some the finest sausage in Italy. It's a smooth, subtly flavored sausage made from finely chopped pork and beef, larded with backfat. The meat is then both smoked and dried.

PEPPERONI: A dry sausage made of beef and pork with lots of red pepper, black pepper, and garlic.

ROSETTE DE LYON: The most famous salami in France, it is made from hand-cut pork and has a rich winey flavor. Look for the Jean de France label.

SALAMI: Mixed meats with varying degrees of garlic and other spices. May be cured and smoked, cured and dried, or cooked.

SALCHICHON: A meaty Spanish salami made from lean pork and pork belly; seasoned with salt and black pepper, marinated, stuffed into a natural casing, and aged 6 to 8 months. The result is very meaty and full-flavored yet with a surprising sweetness.

SETTECENTO GENOA: Another type of hard Genoa salami.

SICILIAN: Finely ground pork trimmings with white and black pepper. Smoked and dried, spicy and flavorful.

SOPPRESSATA: A pungently flavored Italian salami, studded with whole peppercorns and garlic and marinated in red wine.

TIROLER: Cooked sausage, like salami.

TOSCANO: A hearty Italian salami made from chopped lean pork blended with pork fat. Very common.

Pâté Maison is rich and fragrant.

PATE MAISON

Our version of the classic smooth chicken liver pâté has long been a winner. The spices, Calvados, and currants provide such interesting flavor that this is a cocktail buffet favorite. Spread it on thinly sliced French bread, crackers, or buttered toast.

2 small celery ribs with leaves
4 whole black peppercorns
1 teaspoon salt
1 pound chicken livers
Tiny pinch of cayenne pepper
1 cup (2 sticks) unsalted butter
2 teaspoons dry mustard
½ teaspoon grated nutmeg
¼ teaspoon ground cloves
¼ cup roughly chopped yellow onion
1 small garlic clove
¼ cup Calvados
½ cup dried currants

1. Add the celery and peppercorns to 6 cups water in a saucepan. Add the salt. Bring to a boil, reduce the heat, and simmer for 10 minutes.

PERFECT PATES

French pâtés are becoming as familiar in America as meat loaf, and they are usually not much more difficult to make, once you have the knack.

These rich and spicy meat mixtures vary greatly from cook to cook and are at home at the cocktail party as a sit-down first course, as the main course at a picnic, or as an ingredient in a more complicated dish.

The recipes here illustrate some of the differences between types of pâté. Try them all to find the one that best satisfies your personal taste.

CHARCUTERIE MENU

ASSORTED PEASANT BREADS

UNSALTED BUTTER

CORNICHONS

PICKLED PEARL ONIONS

PICKLED WILD CHERRIES

DIJON, HERB, AND COARSE MUSTARDS

COUNTRY AND SPICED PÂTÉS

BLACK AND WHITE RADISHES

CAROTTES RÂPÉES

SMOKED DRIED SAUSAGES

BRIE, CHÈVRE, AND TRIPLE CRÈME CHEESES

FRESH FRUITS

BUTTER COOKIES

2. Add the chicken livers and simmer very gently for about 10 minutes; the livers should still be slightly pink inside.

3. Drain the livers; discard the celery and peppercorns. Place the livers in a food processor. Add the remaining ingredients except the currants and process until well blended and very smooth.

4. Transfer the mixture to a bowl, stir in the currants, and transfer the pâté to a 3- to 4-cup crock or terrine. Smooth the top of the pâté, cover, and refrigerate for at least 4 hours. Allow the pâté to stand at room temperature for 30 minutes before serving.

About 3 cups pâté, 8 or more portions

CHICKEN LIVER PATE WITH GREEN PEPPERCORNS

6 tablespoons (¾ stick) unsalted butter
½ cup finely minced yellow onion
2 garlic cloves, peeled and chopped
1 teaspoon dried thyme
½ cup celery tops (leaves)
10 whole black peppercorns
2 bay leaves
6 cups water
1 pound chicken livers
2 tablespoons Cognac
½ teaspoon salt
Freshly ground black pepper, to taste
½ teaspoon ground allspice
5 teaspoons water-packed green peppercorns, drained
¼ cup heavy cream

1. Melt the butter in a skillet over medium heat. Add the onion, garlic, and thyme and cook, covered, until the onion is tender and lightly colored, about 25 minutes.

2. Meanwhile add the celery tops, peppercorns, and bay leaves to 6 cups water in a saucepan. Bring to a boil, reduce the heat, and simmer for 10 minutes.

3. Add the chicken livers to the saucepan and simmer gently for about 10 minutes; livers should still be slightly pink inside.

4. Drain the livers, discarding the celery tops, bay leaves, and peppercorns. Place the livers and butter mixture in a food processor. Add the Cognac, salt, pepper, allspice, and 4 teaspoons of the green peppercorns. Process until smooth.

5. Pour in the cream and process again to blend. Transfer to a bowl and stir in the remaining teaspoon of green peppercorns.

6. Transfer the mixture to a 2-cup terrine, cover, and refrigerate for at least 4 hours. Let the pâté stand at room temperature for 30 minutes before serving.

2 cups, at least 8 portions

PATE DE CAMPAGNE WITH WALNUTS

This pâté gains special character from the walnuts. We love to feature it as a first course for holiday time, or on a picnic.

2 pounds fresh pork fat, ground
¾ cup finely chopped yellow onion
1 pound ground lean veal
1 pound ground lean pork shoulder
1¾ tablespoons coarse salt
1 teaspoon freshly ground black pepper
1 teaspoon dried thyme
¾ to 1 teaspoon ground allspice
1 teaspoon dried tarragon
½ to 1 teaspoon dried oregano
4 garlic cloves, peeled and chopped fine
3 juniper berries, crushed
½ cup Cognac
¼ cup Madeira wine
4 eggs, lightly beaten
½ pound beef liver, cut into ½-inch dice
1 cup shelled walnuts
1 pound thinly sliced fresh pork fat, to line loaf pan
2 bay leaves
3 whole juniper berries

1. Melt 2 to 3 tablespoons of the pork fat in a medium-size skillet over medium-low heat. Add the onions and cook until softened, about 10 minutes. Drain the onions.

2. Combine the ground veal, ground pork, remaining ground pork fat, coarse salt, pepper, thyme, allspice, tarragon, oregano, garlic, crushed juniper berries, Cognac, Madeira, eggs, and the onions in a bowl. Blend thoroughly without overworking the mixture. (Do not add the liver yet.) To test for seasoning, sauté over medium heat, cool, and taste a small patty of the mixture. Correct all seasonings.

3. Fold in the diced beef liver and walnuts.

4. Preheat the oven to 350°F. Bring a large heavy pot of water to a boil.

5. Line the bottom and sides of a 9½ x 5 x 3 inch loaf pan with the sheets of pork fat, letting some hang over the sides. Pack the meat mixture into the pan, pressing so that no air pockets remain. The top should mound up slightly. Top with 2 bay leaves and 3 whole juniper berries. Cover with the overhanging edges of the lining fat, then with a sheet of pork fat cut to fit, then with aluminum foil. Press the foil snugly onto the edges of the pan to be sure that the pâté is completely enclosed.

THE BAIN-MARIE

Use of the *bain-marie,* or water bath, is an age-old cooking technique, reportedly developed in Italy. The item being cooked (often a pâté, mousse, custard, or other fragile concoction) is set in a larger pan of hot water and transferred to the oven or stove. The water stabilizes the oven's temperature fluctuations and distributes the cooking heat more efficiently. The most familiar everyday application is the double boiler.

6. Set the loaf pan in a larger pan and place in the lower third of the oven. Pour enough boiling water into the outer pan to come halfway up the sides of the inner pan. Bake for 2½ hours. The pâté is done when it shrinks from the sides of the pan and the juices run a clear yellow; you can check this by uncovering the pâté and pressing a spoon on top. If it isn't done, re-cover, and bake 30 minutes more.

7. When the pâté is done, remove the loaf pan from the boiling water bath, or pour the water from the outer pan. The loaf must now be weighted for several hours; this is done to force out the interior fat and compress the meat so it will slice evenly. To weight the pâté, place another loaf pan or a board of suitable size on top of the pâté. Put 2 bricks or an equivalent weight of heavy canned goods in the pan or on the board. Let cool, then refrigerate without the weights.

8. When the pâté has been chilled thoroughly, remove it from the loaf pan. Remove the fat around it, wrap the loaf in plastic wrap, and return it to the refrigerator; or let it warm slightly at room temperature, then serve. The flavor is enhanced after 1 or 2 days of refrigeration. Let the pâté come to near-room temperature before serving.

At least 10 first-course portions, or 20 cocktail portions

from THE SILVER PALATE NOTEBOOK

It is worth the extra money to be properly staffed. Even if your affair isn't being catered, consider calling a lend-a-hand agency to provide personnel. Make certain they arrive in time to be briefed on logistics, timing, garnishes, and any last-minute food preparation. Let them know your personal style (casual, organized, elegant), and be sure they recognize you as host in case of emergencies.

Make it a rule to clean up the night of the party, whether you have staff to help or not.

SEAFOOD PATE

An elegant first course, accompanied by Tomato Coulis (page 232) or a flavored mayonnaise or vinaigrette, such as Creamy Tarragon-Mustard Dressing (page 274) or Green Herb Dipping Sauce (page 178).

1½ pounds sea scallops, chilled
1 cup thinly sliced well-rinsed leeks
1 teaspoon salt
Several pinches of grated nutmeg
Several dashes of Tabasco sauce
3 cups heavy cream, chilled
½ cup frozen peas, thawed
1 tablespoon lemon zest
3 tablespoons finely minced fresh Italian (flat-leaf) parsley
1 pound fresh salmon, chilled
2 very cold egg whites
1 tablespoon tomato paste
1 tablespoon orange zest
Butter, for the pan
For serving (choose 1): Creamy Tarragon-Mustard Dressing, Green Herb Dipping Sauce, Tomato Coulis

1. Remove the tiny hinge muscles from the scallops. Rinse the scallops thoroughly and pat dry. Reserve 6 of the largest and most perfect. Combine the remaining scallops with ½ cup of the sliced leeks in a food processor and process until smooth.

2. Add ½ teaspoon of the salt, a pinch of nutmeg, and 2 or 3 dashes of Tabasco, and process again.

3. With the motor running, dribble in 1 cup of the chilled heavy cream in a slow steady stream. When all the cream is in, shut off the processor. Remove half of the mixture to a bowl; cover and refrigerate. Add the peas to the remaining mixture in the processor; process until smooth. Transfer to a bowl; stir in the lemon zest and parsley. Cover and refrigerate.

4. Clean the processor bowl. Skin the salmon and remove any bones. Cut the salmon into small dice. Place the salmon and the remaining leeks in the processor and process until smooth.

5. Add the egg whites and tomato paste when the mixture becomes too hard for the processor to mix. Season with the remaining ½ teaspoon salt, a pinch of nutmeg, dashes of Tabasco, and the orange zest, and process until smooth.

6. With the motor running, dribble in the remaining 2 cups heavy cream in a slow steady stream. As soon as all the cream has been added, shut off the processor. Cover and refrigerate.

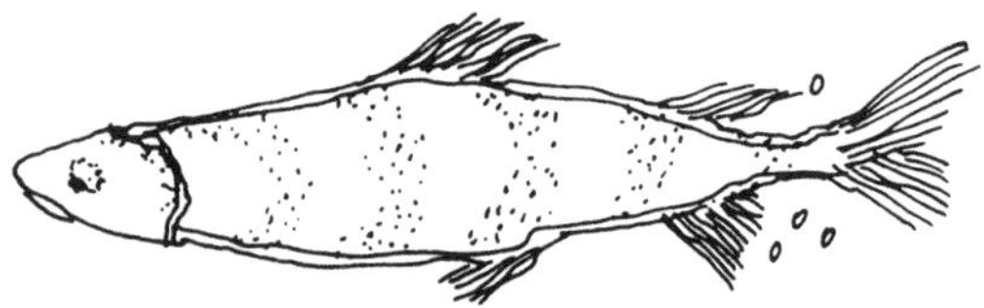

7. Preheat the oven to 350°F. Lightly butter a 9 x 5 x 3 inch loaf pan. Bring a large pot of water to a boil for the water bath.

8. Spoon the plain scallop mixture into the loaf pan. Arrange the reserved scallops in a line down the center of the pan. Press them lightly into the scallop mixture. Spoon the chilled salmon mixture over the scallop layer and smooth with a spatula. Spread the pea and scallop mixture over the salmon layer. Rap the pan firmly on your work surface several times to eliminate air bubbles.

9. Wrap the loaf pan in aluminum foil and set it in a larger baking pan. Pour the boiling water into the baking pan so that it comes about halfway up the sides of the loaf pan. Set the pans on the center rack of the oven and bake until an instant-read thermometer gives an internal temperature of 130°F, 45 minutes.

10. Remove the loaf pan from the hot water and cool to room temperature. Refrigerate overnight.

11. To unmold: Remove the aluminum foil and dip the loaf pan into hot water for about 30 seconds. Run a thin knife carefully around the edge of the pâté, set a large plate on top of the pan, and invert it. The pâté will drop out onto the plate. Turn the pâté top side up.

12. To serve cold, slice and arrange the pâté on plates with a dollop of chosen sauce. To serve hot, slice the pâté when cold, arrange slices on a buttered baking sheet, and cover with foil. Warm gently in a 300°F oven for about 15 minutes. Spoon warmed tomato coulis onto plates and center a slice of warmed pâté on the coulis. Serve immediately.

10 to 12 portions as a first course

Originally the terms "pâté" and "terrine" were used to distinguish meat dishes baked in crusts (pâtés) from those cooked in crockery or a metal dish (terrines). The terms are now used more or less interchangeably.

"Never eat more than you can lift."

—MISS PIGGY

LAYERED VEGETABLE TERRINE

Three layers—tomato, leek, and white bean—combine in a rich, spicy, and satisfying pâté. Serve as is or garnished with Aïoli Sauce (page 50), Tomato-Basil Mayonnaise (page 413), or chilled Tomato Coulis (page 232).

WHITE BEAN LAYER

4 tablespoons (½ stick) unsalted butter
1 cup finely chopped yellow onions
4 garlic cloves, peeled and finely chopped
½ teaspoon salt
½ teaspoon freshly ground black pepper
1 cup canned white cannellini beans
¼ cup Basil Purée (see Note, page 38)
1 whole egg
1 egg yolk

1. Melt the butter in a small heavy saucepan or skillet over low heat. Add the onions, cover, and cook slowly until tender and lightly colored, about 20 minutes.

2. Add the garlic, salt, and pepper to the onions, and cook, uncovered, for another 5 minutes. Remove from the heat.

3. Rinse the beans and drain them well. Combine the beans, onion mixture, and basil purée in a food processor, and process until smooth.

4. Add the whole egg and egg yolk and process again until the eggs are completely incorporated. Transfer to a bowl, cover, and refrigerate until chilled.

INSTANT-READ THERMOMETERS

An instant-read thermometer, unlike a conventional cooking thermometer, does not remain in the food as it cooks. It is merely inserted, gives an "instant" reading, and then is removed. Although instant-read thermometers cost more than conventional thermometers, they last longer and are more accurate.

Layered Vegetable Terrine and Tomato-Basil Mayonnaise—a delightful offering from the garden.

TOMATO LAYER

4 tablespoons (½ stick) unsalted butter
1 cup finely chopped yellow onions
4 medium-size tomatoes (about 1½ pounds)
2 large garlic cloves, peeled and finely chopped
3 tablespoons Basil Purée (see Note)
3 tablespoons tomato paste
1 teaspoon chili powder
Salt and freshly ground black pepper, to taste
1 whole egg
1 egg yolk

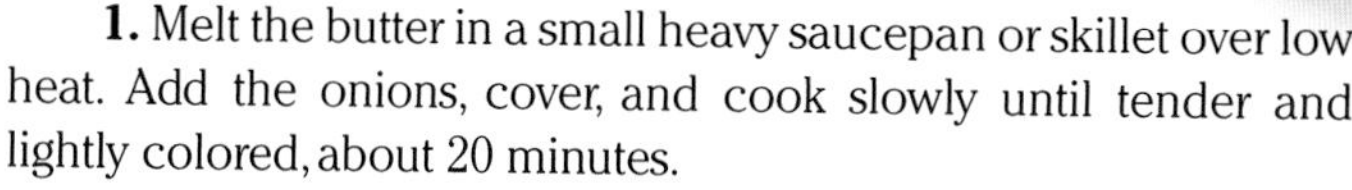

1. Melt the butter in a small heavy saucepan or skillet over low heat. Add the onions, cover, and cook slowly until tender and lightly colored, about 20 minutes.

2. Meanwhile, cut a small X in the bottom of each tomato and drop them into boiling salted water for 10 seconds. Remove with a slotted spoon, drop them into a bowl of ice water, and let cool. The skins will peel off easily when the tomatoes are cool. Cut the peeled tomatoes into halves crosswise, scrape out the seeds, and squeeze out and discard the juice. Chop the tomatoes and add them to the onions. Cook uncovered over medium heat, stirring often, for 20 minutes.

3. Add the garlic, basil purée, tomato paste, chili powder, and salt and pepper, and cook until the mixture is very thick, 15 minutes longer. Taste and correct the seasoning. Transfer the mixture to a bowl and cool to room temperature.

4. Beat the whole egg and egg yolk together in a small bowl and stir into the tomato mixture. Cover and refrigerate until chilled.

Note: *Basil Purée:* Process or blend 7 cups washed and dried fresh basil leaves or 7 cups fresh parsley leaves and 1 tablespoon dried basil, with 3 to 4 tablespoons olive oil. Cover and refrigerate.

LEEK LAYER

6 tablespoons (¾ stick) unsalted butter
4 cups (about 8 medium-size) thinly-sliced, well-rinsed leeks, white part only
2 teaspoons curry powder
2 garlic cloves, peeled and finely chopped
½ cup chopped fresh Italian (flat-leaf) parsley
¾ teaspoon freshly ground black pepper
Salt to taste
1 whole egg
1 egg yolk

1. Melt the butter in a small heavy saucepan or skillet over low heat. Add the leeks, cover, and cook slowly until very tender, about 30 minutes.

2. Add the curry powder, garlic, parsley, pepper, and salt, and cook, uncovered, stirring occasionally, for another 10 minutes. Cool to room temperature.

3. Beat the whole egg and egg yolk together in a small bowl, and stir into the cooled leek mixture. Cover and refrigerate.

"The cook was a good cook, as cooks go; and as cooks go, she went."

—SAKI

APERITIFS

Apéritifs have a bit more kick than table wines, but are less alcoholic than distilled spirits. Often they are infused with herbs and other flavorings in combinations kept secret by their manufacturers. *Vermouths* (we like Lillet) can be garnished with a strip of orange or lemon peel. *Dry Sherry* is delicious just slightly cooled, although many now drink it on the rocks. *Campari* is a brilliantly red, slightly bitter Italian apéritif. Try it with a splash of tonic or soda and a squeeze of fresh lime. (And while you're at it, remember that a splash of soda will lighten your vermouth or sherry, too.) *Pineau des Charentes* has been made in France for over 400 years. It's a slightly sweet blend of white wine and Cognac that we adore. *Pastis* is the working Frenchman's favorite apéritif. The anise-flavored liqueur is mixed with water or soda in a one-to-five ratio. Or shake an egg white, 2 ounces of pastis, and 1 teaspoon of extra-fine sugar together with ice until foamy. Strain into a chilled tall glass, add a splash of soda, and garnish with a mint leaf.

TO COMPLETE THE TERRINE

2 carrots
6 thin asparagus spears
12 large leaves of green cabbage (avoid the coarse outer leaves)
Unsalted butter

1. Bring a large pot of heavily salted water to a boil. Have ready a large bowl of ice water.

2. Scrape the carrots and cut them lengthwise into quarters. Drop them into the boiling water and cook until very tender but not mushy. Lift from the boiling water with a slotted spoon and drop them into the ice water.

3. Trim the woody ends from the asparagus and drop the spears into the boiling water. Cook until tender, remove from the boiling water with a slotted spoon, and drop them into the ice water.

4. Drop the cabbage leaves into the boiling water and press with a spoon to be certain they are submerged and cooking. Blanch them until they begin to become translucent, about 5 minutes. Remove the cabbage leaves from the boiling water with a slotted spoon and drop them into the ice water.

5. When all the vegetables are cool, drain them and pat dry. Lightly butter a 9 x 5 x 3 inch loaf or bread pan. Trim the heavy ribs from the cabbage leaves. Line the loaf pan with the leaves, covering the sides, ends, and bottom, and overlapping the leaves slightly. Be sure you have 2 or 3 leaves left for the top of the terrine.

6. Preheat the oven to 350°F. Bring a large pot of water to a boil for the water bath.

7. Remove the leek, tomato, and bean mixtures from the refrigerator. Stir the leek mixture to be sure the ingredients are well combined and spoon it into the bottom of the loaf pan. Smooth with a spatula and arrange lengths of carrot on top.

8. Stir the tomato mixture and spoon it on top of the leek mixture, being careful not to disturb the carrots. Smooth the tomato mixture and arrange the asparagus spears on top of it.

9. Finally, pour in the bean layer and smooth it. Rap the loaf pan several times on your work surface to expel any air bubbles. Cover the terrine with the remaining cabbage leaves, tucking the excess down the sides of the pan.

10. Wrap the loaf pan in aluminum foil and set it in a larger baking pan. Pour boiling water into the baking pan so that it comes about halfway up the sides of the loaf pan. Set the pans on the center rack of the oven and bake until the center of the terrine feels firm to the touch, 2 hours.

11. Remove the loaf pan from the hot water and unwrap it. Let it cool for 15 minutes, then weight it down by placing another loaf pan on top and putting a weight inside, such as canned goods or coffee mugs, until completely cool. Remove the weights, cover, and chill thoroughly.

12. To unmold, dip the pan briefly into hot water and run a thin knife around the sides of the pan. Set a platter upside down over the terrine and invert; the terrine will drop out onto the plate.

13. Serve cold, sliced and garnished with any of the sauces suggested in the headnote.

8 to 10 portions as a first course

DAZZLERS

For those times when the movers and shakers must be dazzled, when laurels have been bestowed, when transitions must be acknowledged and anniversaries celebrated, something very special indeed is demanded of the host. The casual and easygoing gathering gives way to the event; important people and important events call for important food. This is the time to pull out all the stops and turn your entertaining eye to some of the more elegant and extravagant possibilities the world has to offer.

Caviar, oysters, foie gras, aïoli—even the names excite. We've dealt with these fabulous treats over the years and for us, while the mystery may be gone, the magic always remains. Remember, there's no such thing as being served too much of a good thing, but these are very luxurious and can be served as wonderful garnishes, as well as in lavish amounts. Either way, you and your guests will absolutely love them.

CAVIAR

If you've shopped for caviar and been shocked at prices, you will appreciate the irony that, in the nineteenth century, it was very affordable. And in fact, large quantities of American caviar were exported to Europe! Then recently, we enjoyed decades of importing caviar from the Beluga sturgeon of Russia and Iran. And, just as we mastered the lingo—"beluga," "osetra," "sevruga," "malossol," and "pressed"—the marketplace changed again. For a while the U.N. banned exporting caviar from wild, over-fished—and now endangered—Beluga sturgeon from the Caspian and Black seas.

Today, caviar from farmed Iranian, Manchurian, Romanian, and Siberian sturgeon has become increasingly popular with chefs and home cooks alike. These are complemented by many other fish with very tasty roe including burbot and vendace from Finland; cod from Norway; tuna roe (bottarga) from the Mediterranean; red salmon from Alaska and the Pacific Northwest; hackleback from Tennessee and Kentucky; paddlefish, trout, flounder, shad, herring, scallops, crabs, crawfish, artic char, brook trout, albino sturgeon, and golden whitefish from the Great Lakes and Canada. The roes range in colors of pink, salmon, golden, white, and gray, making for great drama on a caviar buffet. Remember, when shopping, that it is only the eggs from the sturgeon that can be labeled simply caviar, others processed in the same manner must be labeled with the name of the fish preceding the word. The latest and most promising news for U.S. consumers is the success in farming California white sturgeon. Its flavor is the most reminiscent of the wild Beluga and the quantities harvested indicate that the American caviar market will be booming for some time to come. Caviar is back as an elegant, tasty, and affordable American appetizer.

THE CAVIAR CODE

Always buy your caviar from a reputable dealer who specializes in it and therefore "turns the inventory" frequently. Smell and taste the product if at all possible; caviar should not be oily and should never smell or taste fishy or salty. (Caviar labeled *malossol* has been lightly salted.) The eggs should be shiny, translucent, perfectly

whole and firm, so that you can feel the pearls with your tongue. Keep caviar refrigerated (not frozen) and open fifteen minutes before serving, centering the open tin on a bed of crushed ice, with the lid alongside.

SERVING CAVIAR

Purists take their caviar straight, on a mother-of-pearl spoon (silver imparts a metallic taste). Other serving options include fresh toast points or sliced pumpernickel, a dab of sour cream, minced hard-cooked eggs, finely chopped red onion, lemon wedges, and chopped parsley. If you're not using caviar as garnish, and pulling out all of the stops, it's best to place it all on a buffet and let your guests select their own means of indulgence.

OYSTERS

Oysters once flourished in American waters. The Indians harvested them extravagantly, and they were an inexpensive staple for years. Polluted waters endangered the oyster for a while, but each year they are increasingly available, and cultivated beds will soon ensure that if we wish to eat 100 oysters at one sitting as Diamond Jim Brady once did, we can.

Oyster lovers have their favorites and will debate the various merits of the flat versus the hollow, the pale silver and expensive Belon, the green French Marenne, the pungent ivory Limfjord as well as the popular Blue Point, Chatham, Papillion, Cotuit, Box, Kent Island, Claire, Chincoteague, Malpeque, Apalachicola, and Canadian Golden Mantle. There are differences in size, flavor, texture, and saltiness. If you get a chance to taste several varieties side by side, you will learn to distinguish your favorites. Oysters must be served freshly opened, kept cold on a bed of ice. We like them served simply with lemon juice and freshly ground black pepper. Cocktail sauce (the kind made with ketchup and horseradish) is taboo (you can't taste the oysters), but a Mignonette Sauce (page 47) is occasionally welcome.

FOIE GRAS

In the midst of all these other luxuries, a few words about *foie gras* seem in order. Foie gras is the exquisite, pale, fattened liver of a force-fed goose or duck. These animals, bred in the southwest corner of France—Gascony and the Périgord—as well as in Hungary and Israel, are now also bred in Upstate New York, Minnesota, and California. Foie gras should have a firm but silken and velvety texture, and taste as rich and sweet as butter.

Imported foie gras sold in tins or jars is available here. But since the U.S. government prohibits the importation of raw foie gras, it is fully or partially cooked and will give you only the faintest clue as to why it is so beloved. Now that foie gras is being produced in various parts of America we can enjoy it at its best. In its purest form, fresh raw foie gras is cooked into a terrine and served cool, thickly sliced with warm thin toast. Alternatively, fresh foie gras can be lightly seared in a sauté pan, then sliced and served with caramelized apples or pears, or fresh figs or grapes.

The classic wine served with foie gras is Sauternes, the sweet white wine from Bordeaux. But chilled Champagne, Chablis, or a red Bordeaux or Syrah would balance the richness of the foie gras nicely.

A visit to the foie gras market in Gascony or Périgord is quite an experience; it is as if you have stepped back centuries. The market is a large wooden building, bustling with people and contrasts. Peasants and foie gras buyers collide on the floor, each trying to attract the other. The plucked and cleaned ducks and geese, which have been force-fed with corn to fatten their livers, are arranged on long tables covered with crisp white cloths. Both birds and livers are for sale, and competition is keen. Baskets of fresh livers are offered for judgment: Was the bird healthy? Was it fed only the best meal and at the proper intervals? Is the resulting liver the right color of pink or ochre? Does it have the proper texture?

To a visitor, the system and the food it produces may seem strangely harsh, but a Frenchman recognizes the making of foie gras as an art steeped in the antiquity of France itself.

Should you be lucky enough to be invited to a private home in this region or to dine in one of the fine restaurants of France, you will taste the treat of your life—the freshest possible foie gras, prepared and served by those to whom it symbolizes a way of life.

Iced vodka (store your bottle in the freezer overnight before serving), Champagne, aquavit, or a very dry white wine are our favorite sips with caviar.

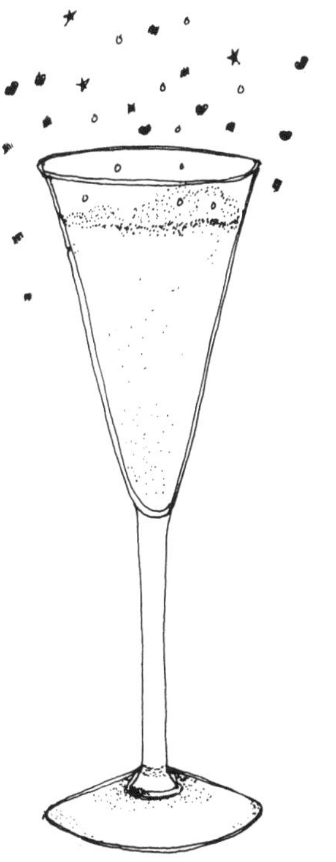

HERBED CAVIAR ROULADE

CREPE

2 teaspoons corn oil
2 eggs
1 cup milk
½ cup unbleached all-purpose flour
Pinch of salt
2 teaspoons chopped fresh chives
1 tablespoon chopped fresh Italian (flat-leaf) parsley
2 teaspoons finely chopped fresh dill

CREPE FILLING

1 cup sour cream
½ cup finely chopped red onion
1 cup finely chopped hard-cooked eggs (3 eggs)
¼ teaspoon freshly ground black pepper
2 ounces black caviar
2 ounces golden caviar
10 sprigs fresh dill, for garnish
10 lemon wedges, for garnish

1. Prepare the crêpe: Preheat the oven to 425°F. Brush an 11 x 17-inch jelly roll pan lightly with the corn oil.

2. In the bowl of an electric mixer, beat the eggs until pale yellow, 15 seconds.

3. With the mixer on, add the milk in a slow, steady stream, then add the flour and mix until smooth, carefully scraping down the sides. Turn the mixer off.

4. Add the salt, chives, parsley, and dill and mix to blend for a few seconds. Let the mixture rest in the bowl at room temperature for 30 minutes.

5. With a rubber spatula, spread the batter evenly on the prepared pan. Bake until set, 12 minutes. Remove from the oven and let cool in the pan. When cool, loosen the bottom with a metal spatula.

6. Prepare the filling: In a medium-size bowl, combine the sour cream, onion, eggs, and black pepper.

7. With a small rubber spatula, gently fold the caviars into the sour cream mixture.

8. Spread the mixture evenly over the crêpe leaving a 1-inch border around the edges. Beginning at the short end, carefully roll up the crêpe.

9. With a serrated knife, cut the crêpe into 1½-inch slices. Place a slice in the center of each plate, and garnish each with a sprig of dill and a wedge of lemon.

8 to 10 portions as an appetizer

"There is more simplicity in the man who eats caviar on impulse than in the man who eats Grape Nuts on principle."

—G. K. CHESTERTON

NEW POTATOES WITH BLACK CAVIAR

12 very small new potatoes (1 pound or less)
4 to 5 cups rock salt
Oil for deep-frying
½ cup sour cream
3½ to 4 ounces black or golden caviar

1. Preheat the oven to 450°F.

2. Wash and dry the potatoes. Arrange them on a bed of rock salt in a shallow baking pan and bake until done, 30 to 35 minutes.

3. Remove the potatoes from the oven and cut them into halves. (Reserve the hot rock salt.) Scoop out the pulp with a melon-ball cutter or small spoon, being careful to keep the shells intact. Mash the pulp slightly in a small bowl and keep warm.

4. Pour oil to a depth of 3 inches into a large saucepan and heat to 375°F on a deep-frying thermometer. Drop the potato shells into the oil and fry until golden brown and crisp, 1 to 2 minutes. Drain well on paper towels.

5. Fill the potato shells with the mashed potatoes, top with a spoonful of sour cream, and add ¼ teaspoon or more of caviar. Serve as a first course atop the hot rock salt on thick salad plates.

6 portions as a first course

CAVIAR ECLAIRS

1 recipe Pâte à Choux (page 408), prepared through Step 3
Butter, for the baking sheet
1 egg, beaten
5 slices of smoked salmon
8 ounces whipped cream cheese
½ cup sour cream
4 ounces black caviar
Finely chopped fresh dill
Freshly ground black pepper, to taste

1. Butter a baking sheet. Fill a pastry bag fitted with a small plain tip with warm Pâte à Choux. Pipe out 2-inch lengths of the pâte à choux. They should look rather like strips of yellow toothpaste. Top each with a second strip of the pâte. Form 20 such miniature éclairs. Brush the tops of the éclairs with beaten egg. Bake according to the pâte à choux directions (Steps 4 and 6), and cool completely.

These luxurious New Potatoes with Black Caviar look simply elegant on their bed of rock salt.

2. Cut each piece of salmon into quarters and reserve.

3. Slice éclairs horizontally into halves. Spread a thin layer of cream cheese in the bottom of each éclair and lay a piece of salmon on top. Spread a thin layer of sour cream on the salmon and top with a dab of caviar. Sprinkle with dill and freshly ground black pepper. Return the tops to the éclairs and serve.

20 éclairs

CAVIAR DIP

6 ounces whipped cream cheese, at room temperature
3 ounces sour cream
1 tablespoon fresh lemon juice
1 teaspoon grated onion
1½ tablespoons finely chopped fresh dill
Pinch of freshly ground black pepper
2 ounces black caviar or natural red salmon caviar

Mix the cream cheese with the sour cream in a small bowl. Gently fold in the lemon juice, onion, dill, and pepper until well blended. Fold in the caviar carefully. Refrigerate until needed.

About 1 cup

OYSTERS AND CAVIAR

Fresh seaweed (see Notes)
18 fresh oysters on the half shell (see Notes)
2 scallions (green onions), well rinsed and thinly sliced into rings
2 ounces black caviar
2 lemons, cut into thin wedges

1. Spread the seaweed in a flat basket. Arrange the oysters, in their shells, on the seaweed.

2. Sprinkle each oyster with 2 or 3 pieces of scallion. Top each with a dab of caviar. Serve very cold, accompanied by fresh lemon wedges.

4 to 6 portions

Notes: Seaweed can be ordered from your fishmonger and is usually free.

Shuck the oysters yourself or have the fishmonger do it.

COOKING WITH CAVIAR

Cooking with caviar and combining it with other ingredients is tricky because the eggs are delicate; unnecessary handling or heat can turn them into mush. There are possibilities, however: fold the caviar into sour cream and serve as a dip; fold into a warm, buttery omelet; roll into a crêpe; spoon into a 2-inch shell of pâte brisée; toss gently with angel hair pasta and crème fraîche; stuff into hollowed cherry tomatoes, hard-cooked eggs, or tiny pastry puffs.

from THE SILVER PALATE NOTEBOOK

Hired entertainment is a lovely touch and need not cost a fortune. A string quartet might feature the son or daughter of a friend. The piano bar player at your favorite hangout might perform as a favor. A pianist, cellist, or harpist might be hired from a nearby music school for a nominal fee and a good reference.

OYSTERS, SPINACH, AND CAVIAR

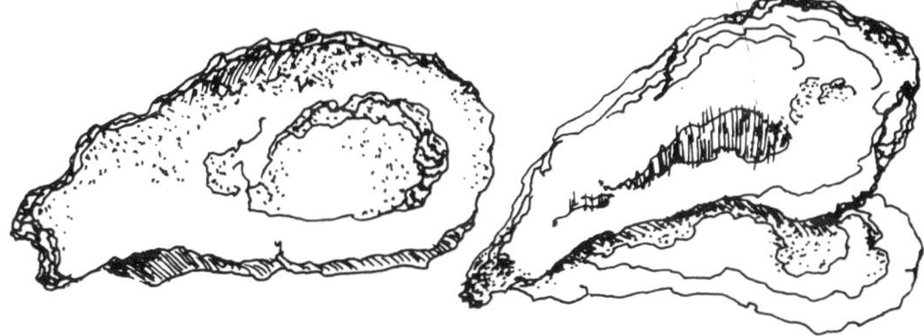

Inspired by Jean-Marie Amat, chef at the restaurant Saint James in Bordeaux, France.

2 large shallots, very finely chopped
½ cup sherry vinegar
32 shucked oysters, including their liquor
32 fresh tender small spinach leaves
6 ounces black American caviar
1 lemon, cut into 8 wedges

1. Marinate the shallots in the sherry vinegar overnight.

2. Gently warm the oysters in their liquor in a small saucepan over medium heat until their edges curl, about 30 seconds. Remove from the heat and cool. Drain.

3. Place the spinach leaves in a strainer, dip into boiling water, and immediately drop into ice water. Drain and pat dry.

4. Wrap 1 spinach leaf around each oyster. Arrange 4 wrapped oysters on each of 8 chilled plates.

5. Drain the shallots and sprinkle them evenly over the oyster bundles. Top each bundle with ½ teaspoon of caviar. Place a lemon wedge on each plate and serve immediately.

8 portions as a first course

"Why, then the world's mine oyster, Which I with sword will open."

—WILLIAM SHAKESPEARE, *THE MERRY WIVES OF WINDSOR*

MIGNONETTE SAUCE

Excellent with oysters.

½ cup dry white wine
½ cup white wine vinegar (see Note)
3 tablespoons chopped shallots
1 teaspoon freshly ground black pepper

Whisk all the ingredients together in a bowl. Let sit at room temperature for 15 to 30 minutes before serving.

1 cup

Note: Or substitute sherry vinegar or raspberry vinegar.

AN AIOLI PLATTER

In Provence, feast days are often celebrated by a lusty community meal in which poached fish, cooked vegetables, and a garlicky aïoli sauce are the main components. This same feast, arranged in smaller quantities, can become a perfect supper for guests who love to linger after drinks. The colors are intense, the flavors powerful. An Aïoli Platter brings the golden sunshine of Provence to your buffet. (Recipe on page 50)

"The air in Provence is impregnated with the aroma of garlic, which makes it very healthful to breathe."

—ALEXANDRE DUMAS

"Life itself is the proper binge."

—JULIA CHILD

VEGETABLES, FISH, AND BEEF FOR AÏOLI PLATTERS

Double batch Aïoli Sauce (recipe follows), made 1 batch at a time
6 small artichokes, trimmed, boiled, chokes removed
7 pounds cod, poached
1 pound carpaccio (thinly sliced and pounded best-quality raw beef tenderloin)
½ pound snow peas, trimmed, blanched, refreshed in cold water
½ pound green beans, trimmed, blanched, refreshed in cold water
1 pound carrots, peeled, cut into 2-inch pieces, blanched, refreshed in cold water
3 pounds cauliflower, cut into florets, blanched, refreshed in cold water
1 pound chickpeas, cooked
3 large red or green bell peppers, stemmed, seeded, and sliced
1 pint cherry or grape tomatoes, washed, stems intact
1 pound zucchini, sliced
1 pound small potatoes, boiled until tender
6 eggs, hard-cooked, peeled, and sliced in half lengthwise
¼ cup capers, drained, for garnish
½ cup chopped fresh parsley, for garnish

1. Spoon some of the aïoli sauce into the center of each artichoke.

2. Place an aïoli-filled artichoke in the middle of each plate and arrange the cod, carpaccio, prepared vegetables, and eggs around it in a spokelike fashion, making sure that each plate has some of everything. Sprinkle with capers and parsley.

12 portions

AÏOLI SAUCE

8 to 10 garlic cloves, peeled
2 egg yolks, at room temperature
Juice of 1 lemon
Salt and freshly ground white pepper, to taste
1 teaspoon Dijon mustard
1½ cups oil (half peanut oil, half olive oil), at room temperature

1. Purée the garlic in a food processor or blender. Whisk the egg yolks in a small bowl until light and smooth, and add to the garlic. Add the lemon juice, mustard, and salt and pepper, and process to a smooth paste.

2. With the machine running, pour the oil very slowly into the mixture in a steady stream. Once all the oil is added, continue blending until you obtain a thick, shiny, firm sauce. Transfer to a storage container, cover with plastic wrap, and refrigerate until ready to use.

CARPACCIO

Carpaccio is lean and tender raw beef, pounded to transparency or sliced paper-thin. If you sweet talk your butcher he may prepare it for you; if not, partially freeze top-quality meat and slice it with your sharpest knife. Put the slices between 2 pieces of wax paper and pound out any irregularities with the flat side of a meat tenderizer or the bottom of a heavy saucepan.

OF GARLIC AND SAINTS

Once a year, at the height of summer, the small towns of Provence celebrate the garlic of the season in a dramatic way. Each town has its own patron saint, who is honored by a three-day festivity—culminating, on the third day, with a Grand Aïoli for all the town's inhabitants.

This aïoli uses raw eggs—use only very fresh eggs that have been refrigerated.

SOUP'S ON

One can stir up memories from childhood of watching Mother or Grandmother preparing kettles of soup. There is nothing like soup to make you feel warm and secure and to recall the love and care that went into those years of nourishing, instinctive cooking.

Soup making has been elevated to the level of haute cuisine, capturing the essences and colors of the freshest vegetables and fruits. All soups can be prepared ahead of time, to be chilled or reheated for serving. Take advantage of a free afternoon or a quiet evening to prepare basic stocks. Freeze them in ice-cube trays or different-size plastic containers for instant use at a later time.

Soups are very logical. All you need is a pot large enough to make the amount of soup you want. Simply blend soup liquids with your favorite meats, beans, vegetables, and fruits. The magic comes when you understand what goes with what; there is no better guide than your own good taste. Originally soup was basic sustenance, a meal in itself. Today, while soup is often served in a small quantity as a first course, it may continue to represent the entrée for a meal for those interested in eating light.

BASIC ADVICE TO SOUP MAKERS

♥ A rich, homemade stock is one of the most generous contributions you can make to a soup.

♥ Remove the soup from the stove and allow it to cool slightly before any puréeing.

♥ Any soup that has a particular herb seasoning should receive a generous dash of that herb just before you are ready to purée. This provides a fresher soup flavor (for example, tomato with dill, sweet pea with mint, potato with arugula).

♥ The image of a long-simmering stock or soup as a catchall for kitchen leftovers is passé, if indeed it ever existed at all. Only the best and freshest of ingredients will become the finest of soups.

♥ Attention to the shape of ingredients and the garnishes used can make a world of difference when serving soup.

♥ Cook onion long and slowly in butter. Spanish onions and leeks add the best flavor.

♥ Take care to balance the flavor of the soup with the rest of the meal. As an elegant first course, anticipatory of the meal to come, soups can provide an easy point of departure for your entertaining imagination.

SOUPS TO START

We love a light and cordial beginning to a meal, a real first course above and beyond cocktail fare; one of the best is soup. Chilled or warm, it is an elegant and cozy way to begin a dinner party. Hot soup will banish the cold of a winter evening; chilled, it will refresh the palate on a summer afternoon.

CURRIED BUTTERNUT SQUASH SOUP

Squash and apples complement each other naturally; curry adds an exotic note. Feel free to experiment with other types of winter or summer squash.

4 tablespoons (½ stick) unsalted butter
2 cups finely chopped yellow onions
4 to 5 teaspoons curry powder
2 medium-size butternut squash (about 3 pounds total)
2 apples, peeled, cored, and chopped
3 cups Chicken Stock (page 416)
1 cup apple juice
Salt and freshly ground black pepper, to taste
1 shredded unpeeled Granny Smith apple, for garnish

1. Melt the butter in a large heavy pot over low heat. Add the onions and curry powder and cook, covered, until the onions are tender, about 25 minutes.

from THE SILVER PALATE NOTEBOOK

The pace of a party is important and up to the host to set. It needs to have a rhythm that's full of surprises. Why not serve the first course at cocktail time? Pass soup in a mug with a basket of grissini. Or spring rolls with dipping sauces, or tiny lamb riblets. Waves of trays of these finger foods could ultimately add up to dinner. Move to another room for a magnificent buffet of wonderful artisanal cheeses, breads, and robust salads. Then guide everyone to the dance floor with music wafting through the air. Or, set up a grill for make-your-own s'mores. Mix things up a bit. Keep your guests amused.

"Tell me what you eat, and I'll tell you what you are."

—JEAN ANTHELME BRILLAT-SAVARIN

2. Meanwhile, peel the squash (a regular vegetable peeler works best). Cut in half horizontally, scrape out the seeds, and chop the flesh.

3. When the onions are tender, pour in the stock, add the squash and chopped apples, and bring to a boil. Reduce the heat and simmer, partially covered, until the squash and apples are very tender, about 25 minutes.

4. Pour the soup through a strainer, reserving the liquid, and transfer the solids to a food processor, or use a food mill fitted with a medium disc. Add 1 cup of the cooking stock and process until smooth.

5. Return the puréed soup to the pot and add the apple juice and about 2 cups more stock, until the soup is of the desired consistency.

6. Season with salt and pepper, simmer briefly to heat through, and serve immediately, garnished with the shredded apple.

4 to 6 portions

CARROT AND ORANGE SOUP

One of the store's most popular soups. Although particularly appropriate for the holidays, it's good and easy to prepare year-round.

4 tablespoons (½ stick) unsalted butter
2 cups finely chopped yellow onions
12 large carrots (1½ to 2 pounds), peeled and chopped
4 cups Chicken Stock (page 416)
1 cup fresh orange juice
Salt and freshly ground black pepper, to taste
Grated orange zest, to taste

1. Melt the butter over low heat in a large heavy pot. Add the onions, cover, and cook until tender and lightly colored, about 25 minutes.

2. Add the carrots and stock and bring to a boil. Reduce the heat, cover, and simmer until the carrots are very tender, about 30 minutes.

> "It is the destiny of mint to be crushed."
>
> —WAVERLEY ROOT

3. Pour the soup through a strainer and transfer the solids to a food processor, or use a food mill fitted with a medium disc. Add 1 cup of the cooking stock and process until smooth.

4. Return the purée to the pot and add the orange juice and 2 to 3 cups more stock, until the soup is of the desired consistency.

5. Season with salt and pepper; add the orange zest. Simmer until heated through. Serve immediately.

4 to 6 portions

MINTED SWEET PEA AND SPINACH SOUP

This rich, elegant soup is a perfect beginning for an important dinner. Although we use frozen peas and spinach with excellent results, the mint really must be fresh.

4 tablespoons (½ stick) unsalted butter
2 cups finely chopped yellow onions
10 ounces frozen chopped spinach, defrosted
3 cups Chicken Stock (page 416)
10 ounces frozen peas, defrosted
½ bunch of fresh mint
1 cup heavy cream
Salt and freshly ground black pepper, to taste

1. Melt the butter in a large heavy pot over low heat. Add the chopped onions, cover, and cook until tender and lightly colored, about 25 minutes.

2. Meanwhile, drain the spinach and squeeze out the excess liquid. Pour the stock into the pot, stir in the peas and spinach, and bring to a boil. Reduce the heat and simmer, partially covered, until the peas are really tender, about 20 minutes.

3. Remove the mint leaves from their stems; there should be 2 cups loosely packed leaves. Rinse thoroughly and pat dry. When the peas are tender, add the mint to the pot, cover, and simmer for another 5 minutes.

4. Pour the soup through a strainer, reserving the liquid, and transfer the solids to a food processor, or use a food mill fitted with the medium disc. Add 1 cup of the cooking stock and process until smooth.

5. Return the puréed soup to the pot. Add the heavy cream and about 1 cup more stock, until the soup is of the desired consistency.

6. Season with salt and pepper, simmer briefly to heat through, and serve immediately.

4 to 6 portions

CREAM OF WATERCRESS SOUP

This soup is rich but light, one of the few versions we know that tastes as fresh as watercress itself. It pairs wonderfully with Filet of Beef (page 118), with both served hot for an evening meal, or with the beef cold and sliced for lunch the next day.

4 tablespoons (½ stick) unsalted butter
2 cups finely chopped yellow onions
½ cup minced shallots
3 cups Chicken Stock (page 416)
1 medium-size potato, peeled and diced
4 bunches of watercress
1 cup heavy cream
Salt and freshly ground black pepper, to taste
Pinch of grated nutmeg, or to taste
Cayenne pepper, to taste

1. Melt the butter in a large heavy pot over low heat. Add the onions and shallots and cook, covered, until tender and lightly colored, about 25 minutes.

2. Add the chicken stock and the potato, bring to a boil, reduce the heat, and simmer, partially covered, until the potato is very tender, about 20 minutes.

3. Meanwhile, remove the leaves and tender stems from the watercress and rinse thoroughly. When the potato is tender, add the watercress to the pot, cover, remove from the heat, and let stand for 5 minutes.

4. Pour the soup through a strainer, reserving the liquid, and transfer the solids to a food processor, or use a food mill fitted with the medium disc. Add 1 cup of the cooking stock and process until smooth.

5. Return the purée to the pot, stir in the heavy cream, and add ½ to 1 cup more stock until the soup is of the desired consistency.

6. Set over medium heat, season with salt, pepper, nutmeg, and cayenne, and simmer just until heated through. Serve immediately.

4 portions

"Beautiful soup! Who cares for fish, game, or any other dish? Who would not give all else for two pennyworth only of beautiful soup?"

—LEWIS CARROLL, *ALICE IN WONDERLAND*

Zucchini is the queen of the garden, often growing so quickly and with such abandon that some are unsure how to cope with the surplus. But zucchini is very versatile and an overabundance is reason to celebrate. It is delicious stuffed with bread crumbs, chopped tomatoes, and Parmigiano-Reggiano cheese, or sliced and quickly sautéed with garlic, olive oil, and a squeeze of lemon. It can be grated raw over salads or into batter for a tea bread, or sauteed with butter and fresh herbs and used to fill an omelet. Experiment with this garden gem—you'll be pleased with the results.

ZUCCHINI-WATERCRESS SOUP

This soup is light, fresh, and versatile; it can begin any number of menus.

4 tablespoons (½ stick) unsalted butter
2 cups finely chopped yellow onions
3 cups Chicken Stock (page 416)
2 pounds (about 4 medium-size) zucchini
1 bunch of watercress
Salt and freshly ground black pepper, to taste
Fresh lemon juice, to taste

1. Melt the butter in a large heavy pot over low heat. Add the onions, cover, and cook, stirring occasionally, until the onions are tender and lightly colored, about 25 minutes.

2. Add the stock and bring to a boil.

3. Scrub the zucchini well with a kitchen brush, trim the ends, and chop coarsely. Drop the zucchini into the stock and return it to a boil. Reduce the heat, cover, and simmer until the zucchini are very tender, about 20 minutes.

4. Meanwhile, remove the leaves and tender stems from the watercress and rinse thoroughly.

5. Remove the soup from the heat, add the watercress, cover, and let stand for 5 minutes.

6. Pour the soup through a strainer, reserving the liquid, and transfer the solids to a food processor or use a food mill fitted with a medium disc. Add 1 cup of the cooking stock and process until smooth.

7. Return the puréed soup to the pot and add about 2 cups more stock (see Note), until the soup is of the desired consistency.

8. Season with salt, pepper, and lemon juice. Simmer briefly to heat through. Serve immediately.

4 to 6 portions

Note: For a richer soup, substitute 1 cup heavy cream for 1 cup of the liquid added after processing.

SOUPS OF THE SEA

Enjoy the bounty of the sea in these subtle bisques and stalwart chowders. The freshest catch of the day, transformed into a soup of the sea, will warm the cockles of your heart.

BOUILLABAISSE

This is the ultimate fisherman's stew, served with a great *rouille*, crusty bread, a green salad, and fresh fruit. It is just the perfect festive meal. We like to round it out with a rough red wine: Chianti, Zinfandel, or a Côtes du Rhône.

½ cup fruity, dark green olive oil
1½ cups well rinsed coarsely chopped leeks
1 cup finely chopped yellow onions
2 cups canned concentrated tomato purée
3 cups chopped fresh tomatoes
2 tablespoons dried thyme
½ cup chopped fresh Italian (flat-leaf) parsley
2 bay leaves
2 cups dry white wine
4 cups Fish Stock (page 417)
Salt and freshly ground black pepper, to taste
6 tablespoons (¾ stick) unsalted butter, at room temperature
2 teaspoons unbleached all-purpose flour
1½ teaspoons whole saffron
2 quarts fresh mussels, scrubbed and debearded
48 Cherrystone clams, scrubbed
3 pounds skinless firm white fish steaks, such as bass, snapper, and cod, cut into large cubes
36 raw shrimp, shelled and deveined
4 lobster tails, fresh or defrosted (1 pound each), shelled and halved crosswise
Garlic croutons (see page 76), for garnish

1. Heat the olive oil in a large soup pot over medium heat. Add the leeks and onions and cook, covered, until the vegetables are tender and lightly colored, about 25 minutes, stirring occasionally.

2. Add the tomato purée, tomatoes, thyme, parsley, bay leaves, wine, fish stock, and salt and pepper. Simmer to blend the flavors,

MAKING AUTHENTIC BOUILLABAISSE

Despite the fuss among purists regarding the making of this great fish soup, the truth is that along the Riviera it is the most common and casually assembled of meals, incorporating whatever the fishing fleet may have brought in. There are as many bad bouillabaisses as there are bad cooks; inversely, the good ones are very good indeed.

You will hear that it is impossible to make bouillabaisse in this country since many of the authentic fish are unavailable. This has frightened away cooks who might otherwise have tried the dish, and it is a false claim. With the exception of the *rascasse* (or rockfish), which seems to be the main point of contention, all commonly used bouillabaisse fish are available here. Often they are called by another name, but if the fishermen feel free to improvise, so can we, and authenticity at the expense of good taste is to be avoided.

A good variety of seafood is also important, and you must really make bouillabaisse for a crowd for it to be worthwhile. Shellfish are not always included in France, but we like them and think they make the dish look more colorful. Prepare the fish stock a day ahead and shop for and dress your fish the morning of the day you plan to serve the bouillabaisse. The actual cooking time is quite short, and you can easily complete the stew after your guests arrive. In fact, this is the kind of dish you can make while guests watch or even assist. Remember, this is a working man's dish, earthy and messy to eat; don't elevate it into something so exalted you never enjoy its simple pleasure.

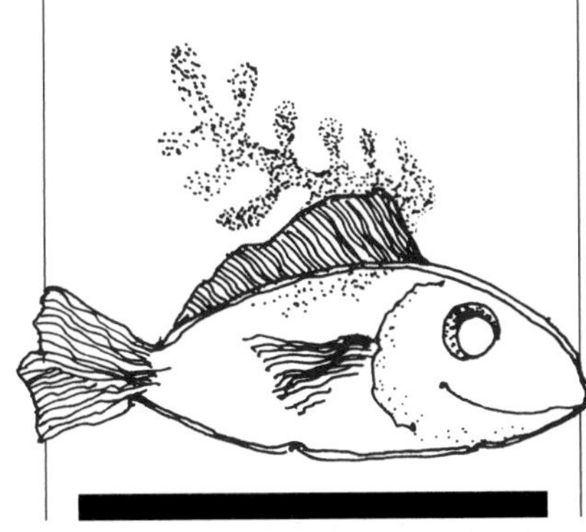

20 minutes. (The soup can be prepared several hours ahead to this point. Return to a simmer before proceeding.)

3. Blend the butter and flour together in a bowl and then whisk the mixture into the tomato mixture.

4. Add the saffron and the mussels and clams in their shells and simmer for 5 minutes. Add the fish, shrimp, and lobster tails and simmer until all the shellfish are opened and the fish is done, another 5 minutes. Do not overcook.

5. Ladle into hot soup plates, discarding any mussels or clams that have not opened. Garnish with the garlic croutons, and serve immediately.

8 to 10 portions

TURBOT EN BOURRIDE

Serve this rich fish soup as the first course of a provençal-style meal, followed by roast leg of lamb, Sautéed Cherry Tomatoes (page 233), and new potatoes roasted with oil and salt.

4 tablespoons (½ stick) unsalted butter
2 leeks, white part only, well rinsed and thinly sliced
1 cup finely chopped yellow onions
3 carrots, peeled and finely chopped
1 cup chopped fresh Italian (flat-leaf) parsley, plus additional parsley for garnish
4 cups Fish Stock (page 417)
Salt and freshly ground black pepper, to taste
2 pounds turbot or halibut, trimmed of skin and bones, cut into 1-inch dice
2 cups Aïoli Sauce (page 50), at room temperature

1. Melt the butter in a pot over low heat. Add the leeks, onions, and carrots and cook, covered, over low heat until the vegetables are tender, about 25 minutes.

2. Add the 1 cup chopped parsley and the fish stock, season with salt and pepper, bring to a boil, reduce the heat and simmer, partially covered, until the vegetables are very tender, 25 minutes.

3. Pour the soup through a strainer set over a bowl, and transfer the solids and ½ cup of the stock to a food processor, or use a food mill fitted with a medium disc. Purée until smooth. Return all the stock and the puréed solids to the pot and reheat over medium heat. Do not boil.

4. Reduce the heat to low, add the diced fish, and let it poach in the hot soup for 5 minutes. Remove the soup from the heat.

5. Slowly whisk 1 cup of the hot soup into the aïoli in a small bowl. Whisk this mixture into the remaining soup and stir constantly over medium heat until slightly thickened, about 3 minutes. Do not let the soup boil or it will curdle.

6. Ladle into heated soup bowls, garnish with the additional chopped parsley, and serve immediately.

6 portions

CALIFORNIA SHELLFISH STEW

This zesty main-dish soup is a cousin of the Mediterranean fisherman's cioppino and an even more distant relative of the great French bouillabaisse. You can vary the shellfish used—lobster, Dungeness crab, squid, and octopus will all work nicely—but do not try to find a substitute for the Zinfandel.

Start with a slice of pâté, follow with a good green salad, and serve plenty of crusty bread for mopping up the juices.

4 tablespoons best-quality olive oil
2 cups finely chopped yellow onions
2 red bell peppers, stemmed, seeded, and coarsely diced
1 green bell pepper, stemmed, seeded, and coarsely diced
6 to 8 garlic cloves, peeled and finely chopped
2 cups Fish Stock (page 417)
2 cups Zinfandel
1 can (2 pounds, 3 ounces) peeled plum tomatoes, drained
1½ tablespoons dried basil
1 teaspoon dried thyme
1 bay leaf
Salt and freshly ground black pepper, to taste
Pinch of crushed red pepper flakes, or to taste
8 mussels
8 small Littleneck or Cherrystone clams
8 large shrimp, peeled and deveined
¾ pound bay scallops
1 cup chopped fresh Italian (flat-leaf) parsley

1. Heat the oil in a large heavy soup pot over low heat. Add the onions, bell peppers, and garlic and cook, covered, until the vegetables are tender, about 25 minutes.

2. Add the fish stock, Zinfandel, and tomatoes and raise the heat.

3. Stir in the basil, thyme, and bay leaf, and season with salt, pepper, and red pepper flakes.

4. Bring the soup to a boil, reduce the heat and simmer, partially covered, for 30 minutes. Stir occasionally, crushing the tomatoes with the stirring spoon. Taste and correct the seasoning. (If you wish to complete the soup through this step the day before serving, it will keep and improve upon refrigeration.)

5. Scrub the mussels and clams well and debeard the mussels. Place them in a heavy pot, add water to a depth of 1 inch, cover, and set over high heat. As they steam open, remove the mussels and clams one by one with a slotted spoon and reserve. Discard any shellfish that haven't opened after 5 minutes. Freeze the shellfish juices for your next batch of fish stock.

6. Rinse the shrimp and scallops and pat dry.

7. At 5 minutes before serving the stew, bring the tomato and wine mixture to a boil. Drop in the shrimp and scallops, then the

CRAZY ABOUT SAFFRON!

Saffron has been treasured throughout history. In the days of ancient Greece it appeared in myth—the mortal Crocus was turned into a saffron-bearing flower after the nymph Smilax rejected his amorous advances. In fourteenth-century Florence, it was easier to use saffron as collateral for a bank loan than coins. The Swiss even started a war over saffron (yes, the Swiss!). Today, it is grown and gathered in Spain, Greece, Kashmir, Morocco, Italy, Switzerland, Iran, and the U.S.

Saffron comes from a particular crocus flower—*crocus sativus*—and it is the crimson red stigmas at the center that are plucked and dried to make the spice we use. It's expensive because the gathering of the crocus and the plucking and the toasting of the stigma is still done by hand. It takes approximately 100,000 flowers to make one pound of saffron. Perhaps it's really a bargain.

Dried saffron threads should be bright red and trumpet shaped with a strong haunting aroma. It is also sold in powdered form, but buy it only from a reputable shop—some dealers sell powdered saffron mixed with less expensive, tasteless turmeric. Saffron is essential in bouillabaisse and Risotto Milanese, and works well in tomato and cream soups, paella, couscous, seafood dishes, and Swedish cakes and breads.

California Shellfish Stew is excellent with a variety of seafood—this version includes lobster, a special treat.

"Of soup and love,
the first is best."

—SPANISH PROVERB

clams and mussels in their shells. Add the parsley, stir well, and remove from the heat. Let stand, covered, for 1 minute.

8. Ladle the stew into heated bowls, dividing the seafood equally, and serve immediately.

4 portions

MANHATTAN CLAM CHOWDER

This saloon and steakhouse favorite is scorned by chowder enthusiasts of the New England school, and in truth it often seems to be no more than a dreary vegetable soup into which some tired clams have accidentally fallen.

We hope this recipe will rescue a tarnished reputation. Made with an abundance of fresh clams, a minimum of vegetables and—in true saloon fashion—a hearty chicken stock, it is a chowder to please the palate and fortify the spirit of even the most discerning New Englander.

4 tablespoons (½ stick) unsalted butter
2 cups finely chopped yellow onions
1 cup chopped celery
5 cups Chicken Stock (page 416)
1½ teaspoons dried thyme
1 bay leaf
Salt and freshly ground black pepper, to taste
1 can (2 pounds, 3 ounces) Italian plum tomatoes, drained and finely chopped
1 cup chopped fresh Italian (flat-leaf) parsley
2 medium-size boiling potatoes, peeled and diced
3 dozen small Littleneck or Cherrystone clams
Grated orange zest, for garnish (optional)

1. Melt the butter in a large heavy pot over low heat. Add the onions and celery and cook, covered, until the vegetables are tender and lightly colored, about 25 minutes.

2. Add the remaining ingredients except the clams and orange zest and simmer, partially covered, until the potatoes are very tender, 30 minutes.

3. Meanwhile, scrub the clams well. Place them in a heavy pot, add water to a depth of 1 inch, cover, and set over high heat. Steam the clams until they open. Remove the clams one by one with a slotted spoon as they open, and reserve. When all the clams are open (discard any that haven't opened after 5 minutes), remove them from their shells.

4. Taste the soup and correct the seasoning. Just before serving, add the clams, simmer for 1 minute to heat through, and ladle into warmed soup bowls. Garnish with orange zest, if desired, and serve immediately.

6 to 8 portions

"It breathes reassurance, it offers consolation; after a weary day it promotes sociability. . . . There is nothing like a bowl of hot soup, its wisp of aromatic steam teasing the nostrils into quivering anticipation."

—LOUIS P. DEGOUY, *THE SOUP BOOK*, 1949

SCALLOP BISQUE

This soup is thickened in the classic French manner with flour, eggs, and cream. Serve it as the first course of an elegant dinner, accompanied by a good white Burgundy or Chardonnay.

7 tablespoons unsalted butter
1 cup well rinsed, thinly sliced leeks, white part only
½ pound mushroom caps, wiped with a damp cloth and thinly sliced
⅓ cup chopped fresh Italian (flat-leaf) parsley
Salt and freshly ground black pepper, to taste
4 cups Fish Stock (page 417)
1 pound bay scallops, rinsed and patted dry
¼ cup all-purpose flour
2 eggs
1 cup heavy cream
¾ cup canned crushed tomatoes
⅓ cup dry sherry
Fresh chives, for garnish

1. Melt 3 tablespoons of the butter in a 4-quart heavy pot over low heat. Add the leeks and cook, covered, for 20 minutes.

2. Add the mushrooms and cook until they begin to render their juices, 5 minutes. Add the parsley, season with salt and pepper, and raise the heat to high. Cook, stirring constantly, until the mushroom juices have evaporated.

3. Add the fish stock to the soup pot, bring to a boil, reduce the heat and simmer, partially covered, for 15 minutes.

4. Remove from the heat, add the scallops and let stand, covered, for 1 minute. Pour the soup through a strainer set over a bowl. Set the scallop mixture aside.

5. Transfer the stock to a small saucepan and bring to a boil.

6. Melt the remaining 4 tablespoons butter in the soup pot over low heat. Add the flour and cook for 5 minutes, stirring constantly. Do not allow the flour mixture to brown.

7. Remove the pot from the heat and pour in the boiling soup stock all at once, beating constantly with a wire whisk. The mixture will bubble furiously and then subside.

8. Set the pot over medium heat and cook, stirring with the whisk, until the mixture has simmered for 5 minutes.

9. Thoroughly whisk the eggs and the cream together in a small bowl. Remove the soup from the heat and slowly whisk 1 cup into the egg and cream mixture. Now whisk this mixture into the remainder of the soup.

10. Set the soup pot over low heat; stir in the crushed tomatoes and sherry. Cook, stirring constantly, until the soup has thickened slightly, about 5 minutes. Do not allow the mixture to boil.

11. Add the reserved scallop mixture and heat for another minute. Taste, correct the seasoning, and ladle into warmed soup bowls. Garnish with the fresh chives and serve immediately.

4 to 6 portions

THE SAGA OF SOUP

French peasants living in the Middle Ages provided the first inspiration for soup as we enjoy it today. Without eating utensils, the peasants were inclined to sop up stewed meat juices with bread. For hundreds of years the evening meal in France was known as *la soupe.* The discovery of soup by the aristocracy was slow, and it wasn't until Louis XIV that soup began to take a more elegant turn. As Louis mistrusted everyone, all of his food had to be tasted. By the time the soup course got to the King, it was inevitably lukewarm or cold. In his inimitable fashion, Louis then deemed that only cold soups be served and thus the wonderful idea of cold soup was born.

SUMMER SOUPS

Soups provide welcome refreshment on hot summer nights. Cool soups are among the many joys of summertime entertaining. Fruits and vegetables are at their best, fragrant and tender with colors that dazzle. Pretty, elegant, and light soups brighten menus, whether served indoors or out. We love them creatively garnished with fruits, vegetables, or flowers, or maybe just a dollop of cream.

BORSCHT

This classic cold soup can begin a many-course European family meal or serve as a cooling luncheon main course year-round.

6 medium-size beets, peeled and cut in half
10 cups cold water
Juice of 3 medium-size lemons
3 tablespoons sugar
2 teaspoons salt
3 eggs
1 cup milk
1 cup sour cream, for garnish
1 cucumber, peeled, seeded, and diced, for garnish

1. Place the beets in a large heavy pot with the 10 cups cold water and bring to a boil. Reduce the heat and simmer partially covered until the beets are tender, 30 to 40 minutes. Skim foam from the cooking liquid as necessary.

2. Remove the beets from the cooking liquid with a slotted spoon and cool to room temperature. Grate the beets and return them to the cooking liquid, along with the lemon juice, sugar, and salt.

3. Simmer the beets for 15 minutes. Remove the pot from the heat and let the soup cool for 15 minutes.

4. Beat the eggs and milk together in a bowl. Gradually whisk

"Soup is cuisine's kindest course."

—KITCHEN GRAFFITI

"Summer has an unfortunate effect upon hostesses who . . . take the season as a cue to serve dinners of astonishingly meager proportions. These they call light, a quality which, while most assuredly welcome in comedies, cotton shirts, and hearts, is not an appropriate touch at dinner."

—FRAN LEBOWITZ

3 cups of the warm borscht into the eggs and milk. Pour this mixture slowly back into the remaining borscht.

5. Cover the soup and refrigerate until very cold. Taste and correct the seasoning; the soup should be nicely balanced between sweet and sour.

6. Ladle into chilled soup bowls. Garnish with the sour cream and diced cucumber and serve immediately.

8 or more portions

CHILLED SHRIMP AND CUCUMBER SOUP

This cool, beautiful soup requires almost no cooking, is ready in minutes, and is light but filling—a perfect summer soup. Other fresh herbs such as parsley and mint can be substituted for the dill.

2 large cucumbers (about 2 pounds), peeled, seeded, and coarsely chopped
¼ cup red wine vinegar
1 tablespoon sugar
1 teaspoon salt
1 pound raw shrimp (the smallest you can find), peeled and deveined
2 tablespoons unsalted butter
¼ cup dry white vermouth
Salt and freshly ground black pepper, to taste
1½ cups buttermilk, chilled
¾ cup chopped fresh dill, or more to taste, plus additional dill for garnish

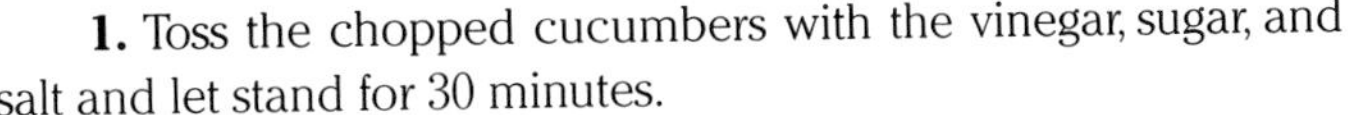

1. Toss the chopped cucumbers with the vinegar, sugar, and salt and let stand for 30 minutes.

2. Rinse the shrimp and pat them dry. Melt the butter in a small skillet over low heat. Add the shrimp, raise the heat, and toss until they turn pink, 2 to 3 minutes. Remove them with a slotted spoon and reserve.

3. Add the vermouth to the skillet and boil until it is reduced to a few spoonfuls. Pour over the shrimp and season them with salt and pepper.

4. Drain the cucumbers and transfer them to a food processor. Process briefly, then add the buttermilk and continue to process until smooth. Add the dill and process briefly, about 1 second.

5. Pour the soup into a bowl, add the shrimp and their liquid, and refrigerate, covered, until very cold. Garnish with additional chopped dill and serve in chilled bowls.

4 to 6 portions

GAZPACHO

We like to ladle gazpacho into chilled heavy mugs as a sippable summer first course while the steaks are grilling. Garnish each portion with a crisp fresh scallion.

6 large ripe tomatoes
2 red bell peppers
2 medium-size yellow onions
2 large shallots
2 large cucumbers
½ cup red wine vinegar
½ cup olive oil
1½ cups canned tomato juice
3 eggs, lightly beaten
½ cup chopped fresh dill
Pinch of cayenne pepper
Salt and freshly ground black pepper, to taste

1. Wash the tomatoes and peppers. Core and coarsely chop the tomatoes; save the juices. Stem, seed, and coarsely chop the peppers. Peel and coarsely chop the onions and shallots. Peel, seed, and coarsely chop the cucumbers.

2. In a bowl whisk together the vinegar, olive oil, reserved tomato juices, canned tomato juice, and eggs.

3. In a blender or a food processor, purée the vegetables in small batches, adding the tomato juice mixture as necessary to keep the blades from clogging. Do not purée completely; the gazpacho should retain some of its crunch.

4. Stir in the dill, cayenne, and salt and pepper. Cover and chill for at least 4 hours.

5. To serve, stir, taste, and correct the seasoning, and ladle into chilled soup bowls or mugs.

8 to 10 portions

GAZPACHO COOLER

Pour 4 ounces (½ cup) of Gazpacho and 6 ounces of Perrier or other sparkling water into a chilled glass and stir. Add ice cubes and garnish with a slice of cucumber.

GREEK LEMON SOUP

This soup is proof that less is more. A pot of *avgolemono* can be ready in about 30 minutes, and for only pennies. While it's delicious hot, it's even better cold, so plan to make it the day before you need it. Serve it in well-chilled bowls and float a paper-thin slice of lemon on top. Hot spinach-filled Phyllo Triangles (page 9) are a perfect accompaniment.

Lively and fresh tasting, Greek Lemon Soup is comforting when hot, refreshing when cool.

> "Soup of the evening, beautiful soup."
>
> —LEWIS CARROLL, *ALICE IN WONDERLAND*

6 cups canned chicken broth
½ cup long-grain rice (not converted or instant)
3 egg yolks
¼ cup fresh lemon juice
Salt and freshly ground black pepper, to taste
Sliced fresh lemon, for garnish
Chopped fresh Italian (flat-leaf) parsley, for garnish

1. Pour the broth into a large heavy pot and bring it gradually to a full boil. Pour in the rice, reduce the heat, and simmer, covered, until the rice is just tender, about 25 minutes. Do not overcook.

2. Meanwhile, whisk the egg yolks and lemon juice together in a small bowl until well combined.

3. When the rice is done, remove the soup from the heat and whisk 2 cups of hot broth into the egg and lemon mixture. Whisk this mixture back into the remaining soup.

4. Return the soup to medium heat and cook, stirring constantly, until it is just steaming. Do not let it reach a boil.

5. Season to taste and serve immediately, or remove from the heat, cool to room temperature, cover, and refrigerate. Correct the seasoning just before serving. Garnish hot or cold with the lemon slices and chopped parsley.

4 to 6 portions

SORREL SOUP

We love the sour taste of sorrel and can never get enough. This summery soup is a snap to throw together in the spare minutes of a busy weekend; it makes a perfect lunch or snack when cold, and a dressy first course when hot.

1 cup (2 sticks) unsalted butter
2 large yellow onions, peeled and thinly sliced
4 garlic cloves, peeled and chopped
10 cups tightly packed fresh sorrel leaves, washed and stems removed
4 cups Chicken Stock (page 416)
¾ cup chopped fresh Italian (flat-leaf) parsley
1 teaspoon salt
1 teaspoon freshly ground black pepper
2 teaspoons grated nutmeg
Pinch of cayenne pepper
1 cup sour cream, for garnish
Snipped fresh chives, for garnish

1. Melt the butter in a soup pot over medium-low heat. Add the onions and garlic and cook, covered, until tender and lightly colored, about 15 minutes.

2. Add the sorrel, cover, and cook until it is completely wilted, about 5 minutes.

3. Add the stock, parsley, salt, pepper, nutmeg, and cayenne, and bring to a boil. Reduce the heat, cover, and simmer for 50 minutes.

4. Transfer the soup to a blender or food processor and purée until smooth.

5. If serving the soup hot, return it to the soup pot. Heat the soup over low heat, stirring constantly, until steaming. Taste and correct the seasoning.

If serving cold, transfer to a bowl, cool, cover, and refrigerate for at least 4 hours. Taste and correct the seasoning before serving.

6. In either case, ladle into bowls and garnish with sour cream and chives before serving.

6 portions

SORREL

There are many varieties of sorrel; all are tart and lemony. Sorrel can be added to soup wherever you want a touch of sourness and a hint of tender green color.

Sourness of sorrel varies, making exact quantities difficult to give. The taste can become overwhelming, so we recommend adding sorrel slowly and tasting as you go.

If your market doesn't stock sorrel (and begging doesn't work), plant your own (seeds are available from many catalogs). Some cookbooks recommend that you substitute spinach if you cannot get sorrel, but there is really no similarity, and the substitution does a disservice to them both.

Avoiding salt? A bit of chopped sorrel will disguise the fact that you've omitted it.

Other possibilities:

- ♥ Toss a few chopped leaves into coleslaw or other salads.
- ♥ Use in place of lettuce in a sandwich.
- ♥ Add a handful of chopped sorrel to any potato or cream soup.
- ♥ Drop leaves into boiling salted water for 1 minute; plunge into ice water, pat dry, and purée. Freeze the purée for a taste of summer in the heart of winter. Or stir the purée into cream cheese and spread on a bagel; scramble into buttery eggs; stir into mayonnaise as a sauce for cold fish.

BLUEBERRY SOUP

Serve this chilled fruit soup as a summertime first course, dessert, or by itself for lunch. Blissfully cool and light.

FOURTH OF JULY PICNIC

BLUEBERRY SOUP

SHRIMP AND GRAPE SALAD WITH DILL

RASPBERRY-MARINATED CARROTS

PUMPERNICKEL BREAD

LIME MOUSSE

BROWNIES

5 cups fresh blueberries, plus additional berries for garnish
4 cups water
4 whole cloves
Peel from 1 orange, white pith removed
2-inch piece of cinnamon stick
⅔ cup honey
Juice of 1 lemon
3 tablespoons Crème de Cassis (black currant liqueur)
1 tablespoon Blueberry Vinegar (page 145)
Crème Fraîche (page 414), for garnish
6 sprigs mint, for garnish

1. Rinse the blueberries and remove any stems, leaves, or green berries.

2. Put the berries in a large heavy pot and add the water, cloves, orange peel, and cinnamon stick. Bring to a boil over medium heat. Stir in the honey, reduce the heat, and simmer, partially covered, until the berries are very tender, about 15 minutes.

3. Remove the pot from the heat and cool the soup to room temperature. Remove and discard the orange peel and cloves. Force the soup through a strainer or a food mill fitted with a medium disc. Stir in the lemon juice, Crème de Cassis, and vinegar. Cover and refrigerate for at least 6 hours.

4. Serve in chilled bowls, garnished with a few whole blueberries, a dollop of crème fraîche, and a mint sprig.

6 portions

CREAM OF MANGO SOUP

Creamy, cool, and slightly sweet, this soup makes a deliciously light lunch for a late-summer afternoon.

2 eggs, well beaten
¼ cup sugar
1 tablespoon vanilla extract
Juice and grated zest of 1 lemon
1 ripe mango, peeled, pitted, and coarsely chopped
2 cups heavy cream
3 cups milk
Blueberries, for garnish
Coarsely chopped strawberries, for garnish

1. Combine the eggs, sugar, vanilla, lemon juice and jest, and mango in a food processor, and process until smooth.

2. Whisk the cream and milk together in a large bowl until frothy. Slowly add the mango mixture, whisking constantly.

3. Cover and chill well.

4. To serve, stir, ladle into chilled bowls, and garnish each serving with the blueberries and chopped strawberries.

6 portions

"I live for good soup,
not fine words."
—MOLIÈRE

SOUP GARNISHES

The challenge is to provide a garnish that offers a clear but complementary contrast in taste, texture, and color without overwhelming the soup itself. In general the more complex the soup, the simpler the garnish and vice versa. Fresh herbs, pasta, a sprinkling of vegetables or grated cheese, fruits, cream, liquor, floating flowers, or fish or meat—all should complement, not complicate, the balanced flavors already developed in the soup.

Life* is *just a bowl of cherries!

SUMMER TOMATO AND MELON SOUP

3 cups peeled, seeded, and diced ripe tomatoes
2 medium-size ripe cantaloupes, seeds and rind removed, diced
2 large cucumbers, peeled, seeded, and chopped
Grated zest of 1 small orange
¼ cup finely chopped fresh mint, plus additional fresh mint as garnish
1 cup sour cream or Crème Fraîche (page 414)

1. Combine the tomatoes, melons, and about 1½ cucumbers in a blender or food processor. (Reserve ½ cucumber for garnish.) Process until smooth. Transfer to a bowl.

2. Stir in the orange zest and the ¼ cup mint. Whisk in the sour cream or crème fraîche and chill.

3. To serve, ladle into bowls and garnish with a bit of the chopped cucumber and a sprig of mint.

6 to 8 portions

SWEET BLACK CHERRY SOUP

7 cans (about 9 ounces each) pitted sweet dark cherries
Grated zest of 1 medium-size orange
4 teaspoons fresh lemon juice
3 tablespoons Grand Marnier
1 teaspoon salt
1 cup Crème Fraîche (page 414)

1. Reserve 1 can of cherries for the garnish. Drain the rest and reserve the syrup.

2. Purée the cherries in a food processor until fine, about 30 seconds. Remove to a bowl.

3. Add 1½ cups of the reserved cherry syrup, the orange zest, lemon juice, Grand Marnier, and salt. Whisk in ½ cup crème fraîche; save the remaining crème fraîche for garnish. Chill until serving time.

4. Drain the remaining can of cherries and divide them into 6 portions. The cherries may be cut in half. Ladle the soup into bowls and garnish with some crème fraîche on each serving. Float the whole or halved cherries on the top.

6 portions

SUNDAY NIGHT SOUPS

There's something about those final moments of preparing for the week ahead that calls for the comfort of a Sunday night soup supper. A soup meal—crusty warm bread, a cheese board, green salad, dessert mousse, and, of course, your own *soupe du jour*—can be enjoyed in front of a roaring fire or at a candlelit table, and will make the transition from the weekend to the work week a little easier to swallow.

WINTER BORSCHT

Make this the day before, if you can, and let it improve in the refrigerator overnight.

2 pounds fresh beets, peeled and grated
1 meaty beef shin bone (about 5 pounds), cut into 5 pieces
Salt
3 cups chopped tomatoes
2 cups coarsely chopped yellow onions
1 medium-size cabbage, shredded
1 carrot, peeled and cut into small dice
1 bunch of fresh dill, chopped
Freshly ground black pepper, to taste
2 cups sour cream, for garnish

1. Put the beets in a large heavy pot and add cold water to cover. Set over medium heat, bring to a boil, reduce the heat, and simmer, partially covered, until the beets are tender, about 20 minutes. Skim any foam from the cooking liquid as necessary. When the beets are done, reserve them and their cooking liquid.

"'It's a comforting sort of thing to have,' said Christopher Robin."

—A. A. MILNE, *THE HOUSE AT POOH CORNER*

BRIDGE AND POKER SANDWICHES

The dramatic decisions that make up any good card game will sooner or later result in giant appetites, whoever is holding the aces. No one wants to spend too much time away from a winning streak, but everyone wants to eat. We suggest you make it hearty, a bit gooey, and delicious, so no one loses. (Recipes for italicized ingredients can be found in the Index.)

- ♥ Put *Ratatouille* and Italian hot sausage on French bread.
- ♥ Layer freshly sliced mushrooms, meat loaf, and *Tomato-Basil Mayonnaise* on pumpernickel.
- ♥ Combine roast turkey with guacamole or *Avocado Dip* on pumpernickel.
- ♥ Try roast *Filet of Beef,* tomato, cucumber with chives, prepared horseradish, and sour cream on white bread.
- ♥ Layer prosciutto and Provolone cheese on Italian bread sliced lengthwise. Spread with *Pesto Mayonnaise* and broil open faced until hot and bubbly.
- ♥ Spread crunchy celery rémoulade on rye bread; top with thin-sliced corned beef and even thinner slices of Swiss cheese. Run under the broiler until hot and bubbly.
- ♥ Combine Black Forest ham, ripe Brie cheese, and your favorite mustard on *Raisin Pumpernickel Bread.* Butter the outside and grill in a hot skillet.
- ♥ Mix crunchy-cooked broccoli, scallions, and toasted cashews with *Sesame Mayonnaise.* Spread on English muffins, sprinkle with grated Parmigiano-Reggiano cheese, and broil until hot and bubbly.
- ♥ Layer turkey breast, avocado, and jalapeño Jack cheese between slices of sourdough bread. Butter the outside and grill in a hot skillet.
- ♥ Spread rye bread with mayonnaise, make layers of sliced onion, avocado, tomato, mild green chiles, and 2 strips of bacon. Top with Cheddar cheese and broil until the cheese is hot and bubbly.

2. Put the beef shin in another large pot. Cover with cold water, add 1 tablespoon salt, and set over medium heat. Bring to a boil, reduce the heat, and simmer, uncovered, until tender, 1½ hours. Skim any foam from the cooking liquid and add additional water as necessary as the cooking liquid evaporates.

3. Add the tomatoes, onion, cabbage, carrot, and dill (reserve some for garnish) to the beef; simmer, partially covered, for 30 minutes.

4. Add the reserved beets and their cooking liquid and simmer, partially covered, for another 20 minutes. Remove from the heat and cool slightly.

5. Lift the pieces of shin from the soup pot. Remove the meaty bits clinging to the bone and return the meat to the pot. Season the soup with salt and pepper.

6. Return the pot to medium heat and simmer for 5 minutes. Serve immediately, garnished with the sour cream and the reserved dill.

10 to 12 portions

BEEF AND RED WINE BROTH

Perfect in a thermos at a football game or on a winter hike.

4 tablespoons (½ stick) unsalted butter
1½ cups chopped yellow onions
2 carrots, peeled and chopped
1 parsnip, peeled and chopped
8 to 10 garlic cloves (about half of a small head), peeled and chopped
¾ cup chopped fresh Italian (flat-leaf) parsley
5 cups Beef Stock (page 416), or a combination of beef stock and Chicken Stock (page 416)
1 cup dry red wine
Salt and freshly ground black pepper, to taste
1 cup small pasta, such as shells or orzo
Grated Parmigiano-Reggiano cheese, for garnish (optional)

1. Melt the butter in a large heavy pot over low heat. Add the onions, carrots, parsnip, and chopped garlic and cook, covered, until the vegetables are tender and lightly colored, about 25 minutes.

2. Add the chopped parsley, beef stock, and wine and season with salt and pepper. Bring to a boil over medium heat, reduce the heat, and simmer, partially covered, for 20 minutes.

3. Meanwhile, bring a quart of salted water to a boil, drop in the pasta, and cook until tender. Drain and reserve.

4. Pour the soup through a strainer and discard the solids. Return the broth to the pot, add the cooked pasta and simmer, partially covered, for 10 minutes. Serve immediately, sprinkled with the grated Parmigiano-Reggiano if desired.

4 to 6 portions

BLUE CHEESE SOUP WITH BACON

A hearty first course or luncheon main dish.

6 tablespoons (¾ stick) unsalted butter
2 cups chopped yellow onions
1 leek, white part only, well rinsed and finely sliced
3 celery ribs, chopped
3 carrots, peeled and chopped
1 medium-size potato, peeled and diced
1 cup dry white wine or dry vermouth
3 cups Chicken Stock (page 416)
½ to ¾ pound imported Roquefort or other blue cheese
Salt and freshly ground black pepper, to taste
6 to 8 bacon strips, sautéed crisp and crumbled, for garnish

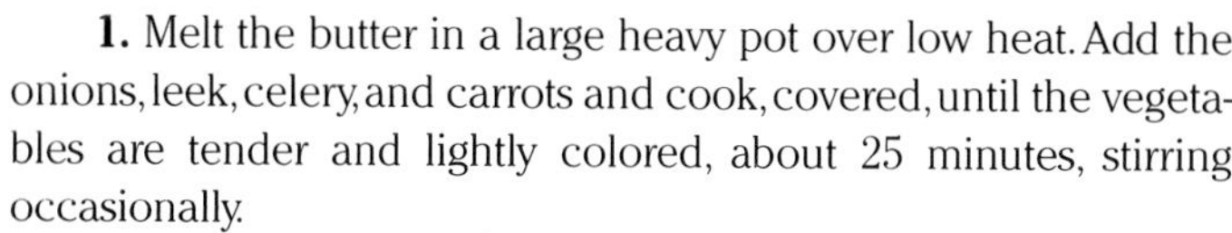

1. Melt the butter in a large heavy pot over low heat. Add the onions, leek, celery, and carrots and cook, covered, until the vegetables are tender and lightly colored, about 25 minutes, stirring occasionally.

2. Add the potato, white wine, and stock, bring to a boil, reduce the heat, and simmer, partially covered, until very tender, about 20 minutes.

3. Remove the soup from the heat and crumble in ½ pound of the cheese. Stir until the cheese has melted into the soup, then pour the soup through a strainer, reserving the liquid. Transfer the solids to a food processor or use a food mill fitted with a medium disc. Add 1 cup of the cooking stock and process until smooth.

4. Return the soup to the pot, pour in the rest of the liquid, and simmer over medium heat. Taste and correct the seasoning; you may want to add a little more cheese, and the soup may need salt and pepper.

5. Ladle into bowls, garnish with the bacon crumbles, and serve immediately.

4 to 6 portions

CROUTONS

Sometimes the simplest garnish is the best. A crisp crouton, made of good-quality bread and well toasted or sautéed, can make or break a soup (or salad).

Cut the bread into ½-inch cubes and spread it on a baking sheet. Toast it in a 400°F oven, stirring occasionally, until crisp and brown, 10 to 15 minutes.

Or, melt butter in a large skillet. Sauté a bit of garlic in the butter first if appropriate, add the bread cubes, and sauté over medium heat, stirring and tossing the cubes until golden brown. Transfer the croutons to paper towels and drain before using.

Blue cheese and bacon—a classic pair, with good reason.

PEASANT VEGETABLE SOUP

Serve this as a fall or winter supper, accompanied by hearty bread, and follow with a green salad and a fruit dessert. Accompany with a glass of Beaujolais or another uncomplicated wine, or a mug of cold dark beer. It tastes even better if made the day before you plan to serve it.

"Only the pure of heart can make a good soup."

—LUDWIG VAN BEETHOVEN

1½ cups dried white beans, such as Great Northern
4 tablespoons bacon fat or lightly salted butter
1 cup finely chopped yellow onions
3 leeks, white part only, well rinsed and thinly sliced
2 celery ribs, coarsely chopped
3 carrots, peeled and chopped
1 teaspoon dried thyme
1 dried bay leaf
Freshly ground black pepper, to taste
8 cups Chicken Stock (page 416) or Beef Stock (page 416), or a combination of the two
3 parsnips, peeled and chopped
1 ham hock
½ small green cabbage, shredded (about 2 cups)
½ cup chopped fresh Italian (flat-leaf) parsley
4 garlic cloves, peeled and chopped
Salt, to taste

1. Sort through the beans and discard any pebbles you may find. Soak the beans overnight in water that covers them by 3 inches.

2. Melt the bacon fat or butter in a large heavy pot over low heat. Add the onions, leeks, celery, and carrots and cook, covered, until the vegetables are tender and lightly colored, about 25 minutes, stirring occasionally.

3. Stir in the thyme, bay leaf, and a grinding of black pepper, and pour in the stock. Add the parsnips, ham hock, and soaked beans, and bring the soup to a boil. Reduce the heat and simmer, partially covered, until the beans are tender, about 40 minutes. Remove the ham hock and allow it to cool slightly. Cut the meat off the bone, cut it into chunks, and return the meat to the pot.

4. Add the cabbage, parsley, and garlic, and simmer for another 10 minutes. Taste, correct the seasoning (add salt at this point if the soup needs it), and serve immediately.

8 to 10 portions

> **"*Bouquet Garni:* a small bundle of herbs, as thyme, parsley, bay leaf and the like, often tied in a cheesecloth bag and used for flavoring soups, stews, etc."**
>
> *—THE RANDOM HOUSE DICTIONARY OF THE ENGLISH LANGUAGE*

BASQUE RICE AND PEPPER SOUP

¾ cup olive oil
3 cups finely chopped yellow onions
2 cups peeled chopped carrots
6 garlic cloves, peeled and chopped
7 cups Beef Stock (page 416)
½ cup long-grain rice (not converted or instant)
½ cup medium-dry sherry
2 red bell peppers, stemmed, seeded, and cut into julienne
2 green bell peppers, stemmed, seeded, and cut into julienne
Salt and freshly ground black pepper, to taste

To take the chill out of an afternoon of cross-country or downhill skiing, it's best to plan ahead and take a thermos of soup along with you. A picnic in the snow will give you a second burst of energy to make the most of a winter afternoon.

1. Heat the olive oil in a large heavy pot. Add the onions, carrots, and garlic and cook, covered, over low heat until the vegetables are tender and lightly colored, about 25 minutes; stir occasionally.

2. Uncover, add the beef stock, raise the heat, and bring to a boil. Reduce the heat, cover, and simmer for 20 minutes.

3. Pour the soup through a strainer, pressing hard with the back of a spoon to extract as much liquid as possible. Discard the solids and return the broth to the pot. Add the rice, sherry, peppers, and salt and pepper. Simmer, partially covered, until the rice is tender, about 25 minutes.

4. Taste, correct the seasoning, and serve immediately.

4 to 6 portions

CURRIED CREAM OF CHICKEN SOUP

6 tablespoons (¾ stick) unsalted butter
2 cups finely chopped yellow onions
2 carrots, peeled and chopped
2 tablespoons curry powder, or more to taste
5 cups Chicken Stock (page 416)
6 parsley sprigs
1 chicken (2½ to 3 pounds), quartered
½ cup long-grain rice (not converted or instant)
Salt and freshly ground black pepper, to taste
1 cup half-and-half
10 ounces frozen peas, defrosted

1. Melt the butter in a large heavy pot over low heat. Add the onion, carrots, and curry powder and cook, covered, until the vegetables are tender, about 25 minutes; stir occasionally.

2. Add the stock, parsley, chicken, and rice. Bring the soup to a boil, reduce the heat, and cover. Cook at a simmer until the chicken is done, skimming any foam from the cooking liquid as necessary, 25 to 30 minutes.

3. Cool the chicken in the stock. Remove the meat from the bones and dice it; reserve the meat.

4. Pour the soup through a strainer and transfer the solids to a food processor, or use a food mill fitted with a medium disc. Add 1 cup of the cooking liquid and process until smooth. Reserve the rest of the liquid.

5. Return the puréed soup to the pot and add the half-and-half. Stir in about 4 cups more cooking stock, until the soup reaches the desired consistency.

6. Add the reserved diced chicken and defrosted peas and simmer the soup until the peas are tender, 15 minutes. Season with salt and pepper, and serve immediately.

4 to 6 portions

PASTA
PERFECT

PIPING HOT PASTA

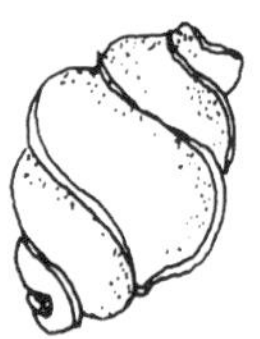
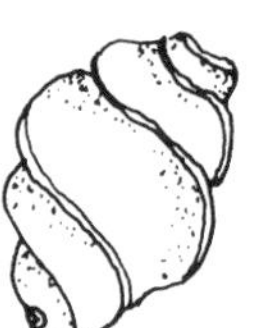

Not even the Italians know how many shapes pasta comes in. They have long considered it among their works of art, and the celebration of color and shape that seems to dominate Italian life is found in their pasta as well.

Thomas Jefferson first imported the pasta machine to America, just at the time that Yankee Doodle was calling the feather in his cap "Macaroni." Even then pasta was an Italian staple, although well-traveled Englishmen had long since made it a favorite "exotic" food back in London. No longer exotic, pasta feels more like a welcome member of the American food family.

PASTA GLOSSARY

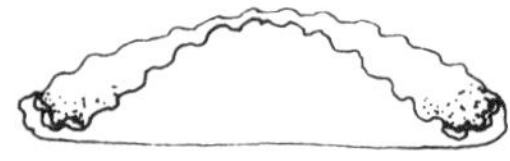

AGNOLOTTI: "Priests' caps"; these are crescent-shaped, meat-filled ravioli.

ANELLINI: The tiniest pasta rings.

BAVETTINE: Narrow linguine.

BUCATINI: Short, straight macaroni.

CANNELLONI: Large, round tubes for stuffing.

CAPELLINI: "Angel hair," the finest of all pasta.

CAPELVENERE: Fine noodles.

CAPPELLETTI: Stuffed "hats."

CAPPELLI DI PAGLIACCIO: "Clowns' hats."

CAVATELLI: Short, crinkle-edged shells.

CONCHIGLIE: "Conch shells."

CORALLI: Small tubes for soup.

CRESTE DI GALLI: "Cockscombs."

DITALI: "Thimbles"; short macaroni.

FARFALLE: "Butterflies"; bow-ties.

FARFALLONI: "Big butterflies" or bow-ties.

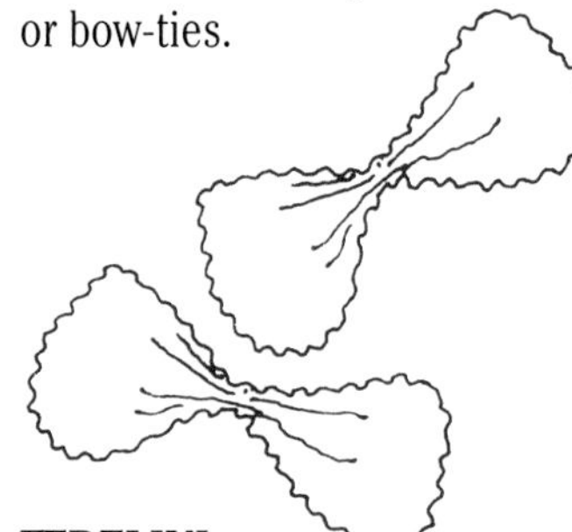

FEDELINI: "Little faithful ones"; very fine rods of spaghetti.

FETTUCCE: "Ribbons"; widest of the fettuccine family.

FETTUCCINE: "Narrow ribbons" of egg noodle.

FUSILLI: "Little springs"; spindles or spirals.

LANCETTE: "Little spears."

LASAGNE: Extra broad noodles, about 2 inches wide; smooth or ripple-edged.

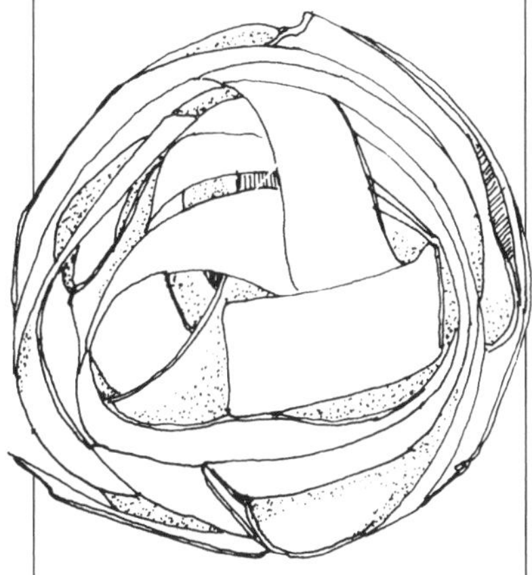

LINGUE DI PASSERI: "Sparrows' tongues."

LINGUINE: "Little tongues"; thick, narrow ribbons.

LUMACHE: "Snails"; shell-shaped.

MACCHERONI: Macaroni of all types; hollow or pierced.

MACCHERONI ALLA CHITARRA: Also called *tonnarelli;* noodles cut with the steel wires of a special guitarlike tool.

MAFALDA: Broad noodle, rippled on both sides; wider than fettuccine.

MAGLIETTE: "Links"; slightly curved, short lengths of hollow pasta.

MALTAGLIATI: Irregularly cut shapes.

MANICOTTI: "Muffs"; giant tubes for stuffing.

MARGHERITA: "Daisies"; narrow noodles, rippled on one side.

MARUZZE: "Seashells."

MEZZANI: Short, cut, curved macaroni.

MOSTACCIOLI: "Little moustaches."

OCCHI DI LUPO: "Wolf's eyes"; large tubes.

OCCHI DI PASSERI: "Sparrows' eyes"; tiny circles.

ORECCHIETTE: "Little ears."

ORZO: Rice-shaped or barley-shaped pasta.

PAPPARDELLE: Broad noodles, traditionally served with game sauces.

PASTA FRESCA: Fresh egg pasta.

PASTA VERDE: Green pasta, usually incorporating spinach in the dough.

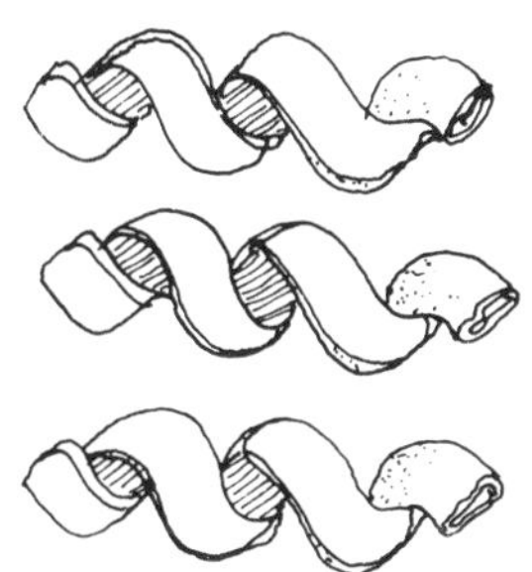

PASTINA: "Tiny dough"; minute pasta shapes used in soup, many with charming names: *acini de pepe* ("peppercorns"); *alfabeto* ("alphabet"); *amorini* ("little cupids"); *arancini* ("little oranges"); *astri* ("little stars"); *avena* ("oats"); *crocette* ("little crosses"); *elefanti* ("elephants"); *funghini* ("little mushrooms"); *pulcini* ("little chickens"); *rosa marina* ("rose of the sea"); *rotini* ("little wheels"); *semi de mela* or *melone* ("apple or melon seeds"); *stellini* ("little stars"); *stivaletti* ("little boots").

PENNE: "Pens" or quills; tubes cut diagonally at both ends.

PERCIATELLI: Long thin hollow macaroni; looks like thick spaghetti.

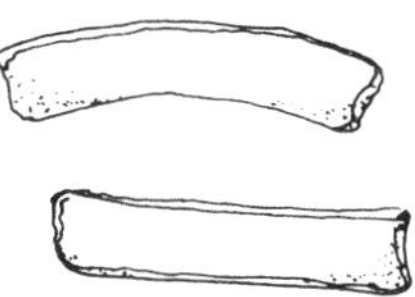

PEZZOCCHERI: Thick, dark buckwheat noodles.

QUADRETTINI: Small flat squares.

RAVIOLI: Pasta squares filled with meat, cheese, and/or vegetables.

RICCIOLINI: "Little curls."

RIGATONI: Large grooved macaroni.

ROTELLE: "Small wheels."

RUOTE: Spiked wheels with hubs.

SPAGHETTI: Variety of long thin rods, including capellini (very, very thin), *spaghettini* (thin), and *spaghettoni* (the thickest).

TAGLIATELLE: Family of egg noodles similar to fettuccine.

TORTELLINI: Small, stuffed pasta similar to cappelletti.

TRENETTE: A narrower, thicker version of tagliatelle.

TUBETTI: "Small tubes"; hollow.

VERMICELLI: Very fine spaghetti.

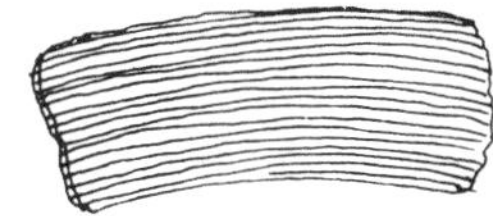

ZITI: "Bridegrooms"; slightly curved, large tubes.

PASTA PRIMAVERA GREGORY

A light and lovely tangle of pasta and fresh vegetables. Serve pasta primavera as the first course or light main course of a spring dinner on the terrace. Feel free to substitute your favorite fresh vegetables and herbs in the appropriate quantities.

½ pound green fettuccine
½ pound regular egg fettuccine
⅓ cup best-quality olive oil
½ cup finely chopped red onion
¾ pound snow peas
⅓ pound sugar snap peas
¾ pound sliced prosciutto, cut into coarse julienne
2 ripe plum tomatoes, quartered
2 red bell peppers, stemmed, seeded, and cut into fine julienne
8 scallions (green onions), well rinsed, trimmed, cut diagonally into ½-inch pieces
½ cup snipped chives, basil, or other fresh herbs
Salt and freshly ground black pepper, to taste
4 tablespoons raspberry vinegar, or to taste
¼ cup grated Parmigiano-Reggiano cheese
1 cup imported black olives (any kind)
Grated zest of 1 orange, lemon, or lime

1. Bring 4 quarts salted water to a boil in a large pot. Stir in all the fettuccine. Cook until tender but still firm, and drain immediately. Transfer the pasta to a large mixing bowl, add the olive oil and chopped onion, and toss gently to combine. Set aside to cool to room temperature.

2. Bring another 4 quarts salted water to a boil. Add the snow peas and sugar snap peas. Cook for 1 minute, drain, and plunge the peas immediately into a large bowl of ice water. Let stand for 10 minutes. Drain the peas and pat thoroughly dry.

3. Add the peas to the pasta in the mixing bowl along with the prosciutto, tomatoes, bell pepper, scallions, and chives or herbs. Season with salt and pepper, sprinkle on the raspberry vinegar, and toss gently.

4. Toss the pasta and vegetables with the grated cheese, taste, and correct the seasoning. Arrange the pasta on a large serving platter. Scatter the olives and citrus zest over the pasta and serve at room temperature.

6 portions

FIREWORKS PICNIC

GOLDEN AMERICAN CAVIAR AND PUMPERNICKEL ROLLS

CRISP CRUDITÉS WITH *SESAME MAYONNAISE*

SLICED FILET OF BEEF

MINTY CUCUMBER SALAD

PASTA PRIMAVERA GREGORY

ASSORTED CHEESES

MINIATURE LOAVES OF FRENCH OR PUMPERNICKEL BREAD

DESSERT MOUSSES

ASSORTED COOKIES

PASTA SAUCE RAPHAEL

Serve this spicy tomato-and-artichoke sauce over tortellini. We like it cold as well as hot, and often recommend it for picnics.

1 pound ripe meaty tomatoes
Half a jar (6 ounces) marinated artichoke hearts
2 tablespoons best-quality olive oil
½ cup coarsely chopped yellow onion
1 garlic clove, peeled and finely chopped
2 tablespoons finely chopped fresh Italian (flat-leaf) parsley
1 tablespoon dried basil
1 teaspoon dried oregano
¼ to ½ teaspoon crushed red pepper flakes
2 teaspoons whole black peppercorns, crushed
1 teaspoon salt, or to taste
1 tablespoon grated Romano cheese

1. Bring a large pot of salted water to a boil. Drop the tomatoes, a few at a time, into the boiling water. Scald for 10 seconds, then with a slotted spoon transfer to a bowl of ice water. Scald all the tomatoes in this fashion, then drain, cool, and slip off the skins. Cut crosswise into halves, squeeze out the seeds and juice, and chop coarsely. Reserve.

2. Drain the artichokes and reserve the marinade.

3. Heat the olive oil in a large saucepan and sauté the onion, garlic, parsley, basil, oregano, and red pepper flakes over medium heat for 5 minutes.

4. Add the black peppercorns to the onion mixture.

5. Add the tomatoes to the sauce, season with the salt, and simmer, uncovered, over medium heat for 1 hour.

6. Add the reserved artichoke marinade and simmer, stirring often, for another 30 minutes.

7. Stir in the artichokes and continue to simmer until the sauce is rich and thick, another 20 minutes or so. Stir in the Romano cheese, and taste and adjust the seasoning. Serve over your favorite pasta. (If serving pasta Raphael cold, toss with sauce and cool to room temperature.)

Enough sauce for 1 pound pasta

TO COOK PASTA

One of the keys to cooking pasta is to have it "swimming" in water, so begin with at least 1 gallon per each pound of pasta, and use a large enough pot. Bring the water to a full boil, add 1 tablespoon salt, stir, then drop in the pasta and stir again. You want to keep the water boiling rapidly, without boiling over, and the pasta moving during the cooking. Stir occasionally to keep the pasta from sticking. Fresh pasta will be done in the time it takes the water to return to a full boil. Dried pasta will take longer, depending on the shape and size. Pasta should not be over- or undercooked. The Italian expression *al dente* or "to the tooth" means that pasta is cooked just to the point that it is completely tender, yet still firm, with a tiny chalky white core. We like to test it by biting into a strand. By the time we drain the pasta in a colander, sauce it, and serve it, it's done to perfection.

"Everything you see I owe to spaghetti."

—SOPHIA LOREN

SPAGHETTI WITH OIL AND GARLIC

Our favorite version of this pasta dish.

12 garlic cloves, peeled
¼ cup best-quality olive oil
1 pound spaghetti
1½ cups Chicken Stock (see page 416) or canned chicken broth
1 cup finely chopped fresh Italian (flat-leaf) parsley
Freshly ground black pepper, for garnish
Grated Parmigiano-Reggiano cheese, for garnish

1. Mince 6 of the garlic cloves and set them aside. Slice the remaining garlic.

2. Heat the oil in a small skillet over medium heat. Add the sliced garlic and cook, stirring occasionally, until golden brown.

3. Bring 4 quarts salted water to a boil in a large pot. Add the spaghetti and cook until tender but still firm; do not overcook. Drain the pasta well and return to the pot.

4. Add the chicken broth to the pasta and simmer until most of the broth has been absorbed, 5 minutes or so.

5. Stir in the heated olive oil and sliced garlic, then the minced garlic and the chopped parsley. Toss thoroughly.

6. Divide the pasta evenly among heated plates or shallow soup bowls. Pour any remaining broth over the pasta, and serve immediately, accompanied by lots of freshly ground black pepper and grated cheese.

6 first-course portions

PASTA WITH SAUSAGE AND PEPPERS

Everyone should have a hearty pasta sauce like this one in their repertoire. A printed recipe for a dish this casual may seem superfluous to those who throw together such simmered sauce improvisations on the spur of the moment. We think balance and harmony are as important here as anywhere else; however, feel free to change the herbs, omit the hot peppers, or increase the garlic as you see fit, in order to make the dish your own.

We like to serve this over short tubular pasta such as ziti or rigatoni. While it's perfectly delicious with the traditional sprinkling of grated Parmigiano-Reggiano cheese, we suggest you try topping it with a dollop of fresh ricotta and a grinding of black pepper for a change of pace.

2 pounds sweet Italian sausage
3 tablespoons best-quality olive oil
1 cup finely chopped yellow onions
3 red bell peppers, stemmed, seeded, and cut into medium-size julienne
1 cup dry red wine
1 can (2 pounds, 3 ounces) Italian plum tomatoes, including the liquid
1 cup water
1 tablespoon dried oregano
1 teaspoon dried thyme
Salt and freshly ground black pepper, to taste
Pinch of crushed red pepper flakes, or to taste
1 teaspoon fennel seeds
½ cup chopped fresh Italian (flat-leaf) parsley
6 (or more) garlic cloves, peeled and finely chopped

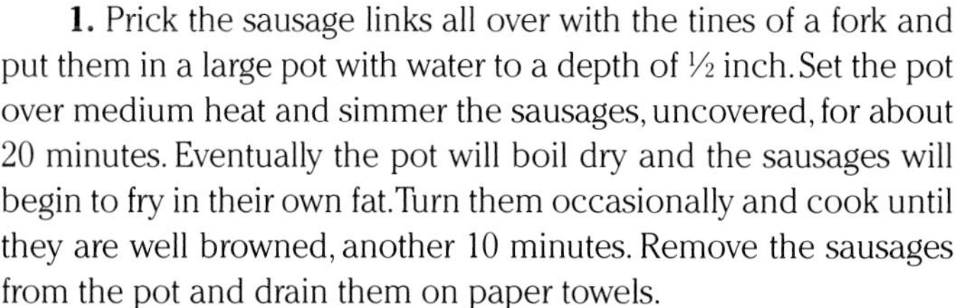

1. Prick the sausage links all over with the tines of a fork and put them in a large pot with water to a depth of ½ inch. Set the pot over medium heat and simmer the sausages, uncovered, for about 20 minutes. Eventually the pot will boil dry and the sausages will begin to fry in their own fat. Turn them occasionally and cook until they are well browned, another 10 minutes. Remove the sausages from the pot and drain them on paper towels.

2. Pour the sausage fat out of the pot but do not wash the pot. Set it over low heat, add the olive oil and onions, and cook them, covered, until tender, about 25 minutes.

3. Add the peppers, raise the heat, and cook uncovered for another 5 minutes, stirring often.

4. Add the wine, tomatoes, water, oregano, and thyme, and season with salt, black pepper, and red pepper flakes. Bring to a boil, reduce the heat, and simmer, partially covered, for 30 minutes.

5. Meanwhile, slice the sausages into ½-inch-thick rounds. When the sauce has simmered for 30 minutes, add the sausages and fennel seeds and simmer, uncovered, for another 20 minutes.

6. Add the parsley and chopped garlic and simmer for another 5 minutes.

2 quarts sauce, enough for about 2 pounds pasta

"Live within your harvest."

—PERSIAN PROVERB

PASTA PUTTANESCA

This racy pasta sauce is named for Italian ladies of the night (the *puttane*). It's quick and cheap and we hope it offends no one to say so.

Puttanesca, with its zesty nuggets of garlic, capers, olives, and anchovies, is not for the faint-hearted. Serve it to food-loving friends and pour an earthy red wine. With practice you can have this sauce ready to eat in 20 minutes. This is our friend Bobbie's recipe. She can make it blindfolded.

CAPERS

Capers are the piquant, aromatic buds of wild thorny bushes that grow all over the Mediterranean. They flourish in dry, sunny climates, and are harvested by hand at the height of summer's heat. Harvested berries are graded in size from the smallest (nonpareils) to the largest (about the size of a grape), and are then immersed in vinegar or enrobed in salt. All capers have big, bold flavor.

Small capers are great sprinkled atop smoked salmon; with tuna; added to a gremolata for grilled fish; in egg, potato, or Greek salads; or anywhere your heart desires. We love to serve the large capers, with their stems on, alongside a bowl of olives with aperitifs. They're a tasty conversation piece in and of themselves.

1 pound spaghetti, linguine, or other thin dried pasta
2 cans (2 pounds, 3 ounces each) Italian plum tomatoes
¼ cup best-quality olive oil
1 teaspoon dried oregano
⅛ teaspoon crushed red pepper flakes, or to taste
½ cup tiny black niçoise olives
¼ cup drained capers
4 garlic cloves, peeled and chopped
8 anchovy fillets, coarsely chopped
½ cup chopped fresh Italian (flat-leaf) parsley, plus extra for garnish
Salt, to taste

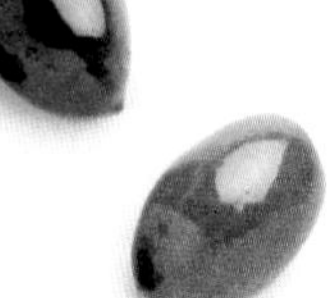

1. Bring 4 quarts salted water to a boil in a large pot. Stir in the spaghetti. Cook until tender but still firm. Drain immediately and transfer to 4 heated plates.

2. While the spaghetti is cooking, drain the tomatoes, cut them crosswise into halves, and squeeze out as much liquid as possible.

3. Combine the tomatoes and olive oil in a skillet and bring to a boil. Keep the sauce at a full boil and add the oregano, pepper flakes, olives, capers, garlic, anchovies, and ½ cup parsley, stirring frequently.

4. Reduce the heat slightly and continue to cook, until the sauce has thickened to your liking, 3 to 5 minutes. Taste and add salt, if desired. Serve immediately over the hot pasta and garnish with the additional chopped parsley.

4 main-course portions

CREAMY PASTA SAUCE WITH FRESH HERBS

This delicate sauce is perfect over angel hair pasta.

1½ cups heavy cream
4 tablespoons (½ stick) unsalted butter
½ teaspoon salt
⅛ teaspoon freshly grated nutmeg
Pinch of cayenne pepper
1 cup finely chopped mixed fresh herbs [our favorite combination is basil, mint, watercress, Italian (flat-leaf) parsley, and chives]
¼ cup grated Parmigiano-Reggiano cheese

1. Combine the cream, butter, salt, nutmeg, and cayenne in a heavy saucepan and simmer until the sauce is slightly reduced and thickened, 15 minutes.

2. Whisk in the fresh herbs and the cheese and simmer for another 5 minutes. Taste and correct the seasoning. Serve immediately.

2 cups sauce, enough for 1 pound angel hair pasta, 6 or more portions as a first course

"I'd rather have roses
on my table than
diamonds on my neck."
—EMMA GOLDMAN

LINGUINE WITH WHITE CLAM SAUCE

Whether you go clamming in the surf or at the fish market, this is the perfect recipe.

¾ cup best-quality olive oil
6 garlic cloves, peeled and minced
4 dozen small clams, such as Littlenecks or Cherrystones, scrubbed, shucked, and chopped coarsely, all liquor reserved
About 2 cups bottled clam juice
½ cup finely chopped fresh Italian (flat-leaf) parsley
1½ teaspoons dried oregano
Salt and freshly ground black pepper, to taste
24 fresh clams, in their shells, for garnish (optional)
1 pound linguine

1. Heat the olive oil in a deep heavy pot over low heat. Add the garlic and cook until golden, about 5 minutes.

2. Combine the reserved clam liquor and enough bottled clam juice to make 3 cups. Add this to the pot along with the parsley, oregano, and salt and pepper. Simmer, partially covered, for 10 minutes. The sauce may be prepared ahead to this point.

3. Meanwhile, scrub the garnishing clams, if you are using them, and put them in another pan with water to a depth of 1 inch. Cover, and set the pan over high heat. Shake the pan or stir the clams and remove them as they open. Reserve them in their shells. Discard any clams that don't open.

4. Bring 4 quarts salted water to a boil in a large pot. Drop in the linguine and cook until tender but still firm.

5. Meanwhile, reheat the sauce if you have allowed it to cool. Add the chopped clams and heat gently; clams should not overcook or they will become tough.

6. Drain the linguine and toss it with the sauce. Serve it in the pot, topped by the clam garnish, or transfer to individual wide soup bowls and garnish each serving with the clams in their shells.

6 portions

from THE SILVER PALATE NOTEBOOK

If fresh herbs are plentiful, use them in bouquets around the house; their dark green or gray leaves are beautiful with flowers.

Make an edible centerpiece of herbs such as basil, dill, and mint: wash fresh herbs, shake dry, and arrange with salad greens in a bowl of crushed ice.

PASTA CARBONARA

An authentic version of this classic dish would use the Italian bacon pancetta, or perhaps prosciutto. With a glass of rough red wine, it is one of the best late-night suppers we know. The use of American bacon can, however, transform pasta carbonara into something else altogether—a wonderful breakfast dish. However and whenever you serve this dish, it is hearty and satisfying.

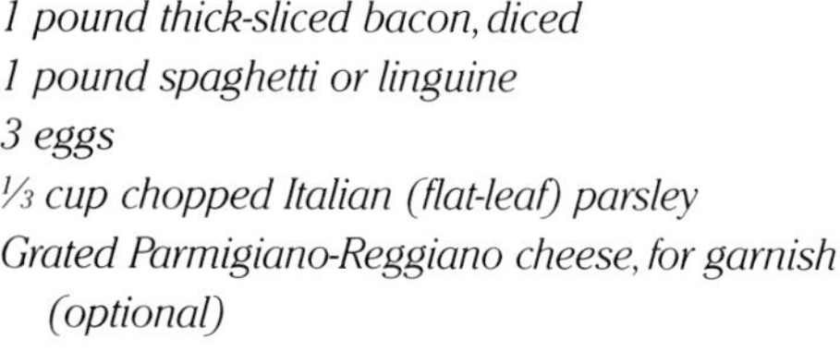

1 pound thick-sliced bacon, diced
1 pound spaghetti or linguine
3 eggs
⅓ cup chopped Italian (flat-leaf) parsley
Grated Parmigiano-Reggiano cheese, for garnish (optional)
Freshly ground black pepper, to taste

1. Sauté the diced bacon in a small skillet until crisp. Remove with a slotted spoon and drain well on paper towels.

2. Bring 4 quarts salted water to a boil in a large pot. Drop in the spaghetti and stir with a wooden spoon to separate the strands. Let the water return to the boil. Cook until tender but not mushy, about 8 minutes, although cooking time will vary.

3. Meanwhile, beat the eggs thoroughly in a large serving bowl. Have the cooked bacon and the chopped parsley at hand.

4. When the pasta is done, drain it immediately in a colander, shaking briefly to eliminate excess water.

5. Pour the drained hot spaghetti into the bowl of eggs and immediately begin tossing it. As the strands of pasta become coated with the beaten eggs, their heat will cook the eggs.

6. Sprinkle on the bacon dice and chopped parsley, toss again, and serve immediately. Grated cheese is delicious (but optional at breakfast); freshly ground black pepper is essential.

4 to 6 portions

AMERICANS LOVE PASTA

Americans eat more pasta than Italians do—at least at one sitting. Italians usually serve two ounces per person; Americans lean toward three or four or more. But then, Italians serve pasta as a first course; we generally reserve it for a main. Italians also sauce their pasta less liberally than we do. They want the sauce to accent but never overwhelm the pasta. That's because the taste and character of the pasta is so important to them. Italian pasta is made of durum wheat (durum semolina), which is a granular, not powdery, grain. American pasta is made from softer wheat. Some of our favorite brands are Martelli, Cipriani, Cavalieri, Latini, Rustichella, and De Cecco.

TORTELLINI WITH GORGONZOLA CREAM SAUCE

Here pungent Gorgonzola is mellowed by heavy cream in a sauce for tortellini. No additional grated cheese is required at the table, but provide your guests with a pepper mill.

AN ITALIAN FLAG MENU

TOMATO DILL SOUP

TORTELLINI WITH GORGONZOLA CREAM SAUCE

ROAST SHOULDER OF VEAL

WATERCRESS AND ENDIVE SALAD

STRAWBERRIES WITH *CHAMPAGNE SABAYON*

1½ cups dry white vermouth
2¼ cups heavy cream
Freshly ground black pepper, to taste
Big pinch of freshly grated nutmeg
1½ pounds fresh tortellini
¾ pound sweet Gorgonzola cheese, crumbled
1½ tablespoons grated Parmigiano-Reggiano cheese

1. Bring the vermouth to a boil in a small heavy saucepan and reduce by half.

2. Add the heavy cream, bring to a boil, and lower the heat to a simmer. Season with freshly ground black pepper, add the nutmeg, and simmer uncovered until reduced by one third, about 15 minutes.

3. Bring 6 quarts salted water to a boil in a large pot. Add the tortellini and cook until tender. Drain and return to the hot pot.

4. Remove the cream sauce from the heat, stir in half of the Gorgonzola and all the Parmigiano-Reggiano, and pour over the tortellini. Set over medium heat and cook gently, stirring constantly, until the cream has thickened slightly and the tortellini have absorbed some of the sauce, 5 to 8 minutes.

5. Divide the tortellini among 6 heated plates, sprinkle each with the reserved Gorgonzola, and serve immediately.

6 portions as a first course or light main course

"Nothing else, not opera or Renaissance art or Roman ruins or even pizza so exemplifies Italy as pasta."

—BURTON ANDERSON, *TREASURES OF THE ITALIAN TABLE*

GREEN LASAGNA

This beautiful dish of pasta is an intriguing departure from the usual lasagna, and yet respects the traditions of freshness and lightness that permeate the best Italian cooking. The combination of soft, fresh goat cheese and fresh basil is one we find especially exciting, and the contrast of flavor and color is wonderful. This is not a main-course pasta; serve it as a first course, followed by a light entrée of fish, veal, or chicken.

¾ pound fresh spinach pasta, uncut, about 3 sheets
2 packages (10 ounces each) frozen chopped spinach, defrosted
1 cup ricotta cheese
⅓ cup grated Parmigiano-Reggiano cheese
Salt and freshly ground black pepper, to taste
½ cup Basil Purée (see Note, page 38)
About 11 ounces Montrachet cheese or other soft chèvre
3 tablespoons heavy cream
1½ cups medium Béchamel Sauce (page 415)

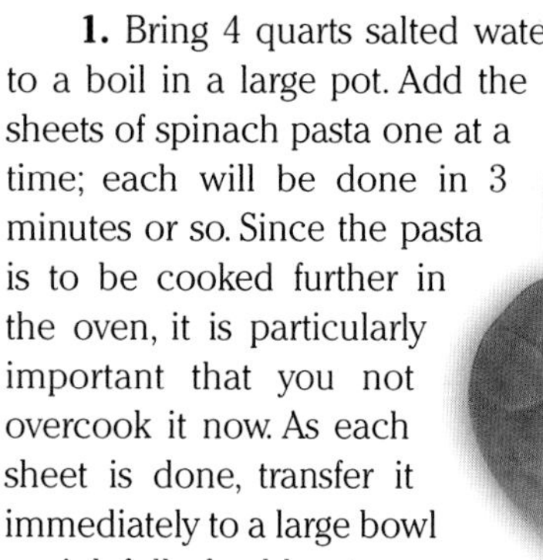

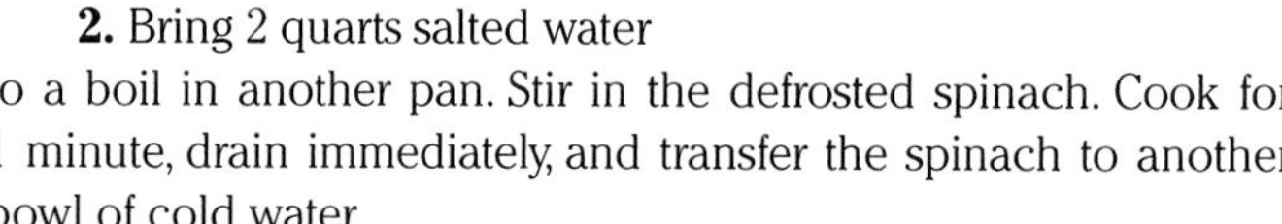

1. Bring 4 quarts salted water to a boil in a large pot. Add the sheets of spinach pasta one at a time; each will be done in 3 minutes or so. Since the pasta is to be cooked further in the oven, it is particularly important that you not overcook it now. As each sheet is done, transfer it immediately to a large bowl or sink full of cold water.

2. Bring 2 quarts salted water to a boil in another pan. Stir in the defrosted spinach. Cook for 1 minute, drain immediately, and transfer the spinach to another bowl of cold water.

3. Mix the ricotta and 2 tablespoons Parmigiano-Reggiano together in a small bowl. Season with salt and pepper and set aside.

4. In another bowl, cream together the basil purée, three-quarters of the chèvre, and the heavy cream. Set aside.

5. Drain the spinach and squeeze out as much water as possible with your hands. Stir the spinach into the ricotta mixture and correct the seasoning; you may need more pepper or Parmigiano-Reggiano; you will probably not need more salt.

6. Drain the sheets of pasta, cut them lengthwise into 2-inch-wide strips, and pat thoroughly dry on paper towels.

7. Preheat the oven to 375°F.

8. Smear one third of the béchamel evenly over the bottom of a 9 x 13-inch baking dish. Arrange about one third of the pasta strips over the béchamel, trimming them as necessary to make an exact fit. Spread all of the spinach and ricotta mixture evenly over the pasta strips, being sure to cover the pasta completely to the edges. Cut a second layer of pasta strips and arrange them over the spinach mixture. Spread half of the remaining béchamel over the second layer of pasta and spread all of the basil and goat cheese mixture over the béchamel. Top this with the final layer of pasta, again trimming and fitting the strips. Spread the remaining béchamel evenly over the top layer of pasta and crumble the remaining chèvre over the béchamel. Sprinkle with the remaining Parmigiano-Reggiano.

9. Set the baking dish in the upper third of the oven. Bake the lasagna until it is bubbling and the top is lightly browned, 10 to 15 minutes. (The short baking time is perfectly adequate for this light, fresh lasagna; do not overcook it.) Serve immediately.

6 portions

from THE SILVER PALATE NOTEBOOK

No one needs a reason to throw a party, but adopting a reason or a theme can make it much more fun. Originality is what counts. Roll up the rug, decorate to the hilt, ask the guest of honor to perform, fill the house with candlelight, play period music, take it outdoors, set up board games or croquet, ask guests to bring a poem, a swimsuit, or a favorite appetizer.

The calendar is loaded with occasions beyond traditional holidays that are worth celebrating. There's Academy Awards night, Election night, the finals of the U.S. Open, Super Bowl Sunday, the summer solstice, a new job, Bastille Day, the arrival of Beaujolais Nouveau, the publication of a friend's book, or the arrival of a new neighbor.

You can always let the menu create the theme. Take your friends someplace wonderful: Serve Chinese and use only chopsticks; beguile with Sangria and continual waves of tapas; or dazzle with white peach Bellinis and three different pastas. Everyone loves to travel . . . especially if someone else has done all of the planning and there's no packing. If you set the stage for fun, there's no doubt it will be contagious.

PASTA WITH LOBSTER AND TARRAGON

A beautiful and sophisticated pasta dish, perfect as the first course of an important dinner. Begin with caviar or oysters, follow the pasta with Roast Shoulder of Veal (page 124) or Filet of Beef (page 118), and fresh raspberries and cream.

2 tablespoons best-quality olive oil
½ cup finely chopped yellow onion
1 can (2 pounds, 3 ounces) Italian plum tomatoes
2 teaspoons dried tarragon
Salt and freshly ground black pepper, to taste
1 cup heavy cream
1 pound spaghetti
Pinch of cayenne pepper
½ pound cooked lobster meat (about 1½ cups; the equivalent of a 3- to 4-pound lobster)
Fresh parsley, basil, or tarragon sprigs, for garnish

1. Heat the oil in a saucepan over medium heat. Add the onion, reduce the heat, and cook, covered, until tender, about 25 minutes.

2. Chop and drain the tomatoes and add them to the onions. Add the tarragon, season with salt and pepper, and bring to a boil. Reduce the heat, cover, and simmer, stirring occasionally, for 30 minutes.

3. Remove the mixture from the heat and let it cool slightly. Purée it in a food processor, or use a food mill fitted with a medium disc.

4. Return the purée to the saucepan, stir in the heavy cream, and set over medium heat. Simmer the mixture, stirring often, until slightly reduced, 15 minutes. Taste the sauce, correct the seasoning, and stir in the cayenne and lobster meat. Simmer further, just until the lobster is heated through, 3 to 5 minutes.

5. Meanwhile, in a large pot, bring 4 quarts salted water to a boil. Stir in the pasta, and cook until tender but still firm. Drain immediately and arrange on warmed serving plates. Spoon the sauce over the pasta and garnish with a sprig of parsley, basil, or tarragon. Serve immediately.

6 portions as a first course, or 4 as a main course

from THE SILVER PALATE NOTEBOOK

We like to use fresh tomato spaghetti with this dish, making it a symphony of reds and pinks. Regular spaghetti is fine, however, and tastes just as good. This is another of those pasta dishes requiring no grated cheese; just pass the peppermill.

SUMMER PASTA

New light sauces and the increasing use of vegetables and fish have opened up a whole new world of pasta, with contrasts in flavor, texture, and temperature. There are cool sauces on hot pasta, cool sauces on cool pasta, and we hardly feel lukewarm about any of these exciting combinations.

LINGUINE WITH TOMATOES AND BASIL

We first had this uncooked pasta sauce when we were guests in a beautiful home on Sardinia. Such a recipe could only be the result of hot, lazy days and abundant ripe tomatoes and basil. The heat of the pasta warms and brings out the flavors of the sauce in a wonderfully subtle way. Delicious and easy.

4 large ripe tomatoes, cut into ½-inch cubes
1 pound Brie, rind removed, torn into irregular pieces
1 cup fresh basil leaves, rinsed, patted dry, and cut into strips
3 garlic cloves, peeled and finely minced
1 cup plus 1 tablespoon best-quality olive oil
½ teaspoon salt, plus additional to taste
½ teaspoon freshly ground black pepper
1½ pounds linguine
Freshly grated Parmigiano-Reggiano cheese, for garnish (optional)

1. At least 2 hours before serving, combine the tomatoes, Brie, basil, garlic, the 1 cup olive oil, and ½ teaspoon each salt and pepper in a large serving bowl.

2. Bring 6 quarts salted water to a boil in a large pot. Add 1 tablespoon olive oil and the linguine, and boil until tender but still firm, 8 to 10 minutes.

3. Drain the pasta and immediately toss with the tomato sauce. Serve at once, passing the peppermill, and the grated Parmigiano-Reggiano cheese, if you like.

4 to 6 portions

In this dish, linguine is the palette for a vibrant array of colors and flavors. This "raw" sauce requires little more than the season's best produce, casually tossed together—use the lushest tomatoes and most fragrant basil you can find.

"Summer cooking implies a sense of immediacy, a capacity to capture the essence of the fleeting moment."

—ELIZABETH DAVID

PASTA AND SEAFOOD SALAD WITH BASIL

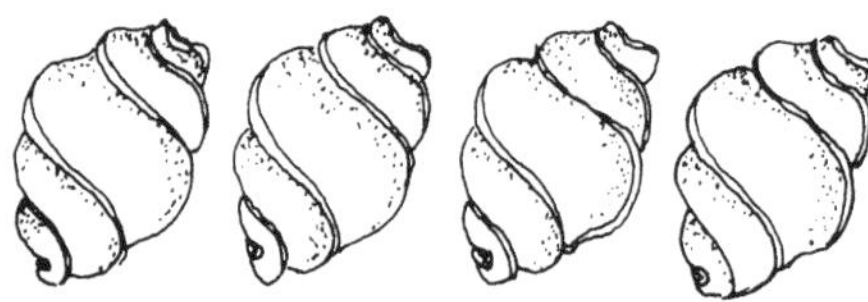

This is perfect summer fare—a casual but dressy one-dish meal that is quick to cook and undemanding to serve. Drop-in guests can give a hand with the chopping or just help themselves to a plateful without fuss or muss. A cool and uncomplicated glass of wine (try one of the California rosés made from Zinfandel or Cabernet grapes) and a piece of crusty bread are all you need to accompany this salad.

1 pound medium-size raw shrimp, shelled and deveined
1 pound bay scallops, rinsed
2 or 3 small squid, cleaned (optional; see Note)
½ pound pasta of some interesting shape, such as shells, spaghetti twists, and corkscrews
1 cup tiny peas (defrosted if frozen; rinsed and patted dry if fresh)
½ cup diced red bell pepper
½ cup minced red onion
½ cup best-quality olive oil
3 to 4 tablespoons fresh lemon juice
½ cup Basil Purée (see Note, page 38)
Salt and freshly ground black pepper, to taste
1 cup imported black olives, such as kalamata or alfonso, for garnish

1. Bring a large pot of salted water to a boil, drop in the shrimp and scallops, cook for 1 minute, and drain immediately.

2. Cut the bodies of the squid, if using, into ½-inch rings. Divide each cluster of tentacles in half. Bring another pot of salted water to a boil, drop in the squid, and simmer for 5 minutes. Drain.

3. Bring a third pot of salted water to a boil. Drop in the pasta, and cook until tender but still firm. Drain.

4. Be certain the seafood and pasta are well drained and free of any excess water. Toss them together in a large bowl.

5. Add the peas (no need to cook them), bell pepper, and onion and toss again.

6. In a small bowl whisk together the olive oil, lemon juice, and basil purée and season with salt and pepper. Pour the dressing over the salad and toss well to distribute. Taste and correct the seasoning if necessary.

7. Mound the salad on a serving platter and scatter the olives over it. Serve immediately, or cover and refrigerate. Allow the salad to return to room temperature before serving.

4 to 6 portions

Note: Omit the squid if you must, but it gives the salad a taste, texture, and visual appeal for which there is no substitute.

NUPTIAL BRUNCH

FIGS AND PROSCIUTTO

ASPARAGUS WITH *BLUEBERRY VINAIGRETTE*

SPINACH PASTA WITH SALMON AND CREAM SAUCE

RAISIN PUMPERNICKEL BREAD WITH UNSALTED BUTTER

CAMPARI ICE

PESTO POSSIBILITIES

We love pesto, but remember, it packs a punch. We generally use a light touch when adding it to a dish.

- ♥ Fold a tablespoon or two of pesto into mashed or smashed potatoes.
- ♥ Add a few tablespoons of pesto as a layer in meat loaf.
- ♥ Drizzle pesto over grilled shrimp.
- ♥ Stir pesto into linguine with sautéed hot and sweet Italian sausages, asparagus, and freshly grated Parmigiano-Reggiano cheese.
- ♥ Swirl a tablespoon of pesto into a bowl of fondue.
- ♥ Use a smidgen of pesto to finish a gnocchi or risotto dish.
- ♥ Dollop a teaspoon of pesto onto roma tomato halves stuffed with mozzarella. Top with shards of Parmigiano-Reggiano cheese and bake gently.
- ♥ Drizzle pesto over slices of summer tomatoes layered with fresh buffalo mozzarella and arugula.
- ♥ Spoon pesto over any green vegetables or stir a tablespoon or two into sautéed greens.
- ♥ Mix 2 tablespoons pesto with 2 tablespoons crème fraîche or sour cream, and dollop into your favorite summer soup.
- ♥ Whisk 1 tablespoon pesto into 4 eggs as you scramble them.
- ♥ Season mayonnaise with a tablespoon or two of pesto when making potato salad.
- ♥ Brush broiled chicken with pesto about 10 minutes before the end of cooking time. Serve with sautéed tomatoes.
- ♥ Whisk together 2 tablespoons pesto, 4 tablespoons crème fraîche, and 1 tablespoon Dijon mustard for superb saucing for poached fish.

SPINACH PASTA
WITH SALMON AND CREAM SAUCE

This elegant dish is not particularly Italian, but the subtle flavors and ravishing colors combine to make it unique.

2 cups heavy cream
4 tablespoons (½ stick) unsalted butter
1 teaspoon salt
Pinch of freshly grated nutmeg
1 pound fresh spinach pasta (narrower noodles preferred)
1 tablespoon grated Parmigiano-Reggiano cheese
1½ to 2 cups flaked poached salmon, all skin and bones removed
⅓ cup chopped fresh dill, plus additional sprigs for garnish

1. Bring the cream and half the butter to a simmer in a small saucepan. Add the salt and the nutmeg, and continue to simmer until the cream is reduced by about one third.

2. Bring 4 quarts salted water to a boil in a large pot. Drop in the pasta. Remember, fresh pasta is ready in 2 to 3 minutes.

3. Meanwhile, stir the grated cheese, then the salmon and the ⅓ cup chopped dill into the cream, and remove from the heat.

4. Drain the pasta, return it to the hot pot and toss with the remaining butter until the butter is melted. Divide the pasta among 6 heated plates and spoon the cream sauce over each portion. Garnish with a sprig of dill and serve at once.

6 first-course portions

PESTO

This pesto is equally at home on pasta, fluffed into hot rice, or stirred into homemade mayonnaise as a sauce for cold poached fish or crudités.

2 cups fresh basil leaves, rinsed and patted dry
4 good-size garlic cloves, peeled and chopped
1 cup shelled walnuts
1 cup best-quality olive oil
1 cup freshly grated Parmigiano-Reggiano cheese
¼ cup freshly grated Romano cheese
Salt and freshly ground black pepper, to taste

1. Combine the basil, garlic, and walnuts in a food processor and pulse to chop.

2. Leave the motor running and add the olive oil in a slow, steady stream.

3. Shut the motor off, add the cheeses, and a big pinch of salt and a liberal grinding of pepper. Process briefly to combine, then scrape out into a bowl and cover until ready to use.

2 cups, enough to sauce 2 pounds pasta

PASTA WITH PESTO

1 pound linguine or fettuccine
¼ cup heavy cream
1 cup Pesto (recipe precedes)
Freshly ground black pepper
Freshly grated Parmigiano-Reggiano or Romano cheese (optional)

1. Bring 4 quarts salted water to a boil in a large pot. Add the pasta and boil until tender but firm.

2. Stir 2 tablespoons of the hot pasta water and the heavy cream into the pesto. Drain the pasta in a colander and return it to the hot pot. Stir in the pesto and toss well to combine.

3. Serve immediately on warm plates. More freshly ground pepper is welcome, but cheese is not really necessary.

6 to 8 moderate first-course portions, 4 generous main-course portions

SPICY SESAME NOODLES

Our unorthodox but delicious version of a Chinese classic.

1 pound thin linguine, or other thin pasta
¼ cup peanut oil
2 cups Sesame Mayonnaise (page 177)
Drops of Szechuan hot chile oil, to taste (see Note)
8 scallions (green onions), trimmed, well rinsed, and cut diagonally into ½-inch pieces
Blanched asparagus tips, broccoli florets, or snow peas, for garnish (optional)

1. Bring 4 quarts of salted water to a boil in a large pot. Drop in the linguine and cook until tender but still firm. Drain, toss in a mixing bowl with the peanut oil, and let cool to room temperature.

2. Whisk together the sesame mayonnaise and drops of chile oil, to taste, in a small bowl. Do not hesitate to make the mayonnaise quite spicy (start with 4 drops and taste before adding more); the noodles will absorb a lot of heat.

3. Add the scallions to the pasta, pour in the sesame mayonnaise, and toss gently. Cover and refrigerate until serving time.

4. Toss the noodles again and add additional sesame mayonnaise if they seem dry. Arrange in a serving bowl and garnish with asparagus, broccoli, or snow peas. Serve immediately.

6 portions

Note: Available in Asian groceries and specialty food shops.

PESTO PERFECT

The first batch of pesto—that marvelous Genoese basil sauce for pasta—officially welcomes summer back to our kitchen. Like tender shoots of early spring asparagus, or the tangy crunch of an apple as autumn slides into winter, basil and pesto are sure signs of seasonal change.

In Genoa, the preparation of this sauce is steeped in years of tradition. It must be pounded with a marble pestle in a marble mortar (the method we prefer, when we have time); only the Genoese basil, bathed by salty sea air as it grows, will do; the purest versions contain nothing but basil, cheese, garlic, and olive oil.

But we let our imaginations run wild, too, using different herbs or vegetables (parsley, tarragon, mint, oregano, arugula, and spinach), different nuts (hazelnuts, macadamias, walnuts, or sunflower, pumpkin, or sesame seeds), and a variety of oils and cheeses. Sometimes we push the envelope even further to include a variety of sun-dried tomatoes, roasted red peppers, chipotle peppers, artichokes, kalamata olives, sweet green peas, or ginger. There are no limits. These new pestos simply dazzle every dish they touch.

THE MAIN COURSE

CHICKEN EVERY WAY

At the turn of the nineteenth century and for a considerable time afterward, chicken was an expensive treat, served on special occasions and made much of. There were even recipes that extended chicken salads and stews with that economy meat, veal! Times have certainly changed. Chicken today is as easy on the pocketbook as it is on the calorie counter, and the only danger is that with all the chicken we consume, we might let it become dull. Fortunately, chicken is compatible with so many different seasonings and cooking methods that only the lazy cook risks turning out a boring chicken dish.

There was always a chicken dish *du jour* on The Silver Palate's menu, and our never-ending efforts to intrigue our customers resulted in the following collection of recipes. We think they'll intrigue you too, and prove once again the adaptability of the versatile chicken.

THE CHICKEN CHART

Today there are conventional, organic, free-range, Amish, kosher, and heritage (antique breed) chickens to choose from. There's only one way to find your favorite: Sample them all.

CORNISH GAME HENS: 1- to 2-pound chickens that are a cross between two breeds. Generally roasted; one per person.

POUSSIN: 16- to 20-ounce young chickens that cook up very moist. One per person.

BROILERS/FRYERS: 2½ to 3½ pounds. Butchers use these terms interchangeably. If you prepare them well, these chickens may be cooked either way. Look for yellow fat and plump breasts. The most commonly available chicken.

GUINEA HENS: 2½ to 3 pounds with slightly richer meat than most breeds of chicken.

ROASTERS/PULLETS: 4½- to 6-pound chickens. Perfect for roasting, with more meat per pound.

FOWL OR STEWING HENS: Up to 8 pounds; best for stock or chicken salads. They require longer, slower cooking, but have great flavor. Hard to find today.

CAPONS: 8- to 10-pound cocks that have grown fat and tender. Mild flavor; perfect for stuffing.

COUNTRY WEEKEND LUNCH

CHEESE STRAWS

CRUDITÉS AND ASSORTED DIPS

CHICKEN MARBELLA

SEMOLINA BREAD

BOUCHERON CHEESE

LIME MOUSSE

CHOCOLATE CHIP COOKIES

CHICKEN MARBELLA

This was the first main-course dish to be offered at The Silver Palate shop, and the distinctive colors and flavors of the prunes, olives, and capers have kept it a favorite for years. It's good hot or at room temperature. When prepared with small drumsticks and wings, it makes a delicious appetizer.

The overnight marination is essential to the moistness of the finished product: The chicken keeps and even improves over several days of refrigeration; it travels well and makes excellent picnic fare.

½ cup olive oil
½ cup red wine vinegar
1 cup pitted prunes
½ cup pitted Spanish green olives
½ cup capers with a bit of juice
6 bay leaves
1 head of garlic, peeled and finely puréed
¼ cup dried oregano
Coarse salt and freshly ground black pepper, to taste
4 chickens (2½ pounds each), quartered
1 cup brown sugar
1 cup dry white wine
¼ cup fresh Italian (flat-leaf) parsley or fresh cilantro, finely chopped

1. Combine the olive oil, vinegar, prunes, olives, capers and juice, bay leaves, garlic, oregano, and salt and pepper in a large bowl. Add the chicken and stir to coat. Cover the bowl and refrigerate overnight.

2. Preheat the oven to 350°F.

3. Arrange the chicken in a single layer in one or two large, shallow baking pans and spoon the marinade over it evenly. Sprinkle the chicken pieces with the brown sugar and pour the white wine around them.

4. Bake, basting frequently with the pan juices, until the thigh pieces yield clear yellow (rather than pink) juice when pricked with a fork, 50 minutes to 1 hour.

5. With a slotted spoon, transfer the chicken, prunes, olives, and capers to a serving platter. Moisten with a few spoonfuls of the pan juices and sprinkle generously with the parsley or cilantro. Pass the remaining pan juices in a sauceboat.

16 pieces, 10 or more portions

Note: To serve Chicken Marbella cold, cool to room temperature in the cooking juices before transferring the pieces to a serving platter. If the chicken has been covered and refrigerated, reheat it in the juices, then allow it to come to room temperature before serving. Spoon some of the reserved juice over the chicken.

RASPBERRY CHICKEN

Boneless chicken breasts are quick and economical to serve but often dull to eat. In this recipe, ready in minutes, raspberry vinegar lends a bit of welcome tartness, mellowed by chicken stock and heavy cream. A handful of fresh raspberries, poached briefly in the sauce just before serving, adds an elegant note. Wild rice and a simply sautéed green vegetable would be good accompaniments.

2 whole boneless, skinless chicken breasts (about 2 pounds)
2 tablespoons unsalted butter
¼ cup finely chopped yellow onion
¼ cup raspberry vinegar (see Note)
¼ cup Chicken Stock (page 416) or canned chicken broth
¼ cup heavy cream or Crème Fraîche (page 414)
1 tablespoon canned crushed tomatoes
16 fresh raspberries (optional)

1. Cut each chicken breast into halves along the breastbone line. Remove the fillet, the finger-size muscle on the back of each half, and reserve for another use. Flatten each breast half or *suprême* by pressing it gently with the palm of your hand.

2. Melt the butter in a large skillet over low heat. Raise the heat, add the suprêmes, and cook until they are lightly colored, about 3 minutes per side. Remove from the skillet and reserve.

3. Add the onion to the fat in the pan and cook, covered, over low heat until tender, about 15 minutes.

4. Add the vinegar, raise the heat, and cook, uncovered, stirring occasionally, until the vinegar is reduced to a syrupy spoonful. Whisk in the chicken stock, heavy cream or crème fraîche, and crushed tomatoes and simmer for 1 minute.

5. Return the suprêmes to the skillet and simmer them gently in the sauce, basting often, until they are just done and the sauce has been reduced and thickened slightly, about 5 minutes; do not overcook.

6. Remove the suprêmes with a slotted spoon and arrange on a heated serving platter. Add the raspberries to the sauce in the skillet and cook over low heat for 1 minute. Do not stir the berries with a spoon, merely swirl them in the sauce by shaking the skillet.

7. Pour the sauce over the suprêmes and serve immediately.

2 to 4 portions

Note: Available in specialty food stores. The intensity of vinegars varies from brand to brand. Be prepared to adjust this quantity to suit your own taste.

"Pic´nic (G. *picknick,* Fr. *pique-nique*) 1. an excursion or outing with food usually provided by members of the group and eaten in the open. 2a. a pleasant or amusing experience. b. an easy task or feat."

We think Mr. Webster has defined the word but hasn't done much for the experience. Our rendering of a *pique-nique* includes a group of fun-loving friends, a spontaneous break from the ordinary, and a chance to appreciate simple delightful things.

A picnic need not be lunch in the park. It can be held on the terrace at midnight, watching shooting stars and fireflies; it can also be an afternoon gathering by the pool, or a luscious breakfast shared with the sunrise. The best picnicking is done with food that looks and tastes delicious and travels beautifully. Because this portable quality was the true essence of our shop, the recipes in this book are, for the most part, easy to eat, pleasing to the palate, and able to survive from the kitchen to the outdoors while still tasting wonderful. Simple food need not be unimaginative.

GLAZED BLUEBERRY CHICKEN

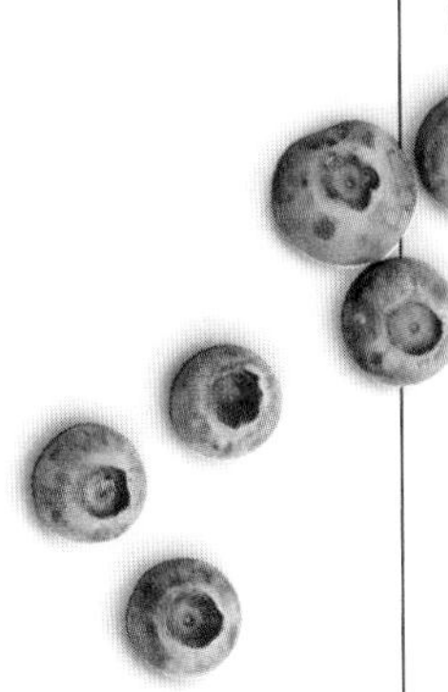

½ cup Blueberry Vinegar (see page 145)
1 teaspoon dried thyme
1 chicken (2½ to 3 pounds), quartered
Salt and freshly ground black pepper, to taste
⅓ cup blueberry chutney (see Note) or preserves
1 tablespoon chopped fresh Italian (flat-leaf) parsley, for garnish

1. Combine the blueberry vinegar and thyme in a large bowl. Add the chicken, turn to coat with the marinade, and marinate for 2 hours, turning occasionally.

2. Preheat the oven to 300°F.

3. Arrange the chicken pieces, skin side up, in a baking pan, reserving the marinade. Season the chicken lightly with salt and pepper and coat it lightly with the blueberry chutney or preserves.

4. Bake the chicken on the center rack of the oven until it is cooked through, about 1 hour, basting occasionally with the marinade. Do not baste in the last 15 minutes of baking.

5. Transfer the chicken to a serving platter. Serve immediately or at room temperature, sprinkled with the parsley.

2 to 4 portions

Note: Available at specialty food shops.

CHUTNEY

Chutneys are descended from the medieval custom of fruit relishes preserved with sugar, vinegar, and spices. The simple notion of grinding a bit of black pepper on melon or strawberries has the same origin. Today chutneys are sweet, tart, and complex, full of flavor and chunky in texture.

Many fruits and vegetables, sometimes in combination, make good chutneys; some we've run across include tomato, peach, cherry, fig, date, eggplant, plum, blueberry, cranberry, mango, onion, apple, carrot, tomato-apple, and jalapeño.

Be adventurous; don't wait until you're serving curry to enjoy a chutney. They complement food, and stimulate the appetite and taste buds. Try chutney with roasted meats or poultry, hot or cold; on a hamburger, in an omelet, or with cheese on a cracker. We think that American cooks have just begun to tap into the flavorful advantages of chutney.

SUMMER CHICKEN

We were pleasantly surprised to find that mustard and basil were beautifully compatible in this one-dish meal.

1 roasting chicken (3½ pounds; save giblets for another use)
1 bunch of fresh basil, washed carefully
5½ cups Chicken Stock (page 416) or canned chicken broth
1 cup coarsely chopped yellow onions
2 carrots, peeled and chopped
5 parsley sprigs
Salt and freshly ground black pepper, to taste
4 small white onions
4 new potatoes, scrubbed
4 medium-size carrots, peeled and cut into 2-inch lengths
¾ pound fresh green beans, cleaned and tipped
6 tablespoons (¾ stick) unsalted butter
3 tablespoons all-purpose flour
⅓ cup Dijon mustard
⅓ cup Crème Fraîche (page 414) or heavy cream
2 tablespoons chopped fresh Italian (flat-leaf) parsley

1. Wash the chicken, pull off all the fat that can be removed, stuff the cavity with the basil, and truss. Set the chicken, breast side up, in a heavy saucepan just large enough to hold it comfortably. Pour in the chicken stock (the stock need not completely cover the chicken) and bring to a moderate boil. Reduce the heat to a gentle simmer and skim any accumulated fat or scum.

2. Add the chopped onion, chopped carrots, and parsley sprigs and season lightly with salt and pepper. Partially cover, reduce the heat, and cook at a gentle simmer until the chicken juices run a clear yellow when the thigh is pricked with a fork, 40 minutes.

3. Meanwhile bring a large pot of salted water to a boil and drop in the white onions. Simmer for 10 seconds, lift out with a slotted spoon, and drop into a large bowl of ice water. Next, add the potatoes and cook until tender; drop into the ice water. Repeat this process with the carrot pieces, cooking them until they're tender but crisp, and then with the green beans. Reserve all the vegetables in the ice water.

4. When the chicken is done, remove it from its broth with a slotted spoon, cover, and keep warm.

5. Measure out 2 cups of the chicken stock and bring it to a boil in a small saucepan. In another small pan melt 2 tablespoons of the butter over medium heat. When the butter is foaming, sprinkle in the flour. Cook without browning, stirring constantly, for about 5 minutes. Remove from the heat and pour in the boiling chicken broth all at once. The sauce will bubble furiously for a minute. Whisk the sauce as it bubbles and subsides and then return it to low heat. Bring the sauce up to a boil, stirring constantly, and cook for 5 minutes.

6. Remove the basil from the chicken's cavity and chop it fine. Whisk the basil, mustard, and crème fraîche into the sauce, remove the sauce from the heat, cover, and keep warm.

7. Melt the remaining 4 tablespoons butter in a heavy skillet over low heat. Drain the blanched vegetables and warm them gently in the butter until hot through, no more than 5 minutes. Season lightly with salt and pepper. Sprinkle with the chopped parsley.

8. Carve the chicken into serving pieces and arrange on a platter. Surround the chicken with the warmed vegetables, spoon some of the sauce over the chicken, and offer the remaining sauce on the side. Serve immediately.

4 portions

CHICKEN DIJONNAISE

This mustard-flavored chicken is easy and versatile. Although the recipe uses a combination of Dijon and coarse mustards, you may substitute any mustard that appeals to your fancy. Since there are hundreds on the market, flavored in countless ways, the possibilities can occupy you for years.

MUSTARD MAKERS

The mustard of Dijon, France, has been made in Burgundy since 1336. It was then that the wine vinegar traditionally added to mustard was replaced with *verjus,* or the "green juice" of not-quite-ripe grapes. The result was the much smoother, milder mustard we know today as Dijon.

We particularly like the mustards of Edmond Fallot, whose family has been making it in the heart of Beaune since 1840. All of the family's mustards—ground, seed style, green peppercorn, tarragon, basil, and red wine—are superb. They're worth searching out.

1 chicken (2½ to 3 pounds), quartered
⅓ cup mustard (we like half Dijon and half coarse Pommery mustard)
Freshly ground black pepper, to taste
⅓ cup vermouth or dry white wine
½ cup Crème Fraîche (page 414) or heavy cream
Salt, to taste

1. Coat the chicken with the mustard and set it in a bowl, covered, to marinate at room temperature for 2 hours.

2. Preheat the oven to 350°F.

3. Arrange the chicken, skin side up, in a flameproof baking dish. Scrape out any mustard remaining in the bowl and spread it evenly over the chicken. Season lightly with pepper and pour the vermouth or wine around the chicken.

4. Set the dish on the center rack of the oven and bake, basting occasionally, until the chicken is done, 1 hour. You may have to bake the dark meat sections for another 5 to 10 minutes.

5. Scrape the mustard off the chicken and back into the baking dish. Transfer the chicken pieces to a serving platter, cover, and keep warm.

6. Skim as much fat as possible from the cooking juices and set the baking dish over medium heat. Bring to a boil, whisk in the crème fraîche or heavy cream, and lower the heat. Simmer the sauce until it is reduced by about one third, 5 to 10 minutes. Season lightly with salt and pepper. Taste, correct the seasoning, and spoon the sauce over the chicken. Serve hot or at room temperature.

2 to 4 portions

"What is sauce for the goose may be sauce for the gander, but it is not necessarily sauce for the chicken, the duck, the turkey or the Guinea hen."

—ALICE B. TOKLAS

SESAME CHICKEN

1 chicken (2½ to 3 pounds), quartered
2 teaspoons herbes de Provence
Salt and freshly ground black pepper, to taste
½ cup buttermilk
¾ cup unseasoned dry bread crumbs
¾ cup toasted sesame seeds (see page 202)
⅓ cup finely chopped fresh Italian (flat-leaf) parsley
4 tablespoons (½ stick) unsalted butter, melted

1. Arrange the chicken in a bowl just large enough to hold it. Sprinkle on the herbes de Provence, season with salt and pepper, and pour the buttermilk over the chicken. Marinate, covered, in the refrigerator for 2 to 3 hours, turning occasionally.

2. Preheat the oven to 350°F.

3. In a small bowl stir together the bread crumbs, sesame seeds, and parsley.

4. Lift the chicken pieces from the marinade, one at a time, and roll in the bread-crumb and sesame-seed mixture, coating each piece well. Arrange the pieces in a shallow baking pan, and season lightly with salt and pepper.

5. Bake the chicken on the center rack of the oven, basting with the melted butter, until it is golden brown and done, 1 hour. Dark meat may take a few minutes longer. Serve immediately, or cool to room temperature before eating.

2 to 4 portions

LEMON CHICKEN

This chicken has a crisp golden crust and the zing of fresh lemon. It's great hot, and also terrific cold, making it perfect picnic fare.

2 chickens (2½ pounds each), cut into quarters
2 cups fresh lemon juice
2 cups unbleached all-purpose flour
2 teaspoons salt
2 teaspoons paprika
1 teaspoon freshly ground black pepper
½ cup corn oil
2 tablespoons grated lemon zest
¼ cup brown sugar
¼ cup Chicken Stock (page 416)
1 teaspoon lemon extract
2 lemons, sliced paper-thin

1. Combine the chicken pieces and lemon juice in a bowl just large enough to hold them comfortably. Cover and marinate in the refrigerator overnight, turning occasionally.

2. Drain the chicken thoroughly and pat dry. Fill a plastic bag with the flour, salt, paprika, and black pepper, and shake well to mix. Put 2 pieces of chicken into the bag at a time and shake, coating completely. Shake off any excess flour.

3. Preheat the oven to 350°F.

4. Heat the corn oil in a frying pan or cast-iron Dutch oven over medium heat until hot. Fry the chicken pieces, a few at a time, until well browned and crisp. This will take about 10 minutes per batch.

5. Arrange the browned chicken in a single layer in a large shallow baking pan. Sprinkle evenly with the lemon zest and brown sugar. Mix the chicken stock and lemon extract together and pour around the chicken pieces. Set a thin lemon slice on top of each piece of chicken.

6. Bake the chicken until tender, 50 minutes.

6 or more portions

LEMONS

Lemons remind us of all things cool, fresh, and sparkling. They just naturally heighten flavors by helping to awaken your taste buds. You'll find the best flavor and the most juice in small, round or oval, smooth-skinned Eureka or Lisbon lemons. The Meyer lemon, which is believed to be a hybrid of a lemon and an orange, is less acidic than the more common Eureka and Lisbon varieties, and therefore sweeter. Store lemons at room temperature and you will obtain more juice from them, unless you're planning to keep them for some time. Some stimulating ideas:

- ♥ Squeeze fresh lemon juice over steamed vegetables before you toss them with butter.
- ♥ Sprinkle lemon juice over new potatoes before tossing with butter and fresh dill.
- ♥ Always serve lemon with shellfish or French fried potatoes.
- ♥ Serve lemon with most cold or hot soups; it intensifies the flavor.
- ♥ Add lemon to sour cream for dips; it perks up the flavor.
- ♥ Substitute lemon juice for vinegar in salad dressing.
- ♥ Drizzle fresh lemon juice over scrambled eggs, then sprinkle with fresh Italian (flat-leaf) parsley.
- ♥ Serve lemon and black pepper with oysters, clams, or smoked salmon.
- ♥ Squeeze lemon over cut-up apples, avocados, mushrooms, bananas, or pears so they don't turn brown.
- ♥ Freeze lemonade ice cubes and add to iced tea, lemonade, or white wine spritzers.
- ♥ Add thinly sliced lemon wedges to a bottle of vodka or gin and put in the freezer. It will be ready to drink in 2 weeks.
- ♥ Stud a lemon with cloves, covering it completely, and tie with a tartan ribbon to make a long-lasting pomander to freshen your closet.

CHICKEN MONTEREY

Officially this is a fricassee—that is, the chicken is first partially cooked in butter or oil and is then finished in a liquid, in this case a mixture of orange juice, tomatoes, and chicken stock. There is a bit of garlic, a touch of rosemary, and a colorful garnish of sautéed vegetables. The whole dish is bright and fresh, reminding us of holidays in the sun.

Parsleyed Rice (page 419), buttered pasta, or steamed new potatoes would all be good starchy accompaniments, but you could just offer lots of crusty bread for mopping up the tasty sauce.

5 tablespoons best-quality olive oil
1 chicken (2½ to 3 pounds), quartered
Salt and freshly ground black pepper, to taste
1 cup finely chopped yellow onions
2 carrots, peeled and chopped
4 garlic cloves, peeled and minced
1 cup Chicken Stock (page 416) or canned chicken broth
½ cup fresh orange juice
½ cup canned crushed tomatoes
1 tablespoon dried rosemary
1 medium-size red bell pepper, stemmed, seeded, and julienned
½ large zucchini and ½ large yellow summer squash, cleaned and sliced diagonally
⅓ cup chopped fresh Italian (flat-leaf) parsley, for garnish
Grated zest of 1 orange, for garnish

1. Heat 3 tablespoons of the oil in a large skillet over low heat. Pat the chicken pieces dry, season them with salt and pepper, and cook for 5 minutes. Turn the chicken, season again, then cook for another 5 minutes. Do not attempt to brown the chicken or you will overcook it; it should be pale gold. Remove the chicken from the skillet and reserve.

2. Add the onions, carrots, and garlic to the oil remaining in the skillet and cook, covered, over low heat until the vegetables are tender, about 25 minutes.

3. Uncover the skillet and add the stock, orange juice, tomatoes, and rosemary. Season to taste with salt and pepper and simmer the mixture, uncovered, for 15 minutes.

4. Return the chicken pieces to the pan and simmer until the chicken is nearly done, 30 or 35 minutes. Baste the pieces with the sauce and turn them once at the 15-minute mark. (If you wish, you may complete the recipe to this point the day before serving. Refrigerate the chicken in the sauce and reheat gently before proceeding.)

5. Heat the remaining 2 tablespoons of olive oil in another skillet and sauté the pepper julienne for 5 minutes. Add the sliced zucchini and yellow squash and season with salt and pepper. Raise the heat and toss the vegetables in the oil until they are tender but still firm, another 5 minutes or so.

"As for rosemary, I let it run all over my garden walls, not only because my bees love it but because it is the herb sacred to remembrance and to friendship, whence a sprig of it hath a dumb language."

—SIR THOMAS MORE

6. With a slotted spoon, transfer the vegetables to the skillet with the chicken and simmer together for 5 minutes. Sprinkle with the chopped parsley and orange zest and serve immediately.

2 to 4 portions

FRUIT-STUFFED CORNISH HENS

These small hybrid birds—the product of American ingenuity—have always seemed particularly festive to us. While they are most widely available frozen, fresh are now available as well, and either makes a meal more special. When properly cooked and filled with a flavorful stuffing, they are moist and golden brown, making a stunning and tasty centerpiece.

6 fresh Cornish hens
2 large oranges
1 cup (2 sticks) unsalted butter
½ cup yellow onion, peeled and diced
2 tart apples, cored and diced (do not peel)
1 cup seedless green grapes
¼ cup minced fresh Italian (flat-leaf) parsley
½ cup crumbs, from good-quality French-type bread
¾ teaspoon dried thyme
Salt and freshly ground black pepper, to taste
Paprika
6 strips of bacon, halved crosswise
1 cup dry sherry or Madeira
Fresh watercress, for garnish

1. Rinse the hens well under cold running water and pat dry.

2. Grate the zest from the oranges and reserve. Cut the oranges into halves and rub the cut halves over the insides and outsides of the hens, moistening them with the orange juice. Set the hens aside.

3. Melt half of the butter in a skillet over low heat. Add the diced onion and cook, covered, until tender and lightly colored, about 15 minutes.

4. Combine the apples, grapes, parsley, bread crumbs, reserved orange zest, and ½ teaspoon of the thyme in a small bowl; pour the butter and onions over the mixture. Season with salt and pepper and toss gently to combine.

5. Preheat the oven to 350°F.

6. Stuff the hens with the stuffing and truss or skewer them shut. Arrange the hens in a shallow roasting pan just large enough to hold them, or use 2 smaller baking dishes, and season the outside of the birds with salt, pepper, the remaining ¼ teaspoon thyme, and a sprinkle of paprika. Arrange 2 pieces of bacon in an X on the breast of each hen. Dot with the remaining butter, pour the sherry or Madeira into the pan, and set it on the center rack of the oven.

CHRISTMAS DAY MENU

SEAFOOD PÂTÉ

CHICKEN LIVER PÂTÉ WITH GREEN PEPPERCORNS

GOUGÈRES

ZUCCHINI-WATERCRESS SOUP

FRUIT-STUFFED CORNISH HENS

NUTTED WILD RICE

BEET AND APPLE PURÉE

CHESTNUT MOUSSE

DATE-NUT PUDDING

"Laughter is an instant vacation."

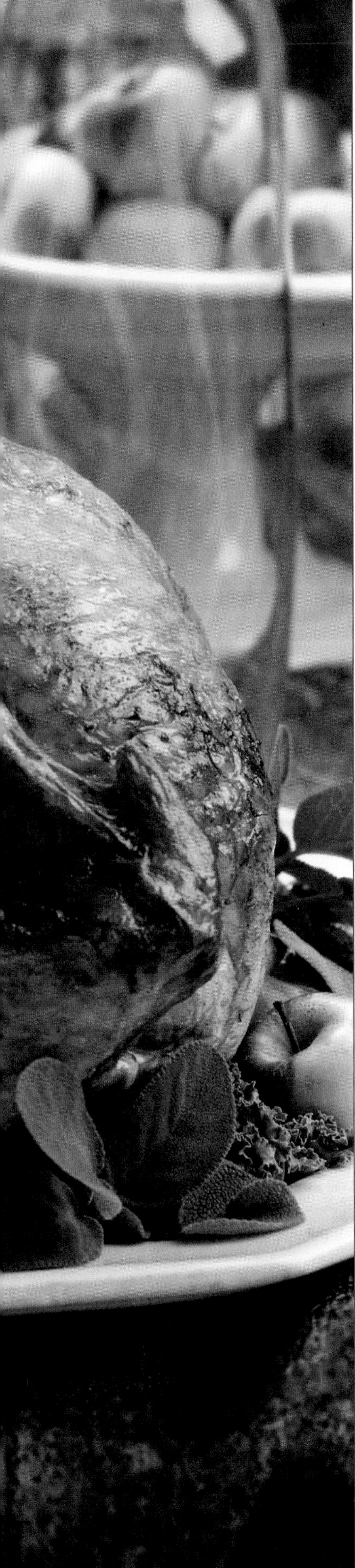

7. Bake for about 1 hour, basting frequently, until the hens are golden brown and done. Transfer them to a serving platter and garnish with the watercress. Remove the grease from the sauce in the roasting pan and reduce over medium heat to two-thirds the amount. Pass the sauce in a gravy boat.

6 portions

OUR FAVORITE WAY TO ROAST A TURKEY

We promise wonderful results and a very moist bird.

GIBLET BROTH (MAKE ONE DAY AHEAD)

Giblets and neck from turkey, well washed
1 cup extra giblets (about ¾ pound)
4 chicken backs (about 1¾ pounds)
2 celery ribs, with leaves
2 medium-size onions, unpeeled
2 garlic cloves, bruised
4 sprigs fresh Italian (flat-leaf) parsley
4 whole cloves
3 whole black peppercorns
1 bay leaf
Salt, to taste

TURKEY (MAKE SERVING DAY)

1 fresh turkey (18 pounds)
1 orange, halved
Paprika, to taste
Salt and freshly ground black pepper, to taste
10 to 12 cups Corn Bread–Sausage Stuffing with Apples (page 117)
6 tablespoons (¾ stick) unsalted butter, at room temperature

GIBLET GRAVY (MAKE SERVING DAY)

4 tablespoons (½ stick) unsalted butter
¼ cup all-purpose flour
2 tablespoons Madeira or dry sherry
1 teaspoon dried thyme
Salt and freshly ground black pepper, to taste
1 tablespoon chopped fresh Italian (flat-leaf) parsley
2 to 3 large bunches of fresh sage, for garnish

1. The day before serving, prepare the giblet broth (set aside the liver for another use). Place all the broth ingredients in a heavy saucepan and add water to just cover. Bring to a boil, reduce the heat, and simmer until the giblets are tender, skimming any foam that rises to the surface, about 1 hour. Strain the broth over a bowl, reserving the giblets, turkey neck, and chicken backs; discard the vegetables. You should have about 3½ cups of broth.

2. When it is cool enough to handle, shred the meat from the turkey neck and chicken backs, discarding any skin. Finely chop the giblets. Mix the meats and giblets together, cover, and refrigerate until needed.

3. Preheat the oven to 325°F.

4. On serving day, prepare the turkey: Rinse the turkey well inside and out, and pat it dry with paper towels. Remove any excess fat.

5. Squeeze the orange halves inside the body and neck cavities. Sprinkle the cavities with paprika, salt, and pepper. Stuff the cavities loosely with the stuffing, using about 3 cups for the neck and 8 cups for the body. Close with turkey lacers or sew closed with a large needle and heavy thread. Tie the legs together with kitchen string.

6. Rub the turkey all over with the butter and sprinkle with paprika, salt, and pepper.

7. Place the turkey, breast side up, on a rack in a large ovenproof roasting pan. Pour 2 cups of the reserved giblet broth into the bottom of the pan, and cover the turkey loosely with aluminum foil. Cover the remaining broth and refrigerate it. Place the turkey in the oven and roast for 1½ hours.

8. Remove the foil and roast the turkey, basting with the pan juices every 30 minutes, for 2½ hours.

9. Raise the oven temperature to 350°F and roast until an instant-reading thermometer inserted into the thickest part of the thigh reads 180°F, another 1 to 1¼ hours. The temperature in the deepest part of the breast should read 160°F. The juices should run clear when the thigh is pricked with a small sharp knife.

10. Remove the turkey, place it on a platter, and let it rest about 20 minutes, loosely covered with aluminum foil. Reserve the juices in the pan.

11. Remove the stuffing from the body and neck cavities and cover it with aluminum foil to keep warm.

12. Prepare the giblet gravy: Heat the pan juices in the roasting pan over medium heat, scraping up all of the brown bits on the bottom of the pan. Pour the juices through a gravy separator to remove the fat, or skim the fat off with a metal spoon. Pour the defatted juices into a measuring cup.

13. Melt the butter in a heavy saucepan over medium heat. Whisk in the flour and continue whisking until it browns slightly, 2 to 3 minutes. Whisking constantly, slowly pour in 2 cups of the reserved pan juices, and continue whisking until smooth. Bring the gravy to a boil, then reduce the heat to medium low and add the Madeira, thyme, salt, pepper, parsley, and reserved giblet mixture (from Step 2). Simmer, stirring, until the gravy has thickened, about 10 minutes. If you prefer a thinner gravy, add more of the remaining 1½ cups giblet broth until the desired consistency is achieved. Adjust the seasonings. Transfer the gravy to a gravy boat.

14. Present the turkey before carving it. Arrange the carved meat on a large decorative platter. Garnish with the fresh sage and serve with the gravy.

16 portions

THANKSGIVING DAY MENU

MINIATURE CHÈVRE TARTS

CHEESE STRAWS

WILD MUSHROOM SOUP

PURÉED BROCCOLI WITH CRÈME FRAÎCHE

SWEET POTATO AND CARROT PURÉE

OUR FAVORITE TURKEY

CORN BREAD–SAUSAGE STUFFING WITH APPLES

CRANBERRY BREAD

HARVEST TART

PUMPKIN PIE

CHOCOLATE TRUFFLES

"A good home must be made, not bought."

—JOYCE MAYNARD

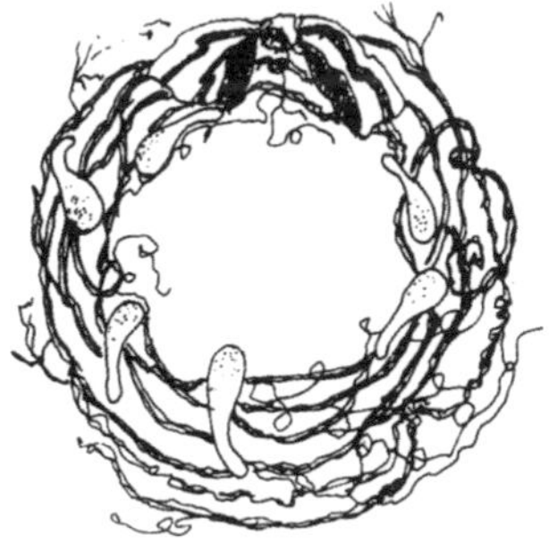

Thanksgiving is a purely American holiday, where thanks can be given for, among other things, the abundance of food in this land. To us, Thanksgiving tradition means a turkey and a dazzling array of seasonal trimmings—truly a harvest celebration.

CORN BREAD–SAUSAGE STUFFING WITH APPLES

This agreeably all-American stuffing is good with any poultry.

12 tablespoons (1½ sticks) unsalted butter
2½ cups finely chopped yellow onions
3 tart apples (Jonathan and Winesap are good), cored and chunked; do not peel
1 pound lightly seasoned bulk sausage (breakfast sausage with sage is best)
3 cups coarsely crumbled corn bread (preferably homemade; page 303)
3 cups coarsely crumbled whole-wheat bread
3 cups coarsely crumbled white bread (French or homemade preferred)
2 teaspoons dried thyme
1 teaspoon dried sage
Salt and freshly ground black pepper, to taste
½ cup chopped fresh Italian (flat-leaf) parsley
1½ cups shelled pecan halves

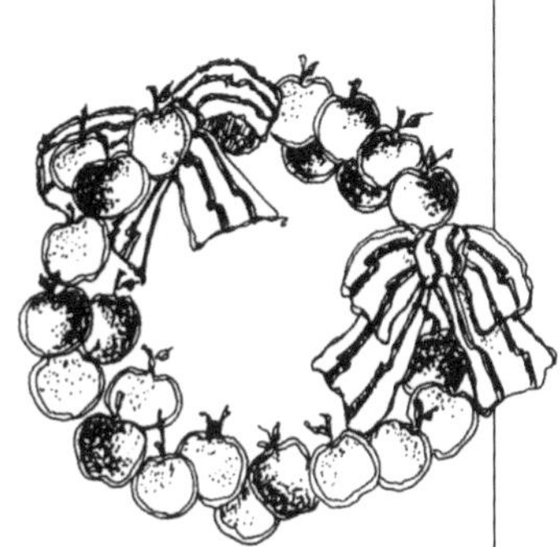

1. Preheat the oven to 325°F.

2. Melt half of the butter in a skillet over medium heat. Add the chopped onions and cook, partially covered, until tender and lightly colored, about 25 minutes. Transfer the onions and butter to a large mixing bowl.

3. Melt the remaining butter in the same skillet. Add the apple chunks and cook over high heat until lightly colored but not mushy. Transfer the apples and butter to the mixing bowl.

4. Crumble the sausage into the skillet and cook over medium heat, stirring, until lightly browned. With a slotted spoon, transfer the sausage to the mixing bowl and reserve the rendered fat.

5. Add the remaining ingredients to the ingredients in the mixing bowl and combine gently. Cool completely before stuffing the bird; refrigerate if not used promptly.

6. If you do not wish actually to stuff the bird (goose or duck, for example, can make the stuffing greasy), spoon it into a casserole. Cover the casserole and set into a large pan. Pour hot water around the casserole to come halfway up the sides. Bake for 30 to 45 minutes, basting occasionally with the cooking juices from the bird or with the reserved sausage fat if necessary.

Enough stuffing for a 20-pound turkey, 12 to 14 portions

SWEET AND SAVORY MEATS

At The Silver Palate we always had a range of meat entrées, some spiced and wrapped in herbs, some sweetened with fruit. We accented meats in a variety of ways, so that their richness could be more fully appreciated.

In fact, sweet and savory meats have an ancient and global tradition. Dishes of the Orient, the Middle East, and Africa have always demonstrated the affinity between meats and fruit, often using fruit as much for color and texture as for their natural sweetness. The finished dish is seldom actually sweet; rather, the acids and sugars act to bring out the natural flavors of other ingredients in the dish. In much the same way, mustards, vinegars, and chutneys enliven meat dishes, and we use them freely in our cooking.

FILET OF BEEF

For those times when you want a dazzling main course, nothing beats a simply roasted beef tenderloin. The choices of beef are numerous—local grass-fed, organic, Black Angus, "prime," Kobe, Wagyu—but always buy from a source you trust. Simple sides such as Crisply Roasted Asparagus with Gremolata (page 182) are just perfect.

1 oven-ready beef filet (about 4½ pounds), wrapped in fat
1 garlic clove, peeled and cut into thin slivers
Salt and freshly ground black pepper, to taste

1. Preheat the oven to 425°F.

2. With the tip of a sharp knife, cut slits in the meat and insert slivers of the garlic. Season the meat generously with salt and pepper, and set it in a shallow roasting pan just large enough to hold the meat comfortably.

3. Bake for 10 minutes. Reduce the heat to 350°F and bake for another 25 minutes for rare meat (120°F on an instant-read thermometer), or another 35 minutes for medium (130°F on an instant-read thermometer).

4. Remove the roast from the oven and let it stand for 10 minutes before slicing. Or cool completely to room temperature and slice for serving cold.

8 to 10 portions

"'Roast Beef Medium' is not a food. It is a philosophy."

—EDNA FERBER

GLAZED CORNED BEEF

1 corned beef (3 pounds)
1 cup dark orange marmalade
¼ cup Dijon mustard
¼ cup brown sugar

1. Place the corned beef in a large pot and cover with boiling water. Bring to a boil, lower the heat, cover partially, and simmer as slowly as possible until very tender when tested with a fork, about 3 hours.

2. Preheat the oven to 350°F.

3. Mix the marmalade, mustard, and sugar together in a small bowl.

4. When the meat is done, remove it from the pot and drain. Place the meat in a baking pan and pour the marmalade mixture over it, coating thoroughly.

5. Bake until the glaze is crisp and brown, 30 minutes. Serve hot or at room temperature.

6 to 8 portions

"My favorite thing is to go where I have never gone."

—DIANE ARBUS

PORK CHOPS WITH BLACK CURRANT PRESERVES

This recipe calls for a tart and chunky black currant preserve. We like to serve two vegetable purées with the chops.

¼ cup black currant preserves
1½ tablespoons Dijon mustard
6 center-cut pork chops (1 to 1½ inches thick)
Salt and freshly ground black pepper, to taste
⅓ cup white wine vinegar
Watercress, for garnish

1. Mix the preserves and mustard together in a small bowl. Set aside.

2. Heat a nonstick skillet just large enough to hold the pork chops comfortably over medium heat. Add the chops and brown them lightly on both sides. Season with salt and pepper and spoon the currant and mustard mixture evenly over them.

3. Cover the chops, reduce the heat, and cook until the chops are done, 20 minutes. Transfer them to a platter and keep them warm in the oven.

WELCOME HOME BUFFET

FRESH PURPLE FIGS WRAPPED IN PROSCIUTTO WITH FRESH LIMES

SPICY SHRIMP

SEASONAL CRUDITÉS WITH *TAPENADE DIP*

BAKED HAM WITH GLAZED APRICOTS

ASSORTED MUSTARDS

CHOCOLATE MOUSSE WITH DEVON CREAM

from THE SILVER PALATE NOTEBOOK

A buffet should be bountiful. Make sure the table is generously filled—bowls should be full, breads generously sliced, centerpieces large enough to hold their own, and the table itself of a size to look like the proverbial groaning board without looking overdone.

No event should leave you with an embarrassing amount of leftover food, but no one likes to run out midway through the evening either. If you're cooking your own food, prepare extra. Your family will be happy for the leftovers—and so will your freezer.

4. Remove the excess fat from the skillet. Add the vinegar, set the pan over medium heat, and bring the juices to a boil, stirring and scraping up any brown bits. When the sauce is reduced by about one third, pour it over the chops and serve immediately, garnished with the watercress.

3 to 6 portions

BAKED HAM WITH GLAZED APRICOTS

From day one, The Silver Palate shop always featured this baked glazed ham and every single day it sold out. This is a cocktail buffet and picnic favorite with endless possibilities for leftovers. Don't save it just for holidays.

1 ready-to-eat ham with bone in (12 to 16 pounds)
Whole cloves, to cover the surface of the ham
¼ cup Dijon mustard
1 cup dark brown sugar
3 cups apple juice
1 pound dried apricots
1 cup Madeira
Favorite mustards, for serving
Favorite chutneys, for serving

1. Preheat the oven to 350°F.

2. Peel the skin from the ham and trim the fat, leaving about a ¼-inch layer to protect the meat. With a sharp knife score the fat in a diamond pattern.

3. Set the ham in a shallow baking pan, insert a whole clove in the crossed point of each diamond, and pat the mustard evenly over the top and sides of the ham. Sprinkle the top with the brown sugar and pour the apple juice into the bottom of the pan.

4. Bake the ham for 1½ hours, basting frequently.

5. Meanwhile, combine the apricots and Madeira in a small saucepan. Bring to a boil, cover, and remove from the heat.

6. At 30 minutes from the end of the baking time, add the apricots and their liquid to the roasting pan and continue to bake and baste the ham.

7. Transfer the ham to a large platter. Attach the apricots to the top of the ham with toothpicks. Skim the fat from the pan juices and pour the juices into a sauceboat. Accompany the ham with the mustards, chutneys, and pan juices.

20 to 25 portions

ROAST LAMB WITH PEPPERCORN CRUST

The mixture of mustard and three peppercorns gives this roast a crisp and piquant crust.

3 tablespoons crushed dried peppercorns, an equal mix of white, black, and green
1 tablespoon fresh rosemary leaves, or 1½ teaspoons dried
½ cup fresh mint leaves
5 garlic cloves, crushed
½ cup raspberry vinegar (see Note)
¼ cup soy sauce
½ cup dry red wine
1 boned but untied leg of lamb (about 5 pounds after boning)
2 tablespoons Dijon mustard

"I hate people who are not serious about their meals."

—OSCAR WILDE

Roast Lamb—always inviting and delicious.

THE SPICE OF LIFE

Exotic peppercorns, each with a distinctive flavor and aroma, are taking their place on spice shelves.

♥ Ecuadoran Black: known for excessive heat and pungency.

♥ Green Peppercorns: these are the tender, full-grown yet underripe berries of the pepper plant. They're mildly pungent but with a touch of heat.

♥ Lampong Black (Sumatra, Indonesia): this is a popular black pepper with a rich aroma and moderate to strong heat. It is picked when mature and dried in the sun.

♥ Long Pepper (India, Southeast Asia): berries cluster together on a long rod, somewhat similar in appearance to a small pine cone. It has medium-hot/sweet overtones.

♥ Penja White (Cameroon): a delicate peppercorn with hints of musk and wood.

♥ Pink Pepper Berries: These come from the Peruvian pepper tree and its cousin, the Brazilian pepper tree, both botanically unrelated to the true peppercorn-bearing Piper nigrum. Not really pepper, but with a sweet mysterious flavor. Ravishing pink, they are often blended with peppercorns in a medley.

♥ Red Peppercorns (China): developed by being left on the vine longer to ripen.

♥ Sarawak Black (Borneo, Indonesia): has a fresh aroma with tones of hickory, fruit, and pine. It is mild and can be used in desserts.

♥ Szechuan (China): similar to a true peppercorn, but actually the berries of a prickly ash tree. Tastes pungent with lemony notes.

♥ Tellicherry Black (Northwest India): bold, pungent aroma and lightly hot with sweet flavors. The finest black pepper.

♥ Vietnamese Black: smoky and complex with citrus highlights.

♥ White Peppercorns: the interior kernels of pepper berries. Made from the mature berries that are harvested when ripe, soaked in water to remove their outer skins, then dried. Not as hot as black pepper, but more aromatic.

1. Combine 1 tablespoon of the crushed peppercorns, the rosemary, mint, garlic, vinegar, soy sauce, and red wine in a large shallow bowl. Add the lamb and turn to coat with the marinade. Marinate the lamb, covered, in the refrigerator, for 8 hours, turning occasionally.

2. Preheat the oven to 350°F.

3. Remove the roast from the marinade and drain; reserve the marinade. Roll the roast, tying it with kitchen twine.

4. Spread the mustard over the meat and pat 2 tablespoons of crushed peppercorns into the mustard. Set the roast in a shallow roasting pan just large enough to hold it comfortably and pour the reserved marinade carefully around but not over the roast.

5. Bake for 1½ hours, or 18 minutes per pound, basting occasionally. The roast will be medium rare. Bake for another 10 to 15 minutes for well-done meat. Let the roast stand for 20 minutes before carving. Serve the pan juices in a gravy boat along with the lamb.

6 to 8 portions

Note: Available in specialty food stores.

ASIAN LAMB CHOPS

3 tablespoons dark sesame oil (see Note)
6 thick shoulder-cut lamb chops, trimmed of excess fat
¾ cup finely chopped yellow onion
3 garlic cloves, peeled and minced
3 tablespoons soy sauce
3 tablespoons chile paste (see Note)
¾ cup tart orange marmalade
1½ tablespoons rice wine vinegar (see Note)
1 tablespoon minced fresh ginger

1. Heat the sesame oil in a large skillet over medium heat. Add the chops and brown them lightly on both sides. Transfer the chops to paper towels to drain.

2. Add the onion and garlic and cook, covered, over low heat until tender and lightly colored, 20 minutes.

3. Add the soy sauce, chili paste, marmalade, vinegar, and ginger. Simmer for 2 minutes, stirring constantly.

4. Return the chops to the skillet, cover, and cook over low heat, turning once, until done, about 7 minutes. Serve immediately, spooning the sauce over the chops.

3 to 6 portions

Note: Available in Asian or specialty food stores.

VEAL WITH SHERRY AND LEMON MARMALADE

4 tablespoons (½ stick) unsalted butter
2 tablespoons vegetable oil
4 loin veal chops (1 inch thick)
Salt and freshly ground black pepper, to taste
⅓ cup finely chopped yellow onion
⅓ cup medium-dry sherry
⅓ cup Chicken Stock (page 416)
2 tablespoons lemon marmalade
¼ cup heavy cream or Crème Fraîche (page 414)
Watercress, for garnish

1. Heat the butter and oil in a large skillet until very hot. Add the veal chops and sear them until brown on both sides, 2 minutes per side. Season both sides with salt and pepper.

2. Reduce the heat to medium and cook the chops, turning occasionally, until they are slightly underdone and still juicy, 3 to 5 minutes total. Remove them from the skillet, cover, and keep warm while making the sauce.

3. Add the onion to the butter and oil remaining in the skillet and cook, covered, over medium heat until tender, about 15 minutes.

4. Add the sherry, stock, and marmalade to the skillet and bring to a brisk boil, stirring up any browned bits. When the mixture is reduced by one third, whisk in the heavy cream or crème fraîche and simmer for 5 minutes. Taste and correct the seasoning.

5. Transfer the veal chops to a heated serving platter and spoon some of the sauce over them. Garnish with the watercress and serve immediately, accompanied by additional sauce.

4 portions

SALT FROM THE SEA

There are a dazzling number of sea salts available now and we've acquired an affinity for them. We use some in cooking and some as condiments, sprinkling just a few grains atop a finished dish to make it sparkle.

Maldon sea salt is a pure flaky white salt from the southeast corner of England. The small pyramid-shaped salt crystals have a mellower, sweeter, softer flavor, particularly good sprinkled on cooked mild fish dishes and salads.

We like Breton gray salt or *sel gris,* the majority of sea salt harvested along the Atlantic Coast of France. It retains a complex mineral taste that can be quite bold.

The queen of French sea salts is *fleur de sel,* a powdery white snowflakelike crystal that forms atop the sparkling summer waters off Normandy, Brittany, and the Isle de Re. Very delicate, it is to be used sparingly.

Other sea salts include: Sicilian; Hawaiian pink and black; Balinese cinnamon-smoked and coconut and kaffir lime–smoked; Northwest alder-smoked; Cyprus flake; black smoked from Brazil; and pink Murray River from Australia.

Try a little sea salt over roasted fruits, or on chocolate truffles or buttery caramels. The secrets of the sea are enormous.

Lemon marmalade is a lively and unexpected foil for hearty veal chops.

ROAST SHOULDER OF VEAL

In this recipe, the bacon and wine keep the roast moist, while the mustard adds zest.

4½ pounds boned and tied shoulder of veal (weighed after boning)
1 small garlic clove, cut into thin slivers
¼ cup Dijon mustard
1 teaspoon dried thyme
Salt and freshly ground black pepper, to taste
8 strips of bacon
8 tablespoons (1 stick) unsalted butter, at room temperature
¾ cup dry white wine

1. Preheat the oven to 350°F.

2. Cut tiny slits in the veal with the tip of a sharp knife and insert the garlic slivers. Set the roast on a rack in a shallow baking pan just large enough to hold it comfortably. Rub the mustard all over the veal and sprinkle with the thyme and salt and pepper.

3. Wrap the bacon around the roast to cover it completely, tucking the bacon ends under the meat. Spread the butter generously over the bacon and meat and pour the white wine into the pan.

4. Bake until the juices run clear when pricked with a skewer, 2 hours and 15 minutes, or about 30 minutes per pound. Baste frequently. Let the roast stand for 20 minutes before carving. Serve the pan juices in a gravy boat along with the veal.

6 to 8 portions

VEAL SCALLOPS IN MUSTARD-CREAM SAUCE

A main course of sautéed veal, sauced with a bit of mustard, white wine, and cream, can be ready in minutes. Use your favorite mustard to personalize the dish.

4 tablespoons (½ stick) unsalted butter
2 tablespoons vegetable oil
3 scallions (green onions), well rinsed and chopped
1½ pounds veal scallops (8 very large scallops, or 10 to 12 smaller scallops), pounded flat
Salt and freshly ground black pepper, to taste
⅓ cup dry white wine
⅓ cup mustard (avoid "ballpark"-type mustards)
½ cup Crème Fraîche (page 414) or heavy cream
1 large firm ripe tomato, peeled, seeded, and chopped, for garnish

1. Heat the butter and oil together in a large skillet over low heat. Add the scallions and cook for 5 minutes without browning.

2. Raise the heat, add the veal, and season with salt and pepper. Cook the veal for 1 minute per side; do not overcook, and do not worry if it does not actually brown. Remove the veal from the skillet and keep warm.

3. Add the wine to the skillet and bring it to a boil. Cook until the mixture is reduced to a few syrupy spoonfuls. Whisk in the mustard and the crème fraîche or heavy cream and

DEGLAZING A PAN

To deglaze a pan, add wine, water, or vinegar to a skillet in which food has been browned and stir or scrape up the juices with a whisk or fork. Whisk in butter, herbs, or cream, simmer to reduce, and you have a light sauce, ready in minutes.

TRADITIONS

The whole roasted animal is in many cultures the epitome of gracious hospitality—it is a tradition that goes back to welcoming the prodigal son by slaughtering the fatted calf for a feast.

from THE SILVER PALATE NOTEBOOK

Successful flavoring depends on creativity. To build your confidence, experiment. Taste an unfamiliar fresh herb, and if you like it, add just a little, then a little more to a familiar recipe. It may become your favorite version. Toss orange or lime zest in a rice dish. Zest a lemon over broccoli. Add a few sprigs of thyme or a dash of balsamic vinegar to green bean steaming water. The ideas are endless. You may want to experiment with small batches at first, but as your confidence and your palate develop, you'll learn to create more boldly, trusting your instincts. You, too, will become a curious cook—the very best kind.

boil for 2 minutes. Taste the sauce and correct the seasoning.

4. Arrange the veal on a serving platter or on individual plates and spoon the sauce over them. Sprinkle with the chopped tomato and serve immediately.

4 to 6 portions

ROAST SUCKLING PIG

There is hardly a more spectacular main course than a roast suckling pig. Given a few days' notice, most butchers can order one for you, and very little additional work is required to produce this unique dish. It is delicious served with Black Bean Soup (page 188), Saffron Rice (page 419), and watercress salad.

3 limes, cut into halves
1 suckling pig (15 pounds), well cleaned
18 garlic cloves, peeled
2 tablespoons dried oregano
⅓ cup capers plus 3 tablespoons caper brine
2 tablespoons olive oil
1 teaspoon salt
1 teaspoon freshly ground black pepper
1 teaspoon curry powder
½ cup firmly packed fresh cilantro leaves
1 tiny apple or crabapple, for garnish
Watercress, for garnish
Kumquats, for garnish

1. The day before you're cooking the pig, rub the lime halves all over the body, squeezing the lime juice liberally; rub the cavity with the limes, too.

2. With a knife tip cut slits ¾ inch deep all over the body of the pig. (Do not prick the head.) Cut 5 garlic cloves into 8 pieces each and stuff the pieces into the slits in the pig.

3. In a medium-size bowl mix together the remaining 13 garlic cloves, finely minced, the oregano, capers, olive oil, salt, pepper, and curry powder. Stuff half of the mixture into the cavity of the pig and rub the remainder all over the outside. Place the cilantro inside the cavity. Let the pig rest, covered, in the refrigerator for 24 hours.

4. Preheat the oven to 400°F.

5. Place the pig on a rack in a large roasting pan and bake for 30 minutes. Turn the heat down to 350°F and roast until the juices run clear when the pig is pricked with a knife, 3½ hours.

6. Place the apple in the pig's mouth, and serve on a large platter, decorated with the watercress and preserved or fresh kumquats.

10 portions

FORK SUPPERS

We have seen many a buffet ruined because an awkward or overly complex dish—often the meat course—was simply impossible to eat from a lap-held plate. Some menus avoid this problem by offering an array of salads or other bite-size foods, which can often leave one hungry.

With a little thought and planning, however, you can provide a meaty main dish that is simple, elegant, and convenient to eat. The following entrées will fit the bill, and in addition to being tender enough to eat with just a fork, they can all be prepared in advance—a boon to host and guest alike.

FLANK STEAK MOSAIC

1 cup dry red wine
¼ cup soy sauce
1 garlic clove, minced
1 large flank steak (2 to 3 pounds), butterflied
2-egg omelet (see page 386), cut into ½-inch strips
½ pound carrots, peeled and cut into julienne
½ pound green beans, trimmed and blanched
Pitted green olives
1 can (1¾-ounces) pimientos, cut into ¼-inch strips
5 strips of bacon

1. Mix together the wine, soy sauce, and garlic in a large bowl. Add the flank steak and marinate it, covered, in the refrigerator for 2 hours.

2. Preheat the oven to 350°F.

3. Working left to right, arrange 2 rows of omelet strips the length of the steak. Top the 2 rows with 2 or 3 layers more of omelet strips. Lay the carrots in rows alongside the omelet—3 wide and 3 high. Repeat with the green beans. On the other side of the omelet, place 1 row of olives and, next to them, 1 row of pimientos, 3 layers high.

4. Roll the steak tightly toward you, tucking the meat closely around the vegetables. Wrap the bacon around the roll and tie securely at ½-inch intervals.

5. Bake the roast for 30 minutes, basting twice with the reserved marinade. Put under the broiler briefly to brown the bacon. Cool, and cut into ½-inch-thick slices.

6 to 8 portions

Fruit-Stuffed Loin of Pork makes a delicious main course for an autumn dinner, served hot with a bit of the pan juices spooned over it. It is also good cold; the rich flavors of the pork and the sweetly tart taste of the fruit are even more apparent. Take it along on a picnic, or slice it thin for elegant sandwiches. It is a *Silver Palate Cookbook* signature dish.

FRUIT-STUFFED LOIN OF PORK

Approximately 1 cup pitted prunes
Approximately 1 cup dried apricots
4 pounds boneless pork loin roast, prepared with a pocket for stuffing
1 garlic clove
Salt and freshly ground black pepper, to taste
8 tablespoons (1 stick) unsalted butter, at room temperature
1 tablespoon dried thyme
1 cup Madeira
1 tablespoon molasses
Watercress, for garnish

1. Preheat the oven to 350°F.

2. Using the handle of a wooden spoon, push the dried fruits into the pocket in the roast, alternating the prunes and apricots.

3. Cut the garlic into thin slivers. Make deep slits in the roast with the tip of a knife and push the garlic into the slits. Tie the roast with twine and rub the surface with salt and pepper.

4. Set the roast in a shallow baking pan and smear the butter over the roast. Sprinkle with the thyme.

5. Stir the Madeira and molasses together in a small bowl and pour over the roast. Set the pan on the center rack of the oven and bake for 1½ hours (approximately 20 minutes per pound), basting frequently.

6. When the roast is done (do not overcook), remove it from the oven and let it stand, loosely covered with foil, for 15 to 20 minutes. Cut into thin slices, arrange the slices on a serving platter, and spoon the pan juices over them. Garnish the platter with the watercress and serve immediately.

8 to 10 portions

"One of the very nicest things about life is the way we must regularly stop whatever it is we are doing and devote our attention to eating."

—LUCIANO PAVAROTTI AND WILLIAM WRIGHT

VEAL ROLL

This veal roll, with its own tomato sauce, is a beautiful and unusual main dish. Accompany it with a starch such as buttered pasta, and a green vegetable, hot or cold.

2 pounds veal scallops, pounded flat
½ pound boiled ham, thinly sliced
Olive oil, to season the veal
Juice of 1 lemon
Freshly ground black pepper, to taste
½ pound mortadella sausage, thinly sliced
½ pound Genoa salami, thinly sliced
10 hard-cooked eggs
¼ cup minced Italian (flat-leaf) parsley
¼ cup unseasoned dry bread crumbs
2 garlic cloves, minced
Salt, to taste
5 strips of bacon
4 cups Quick Tomato Sauce (page 418)
1 cup dry white wine

1. Preheat the oven to 350°F.

2. Unroll an 18-inch length of aluminum foil on your working surface.

3. Arrange the veal scallops in a rectangle, 6 x 12 inches, overlapping the scallops as necessary. Arrange the boiled ham in a similar layer over the veal. Sprinkle with the oil, lemon juice, and black pepper. Layer with the slices of mortadella and salami.

4. Trim the ends of the hard-cooked eggs so that the yolk is exposed. Arrange the eggs in a line lengthwise down the center of a rectangle, being certain the cut edges of the eggs touch closely. Sprinkle the parsley down one side of the eggs, and the bread crumbs mixed with the garlic down the other side. Drizzle a little oil over the eggs and sprinkle with salt and pepper.

5. Pick up the long edge of the foil and bring it over the eggs. Tuck the meat under the eggs, making a tight roll, and continue to make a roll, ending with the seam side down. Discard the foil, drape the bacon over the roll, and tie securely with kitchen twine at ½-inch intervals.

6. Set the roll in a roasting pan. Mix the tomato sauce and wine and pour over the roll. Cook for 1 hour, basting often. Remove from the oven and let stand, covered with foil, for 20 minutes.

7. Cut the roll into thin slices and serve with the pan juices as a sauce. Pass the additional sauce in a gravy boat.

8 to 10 portions

from THE SILVER PALATE NOTEBOOK

For buffet meals, tie your eating utensils in napkins with a pretty ribbon, and bunch them in a basket. Let it decorate your table and save space, too.

Stack your collection of trays—no matter how eclectic—near the buffet table. They make it much easier for your guests to relax and enjoy the food without having to balance dishes on their knees.

GAME

Game was once plentiful in America, and every rural family hunted as a matter of course. Now wild herds are much reduced and hunting is a sport with seasons. We greatly respect wild game for its unique flavor and leanness, but today, with both wild and farm-raised game available, game no longer is limited to cooks with a hunter in the family or to a season. We find ourselves turning more often to our butcher to supply our game throughout the year. A rabbit in every pot and venison in every freezer seems to us to be a very good thing. The taste will be different without a truly wild edge, but milder game attracts more fans and also frees the inexperienced cook from some of the pitfalls of game cookery. The meat you buy from the butcher won't be tough, old, and impossibly stringy the way meat from wild game might be. So, in a very different way from our forebears, we give thanks for game and enjoy its lean meat and rich flavors. The following recipes will help you celebrate the adventure.

"[Pheasant] is the King of earthly poultry."

—OLIVIER DE SERRE

PHEASANT WITH LEEK AND PECAN STUFFING

We think pheasant is one of the most delicious of the domestically raised game birds available to us. It is rich and meaty, with a firm texture no longer found in chicken. If care is taken during roasting, the meat is moist and succulent.

2 young pheasants (about 4 pounds each), thoroughly defrosted if frozen
1 tablespoon olive oil
½ cup finely chopped yellow onion
1 large carrot, peeled and finely chopped
2 tablespoons plus 1 teaspoon dried marjoram
¼ teaspoon dried thyme
1 bay leaf
6 sprigs of fresh Italian (flat-leaf) parsley
3 cups Chicken Stock (page 416) or canned chicken broth
Salt and freshly ground black pepper, to taste
12 tablespoons (1½ sticks) unsalted butter
10 medium-size leeks, white part only, well rinsed and thinly sliced
6 cups crumbs from good-quality white bread
2 cups toasted pecans (see page 202)
1 cup finely chopped fresh Italian (flat-leaf) parsley
4 strips of pancetta, 1 ounce each
½ cup heavy cream

1. Rinse the pheasants thoroughly inside and out and pat dry with paper towels. Chop the neck, heart, and gizzard (save the liver for another use).

2. Heat the olive oil in a small saucepan over medium heat. Brown the neck and giblets well in the oil, turning frequently. Add the onion, carrot, and the 1 teaspoon of marjoram. Reduce the heat to low and cook, covered, until the vegetables are tender, about 25 minutes.

3. Uncover the pan, add the thyme, bay leaf, parsley, and stock, and season with a pinch of salt and freshly ground black pepper. (Canned broth and pancetta are both quite salty; do not salt the sauce again until just before serving.) Bring to a boil, reduce the heat, and simmer, partially covered, for 45 minutes. Strain the stock, discarding the solids, and reserve.

4. Melt the butter in a skillet over low heat. Stir in the sliced leeks and cook, covered, until the leeks are very tender, 30 minutes.

5. Toss the leeks, including their butter, with the bread crumbs, pecans, chopped parsley, and the remaining 2 tablespoons of marjoram. Season lightly with salt and generously with pepper. Toss again; if the stuffing seems dry, moisten it with ¼ cup or so of the reserved broth.

6. Preheat the oven to 375°F.

7. Stuff the pheasants loosely and drape the breasts with the pancetta. Tie it in place with kitchen twine and set the pheasants in a shallow roasting pan.

8. Set the roasting pan on the center rack of the oven and bake for about 1 hour, basting the pheasants occasionally with the fat and juices that accumulate. The pheasants are done when the thighs, pricked with a fork at their thickest part, dribble clear yellow juices. Remove the pheasants from the pan, cover with aluminum foil, and keep warm.

PANCETTA AND GUANCIALE

Pancetta is an Italian bacon, made of pork belly that has been salt cured and spiced, but not smoked. Instead, it is dried for about three months. Guanciale is Italian bacon made from the pig's jowls or cheeks. It, too, is not smoked—it is rubbed with salt and ground red or black pepper and cured for three months. It has a stronger flavor and more delicate texture than pancetta. Your favorite smoked American breakfast bacon can be substituted for either; the flavor will be slightly different, but still very good.

Christmas memories . . . anticipation . . . snow, always, in Michigan . . . a night so clear you can see the Star of Bethlehem . . . favorite relatives . . . hunting in the woods for a tree . . . snacks for Santa's reindeer . . . carols in the snow . . . candlelight services . . . a sleigh ride in the snow . . . and all the good things to eat.

9. Pour the excess fat out of the roasting pan. Pour the reserved stock and the heavy cream into the pan and set over medium heat. Bring to a boil, reduce the heat, and simmer, stirring and scraping up any browned bits, until the sauce is reduced by about one third. Taste and correct the seasoning.

10. Carve the pheasants and arrange the meat on a platter. Mound the stuffing in the center and drizzle the meat and stuffing with a few spoonfuls of the sauce. Serve immediately, passing the remaining sauce in a gravy boat.

6 to 8 portions

VENISON STEW

This rich, complex stew is worthy of your most important holiday celebration. Venison is no longer difficult to come by (we have even seen it cut into stewing pieces and frozen) and for stewing, if you have a choice of cuts, use the chuck or rump—it's the most tender.

MARINADE
2 cups dry red wine
Juice of 1 lemon
Juice of 2 limes
2 large bay leaves
2 whole cloves
1 large yellow onion, peeled and sliced
3 carrots, peeled and chopped
Top leaves of 2 celery ribs
1 large garlic clove, peeled and crushed
½ teaspoon dried tarragon
Pinch of dried thyme
6 whole black peppercorns, crushed
1 juniper berry, crushed
½ teaspoon salt

VENISON
3 pounds lean venison, cut into 1-inch cubes
8 tablespoons (1 stick) unsalted butter (slightly more if needed)
2 tablespoons gin
3 tablespoons ¼-inch dice lean salt pork
¼ pound fresh mushrooms, as small as possible
Salt and freshly ground black pepper, to taste
12 to 18 tiny pearl onions
6 chicken livers

1. Combine the marinade ingredients in a large glass bowl and stir well. Add the venison, cover, and refrigerate for 1 day. Turn the meat 1 or 2 times in the marinade.

2. Remove the meat from the marinade and dry thoroughly with paper towels. Reserve the marinade.

3. Melt 2 tablespoons of the butter in a heavy skillet over medium heat. Brown the cubed venison a few pieces at a time, and with a slotted spoon transfer them to a bowl. Add a little additional butter to the pan as needed.

4. Transfer all the venison to an ovenproof casserole. In a small saucepan, warm the gin, then remove it from the heat. Pour the gin over the venison and, using a long match, ignite it away from anything flammable. Shake the casserole slightly until the flames die out.

5. Sauté the diced salt pork in a small skillet over medium heat until golden. With a slotted spoon transfer the pork to the casserole.

6. Remove the mushroom stems and save for another use or discard. Wipe the mushroom caps with a damp paper towel.

AN AUTUMN FEAST

CHAMPAGNE

SMOKED CAVIAR

SUGARED AND SPICED NUTS

FRESH OYSTERS

VENISON STEW

CHESTNUT PURÉE

SWEET POTATO AND CARROT PURÉE

PURÉED BROCCOLI WITH CRÈME FRAÎCHE

WATERCRESS SALAD WITH WALNUT OIL VINAIGRETTE

STILTON CHEESE
PORT WINE

BAKED APPLES

CHOCOLATE HAZELNUT CAKE WITH CRÈME FRAÎCHE

MARC DE BOURGOGNE
FRAMBOISE
ARMAGNAC

Melt 4 tablespoons of the butter in a small skillet over medium-low heat. Add the mushroom caps and season with salt and pepper. Cook, stirring occasionally, until tender, about 5 minutes. Transfer the mushrooms and cooking liquid to the casserole.

7. Bring 1 quart salted water to a boil. Drop in the pearl onions and boil for 1 minute. Transfer the onions to a bowl of ice water; when cool, peel them and add to the casserole.

8. Strain the marinade and add it to the casserole; stir well. Set the casserole over medium heat. Bring to a boil, reduce the heat, cover, and simmer for 30 to 40 minutes.

9. Meanwhile, melt the remaining 2 tablespoons butter in a small skillet over medium heat and cook the chicken livers until they are firm but still pink inside, about 5 minutes. Cut into large dice.

10. When the venison is tender, add the livers to the casserole. Taste, correct the seasoning, and serve immediately.

4 to 6 portions

RAGOUT OF RABBIT FORESTIERE

Of course use a fresh domestic rabbit for this recipe if you can, but a good brand of frozen rabbit is available in many supermarkets, and is convenient and affordable. No marinating is needed for the domestic product, and aside from the time to soften the dried mushrooms, the stew proceeds quickly. We suggest serving this with a Leek and Potato Purée (page 241) and buttered rice or pasta, followed by a green salad and cheese.

This recipe is not intended for wild rabbit; you'll be happier with the results if you use domestic.

2½ cups Chicken Stock (page 416)
1 ounce dried cèpes (porcini mushrooms)
½ cup best-quality olive oil
2 cups finely chopped yellow onions
3 large carrots, peeled and quartered lengthwise
2 rabbits (a total of 5 to 6 pounds), thoroughly defrosted if frozen and cut into serving pieces
2 tablespoons sugar
¼ cup unbleached all-purpose flour
Salt and freshly ground black pepper, to taste
1 cup dry red wine
1 cup canned crushed tomatoes
1 tablespoon dried thyme
2 bay leaves
6 parsley sprigs
⅓ cup Calvados
1 pound fresh mushrooms
3 tablespoons unsalted butter
5 garlic cloves, peeled and chopped

"We must eat to live and live to eat."

—HENRY FIELDING

1. Heat ¾ cup of the chicken stock to boiling in a saucepan and pour it over the cèpes in a small bowl. Let stand for 2 hours.

2. Heat half of the olive oil in a large, heavy pot. Add the onions and carrots and cook over medium heat, covered, until tender and lightly colored, about 25 minutes. Remove the vegetables with a slotted spoon, leaving as much cooking oil behind in the pot as possible, and set the vegetables aside.

3. Set the pot over high heat. Pat the rabbit pieces dry with paper towels and brown them in batches in the hot oil. Turn the pieces frequently, and add additional oil if the pot seems dry. Return all the rabbit pieces to the pot, sprinkle with the sugar, and continue to sauté until evenly browned, another 5 minutes.

4. Turn the heat down and sprinkle the rabbit with the flour and season with salt and pepper. Continue turning the rabbit pieces until the flour is lightly colored, another 5 minutes or so.

5. Add the red wine and stir and scrape up any browned bits in the bottom of the pot. Stir in the remaining 1¾ cups chicken stock, the crushed tomatoes, thyme, bay leaves, and parsley.

6. Warm the Calvados in a small pan, then move it off the heat and away from anything flammable. Using a long kitchen match, ignite the Calvados. When the flame dies down, add the Calvados to the stew. Bring to a healthy simmer, cover, and reduce the heat. Cook, stirring occasionally, for 30 minutes.

7. Meanwhile, cut the stems from the fresh mushrooms and discard or save them for another use. Wipe the mushroom caps with a damp paper towel and slice. Carefully lift the dried mushrooms from the soaking liquid with a slotted spoon. Chop them finely. Let the liquid sit a few moments and then pour it carefully into the pot, leaving any sediment behind.

8. Melt the butter in a large skillet over medium-low heat, add the fresh and dried mushrooms, and sauté over medium heat for 10 minutes. Season with salt and pepper and reserve.

9. Remove the rabbit pieces from the pot with a slotted spoon and transfer to a plate. Discard the carrots, bay leaves, and parsley and purée the sauce in a food processor or a food mill fitted with the fine disc.

10. Return the puréed sauce and the rabbit pieces to the pot. Add the mushrooms and their liquid and the chopped garlic and set over medium heat. Simmer gently for 15 minutes, stirring occasionally. Taste and correct the seasoning. Transfer the ragout to a serving dish and serve immediately.

6 to 8 portions

BOUQUET GARNI

This little bouquet of dried and fresh herbs (and sometimes spices) is tied around the top with a long kitchen string (or placed in a small cheesecloth bag) so that when cooking is completed it is easily lifted out of the pot. There is no set group of herbs that must be used. It depends on the flavor that will most enhance the dish being prepared. Use such spices as peppercorns, whole cloves, and cinnamon sticks for hot mulled wine, for instance; other combinations will infuse your soup or casserole. Discard the little bouquets or bags after use. Start fresh and imaginatively each time a *bouquet garni* is called for.

CATCH OF THE DAY

From fresh or salt waters, wild or farmed, caught by trawler or line, local varieties or imported, the explosion in the kinds of seafood available today is simply incredible. Even when we need to back away from favorites that are being overfished, the choices are still exciting and plentiful. We're all, justifiably, hooked on the treasures of the sea!

The secret to loving seafood is enjoying it when it's fresh. It's that simple. And unless you have a fisherman in the family, you need to find a local fishmonger you can trust. Always ask where the seafood on display was caught—if the signage doesn't already say—and whether it was frozen when it arrived at the shop. It's important to know what you're buying. Then take it home and enjoy.

SEAFOOD VARIETIES WE PARTICULARLY LIKE

FRESHWATER

Bass; Catfish; Perch; Rainbow or German Brown Trout; Smelt; Walleyed Pike

SHELLFISH

Bay Scallops, Long Island and Nantucket; Blue Claw Crab; Clams; Cockles; Crayfish; King Crab, Alaska; Langoustines; Lobster, Maine; Mussels, Prince Edward Island; Oysters; Periwinkles; Sand Dabs; Sea Scallops, Alaska; Shrimp, Gulf; Softshell Crab; Squid; Stone Crab

SALTWATER

Arctic Char; Black Bass; Black Cod; Bluefish; Dover Sole; Flounder; Grouper; Haddock; Halibut; Mahimahi (dolphinfish); Monkfish; Pompano; Red Mullet; Salmon, Wild or White; Scrod (young cod); Sea Bass; Shad; Skate; Snapper; Striped Bass; Swordfish; Tilapia; Tilefish; Tuna; Turbot; White Sardines

FROM EUROPEAN WATERS, BUT BECOMING AVAILABLE HERE

Coquilles avec Oeufs (sea scallops with roe); Crevette Grise (gray shrimp); Dover Sole; Rouget (red mullet)

SOFTSHELL CRABS AMANDINE

The crabs must be sautéed quickly and served immediately. This makes enough for one but is easy to multiply for more servings.

6 tablespoons (¾ stick) unsalted butter
¼ cup sliced blanched almonds
2 or 3 small softshell crabs, cleaned
Unbleached all-purpose flour, for dredging the crabs
Juice of ½ lemon
2 tablespoons finely chopped fresh Italian (flat-leaf) parsley
Lemon wedges, for garnish

1. Melt 2 tablespoons of the butter in a small skillet over medium-low heat. Add the almonds and sauté, stirring occasionally, until golden brown.

2. Meanwhile, dredge the crabs lightly with flour and shake off the excess. Melt the remaining butter in another skillet over medium-low heat; when it is hot and foaming, add the crabs.

3. Sauté the crabs over high heat, turning occasionally with tongs, until crisp and reddish-brown, about 5 minutes.

4. Transfer the crabs to a heated plate. Squeeze the lemon juice into the skillet and bring the butter and juices to a boil. Add the parsley, stir, and pour over the crabs.

5. Remove the almonds from their butter with a slotted spoon and sprinkle over the crabs. Garnish with the lemon wedges and serve immediately.

1 portion

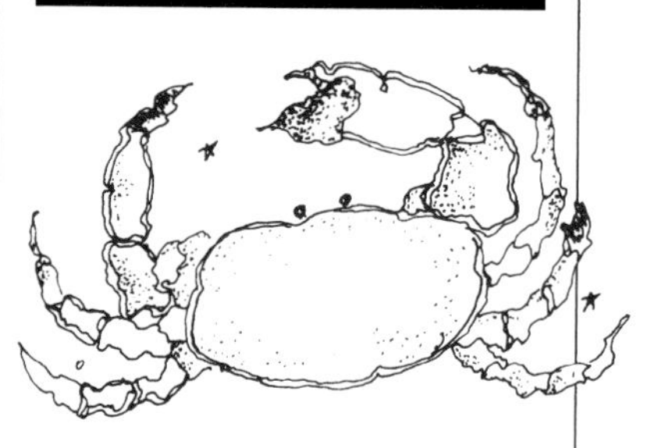

"When my mother had to make enough for eight, she'd just make enough for sixteen and only serve half."

—GRACIE ALLEN

Softshell crabs are always welcome dinner guests. They are seasonal, but can be purchased frozen during the off-season.

HOW TO CLEAN A SOFTSHELL CRAB

Our favorite way to dress a softshell crab is to have the fishmonger do it. This is, however, not always possible, and since the task is not all that disagreeable or demanding we think every good cook should learn the basic steps. The delicious end here certainly justifies the means; wouldn't it be a shame to be on the Maryland shore in the springtime, presented with a batch of fresh crabs, and not know where to begin?

Just such a misadventure happened to Julee once, when she invited 12 friends over to celebrate the beginning of the softshell crab season, brought the crabs home, and then realized, as they glared at her from the sink, that they were very much unlike anything she had ever seen on a plate. On inspiration, she called a chef at a well-known restaurant, who took the time to explain the procedure over the phone. The dinner was a huge success and we continue to follow his good advice:

Rinse the live crabs well under cold water. Snip off their heads approximately ¼ inch behind their eyes. This will kill them instantly and that will be that. Next turn them on their backs and lift and pull away sharply the triangular aprons that are folded on the stomachs like tucked-under tails. Finally peel back the points of the top skin "shells," taking care not to pull them off, and scrape out the spongy gills at each side. Rinse the crabs a final time and pat them dry before grilling, sautéing, or broiling.

SHRIMP WITH APPLES AND SNOW PEAS

Experiment with the many mustards available and personalize this recipe with your favorite. Served with a bit of fluffy white rice this dish is a perfect first course, while in larger portions it is good as a main course or a luncheon dish. Serve a crisp white wine such as those from the Loire—Muscadet, Pouilly-Fumé, Sancerre, or Vouvray.

1 pound snow peas, trimmed and stringed
6 tablespoons (¾ stick) unsalted butter
2 large, firm, tart apples, peeled, cut into thick slices
2 tablespoons sugar
½ cup finely minced yellow onion
2 pounds medium-size raw shrimp, shelled and deveined
¾ cup dry white wine or vermouth
⅔ cup Dijon mustard, or try tarragon, orange, green peppercorn, or sherry mustard
¾ cup heavy cream or Crème Fraîche (page 414)

1. Bring a large pot of salted water to a boil and drop in the cleaned snow peas. When tender but still crunchy, after about 3 minutes, drain them and plunge immediately into ice water. This will stop the cooking process and set their bright green color. Reserve.

2. In a large skillet melt 2 tablespoons of the butter and sauté the apple slices over medium heat until tender but not mushy, about 5 minutes. Sprinkle the slices with the sugar and raise the heat, rapidly turning the apple slices until they are brown and lightly caramelized. Using a spatula, remove the slices from the skillet and reserve.

3. In the same skillet melt the remaining 4 tablespoons butter and gently cook the minced onion, covered, over medium heat until tender and lightly colored, about 25 minutes.

4. Raise the heat, add the shrimp, and stir and toss them rapidly in the butter until they are firm and pink, about 3 minutes. Do not overcook. Remove the shrimp from the skillet and reserve.

5. Pour the wine or vermouth into the skillet and over high heat reduce it by two thirds. Turn down the heat and stir in the mustard with a wire whisk. Pour in the cream or crème fraîche and simmer uncovered, stirring occasionally, until the sauce is reduced slightly, 15 minutes.

6. Drain the snow peas thoroughly and pat dry with paper towels. Add them, along with the reserved apples and shrimp, to the mustard-cream sauce and simmer together for 1 minute. Serve immediately.

6 portions as a first course, 4 portions as a main course

SWORDFISH STEAKS

Swordfish is deliciously meaty; when cooked with a little care, it need not be dry. We bake it according to the Canadian Fisheries method and surround it with a bit of wine or fish stock as additional insurance. The result is moist and flavorful every time. With a fish this rich a sauce is really unnecessary, but a seasoned butter, melting over the steak as it's brought to the table, is a lovely touch. Particularly appropriate are Anchovy Butter and Basil-Mustard Butter (see page 145).

6 swordfish steaks (½ to ¾ pound each), cut 1 inch thick
Approximately 1 cup Fish Stock (page 417) or dry white wine
Salt and freshly ground black pepper, to taste
½ to ¾ cup flavored butter of your choice

1. Preheat the oven to 375°F.

2. Arrange the swordfish steaks in a single layer in 1 or 2 baking dishes just large enough to hold them comfortably. Pour the fish stock or white wine, or a combination of both, around the fish, to a depth equal to half the thickness of the steaks. Season lightly with salt and freshly ground black pepper.

3. Set the dish or dishes on the center rack of the oven and bake for 9 minutes. Check the fish for doneness with a fork, remembering that residual heat will continue to cook the fish even after you take it from the oven; if the fish is not ready, bake a moment or two longer and test again.

4. When done to your liking, transfer the steaks with a spatula to heated plates. Place a tablespoon or two of the flavored butter in the center of each steak and serve immediately.

6 portions

BUYING AND KEEPING FRESH FISH

♥ Most fish are seasonal, so go to the fish market with an open mind. Learn how to substitute within categories of fish from the fishmonger.

♥ Whole fish are more perishable, thus they are usually fresher than fillets.

♥ If you have the choice, buy where reputable restaurants get their fish. If you have no choice, learn to shop with an eagle eye; demand increased variety if it seems limited, and freshness if the fish is over the hill.

♥ Look your fish squarely in the eye and be sure that eye is bright and firm. The gills should be red, the flesh firm and springy when poked with a finger. Truly fresh fish smell fresh—like the ocean—and are not slimy. Fillets should be firm, without the fishy odor that indicates staleness.

♥ The best way to store fish is on ice—similar to the way the markets do. Bring your fish home immediately, rinse under cold running water, enclose in a plastic bag and place on a bed of ice. Plan to use the fish, particularly if it is whole, on the day it is purchased.

BLUEFISH BAKED WITH APPLES AND MUSTARD

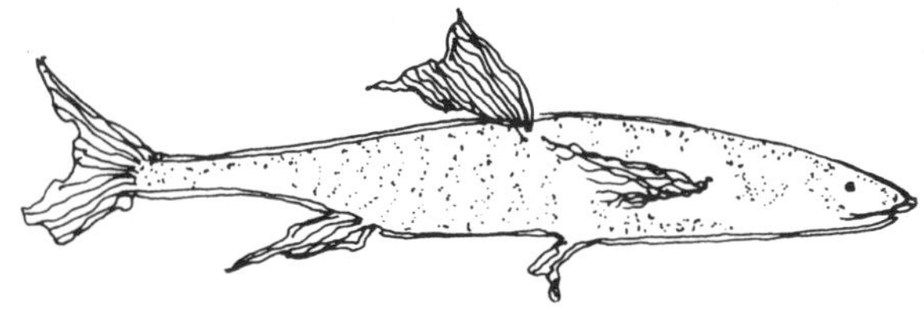

The oily and robustly flavored bluefish stands up well to the sweet and pungent combination of flavors in this recipe.

4 firm, crisp, tart cooking apples
½ cup plus 4 tablespoons (2½ sticks) unsalted butter, chilled
4 bluefish fillets (about 2½ pounds)
Approximately 1 cup coarse mild mustard
1 cup Fish Stock (page 417)
Approximately 2 cups medium-dry white wine
1 tablespoon minced shallots

1. Preheat the oven to 350°F.

2. Peel the apples or not, as you wish, and cut them into thin slices. Melt 4 tablespoons of the butter in a skillet over medium heat. Add the apples, raise the heat to high, and sauté until lightly browned. Remove from the heat and reserve.

3. Lay the bluefish fillets in a shallow baking dish just large enough to hold them in a single layer. Smear the mustard evenly over the fillets. Spread the apples over and around the fish. Pour the fish stock and enough wine around the fillets to come about halfway up their thickness, about ½ cup. The apple slices should be more or less submerged.

4. Set the baking dish on the center rack of the oven and bake for 8 minutes.

5. While the fish is cooking, combine the remaining white wine and the minced shallots in a small skillet and cook over high heat until reduced to about a spoonful, 5 to 7 minutes.

6. Test the fish with a fork. When it is almost, but not quite, done to your liking, remove from the oven.

7. Drain all the liquid from the baking dish into the wine-shallot mixture in the small skillet and turn the heat to high to reduce the liquid. Cover the fish and apples with aluminum foil and keep warm while finishing the sauce.

8. When the liquid in the skillet is reduced by half, turn the heat to very low. Whisk in the remaining 2 sticks of chilled butter, a piece (about a tablespoonful) at a time, always adding the next bit of butter just before the last has been completely incorporated. The sauce will become glossy. When all the butter has been incorporated, turn off the heat and cover the pan.

9. Divide the fillets and apple slices among 4 heated plates, spoon the sauce over all, and serve immediately.

4 portions

"Nothing is really work unless you'd rather be doing something else."

—JAMES BARRIE, *PETER PAN*

BAKED STRIPED BASS WITH FENNEL

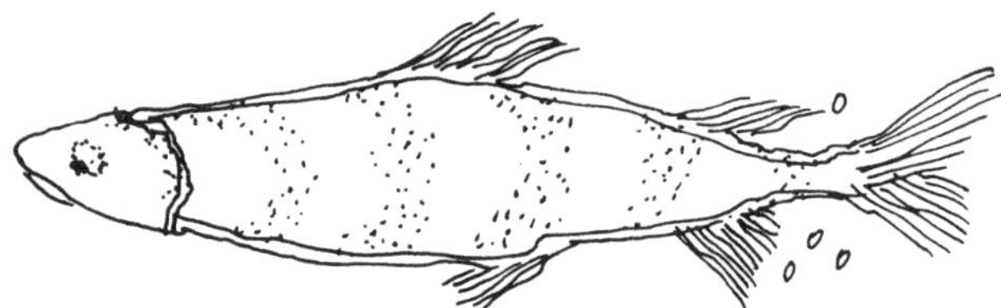

When you want to pull out all the stops, this is the most elegant of fish dishes. Serve it with Sautéed Cherry Tomatoes (page 233) and buttered spinach noodles. Accompany it with an excellent white wine, a first-growth Chablis or a California Chardonnay.

1 large fennel bulb, including stems and feathery leaves
¼ cup best-quality olive oil
2 garlic cloves, peeled and minced
Salt and freshly ground black pepper, to taste
¼ cup chopped fresh Italian (flat-leaf) parsley
1 striped bass (5 to 7 pounds before dressing), backbone removed (see Note), scaled, head and tail intact
Juice of ½ lemon
½ lemon, thinly sliced
½ cup dry white wine or vermouth
1 or 2 bunches of fresh watercress, for garnish

1. Preheat the oven to 400°F.

2. Cut the fennel bulb into slices and the slices into thin strips. Reserve the stems and feathery leaves.

3. Heat the olive oil in a small skillet over medium heat, and sauté the fennel slices and half of the garlic, covered, until just tender, about 10 minutes. With a slotted spoon, transfer the fennel to a bowl, season with salt and pepper, and add the parsley. Reserve the oil.

4. Arrange the bass in an oiled shallow baking dish and spread it open. Lay the cooked fennel mixture down the center of the bass and arrange a few of the reserved ferny sprigs on top of the mixture. Sprinkle with lemon juice, close the fish, and tie it together in two or three places with kitchen twine. Distribute the lemon slices around the bass in the dish.

5. Season the outside of the fish with salt and pepper and rub it with the remaining garlic. Pour the reserved oil over the fish and lay the reserved fennel stems on top. Pour the white wine or vermouth into the pan.

6. Bake the fish on the center rack of the oven for 10 minutes per inch of thickness, measured at the thickest part. Baste often with the accumulated juices from the pan. The bass is done when the flesh is opaque and flakes slightly when probed with a fork.

7. Carefully transfer the bass to a large serving platter, remove the strings, and surround it with fresh watercress. Serve at once.

8 portions

Note: Your fishmonger will do this for you.

Even a fish story needn't be dull. When you tire of sole fillets and tunafish sandwiches, there is literally a whole ocean full of fish to be discovered. You'll find a wonderful new world of firm-textured, juicy, flavorful fish dishes.

SUNDAY SUMMER SUPPER

CARROT AND ORANGE SOUP

BAKED STRIPED BASS WITH FENNEL

BULGUR WHEAT SALAD

EGGPLANT BASIL SALAD

CHOCOLATE HAZELNUT CAKE

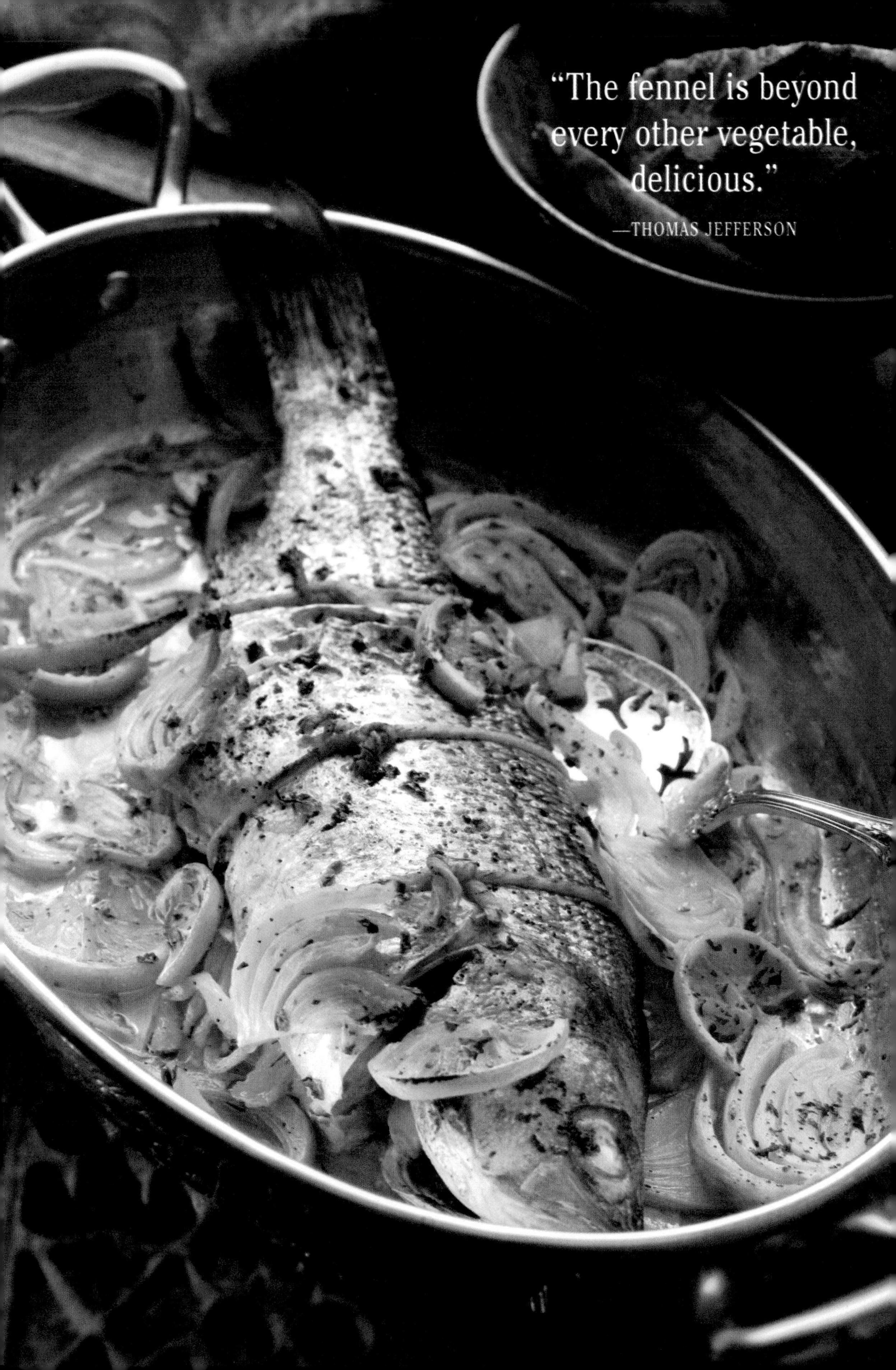
"The fennel is beyond
every other vegetable,
delicious."
—THOMAS JEFFERSON

ESCABECHE

This version of South American pickled fish (also called seviche) looks complicated, but is assembled with little kitchen time. After assembling, it is marinated for four days before you serve it, and will keep for a good two weeks afterward, if well refrigerated. Make it with any firm-fleshed white fish (snapper, tilefish, and scrod are good), and serve it with warmed bread and white rice. Perfect for a summertime picnic on the porch.

2 cups unbleached all-purpose flour
4 pounds fish steaks or fillets (½ inch thick)
1½ cups best-quality olive oil
Juice of 1½ limes
⅔ cup white wine vinegar
⅔ cup dry white wine
2⅔ cups green beans, trimmed and cut into julienne
1⅓ cups carrots, peeled and cut into julienne
⅓ cup green olives, pitted, with juice
½ cup imported black olives, pitted, without juice
⅓ cup capers, drained
1 medium-size red onion, peeled and cut into thin rounds
1 small white onion, peeled and cut into thin rounds
2 green bell peppers, stemmed, seeded, and cut into thin rings
2 red bell peppers, stemmed, seeded, and cut into thin rings
1 tablespoon Asian oyster sauce
3 tablespoons coarsely chopped fresh cilantro
3 tablespoons coarsely chopped fresh dill
1 tablespoon mixed dried pickling spice
1 teaspoon salt
Freshly ground black pepper, to taste
1½ tablespoons brown sugar
3 garlic cloves, peeled and finely chopped
1 tablespoon chopped fresh Italian (flat-leaf) parsley, plus extra for garnish

1. Flour the fish lightly. Heat the oil in a large skillet over medium heat. Add the fish and sauté, in batches if necessary, turning frequently, for 3 to 4 minutes. The fish should be just cooked and starting to brown lightly. Remove from the skillet and drain on paper towels.

2. Transfer the drained fish to a large bowl. Combine all the ingredients and pour over the fish. Cover and refrigerate for 4 days, basting at intervals.

3. Toss again, arrange on a large platter, and garnish with additional chopped parsley. Serve immediately.

12 to 14 portions

COOKING FRESH FISH

Don't be afraid to cook fish at home. If you start with extraordinarily fresh fish, nothing else can compare. Befriend your local fishmonger and ask him "What's freshest today?" That's what you should buy! Remember, he loves fish and chances are loves to educate his customers. If he ever disappoints you, tell him so. He won't do it twice. Alternatively, get to know your most reliable local source for frozen fish. Today so much is frozen "just caught at sea," that it is generally very high quality. Once home, carefully defrost it on a plate in the refrigerator for 12 to 24 hours (depending on size and thickness), frequently draining any liquid that accumulates. Then treat it as fresh and cook it quickly.

Many home cooks overcook fish, drying it out. We still follow the Canadian Fisheries cooking method: It estimates the total cooking time of any fish to be 10 minutes for every inch of thickness, measured at the thickest part. We follow this for whole fish, steaks, or fillets, whether grilled, broiled, fried, poached, or baked. Give it a try; it's amazingly accurate and you'll be proud of the results! Then, you can adjust cooking times to your own taste.

FLAVORED BUTTERS

Try these instead of plain butter in sandwiches and with vegetable, fish, and meat dishes. Start with room temperature butter, and for each flavored butter, either combine the ingredients in a food processor and process until smooth, or cream them together by hand in a small bowl. Cover and refrigerate until ready to use. Use a melon baller, if you like, to make perfect spheres of the butter before chilling.

- ♥ Anchovy Butter: 8 tablespoons (1 stick) unsalted butter, 1 tablespoon (drained) capers, 2 tablespoons anchovy paste (or to taste).
- ♥ Basil-Mustard Butter: 8 tablespoons (1 stick) unsalted butter, ¼ cup coarsely chopped fresh basil leaves, ¼ cup Dijon mustard.
- ♥ Curry-Chutney Butter: 8 tablespoons (1 stick) unsalted butter, 1 teaspoon curry powder, ¼ cup mango chutney.
- ♥ Dill Butter: 8 tablespoons (1 stick) unsalted butter, 3 tablespoons chopped fresh dill, ½ teaspoon lemon juice, ½ teaspoon Dijon mustard.
- ♥ Herb Butter: 8 tablespoons (1 stick) unsalted butter, 1 tablespoon finely chopped fresh herb of your choice.
- ♥ Ravigote Butter: 8 tablespoons (1 stick) unsalted butter, 1 tablespoon (drained) capers, 1 heaping tablespoon each of chopped shallots, chopped fresh parsley, and tarragon, 1 tablespoon snipped fresh chives, ½ teaspoon lemon juice.

COLD POACHED SCALLOPS

Serve the scallops as a first course or as a light main course.

1½ pounds sea scallops, hinge muscles removed
Fresh blueberries, for garnish (optional)
Fresh mint sprigs, for garnish (optional)
Blueberry Mayonnaise (recipe follows)

1. Rinse the scallops briefly and place them in a saucepan that holds them comfortably in one layer. Cover with lightly salted water and bring the water to a simmer. Cook gently for 1 minute. Remove the saucepan from the heat and let the scallops cool to room temperature in their poaching liquid.

2. Rinse and sort through the blueberries, if using, selecting fat perfect berries only. Rinse the mint sprigs, if using, under cold water and pat dry.

3. Drain the scallops and arrange them on small plates. Spoon the blueberry mayonnaise over and around the scallops but do not completely mask them. Garnish randomly with selected blueberries and mint sprigs and serve immediately.

4 to 6 portions

BLUEBERRY MAYONNAISE

BLUEBERRY VINEGAR
½ cup cider vinegar
½ cup fresh blueberries
1 tablespoon honey
1 piece (2 inches) cinnamon stick
4 whole cloves

MAYONNAISE
1¾ cups prepared mayonnaise, such as Hellmann's
2 tablespoons olive oil
Salt and freshly ground black pepper, to taste

1. Prepare the blueberry vinegar one day ahead. Combine the vinegar ingredients in a small saucepan and cook over low heat for 5 minutes. Cool to room temperature and refrigerate, covered, overnight. Strain before using. There should be ¼ cup.

2. Place the mayonnaise in a bowl. Whisking constantly, add the strained vinegar and olive oil. Season with salt and pepper. Refrigerate for up to 2 days before serving.

2 cups

BAKING IN FOIL

Foods baked in aluminum foil packets retain the maximum of their natural moisture and flavor. The packets can be arranged and sealed in advance of cooking, leaving the host free to spend time with his or her guests. And finally, the silvery envelopes look terrific cut open at the table, releasing their savory steam.

Cut the foil into a large heart shape, or use a simple rectangle. Arrange the meat or fish and garnishes inside and fold the foil over, sealing well on all sides. When arranging food in packets, do not overlap the meat or fish pieces or they will not cook evenly. If the packets are prepared far in advance and refrigerated, be certain to let the foods return to room temperature before cooking. If you prefer to use classic cooking parchment rather than foil, butter it well and reduce the cooking times slightly.

LAMB CHOPS WITH MUSHROOMS AND HERBS

1 tablespoon minced garlic
⅓ cup mixed minced fresh mint and parsley, more or less half and half, or to taste
4 tablespoons (½ stick) unsalted butter, at room temperature
6 boned loin lamb chops, cut 1½ inches thick (about 6 ounces each, trimmed weight)
6 thin lemon slices
6 mint sprigs
2 to 3 dozen firm white mushroom caps (about 1 pound)
Salt and freshly ground black pepper, to taste

1. Preheat the oven to 350°F.

2. Mash the garlic, herbs, and half of the butter together into a rough paste. Divide the herb butter among the lamb chops, spreading a bit inside the tails and the rest on top. Tie the chops into tidy rounds with kitchen twine.

3. Arrange each chop on a piece of aluminum foil and place a lemon slice and a mint sprig on top of each. Smear the remaining butter over the mushrooms and arrange them equally among the chops. Season with salt and pepper. Seal the foil packets, and set on a baking sheet.

4. Bake about 20 minutes for medium rare. Transfer the packets to serving plates and allow the guests to open them at the table.

6 portions

Lamb Chops with Vegetables and Fruits are a natural addition to a spring-inspired menu.

LAMB CHOPS

Lamb chops cook to moist perfection in foil packets. The chops should be loin chops, boned but otherwise left in one piece, with the tiny tail intact. After final assembly, secure with a toothpick or tie with thin twine. Each of our three versions includes its own vegetables, and no other accompaniment is really necessary, particularly if you begin with a light pasta dish to provide the starch.

LAMB CHOPS WITH VEGETABLES AND FRUITS

6 boned loin lamb chops, cut 1½ inches thick (about 6 ounces each, trimmed weight)
Salt and freshly ground black pepper, to taste
3 kiwis, peeled and scooped into balls
2 cups seedless red or green grapes
24 asparagus spears, trimmed, blanched, and sliced diagonally
2 thin cucumbers, peeled and scooped into balls
⅓ cup mixed minced fresh mint and parsley, more or less half and half, or to taste

1. Preheat the oven to 350°F.

2. Tie the chops into neat rounds with kitchen twine. Arrange each on a piece of aluminum foil and season with salt and pepper. Scatter the fruits and vegetables equally among the chops. Sprinkle the chopped mint and parsley mixture over all. Seal the foil packets, and set on a baking sheet.

3. Bake about 20 minutes for medium rare. Transfer the packets to serving plates and allow the guests to open them at the table.

6 portions

LAMB CHOPS WITH ARTICHOKES AND ENDIVE

6 boned loin lamb chops, cut 1½ inches thick (about 6 ounces each, trimmed weight)
6 large cooked artichoke hearts, fresh or jarred
Salt and freshly ground black pepper, to taste
¾ cup cooked spinach
Pinch of freshly grated nutmeg
1 tablespoon finely minced garlic
6 tablespoons (¾ stick) unsalted butter
6 whole endives, trimmed, cleaned, and halved lengthwise
⅓ cup finely chopped fresh Italian (flat-leaf) parsley

1. Preheat the oven to 350°F.

2. Arrange each chop on a large piece of aluminum foil. Set 1 artichoke heart in the half-circle formed by the tail of each lamb chop, wrap the tail around it, and secure in place with a short wooden skewer. Season the chops and artichokes with salt and freshly ground black pepper.

3. Season the spinach to taste with salt, pepper, and nutmeg and divide equally in the center of the artichoke hearts.

4. Mash together the garlic and 2 tablespoons of the butter. Spread a bit of garlic butter on top of each lamb chop.

5. Place 2 endive halves next to each chop and dot each half with the remaining butter. Season the endives with salt and pepper and sprinkle the chopped parsley over all. Seal the foil packets, and set on a baking sheet.

6. Bake about 20 minutes for medium rare. Transfer the packets to serving plates and allow the guests to open them at the table.

6 portions

SKEWERED SHRIMP AND SOLE

6 fillets of flounder or sole (about 3 pounds total)
18 medium-size raw shrimp, shelled and deveined
24 asparagus tips, blanched
2 limes, thinly sliced
Salt and freshly ground black pepper, to taste
4 cucumbers, peeled
Chopped fresh dill, to taste
4 tablespoons (½ stick) unsalted butter

1. Preheat the oven to 400°F.

2. Weave the sole fillets lengthwise onto wooden skewers, threading a shrimp between each fold of the sole, 3 to a skewer.

3. Center each sole skewer on a large piece of aluminum foil and wedge the asparagus tips between the shrimp and sole. Halve the lime slices and tuck these between the shrimp and sole for a decorative effect. Season with salt and freshly ground black pepper.

4. Cut the cucumbers with a melon-baller to make as many balls as possible. Scatter the cucumber balls over the fish and sprinkle with the chopped fresh dill. Dot with the butter and seal the packets. Set on a baking sheet.

5. Bake until done, about 10 minutes. Transfer the packets to serving plates and allow the guests to open them at the table.

6 portions

SKEWERED SHRIMP AND PROSCIUTTO

Wrapping prosciutto around the shrimp gives the shellfish a savory, meaty flavor. Prosciutto is cured with salt, and the black olives contribute a burst of flavor, so no additional seasoning is needed.

9 thin slices of prosciutto
3 dozen medium-size raw shrimp, shelled and deveined
2 dozen pitted California black olives
18 thin lemon slices (2 or 3 lemons)
½ cup finely chopped fresh Italian (flat-leaf) parsley
2 or 3 garlic cloves, peeled and finely chopped
Crushed red pepper flakes, to taste
6 tablespoons best-quality olive oil, or more

1. Preheat the oven to 350°F.

2. Cut each slice of prosciutto in half lengthwise and wrap 1 piece of prosciutto around each of the 18 shrimp.

3. Slide 2 olives onto one of 6 skewers. Slide a wrapped shrimp onto the skewer. Wrap a lemon slice around a plain shrimp and slide it onto the skewer. Repeat, using 2 more prosciutto-wrapped shrimp and 2 more lemon-wrapped shrimp. End with 2 more olives. Repeat the skewering procedure with the remaining shrimp, lemons, and olives.

4. Lay each skewer on a large piece of aluminum foil. Sprinkle with the parsley, chopped garlic, and red pepper. Drizzle each skewer with a tablespoon or so of olive oil and seal the packets. Set on a baking sheet.

5. Bake for 10 minutes, or until the shrimp are done. Do not overcook. Transfer the packets to plates and allow the guests to open them at the table.

6 portions

from THE SILVER PALATE NOTEBOOK

Even if you've prepared everything in advance, try to arrange for the aroma of something cooking when guests arrive. Whether it's cloves or herbs simmering in water, the effect is subtly welcoming.

FISH ELVIRA

2 fillets of mild white fish, such as flounder or sole, about ¾ inch thick (about 12 ounces total)
½ cup Crème Fraîche (page 414)
1 medium-size white onion, peeled and thinly sliced
Salt and freshly ground black pepper, to taste
Chopped fresh cilantro, to taste
1 lime, quartered, for garnish

1. Smear the fish fillets with the crème fraîche and set aside in a dish to marinate at room temperature for 1 hour.

2. Preheat the oven to 400°F.

3. Transfer each fish fillet to a large piece of aluminum foil. Spoon any juices and crème fraîche from the marinating dish over the fish. Cover the fillets completely with a thin layer of onion slices. Season with salt and pepper and seal the foil packets. Set on a baking sheet.

4. Bake for 8 to 10 minutes, according to the thickness of the fish. Transfer the packets to serving plates, slit open, and sprinkle the fish with the cilantro. Garnish with lime wedges and serve immediately.

2 portions

One of our favorite restaurants in the world is Elvira's in Nogales, Mexico. It can be truly said that Elvira's is a dive, but in the best sense of the word. Oilcloth covers the tables, a cat wanders through, and genial musicians assault the senses with incomprehensible songs. By way of compensation, the tequila flows freely, the welcome is genuine, and the food is delicious.

One of our favorite dishes there is fish baked in foil with a topping of sour cream and onions. It is a simple dish, dressing up the plainest and mildest piece of fish with delicate zest. The Mexican version of sour cream does not separate when heated, much like the crème fraîche we have preferred to substitute. Slice the onions paper-thin, and sprinkle the fish with lime juice and chopped cilantro, if you like. Mexican beer or tequila is the perfect accompanying beverage.

CHICKEN WITH LEMON AND HERBS

1 cup mixed chopped fresh mint, dill, and parsley, in about equal proportion, or to taste
2 garlic cloves, peeled and minced
6 skinless, boneless chicken breasts (about 4½ pounds total)
Salt and freshly ground black pepper, to taste
2 lemons, cut into 6 slices each
4 tablespoons (½ stick) unsalted butter

1. Preheat the oven to 350°F.

2. Mix the herbs and garlic together in a small bowl. Flatten the chicken breasts by pressing them gently against the work surface with the palm of your hand. Arrange each breast on a large piece of aluminum foil and season with salt and pepper. Sprinkle the herb and garlic mixture over the chicken breasts.

3. Arrange 2 lemon slices over each breast. Dot with the butter and seal the packets. Set on a baking sheet.

4. Set the packets on the center rack of the oven and bake until done, 30 minutes. Transfer to serving plates and allow the guests to open the packets at the table.

6 portions

THE STEW POT

Today, stews are considered "comfort food" and sometimes they're just what we need to slow us down in our busy world. The influence of the Slow Food movement to sustain authentic cooking methods, and the ease of electric slow cookers, have contributed to the trend of gently simmering meats and vegetables. In our world of instant everything, the revival of old-fashioned stews and pot roasts just seems so very luxurious and worth celebrating.

Stews are forgiving food, easygoing, and open to improvisation and substitution. They also reduce pressure in the kitchen, since stews are nearly always better made a day or two in advance of serving. The finished product, long simmered and rich flavored, is always a crowd pleaser. There's something about a stew pot simmering in the kitchen that lets everyone know that a caring cook is in control. Stew says something special to your guests; they feel welcomed, comforted, nourished.

MEDITERRANEAN SUPPER MENU

LEEKS NIÇOISE

BEEF STEW WITH CUMIN

PARSLEYED RICE

ORANGE AND ONION SALAD

LIME MOUSSE

BEEF STEW WITH CUMIN

Depending on the rest of the menu, this hearty stew can seem Latin or Mediterranean because it is intriguingly seasoned with cumin, a spice that has become a staple in our kitchen.

2 cups unbleached all-purpose flour
1 tablespoon dried thyme
1 teaspoon salt, plus additional to taste
½ teaspoon freshly ground black pepper, plus additional to taste
3 pounds beef stew meat, in 1-inch cubes
¼ cup olive oil
1 cup dry red wine
1½ cups homemade Beef Stock (page 416)
1 cup canned crushed tomatoes
2 tablespoons ground cumin
1 teaspoon chili powder
1 bay leaf
8 to 12 white pearl onions
6 garlic cloves, peeled and chopped
½ cup chopped fresh Italian (flat-leaf) parsley, plus additional for garnish
1½ cups green Sicilian olives

1. Preheat the oven to 350°F.

2. Stir the flour, thyme, the 1 teaspoon salt, and the ½ teaspoon pepper together in a shallow bowl. Turn the cubes of stew meat in the flour to coat well, shake off the excess, and transfer to a plate.

3. Heat the olive oil in a large heavy pot over medium heat. Add the beef cubes, a few at a time, and brown them well on all sides. As they are browned, transfer them to paper towels to drain.

4. When all the meat is browned, discard any excess oil but do not wash the pot. Add the wine, beef stock, and crushed tomatoes, and set the pot over medium heat. Bring to a boil, stirring and scraping up the browned bits from the bottom of the pan. Return the beef to the pot, add the cumin, chili powder, and bay leaf and season with salt and pepper.

5. Cover the pot and set it on the center rack of the oven. Bake for 1 hour, stirring occasionally and regulating the oven temperature to maintain the stew at a steady simmer.

6. Meanwhile, bring a large pot of water to a boil. Cut an X in the root end of each pearl onion and drop them into the boiling water for 1 minute. Drain them and drop them into a bowl of cold water. When completely cool, drain and peel them.

7. After the stew has been in the oven for about 1 hour, stir in the onions. Continue to cook the stew, uncovered.

8. After another 15 minutes, stir in the garlic, the ½ cup parsley, and the olives. Continue to cook, uncovered, until the stew is reduced and thickened to your liking and the beef is tender, another 15 to 30 minutes. Transfer to a serving bowl, sprinkle with the parsley, and serve immediately.

6 portions

AUTUMN LUNCHEON

ZUCCHINI-WATERCRESS SOUP

BEEF CARBONNADE

PARSLEYED BUTTERED NOODLES

SWEET POTATO AND CARROT PURÉE

AN ALL-ARUGULA SALAD WITH OUR FAVORITE VINAIGRETTE

ELLEN'S APPLE TART

BEEF CARBONNADE

Our version of this Belgian beef stew is cooked with sweetly caramelized onions and dark beer. It is the kind of rich, hearty but simple food that is equally appropriate for family or guests. It is especially welcome after an autumn hike, at the end of a long day of skiing, or for a snowbound Sunday supper. Serve carbonnade with egg noodles tossed with butter and poppy seeds, sautéed apples, and pumpernickel. Offer the same beer you used in the stew.

Beef stew, such as this dish scented with cumin, is quintessential comfort food.

"There is
no sight on earth
more appealing
than the sight of
a woman making
dinner for someone
she loves."
—THOMAS WOLFE

¼ pound bacon
2 very large yellow onions (1½ to 2 pounds total), peeled and thinly sliced
1 tablespoon sugar
1 cup unbleached all-purpose flour
1 tablespoon dried thyme
1 teaspoon salt
½ teaspoon freshly ground black pepper
3 pounds beef stew meat (chuck is best), in 1-inch cubes
Vegetable oil (optional)
2 cups imported dark beer
Chopped fresh parsley, for garnish

1. Coarsely dice the bacon and sauté it in a large skillet over medium heat until crisp and brown. Remove the bacon with a slotted spoon and reserve.

2. Add the onions to the skillet and cook them, covered, in the rendered bacon fat until tender, about 20 minutes. Uncover the skillet, raise the heat, and sprinkle the onions with the sugar. Toss and stir them until they are well browned. Transfer the onions to a strainer set over a bowl and let stand while you prepare the beef.

3. Stir together on a plate the flour, thyme, salt, and pepper, and roll the cubes of meat around in the mixture until well coated. Shake off the excess and set the cubes on another plate.

4. Press the onions gently with the back of a spoon to extract as much of the cooking fat as possible. Transfer the fat to a large heavy pot. Add additional fat in the form of vegetable oil if it appears you will not have enough for properly browning the beef. Be sparing, however, or the carbonnade will be greasy.

5. Set the pot over high heat; when it is very hot, add 6 to 8 beef cubes. Do not crowd them in the pot or they will not brown properly. Turn the heat down slightly and continue to cook the cubes until browned on all sides. Transfer them with a slotted spoon to a clean plate and proceed with the browning until all the meat is done.

6. Preheat the oven to 325°F.

7. Pour the beer into the pot and use a spoon to stir up all the browned bits on the bottom. Return the beef cubes to the pot along with the bacon and sautéed onions. Bring to a simmer on the stove. Cover and set on the center rack of the oven.

8. Cook, stirring occasionally, until the stew is reduced and thickened and the meat is tender, about 1½ hours. Regulate the oven temperature as needed to maintain a moderate simmer.

9. Taste and correct the seasoning. Turn the stew out into a heated serving dish, garnish with the chopped parsley, and serve immediately.

6 portions

BEAUJOLAIS

Anytime after midnight on the third Thursday of each November it's fun to sample the first of the Beaujolais Nouveau. This is the new wine that just weeks before was a cluster of grapes in a grower's vineyard in Burgundy. Then, harvested quickly, fermented rapidly, and bottled speedily, the resulting wine was carried by motorcycle, balloon, pickup, helicopter, jet, dinghy, elephant, runners, and rickshaw to its final destinations all over the world. It may all seem silly, but half the fun is knowing that on this same day—in homes, cafés, restaurants, pubs, bars, and bistros, citizens the world over celebrate the birth of a new wine. Even when the wine has lost a bit of its youth, it remains a delight. While Beaujolais may not be considered by some to be a serious wine, we think its unstuffy character deserves its own place in the sun—perhaps at your next picnic.

"Cuisine is when things taste like themselves."

—CURNONSKY

POT ROAST

A perfect Sunday supper.

- *3½ pounds beef shoulder or chuck roast, rolled and tied*
- *1 teaspoon freshly ground black pepper, plus additional to rub over the roast before cooking*
- *3 tablespoons best-quality olive oil*
- *1½ to 2 cups Beef Stock (page 416)*
- *2 cups dry red wine*
- *1 bunch of fresh Italian (flat-leaf) parsley, thick stems trimmed and discarded, leaves chopped fine, plus additional for garnish*
- *1 teaspoon salt*
- *7 whole cloves*
- *2½ cups coarsely chopped yellow onions*
- *2 cups peeled carrot chunks (1-inch chunks)*
- *8 medium-size potatoes, peeled and cut into thirds*
- *2 cups canned Italian plum tomatoes, with juice*
- *1 cup diced celery*

1. Preheat the oven to 350°F.

2. Rub the roast with black pepper. Heat the olive oil in a heavy ovenproof casserole or Dutch oven over medium heat. Add the roast and sear for several minutes on all sides, browning well.

3. Pour in the stock and wine and add the parsley, the salt, the 1 teaspoon black pepper, and the whole cloves. Stir in the onions, carrots, potatoes, tomatoes, and celery. The liquid in the casserole should just cover the vegetables. Add additional beef stock if necessary. Bring to a simmer on the stove, then cover, and bake on the center rack of the oven for 2½ hours.

4. Uncover the pot and cook, until the meat is tender, basting frequently, about 1½ hours more.

5. Transfer the roast to a deep serving platter and arrange the vegetables around it. Spoon a bit of sauce over all and garnish the platter with parsley. Pass additional sauce in a gravy boat.

6 portions

"The ornament of the house is the friends who frequent it."
—RALPH WALDO EMERSON

from THE SILVER PALATE NOTEBOOK

There has always been one rule in our kitchens, made in the very beginning, and it still holds true: When cooking, you must taste and taste often! Good cooks taste continually and learn over time to trust their own judgment. Tasting helps you develop into a confident cook.

Don't be afraid to taste a dish several times as it cooks. It is the only way to understand how flavors begin to meld with heat and time. If a dish isn't working, feel free to doctor it with a little more of this or that. If it is working, glorious! Take our recipes, make them your own, and have fun with them. That will be our greatest pleasure.

BRAISED SHORT RIBS OF BEEF

These short ribs are simmered long and slow, bathing the kitchen in a delicious aroma and yielding tender meat that practically falls apart at the touch.

1 teaspoon freshly ground black pepper, plus additional to sprinkle over the ribs before cooking
4 pounds beef short ribs, cut into 2-inch lengths
5 tablespoons best-quality olive oil
8 garlic cloves, peeled and finely chopped
1½ cups canned Italian plum tomatoes, with juice
2 cups peeled and sliced carrots (⅛-inch-thick slices)
3 cups sliced onions
8 whole cloves
½ cup chopped fresh Italian (flat-leaf) parsley
¾ cup red wine vinegar
3 tablespoons tomato paste
2 tablespoons brown sugar
2 teaspoons salt
¼ teaspoon cayenne pepper
Approximately 3 cups Beef Stock (page 416)

1. Sprinkle the pepper over the short ribs. Heat the olive oil in a Dutch oven or casserole over medium heat. Sear the ribs, 3 or 4 at a time, browning well on all sides. As they are browned, drain them on paper towels.

2. Preheat the oven to 350°F.

3. Return half of the ribs to the casserole. Sprinkle with half of the garlic. Layer half of each vegetable over the meat. Add 4 cloves and sprinkle with half of the parsley. Repeat with the remaining ingredients, ending with a layer of chopped parsley.

4. In a bowl mix together the vinegar, tomato paste, brown sugar, salt, the 1 teaspoon black pepper, and the cayenne. Pour it over the meat and vegetables and then add the beef stock just to cover.

5. Cover the casserole, set over medium heat, and bring to a boil. Bake on the center rack of the oven for 1½ hours. Uncover and continue baking until the meat is very tender, 1½ hours longer. Taste, correct the seasoning, and serve immediately.

6 portions

CHILI FOR A CROWD

From the very beginning of The Silver Palate, Sheila's special chili was a winner. Whether you're a busy cook who likes to freeze food for future meals, or a host with a crowd on hand, this southwestern stew is the answer. Offer bowls of sour cream, chopped white onion, and grated Cheddar cheese, and let your guests garnish as they please. We like to serve sourdough bread or Crackling Corn Bread (page 303) on the side, follow the chili with a plain green salad, and of course serve Mexican beer—try Bohemia, Carta Blanca, or the dark Dos Equis.

½ cup best-quality olive oil
1¾ pounds yellow onions, coarsely chopped
2 pounds sweet Italian sausage meat, removed from its casing
8 pounds beef chuck, ground
1½ tablespoons freshly ground black pepper
2 cans (12 ounces each) tomato paste
3 tablespoons minced garlic
3 ounces ground cumin
4 ounces chili powder
½ cup Dijon mustard
4 tablespoons salt
4 tablespoons dried basil
4 tablespoons dried oregano
6 pounds canned Italian plum tomatoes, drained (about 5 cans, each 2 pounds, 3 ounces)
½ cup Burgundy wine
¼ cup fresh lemon juice
½ cup chopped fresh dill
½ cup chopped fresh Italian (flat-leaf) parsley
3 cans (16 ounces each) dark red kidney beans, drained
4 cans (5½ ounces each) pitted black olives, drained

1. Heat the olive oil in a very large heavy pot. Add the onions and cook over low heat, covered, until tender, about 10 minutes.

2. Crumble the sausage meat and ground chuck into the pot and cook over medium-high heat, stirring often, until the meats are well browned. Spoon out as much excess fat as possible.

3. Turn the heat to medium-low and stir in the black pepper, tomato paste, garlic, cumin, chili powder, mustard, salt, basil, and oregano.

4. Add the drained tomatoes, Burgundy, lemon juice, dill, parsley, and kidney beans. Stir well and simmer, uncovered, for another 20 minutes.

5. Taste and correct the seasoning. Add the olives, simmer for another 5 minutes to heat through, and serve immediately.

35 to 40 portions

SUPER BOWL BUFFET

CHEF'S SALAD

CRUSTY FRENCH BREAD WITH *HERBED BUTTER*

CHILI FOR A CROWD, GARNISHED WITH SOUR CREAM, CHOPPED ONIONS, AND GRATED CHEDDAR CHEESE

PARSLEYED RICE

BROWNIES

CHOCOLATE CHIP COOKIES

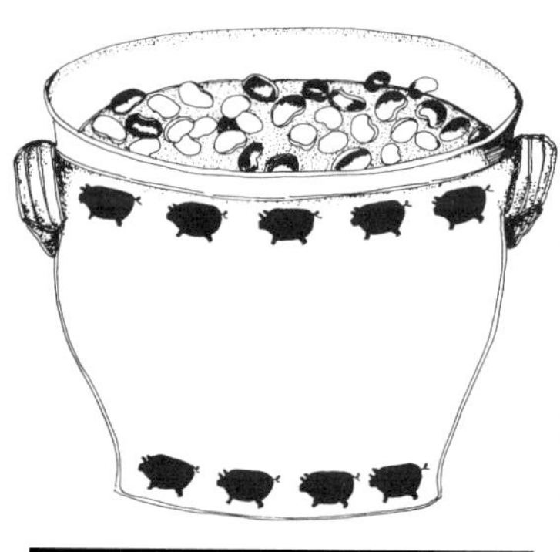

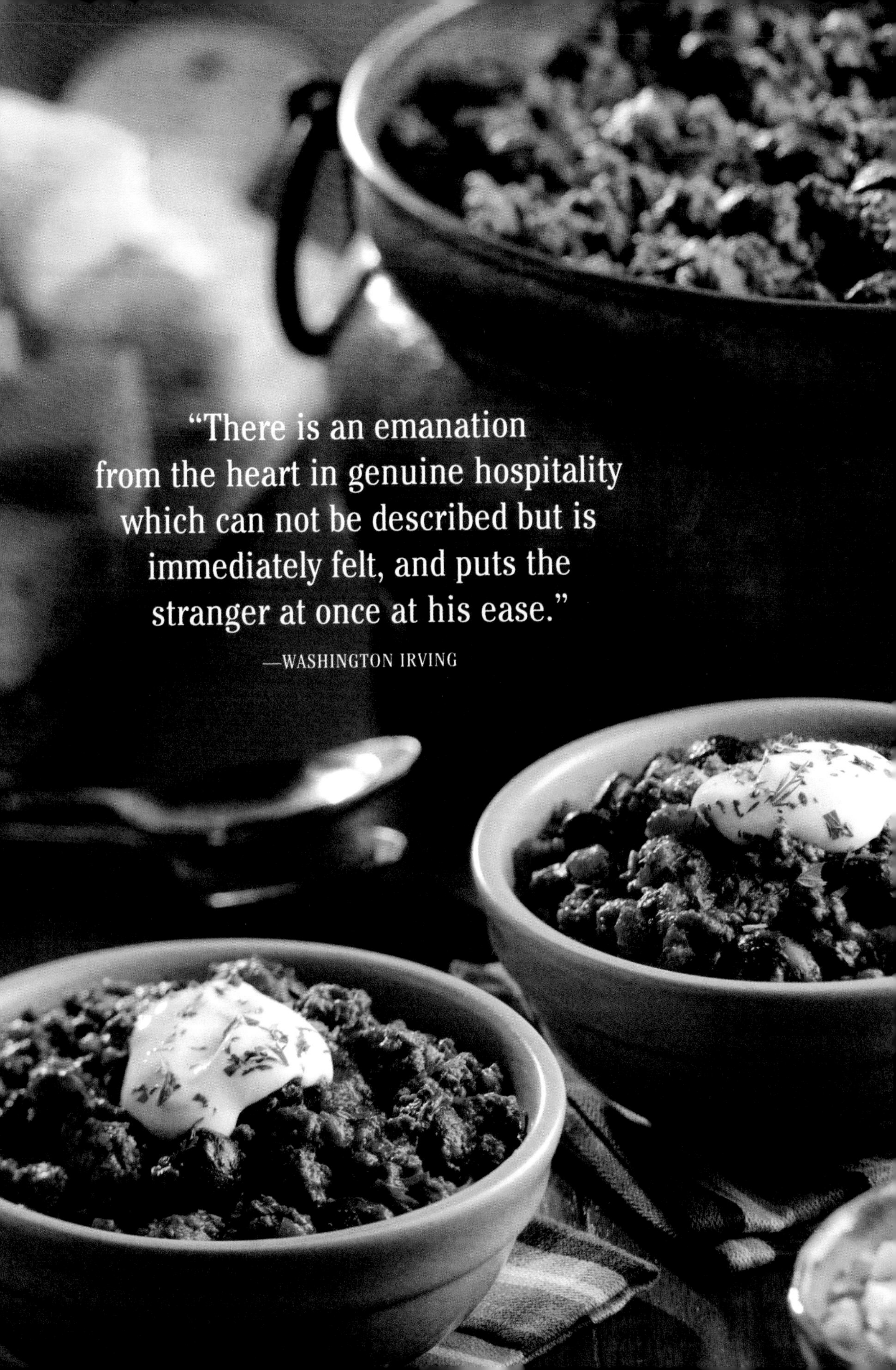
"There is an emanation
from the heart in genuine hospitality
which can not be described but is
immediately felt, and puts the
stranger at once at his ease."
—WASHINGTON IRVING

WINTER PORK AND FRUIT RAGOUT

Serve this delicious casserole with Saffron Rice (page 419), black beans, and a green salad garnished with orange slices.

3 pounds lean boneless pork, in 1-inch cubes
2 dozen dried apricot halves
1 cup dark seedless raisins
1 cup dry red wine
1 cup red wine vinegar
3 tablespoons chopped fresh dill
3 tablespoons chopped fresh mint
1 teaspoon ground cumin
1 teaspoon freshly ground black pepper
1 tablespoon dried thyme
Salt, to taste
⅓ cup best-quality olive oil
4 shallots, peeled and minced
1 cup dry white wine
1 quart Chicken Stock (page 416)
2 bay leaves
¼ cup honey

1. In a large bowl combine the pork, apricots, raisins, red wine, vinegar, dill, mint, cumin, pepper, thyme, and salt. Cover and marinate, refrigerated, for 24 hours. Stir occasionally.

2. Remove the pork and fruit from the marinade. Reserve the fruit in a small bowl. Reserve the marinade separately. Pat the pork dry with paper towels.

3. Heat the olive oil in a large skillet and sauté the meat, a few pieces at a time, until well browned. With a slotted spoon transfer the pork to a deep casserole.

4. Drain the oil from the skillet, add the shallots, and sauté over medium heat for 5 minutes. Add the reserved marinade and bring to a boil, scraping up any browned bits remaining in the skillet. Cook for several minutes, until slightly reduced, and add to the casserole.

5. Preheat the oven to 350°F.

6. Stir in the apricots, raisins, half of the white wine, half of the chicken stock, the bay leaves, and honey; mix well. Set over medium heat, bring to a boil, cover, and set on the center rack of the oven.

7. Bake for 1 hour and 15 minutes. Uncover the casserole, and add additional wine or stock if the meat seems too dry. Bake, uncovered, until the meat is tender and the sauce is rich and thick, another 30 to 45 minutes.

6 to 8 portions

HOLIDAY BUFFET

CHICKEN LIVER PÂTÉ WITH GREEN PEPPERCORNS

TOASTS

WINTER PORK AND FRUIT RAGOÛT

SWEET POTATO AND CARROT PURÉE

WATERCRESS SALAD WITH RASPBERRY VINAIGRETTE

CHESTNUT MOUSSE

LINZERTORTE

Some of these stews could be called classics, but we've made them with lighter sauces and abundant vegetables so that they fit right in with contemporary cooking. Stews are perfect entertaining fare. They have always been part of our repertoire, and are only becoming more popular as time goes by.

BEEF STROGANOFF

Our version of this classic is rich and delicious. Serve it with buttered wide noodles and a simple green vegetable. Garnish the plates with Sautéed Cherry Tomatoes (page 233), and pour a good red wine.

3 cups Crème Fraîche (page 414)
1½ tablespoons Dijon mustard
3 tablespoons tomato paste
3 tablespoons Worcestershire sauce
2 teaspoons imported sweet paprika
¾ teaspoon salt
Freshly ground black pepper, to taste
1 teaspoon demiglace (see Note)
1 pound medium-size firm white mushrooms
10 tablespoons (1¼ sticks) unsalted butter
24 medium-size white pearl onions
3 pounds beef tips (fillet)
Chopped fresh Italian (flat-leaf) parsley, for garnish

1. Combine the crème fraîche, mustard, tomato paste, Worcestershire sauce, paprika, salt, pepper, and demiglace in a medium-size saucepan and simmer slowly until the sauce is slightly reduced, 20 minutes. Remove from the heat and let stand, covered, while completing the recipe.

2. Trim the stem ends off the mushrooms and discard. Wipe the mushrooms with a damp paper towel and slice thin. Melt 3 tablespoons of the butter in a medium-size skillet over medium-low heat. Add the mushrooms and sauté until tender and golden, about 10 minutes. Transfer to a bowl and reserve.

3. Cut a small X in the root end of each pearl onion. Bring a large pot of water to a boil and drop in the onions. Blanch for 10 minutes, drain, and rinse under cold running water. Peel the onions.

4. Melt another 2 tablespoons of the butter in the same skillet over medium heat and sauté the onions, stirring and shaking the skillet often, until they are lightly browned, about 10 minutes. Transfer the onions to the bowl with the mushrooms.

5. Cut the meat into thin slices on the diagonal. Melt the remaining butter in the skillet and sauté the pieces of fillet over high heat until just lightly browned, 3 or 4 minutes. Transfer the pieces to a plate as each batch is browned.

6. To complete, set the crème fraîche sauce over medium heat and bring to a simmer. Add the mushrooms, onions, and any accumulated juices from the bowl, and simmer for 5 minutes.

7. Add the of fillet slices and any accumulated juices and simmer just until the meat is heated through, about 2 minutes. Serve immediately, garnished with the chopped parsley.

6 portions

Note: Available at specialty food shops.

"Good conversation is
as stimulating as black coffee,
and just as hard to sleep after."
—ANNE MORROW LINDBERGH

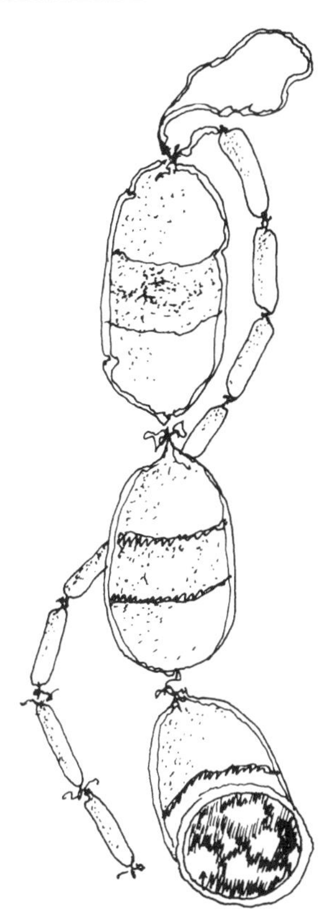

from THE SILVER PALATE NOTEBOOK

Make entertaining and sharing meals a way of life—as natural and sincere as anything else you do. Entertaining need not be fancy or even organized to convey your personal style. Invite a few close friends in for a weekday family dinner. Share a meal, simple and unrushed, around a table with plenty of good conversation and lots of laughter. Most important is that you do it, and often. We find it addictive.

SAUSAGE RAGOUT

Serve this thick, tomato-rich ragoût with buttered pasta or mashed potatoes and follow it with a tart green salad. A hearty red wine—perhaps the one with which you cooked the ragoût—would be the ideal drink.

1½ pounds sweet Italian sausage
1½ pounds hot Italian sausage
¼ cup best-quality olive oil
1 large yellow onion, peeled and coarsely chopped
3 garlic cloves, peeled and minced
2 green bell peppers, stemmed, seeded, and coarsely chopped
2 red bell peppers, stemmed, seeded, and coarsely chopped
8 fresh Italian plum tomatoes, quartered
1 cup Spicy Tomato Sauce (page 419)
½ cup dry red wine
½ cup minced fresh Italian (flat-leaf) parsley, plus additional for garnish
Salt and freshly ground black pepper, to taste

1. Cut the sausages into ½-inch slices. Heat the olive oil in a skillet over medium-low heat and add the sausage pieces. Cook, stirring occasionally, until the sausage pieces are well browned.

2. Add the onion and garlic and cook for another 5 minutes. With a slotted spoon transfer the meat mixture to a deep casserole.

3. Set the casserole over medium heat and add the peppers. Cook, stirring, until the peppers are slightly wilted, about 7 minutes.

4. Add the tomatoes, tomato sauce, wine, and parsley, and season with salt and pepper. Simmer uncovered, stirring occasionally, for 30 minutes.

5. Taste, correct the seasoning, and serve immediately, sprinkled with the chopped parsley.

6 portions

CHOUCROUTE GARNIE

If you are used to thinking of sauerkraut as the obnoxious stuff between the mustard and the hot dog at a baseball game, you have a surprise in store. In this hearty peasant dish, the kraut is rinsed of its salty brine and slowly oven-braised with wine, chicken stock, herbs, and spices. Garnish it with an array of sausages and smoked meats, and serve mashed potatoes with lots of butter, pumpernickel bread, and beer. It is a meal fit for family and company alike.

Although you can use store-bought sausages and kraut, you really must make the chicken stock—it is the secret of the dish's success.

2 pounds sauerkraut (the kind that comes in plastic bags or refrigerated jars; use canned sauerkraut only as a last resort)
½ pound bacon, coarsely diced
1 large yellow onion, peeled and chopped
3 carrots, peeled and sliced
1 tart cooking apple (Newton, Granny Smith, Winesap), cored and grated; do not peel
1 tablespoon caraway seeds (optional)
10 juniper berries
4 parsley sprigs
6 white peppercorns
2 bay leaves
1 cup dry white wine
4 cups Chicken Stock (page 416), plus more if needed
1½ pounds sausage (saucisson, spicy bulk breakfast sausage, bratwurst, knockwurst, and others)
6 smoked pork chops
Chopped fresh Italian (flat-leaf) parsley, for garnish

1. Soak the sauerkraut in a large bowl of cold water for 30 minutes.

2. Meanwhile, fry the bacon in a large skillet over medium heat. When it renders its fat, after about 5 minutes, add the onion and carrots. Raise the heat and cook, stirring occasionally, until the vegetables are about half-cooked and lightly browned. Remove from the heat and reserve.

3. Drain the sauerkraut and squeeze out all the water (be thorough!). Spread the sauerkraut in a nonaluminum roaster or oven-proof casserole with a tight-fitting lid. Stir in the bacon, bacon fat, sautéed vegetables, grated apple, and caraway seeds if you use them.

4. Tie the juniper berries, parsley, peppercorns, and bay leaves in a small cheesecloth bag and bury it in the kraut. Pour in the wine and add enough chicken stock to cover the kraut.

5. Preheat the oven to 325°F.

6. Butter a piece of wax paper (do not use foil) and press it, buttered side down, onto the kraut. Set the roaster over medium heat and bring to a simmer, then cover and set in the oven.

7. Cook the kraut for 5 hours, adding additional stock if the dish seems to be drying out. Refrain from adding stock near the end of the cooking time, since all liquid must be absorbed by the kraut before serving.

8. If you are using bulk sausage, form it into 6 small patties and brown lightly in a skillet over medium heat. If you are using link sausages, prick the skins well with a fork and sauté until lightly browned. Discard the rendered fat in any case.

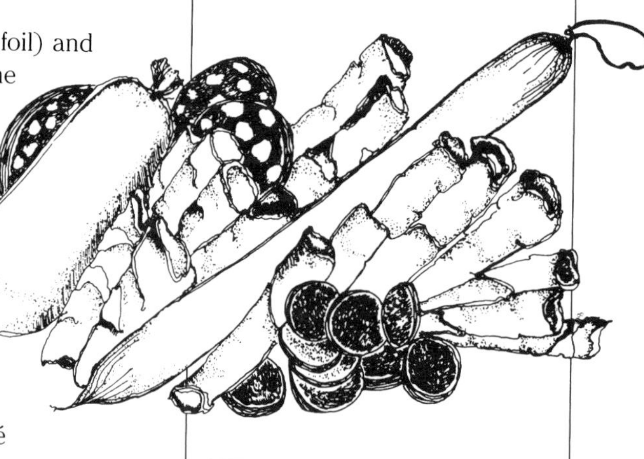

9. About 30 minutes before you estimate the kraut will be done, uncover, lift the wax paper, and distribute the sausages and smoked pork chops over the kraut. Cover and finish cooking. Remove the spice bag and sprinkle with the parsley before serving.

6 portions

DILLED BLANQUETTE DE VEAU

Such a rich but delicate dish should be served with nothing but parsleyed new potatoes. The fresh dill makes all the difference.

SUPPER PARTY MENU

SALMON MOUSSE WITH GREEN HERB DIPPING SAUCE AND RUSSIAN PUMPERNICKEL

DILLED BLANQUETTE DE VEAU

WATERCRESS AND ENDIVE SALAD WITH *WALNUT OIL VINAIGRETTE*

CHOCOLATE MOUSSE WITH CRÈME FRAÎCHE

12 tablespoons (1½ sticks) unsalted butter
3 pounds boneless veal shoulder or shank, in 1-inch cubes
½ cup unbleached all-purpose flour
1 scant teaspoon freshly grated nutmeg, plus additional to taste
1½ teaspoons salt, plus additional to taste
1½ teaspoons freshly ground black pepper, plus additional to taste
3 cups peeled carrots, sliced diagonally (⅛ inch thick)
3 cups coarsely chopped yellow onions
5 tablespoons finely chopped fresh dill
3 to 4 cups Chicken Stock (page 416)
¾ cup heavy cream

1. Preheat the oven to 350°F.

2. Melt 8 tablespoons (1 stick) of the butter in a heavy ovenproof casserole over medium-low heat. Add the veal and cook, turning frequently, without browning.

3. Stir 3 tablespoons flour, the nutmeg, salt, and pepper together in a small bowl, and sprinkle over the veal. Continue to cook over low heat, stirring, for 5 minutes. The flour and veal should not brown.

4. Add the carrots, onions, 3 tablespoons of the dill, and enough stock just to cover the meat and vegetables. Raise the heat to medium, bring to a boil, cover, and bake in the oven for 1½ hours.

5. Remove the stew from the oven and pour it through a strainer placed over a bowl. Reserve the solids and liquid separately.

6. Return the casserole to medium heat and melt the remaining 4 tablespoons of butter in it. Sprinkle in the remaining 5 tablespoons flour and cook over low heat, whisking constantly, for 5 minutes.

7. Whisk the reserved cooking liquid slowly into the butter and flour mixture and bring to a simmer. Cook slowly, stirring constantly, for 5 minutes.

8. Whisk in the cream and the remaining 2 tablespoons dill, and season with salt, pepper, and nutmeg. Return the veal and vegetables to the casserole and simmer together to heat through, about 5 minutes. Transfer to a deep serving dish and serve at once.

6 portions

PIZZA POT PIE

This hearty casserole features typical pizza ingredients—sausages, mushrooms, and tomato sauce—baked together under a tender pizza crust. It is simple and satisfying, and with a green salad makes a complete meal.

2 pounds sweet Italian sausage, in 1-inch pieces
2 pounds hot Italian sausage, in 1-inch pieces
4½ cups Spicy Tomato Sauce (page 419)
2 cups ricotta cheese
½ cup freshly grated Parmigiano-Reggiano cheese
¾ cup chopped fresh Italian (flat-leaf) parsley
2½ tablespoons dried oregano
2 eggs
Freshly ground black pepper, to taste
4 cups grated mozzarella cheese
Pizza Dough for crust (recipe follows), raised once

1. Preheat the oven to 350°F.

2. In a heavy skillet sauté the sausages until brown. Drain well and transfer to a bowl. Stir the tomato sauce into the sausages and reserve.

3. Mix the ricotta, Parmigiano-Reggiano, ½ cup of the parsley, 2 tablespoons of the oregano, 1 egg, and the pepper.

4. In a rectangular ovenproof dish, about 9 x 13 inches, spread half of the sausage mixture. Dot this with half of the ricotta mixture and sprinkle 2 cups of the mozzarella evenly over the entire surface. Sprinkle with half of the remaining parsley and half of the remaining oregano. Repeat.

5. Roll out three quarters of the dough to a thickness of about ⅓ inch, being certain the dough is about 1 inch larger than the baking dish all the way around. Transfer the dough to the top of the pizza and tuck in the excess all around. Beat the remaining egg with 1 tablespoon water and brush some of it on top of the crust.

6. Roll out the remaining dough and cut with cookie cutters to form decorative shapes, if you like. Arrange the shapes on top of the crust, brush again with beaten egg, and bake until the top is golden brown and the edges are bubbling, 35 to 45 minutes.

7. Let the pizza stand for 30 minutes before cutting.

8 or more portions

PIZZA DOUGH

1 package active dry yeast
1 to 1¼ cups lukewarm water (105° to 115°F)
2⅓ cups unbleached all-purpose flour
¾ cup cake flour
⅓ teaspoon freshly ground black pepper
1 teaspoon salt
2 tablespoons olive oil

COOKING WITH HERBS

Our cooking would be very different were it not for herbs! When we began The Silver Palate, it was a great day when our local greengrocer could find fresh tarragon or thyme for us. We'd rejoice at a delivery of fresh cilantro.

Now markets across the country abound with fresh herbs, and farmers' markets offer plants for cooks in the springtime and huge bunches of herbs as they harvest them during the summer. For years we've been lucky enough to have the herb lady delivering a spectrum of lush, fresh herbs to our kitchen door year-round. And to have a good-size herb garden right outside the kitchen door is truly a luxury.

There are very few rules about cooking with herbs other than to get to know each herb intimately—by tasting it—so you know what you like! Some of our tips:

- ♥ Buy small bunches of herbs until you know how much you'll use weekly. You want to use herbs when they're fresh.
- ♥ Always wash and dry herbs until they're bone dry. Then set the stems in a glass of water, cover loosely with a plastic bag, and refrigerate.
- ♥ Scissor snip or tear fresh herbs; don't cut them with a knife or you'll leave a lot of the flavor on the cutting board.
- ♥ Strip the leaves from the thicker stems. Then use the stems for soups and stocks.
- ♥ Don't combine too many different herbs in one dish. We prefer clear and clean flavors.
- ♥ Use herbs for marinades and meat, fish, and poultry rubs.
- ♥ Add herbs as you cook a dish and then again at the end. You'll get cooked-in flavor and a burst of fresh flavor, too.

- ♥ If you're experimenting and are unsure of which herb to use, separate a bit out of your dish, add the herb, cook it separately for a few moments, and taste. Proceed accordingly.
- ♥ Be cautious when buying dried herbs. When exposed to light, air, or heat they lose flavor rapidly, and may become tasteless. A dry-as-dust herb won't do much for your cooking. When in doubt, throw it out.

1. In a small bowl, dissolve the yeast in ½ cup of the lukewarm water and let stand 10 minutes.

2. In a mixing bowl, mix the flours, pepper, and salt together.

3. Add the dissolved yeast to the dry ingredients with the olive oil and ½ cup of the remaining water. Mix with a wooden spoon to form a dough, adding a little more water if needed.

4. Remove the dough from the bowl to a floured pastry board. Knead until the dough is smooth and pliable, 8 to 10 minutes. Flour the board lightly when the dough begins to stick.

5. Wash and dry the mixing bowl, and rub it with olive oil. Place the dough in the bowl and turn it over to coat it thoroughly. Cover the dough with plastic wrap and place in a warm place (75° to 80°F) until doubled in bulk, 2 hours.

6. When the dough has doubled in bulk, punch it down and knead for 15 seconds. Let it rest under a towel for 10 minutes before proceeding with the recipe.

Enough dough for 1 Pizza Pot Pie

NAVARIN OF LAMB

Our *navarin,* made with snow peas, is light and very beautiful.

3 tablespoons best-quality olive oil
1 tablespoon unsalted butter
3 pounds boned lamb, in 1-inch cubes for stew
18 medium-size pearl onions
¾ pound snow peas, trimmed and cleaned
½ cup Cognac
¼ cup sherry vinegar
2 tablespoons potato starch
2 tablespoons red currant jelly
2 tablespoons tomato paste
2 cups rich Beef Stock (page 416)
1 cup dry red wine
1 medium-size yellow onion, thinly sliced
4 large carrots, peeled and cut into 1-inch lengths
5 garlic cloves, peeled and crushed
¼ cup chopped fresh Italian (flat-leaf) parsley
1 teaspoon dried rosemary
1 teaspoon dried thyme
1 teaspoon salt
1 teaspoon freshly ground black pepper
1 bay leaf

1. In a heavy skillet, heat the olive oil and butter over medium heat. Brown the lamb, a few pieces at a time. Transfer with a slotted spoon to a deep ovenproof casserole.

2. Bring 2 quarts of salted water to a boil. Cut a shallow X in the root end of each pearl onion and drop them into the water. Cook until tender but firm, 10 minutes. Drain, transfer to a small bowl, and cover with cold water for 10 minutes. Drain, peel, and reserve.

3. Bring another 2 quarts of salted water to a boil. Drop in the snow peas and cook for 1 minute. Drain and plunge into ice-cold water. Let stand until cool, drain, pat dry, and reserve.

4. When all the lamb is browned, turn off the heat under the skillet. Drain the oil and return all the lamb to the skillet.

5. Preheat the oven to 350°F.

6. Heat the Cognac in a small saucepan. Set the skillet with the lamb away from anything flammable and pour in the Cognac. Ignite the Cognac with a long kitchen match and let it flame until it burns out, about 30 seconds. With a slotted spoon return the meat to the casserole.

7. Add the vinegar, potato starch, currant jelly, tomato paste, beef stock, and red wine to the skillet and stir well. Set over high heat and bring to a boil, stirring constantly, for 5 minutes.

8. Add the sliced onion, carrots, garlic, most of the parsley (reserve a bit for garnish), rosemary, thyme, salt, pepper, and bay leaf to the casserole. Pour the sauce over all, stir well, and cover.

9. Bake for 1½ hours, uncovering the casserole for the last 15 minutes of baking. Toss in the snow peas and pearl onions and serve garnished with the remaining chopped parsley.

6 portions

OSSO BUCO

Serve this meaty veal shank classic with Saffron Rice (page 419) into which you have thrown a handful of peas. Don't forget to savor the bone marrow; it's delicious.

1 cup unbleached all-purpose flour
Salt and freshly ground black pepper, for seasoning and to taste
16 sections of veal shank (10 to 12 pounds total), 2 inches thick
½ cup best-quality olive oil
½ cup (1 stick) unsalted butter
2 medium-size yellow onions, coarsely chopped
6 large garlic cloves, peeled and chopped
½ teaspoon dried basil
½ teaspoon dried oregano
28 ounces canned Italian plum tomatoes, drained
2 cups dry white wine
2 cups Beef Stock (page 416)
¾ cup chopped fresh Italian (flat-leaf) parsley
Grated zest of 2 lemons

1. Season the flour with salt and pepper and dredge the pieces of veal shank well. Heat the oil and butter together in a large casserole or Dutch oven over medium-low heat and sear the veal, browning well on all sides. Transfer the veal to paper towels to drain.

2. Add the onions, garlic, basil, and oregano to the casserole and cook, stirring occasionally, for 10 minutes.

“The art of dining well is no slight art, the pleasure not a slight pleasure.”

—MICHEL DE MONTAIGNE

We like to serve Osso Buco over pea-studded Saffron Rice or risotto.

3. Add the tomatoes and salt and pepper to taste, and cook for another 10 minutes. Skim the excess fat.

4. Add the wine and bring to a boil. Reduce the heat and simmer, uncovered, for 15 minutes.

5. Preheat the oven to 350°F.

6. Return the veal shanks to the casserole and add the beef stock just to cover. Cover the casserole and bake for 1½ hours. Remove the lid and bake, uncovered, until the veal is very tender, another 30 minutes.

7. Sprinkle with the chopped parsley and grated lemon zest and serve immediately.

6 to 8 portions

"A recipe is only a theme, which an intelligent cook can play each time with a variation."

—MADAME JEHANE BENOIT

OXTAIL STEW

Americans are not as fond of oxtail as Europeans are. But if you enjoy a chewy, gelatinous bit of flavorful beef once in a while, this stew is for you. It needs only a light first course (marinated shrimp or raw oysters, for example) and a green salad afterward.

2 oxtails (about 5 pounds total), in 2-inch pieces
¾ cup unbleached all-purpose flour
3 tablespoons best-quality olive oil
3 cups Beef Stock (page 416)
1 cup Burgundy wine
1 cup tomato juice
3 tablespoons tomato paste
2 garlic cloves, minced
1 bay leaf
1 teaspoon dried thyme
½ teaspoon grated nutmeg
1 teaspoon salt
1 teaspoon freshly ground black pepper
2 cups coarsely chopped yellow onions
1 cup diced celery
1 cup carrot rounds, cut ⅛ inch thick
8 medium-size potatoes, cut into thirds
Chopped fresh parsley, for garnish

1. Dredge the oxtails with the flour until thoroughly coated. Shake off the excess.

2. Heat the oil in a heavy Dutch oven over medium-low heat and brown the oxtails well in several batches, setting each batch aside until all are browned; return all the oxtails to the pot.

3. Add the stock, wine, tomato juice, and tomato paste. Stir in the garlic, bay leaf, thyme, nutmeg, salt, and pepper. Add the vegetables, immersing them well in the liquid.

4. Set the Dutch oven over medium heat. Bring to a boil, cover, reduce the heat, and simmer until the oxtails are very tender, 2 hours. Taste and correct the seasoning. Skim the fat from the sauce, garnish with the parsley, and serve immediately.

4 to 6 portions

GREAT
GARDEN
VEGETABLES

"There is no love sincerer than the love of food."

—GEORGE BERNARD SHAW

ARTICHOKES

Artichokes intimidate most, but they hold a dear place in our hearts. They are members of the thistle family and seem armored against our intrusion by their spiky leaves and fuzzy choke. Beyond this barricade, however, is the taste prize—a sweet and tender heart.

The ancient artichoke has been grown in the Mediterranean basin for centuries, another Italian specialty that merged into French gastronomy when Catherine de Medici took it into the court of the French King Henry II. In America, virtually all of the artichokes are grown in Castroville, "The Artichoke Capital of the World," along the coast of California. Artichokes are available year-round, but are at their best in late spring.

Choose only firm, young, and unspotted artichokes. Those with tight leaves and that are heavy in the hand for their size are best. Hold the artichoke close to your ear and rub the leaves together: if the vegetable is fresh, the leaves will squeak. Although some artichokes are huge, the small- to medium-size artichokes have better flavor. Trim off the stem and use kitchen scissors to cut the spiky points off the outside leaves. Rinse under cold water. Cook in boiling salted water until done, 30 to 40 minutes, or until a few test leaves pull out easily. At table, working from the outside in, dip each leaf in lemon butter and savor its meat, slowly working your way to the prize—the heart. Once there, you'll find it's been well worth the quest.

One of our favorite ways to begin an Italian meal: Stuffed Artichokes Fontecchio.

ONE-STEP ARTICHOKES

These artichokes are easy to prepare and add a colorful note as well. Since they're as good cold as hot, plan to make them ahead. We like to take them on picnics with Lemon Chicken (page 110) and Bulgur Wheat Salad (page 262).

6 whole artichokes, trimmed
3 carrots, peeled and finely diced
1 medium-size yellow onion, peeled and finely diced
½ cup olive oil
¼ cup chopped fresh Italian (flat-leaf) parsley
¼ cup fresh lemon juice
1 tablespoon dried oregano
1 tablespoon dried basil
1 teaspoon freshly ground black pepper
½ teaspoon salt

1. Place the artichokes in a deep heavy pot and just cover with water. Add the remaining ingredients (reserve a bit of the parsley for garnish). Cook, partially covered, at a gentle boil until the leaves pull away easily, 40 minutes. Drain the artichokes.

2. Transfer the artichokes to a large serving platter. Strain the cooking liquid and strew the vegetables and herbs over the artichokes. Serve hot, or cool to room temperature.

6 portions

HERB MAYONNAISE

Instead of serving the more traditional Hollandaise Sauce (page 414) with these thistles, try this herb mayonnaise, perfect on cold artichokes served as a summertime first course.

1 cup Homemade Mayonnaise (page 413)
1 cup watercress leaves, rinsed and dried
¼ cup chopped fresh Italian (flat-leaf) parsley
¼ cup snipped fresh chives

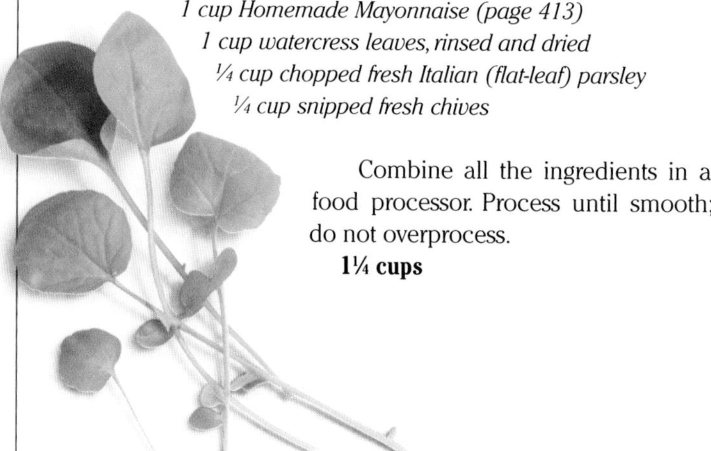

Combine all the ingredients in a food processor. Process until smooth; do not overprocess.

1¼ cups

THE GARDEN'S STORY

Cooking with vegetables is all about cooking with the seasons. Mother Nature has cleverly planned it so that foods from the garden that ripen at the same time inherently taste good together. They are young, light, crunchy, and crisp in the spring; shouting the awakening of the earth, robust, and luscious when filled with summer sunshine's warmth; and deeply rooted when headed for cover in the fall and winter.

Vegetables are playing an ever-increasing role in everyday menus for Americans. No longer just the "color" on the plate, they're often the main event! It is consumers who have made it happen by telling the marketplace just what they wanted: first by actively asking for better quality and being willing to put our money where our mouth is, and second, by making farmers' markets and stands a regular part of the weekly food shopping regimen, singing the praises of organic and local produce, especially those with an heirloom lineage. Today, for the first time since victory gardens in the 1940s, we're finding space to grow a few tomato plants, some lettuces, herbs, radishes, carrots, alpine strawberries, even sweet corn right outside the kitchen door. We've all learned just how fabulous produce that only travels a few feet after picking to table can taste. And, we want it as often as possible.

STUFFING ARTICHOKES

Once artichokes are cooked and the tangle of hairs known as the "choke" is removed, a cavity remains that is a natural container for a wide variety of savory fillings.

For the simplest kind, you can spoon Hollandaise Sauce (page 414) into the cavity. Other stuffing possibilities include Shrimp and Grape Salad with Dill (page 274), Shrimp and Artichoke Salad (minus the artichoke hearts, page 275), and Rice and Vegetable Salad (page 262).

STUFFED ARTICHOKES FONTECCHIO

These meaty stuffed artichokes were a specialty of our Italian chef. They are good hot or cold.

4 large artichokes, trimmed
Juice of 2 lemons
½ cup best-quality olive oil
1 large yellow onion, peeled and finely chopped
4 garlic cloves, peeled and finely chopped
¼ cup finely chopped fresh Italian (flat-leaf) parsley
½ pound sweet Italian sausage, removed from its casing
2 cups unseasoned fine dry bread crumbs
1 cup Chicken Stock (page 416)
½ teaspoon dried oregano
Salt, to taste
½ teaspoon freshly ground black pepper
¼ cup grated Romano cheese
2 eggs
Quick Tomato Sauce (page 418), for serving (optional)
Chopped fresh parsley, for garnish (optional)
Lemon wedges, for garnish (optional)

1. Trim the stems of the artichokes so that they will sit upright. Bring a large pot of salted water to a boil. Add the lemon juice, drop in the artichokes, and cook until a few leaves pull out with only slight resistance, 20 to 30 minutes. (You will cook the artichokes again later in the recipe; do not overcook them now.) Drain the artichokes, invert them, and cool completely.

2. Heat half of the oil in a skillet. Add the onion, garlic, and parsley, and cook over low heat for 15 minutes.

3. Add the sausage and cook for another 15 minutes, stirring to break up lumps, or until the sausage is mostly, but not completely, cooked.

4. Transfer the sausage mixture to a mixing bowl and add the bread crumbs, chicken stock, oregano, salt, black pepper, and Romano cheese. Toss gently and cool to room temperature.

5. Beat the eggs lightly and stir them into the cooled stuffing.

6. Preheat the oven to 350°F.

7. Carefully spread open the cooled and drained artichokes and remove the choke from each with a spoon. Fill the cavities with the stuffing, and force any remaining stuffing down inside the outside leaves. Re-form the artichoke shape as much as possible.

8. Arrange the stuffed artichokes in a shallow baking dish; drizzle them with the remaining olive oil and pour 1 cup of water into the dish. Cover tightly and bake for 40 minutes.

9. Remove the artichokes from the oven and serve hot with tomato sauce; or cool to room temperature and garnish with the chopped parsley and lemon wedges.

4 portions

ASPARAGUS

The spring asparagus hunt can take us to the fields, our gardens, or the market, but it is always a joy. The thrill of sighting the vegetables—tight-tipped, green, violet, white, thick or pencil-thin, tame or wild—heralds the season ahead.

Once found, will our asparagus become soup, pasta sauce, salad, soufflé, or, best of all, nature's most elegant finger food? We rush to enjoy it at its best . . . as quickly after picking as possible. The choices are innumerable but we won't tarry in deliberation. Let the celebration begin!

STRAIGHT TALK ABOUT ASPARAGUS

Much advice is given regarding the cooking of asparagus; most of it can be ignored. This best of all possible vegetables needs only the simplest kind of attention to bring out and preserve its goodness.

Choose thin or thick spears, as you like. They should be firm and green with tightly closed tips. Do not plan on storing uncooked asparagus for more than twenty-four hours. Refrigerate it if you must keep it.

Take each spear by its ends and bend it gently; it will snap approximately at the point where tenderness begins. Reserve the woody stem ends for another use, such as soup, or discard them. Rinse the tip ends under cold running water. If you would like to tie the asparagus into convenient serving-size bundles, do so now, using plain kitchen twine. (Include a few extra spears for testing doneness.)

Bring a large heavy pot of salted water to a full rolling boil. Drop in the asparagus spears or bundles, let the water return to a boil, and cook, uncovered, to the desired doneness. You have some flexibility here as long as you don't overcook the asparagus. Occasionally fish out a spear and bite it (not an unpleasant task) to test if it's ready. This may seem a vague guide, but you'll soon learn that such variables as thickness of stalk make you, and not time, the final judge. If you'll be reheating the asparagus later, you'll want the cooking to stop when it is still fairly crisp; if you're serving it cold with dips, it should be tender but not droopy; if you want to serve it cold in, say, a vinaigrette, it can be quite tender, as long as the spears are not mushy. Have a large bowl of ice water nearby. When the asparagus is perfect, transfer it with tongs to the ice water. This stops the cooking and sets the brilliant green color.

Let stand until thoroughly cool, then drain and pat dry. Cover until ready to use, refrigerating if serving time is several hours off. Asparagus is best eaten the same day as cooked, but will keep for another day, losing only a little of its perfection in your refrigerator.

"Do that in less time than it takes to cook asparagus."

—ROMAN EXPRESSION

When preparing homemade mayonnaise, use the very freshest eggs, and keep them well refrigerated.

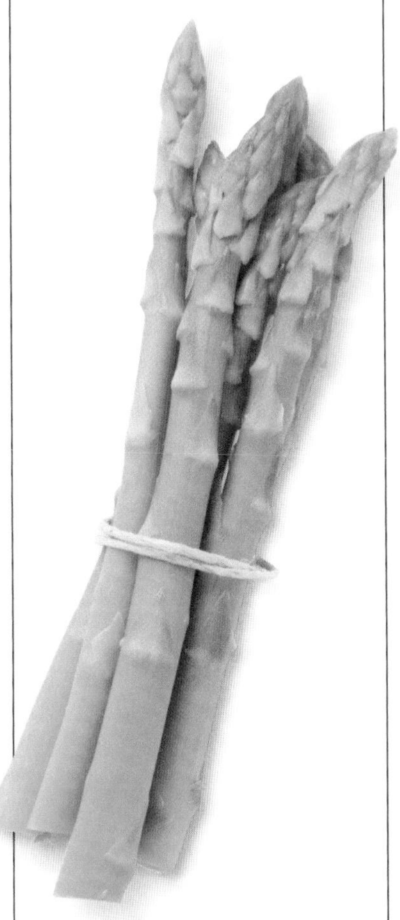

MAYONNAISES FOR ASPARAGUS

Here is a trio of our favorite mayonnaises, light enough not to disguise the wonder of this long vegetable. Arrange asparagus tips for dipping upright in a small basket, as if they had just arrived from the market. As a first course, serve 4 to 6 stalks on a small plate; lightly drizzle 3 to 4 tablespoons of dressing across the center of the asparagus and sprinkle with chopped fresh parsley or another appropriate garnish.

SESAME MAYONNAISE

1 whole egg
2 egg yolks
2½ tablespoons rice vinegar (see Note)
2½ tablespoons soy sauce
3 tablespoons Dijon mustard
¼ cup dark sesame oil (see Note)
2½ cups corn oil
Szechuan-style hot and spicy oil (optional, see Note)
Grated orange zest, for garnish (optional)

1. In a food processor, process the whole egg, egg yolks, vinegar, soy sauce, and mustard for 1 minute.

2. With the motor still running, dribble in the sesame oil and then the corn oil in a slow, steady stream.

3. Season with drops of the hot and spicy oil if you use it, and scrape the mayonnaise out into a bowl. Cover and refrigerate until ready to use.

4. Garnish with the orange zest, if desired, before serving.

About 3½ cups

Note: Available in Asian groceries and other specialty food shops.

MAYONNAISE NICOISE

1 cup Homemade Mayonnaise (page 413)
1 tablespoon capers, drained, plus additional to taste
1 tablespoon tomato paste
1 tablespoon anchovy paste
1 garlic clove, peeled and minced
Large pinch of dried oregano

1. Combine all the ingredients in a food processor.

2. Process until smooth, then stir in additional capers to taste.

1¼ cups

GREEN HERB DIPPING SAUCE

½ bunch of fresh Italian (flat-leaf) parsley
½ bunch of fresh dill
½ bunch of watercress
¼ cup drained, cooked fresh spinach, all liquid squeezed out
2 scallions (green onions), tender greens included, well rinsed and sliced thin
2 cups Homemade Mayonnaise (page 413)
1 cup sour cream
Salt and freshly ground black pepper, to taste

1. Place the parsley, dill, and watercress in a food processor. Chop fine and transfer to a bowl.

2. Process the spinach in the same way and add to the herb mixture.

3. Combine the herbs with the scallions, mayonnaise, and sour cream, folding together gently. Season with salt and pepper. Refrigerate until ready to use.

4 cups

"We must cultivate our garden."

—VOLTAIRE

VINAIGRETTES FOR ASPARAGUS

BLUEBERRY VINAIGRETTE

⅓ cup olive oil
½ cup blueberry vinegar with blueberries (page 145)
¾ teaspoon salt
¾ teaspoon freshly ground black pepper
1-inch piece of cinnamon stick
¼ cup fresh blueberries, or unsweetened frozen, thawed

Combine all the ingredients in a jar. Shake well. Make at least 1 hour before using. Shake again before serving.

1 cup

OUR FAVORITE VINAIGRETTE

1 tablespoon Dijon mustard
¼ cup red wine vinegar
1 teaspoon sugar
½ teaspoon salt
½ teaspoon freshly ground black pepper
Minced fresh parsley and/or snipped fresh chives, to taste
½ cup olive oil

LEMON BUTTER

For a light and piquant accompaniment to steamed or boiled fresh, green vegetables, melt 8 tablespoons (1 stick) unsalted butter with the juice of 2 lemons and 2 tablespoons freshly chopped Italian (flat-leaf) parsley.

AN ASPARAGUS MENU

ASPARAGUS WITH *SESAME MAYONNAISE*

ASPARAGUS WITH *ASPARAGUS SAUCE*

ASPARAGUS STRUDEL WITH TOMATO COULIS

ASPARAGUS-PARMESAN SOUFFLÉ

CHOCOLATE MOUSSE

DEVON CREAM

FRESH STRAWBERRIES

Asparagus makes a natural, edible paintbrush. Serve tender spears alongside your soft-cooked breakfast egg. Dunk the asparagus into the yolk, stir, eat. Repeat until happy.

1. Measure the mustard into a bowl. Whisk in the vinegar, sugar, salt, pepper, and herbs.

2. Continue to whisk the mixture while slowly dribbling in the olive oil until the mixture thickens. Adjust the seasoning to taste. Cover until ready to use. (Vinaigrette is best if made just before it is to be used.) If necessary, whisk again before serving.

1 cup

ASPARAGUS SAUCE

12 asparagus spears, trimmed
1½ tablespoons unsalted butter
4 scallions (green onions), white and green parts, well rinsed and chopped
Salt and freshly ground black pepper, to taste
Pinch of sugar
2 tablespoons heavy cream

1. Cut the asparagus into 1-inch pieces. Parboil in a pot of boiling salted water until just tender, about 8 minutes. Drain

2. Melt the butter in a skillet over low heat. Add the asparagus and chopped scallions, seasoning with salt, pepper, and sugar. Cook, stirring, over medium heat until the scallions are tender, about 5 minutes.

3. Purée the mixture in a food processor or push through a food mill fitted with a fine disc. Place the purée in a saucepan, add the cream, mix well, and keep warm until needed.

4 portions

ASPARAGUS WITH PROSCIUTTO

4 ounces whipped cream cheese
¼ teaspoon finely minced garlic
Pinch of salt
Pinch of freshly ground black pepper
12 thin slices of prosciutto, cut crosswise into halves
24 asparagus spears, cut to 4 inches, lightly cooked

1. Preheat the oven to 350°F.

2. Combine the whipped cream cheese with the garlic, salt, and pepper.

3. Spread each half slice of prosciutto with some of the cheese mixture and roll around an asparagus spear. Arrange on a baking sheet.

4. Heat in the oven until heated through, 3 to 4 minutes. Serve immediately.

6 to 8 portions

ASPARAGUS STRUDEL

¼ pound asparagus, trimmed and cut into 1-inch lengths
2 medium-size leeks, white parts only, rinsed well and thinly sliced
1 tablespoon chopped shallot
1 cup plus 4 tablespoons (2½ sticks) unsalted butter, melted
½ pound Gruyère cheese, grated
2 ounces sliced almonds, toasted
3 eggs, beaten
2 tablespoons chopped fresh mint
2 tablespoons chopped fresh Italian (flat-leaf) parsley
¼ cup chopped fresh dill
2 tablespoons snipped fresh chives
1 teaspoon salt
½ teaspoon freshly ground black pepper
½ teaspoon paprika
Dash of cayenne pepper
2 tablespoons fresh lemon juice
12 leaves of packaged phyllo pastry, thawed if necessary

1. Blanch the asparagus in a large pot of boiling water for 3 minutes. Drain and pat dry. Place in a bowl.

2. Sauté the leeks with the shallot in 4 tablespoons of the butter until transparent. Add to the bowl of asparagus.

"The right food always comes at the right time. Reliance on an out-of-season food makes the gastronomic year an endless boring repetition."

—ROY ANDRIES DE GROOT

3. Add all the other ingredients to the bowl except the remaining melted butter and phyllo. Toss together.

4. Preheat the oven to 350°F.

5. Butter a large cookie sheet with melted butter. Lay 1 leaf of phyllo on a work surface (cover the remaining phyllo with a damp cloth) and quickly brush with melted butter. Repeat until you have 6 layers.

6. Place half of the asparagus mixture along one short end and roll up jelly-roll fashion, tucking the ends in as you go. Place on the cookie sheet. Proceed to make the second strudel with the remaining phyllo, butter, and filling and place it on the cookie sheet, leaving ample space between the rolls. Brush the tops of the rolls with any remaining butter.

7. Bake until golden, 40 to 45 minutes. Cool slightly and slice into 2-inch pieces.

8. Serve as a first course with fresh Tomato Coulis (page 232).

8 portions

CREAM OF ASPARAGUS SOUP

The food mill is really essential for this recipe. A food processor won't adequately purée the asparagus fibers, and forcing the soup through a sieve will take hours. If you don't have a food mill, an inexpensive and incredibly handy little gadget, consider investing in one.

Our favorite asparagus soup, tasting purely and simply of asparagus and nothing else. This recipe is a good way to use the thick and woody asparagus that appears late in the season. The soup is fabulous cold, but it's also pretty wonderful hot: play your cards right and you can have it both ways; the recipe makes a generous 2½ quarts.

8 tablespoons (1 stick) unsalted butter
4 cups chopped yellow onions (about 4 large onions)
2 quarts Chicken Stock (page 416), thoroughly defatted
2 pounds asparagus
Salt and freshly ground black pepper, to taste
½ cup heavy cream or buttermilk (for cold soup)

1. Melt the butter in a large pot over low heat and simmer the onions until very soft and golden, stirring often, about 25 minutes.

2. Add the chicken stock and bring to a boil.

3. Meanwhile, trim the tips from the asparagus and reserve. Cut about 1 inch from the butt ends of the asparagus spears; don't try to remove all of the tough parts, just the very woody ends. Chop the spears into ½-inch pieces and drop into the boiling chicken stock, cover, reduce the heat, and simmer until the asparagus is very soft, 45 minutes.

4. Force the soup, broth and all, through the medium disc of a food mill. Return the purée to the pot, add the reserved asparagus tips, and simmer until they are tender but still firm, 5 to 10 minutes. If serving the soup hot, season with salt and pepper and serve.

5. If serving the soup cold, remove from the heat, cool, stir in the cream or buttermilk, and refrigerate, covered. Season with salt and pepper. Serve very cold.

8 to 10 portions

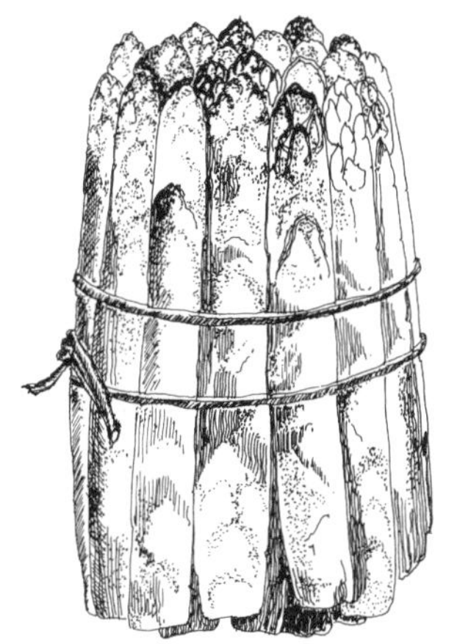

CRISPLY ROASTED ASPARAGUS WITH GREMOLATA

GREMOLATA
2 tablespoons chopped fresh Italian (flat-leaf) parsley
Finely grated zest of 1 large lemon
2 teaspoons finely minced garlic

ASPARAGUS
1 pound medium-size asparagus, woody ends removed
2 tablespoons extra-virgin olive oil
Coarse salt and freshly ground black pepper, to taste
2 lemons, halved crosswise, for garnish

1. To prepare the gremolata: Combine all the ingredients in a small bowl with a fork. Cover and set aside. (Makes ¼ cup.)

2. Preheat the oven to 400°F.

3. Place the asparagus in a roasting pan in a single layer, facing the same direction. Toss with the olive oil and season with salt and pepper. Cover with aluminum foil and bake on the center rack of the oven for 10 minutes. Remove the foil and bake for 10 minutes longer. Remove to a serving dish and sprinkle with the gremolata. Serve with the lemon halves.

4 portions

As good as asparagus is cold, it is equally delicious hot. Asparagus cloaked in a lemony Hollandaise Sauce (page 414) is a pairing made in heaven. Asparagus in butter, with or without a shower of your favorite chopped herb over all, is simple perfection. Other partnerships are equally successful.

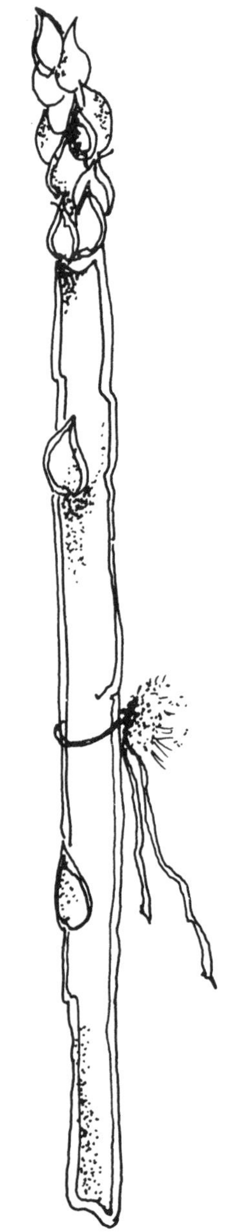

ASPARAGUS-PARMESAN SOUFFLE

2 cups 1-inch pieces of asparagus tips and tender stems
4 tablespoons (½ stick) unsalted butter
½ cup finely chopped yellow onion
1 cup milk
3 tablespoons unbleached all-purpose flour
4 egg yolks
⅔ cup freshly grated Parmigiano-Reggiano cheese
Salt and freshly ground black pepper, to taste
Grated nutmeg, to taste
5 egg whites
Cream of tartar or fresh lemon juice

1. Preheat the oven to 425°F.

2. Bring a large heavy pot of salted water to a boil, drop in the pieces of asparagus, and cook until tender but not mushy, about 10 minutes. Drain and plunge into ice water. When cool, drain then purée in a food processor.

ASPARAGUS AND EGGS

An early Spring morning asparagus hunt. Success with a generous basketful of thin spears, a dozen eggs, from the coop or the fridge. Why wait for dinner when you can savor asparagus for breakfast, too?

AN ASPARAGUS OMELET

Simple things like eggs and butter emphasize the simple goodness of asparagus. Cook the asparagus lightly, warm it in plenty of butter, and arrange across a plain omelet before folding.

ASPARAGUS AND EGG SALAD

Asparagus and eggs again, this time a glorified version of an old favorite, egg salad. Lots of eggs, lots of good mayonnaise, onion if you like, and an indispensable touch of mustard. Stir in tender asparagus tips, or strew them with a lavish hand over the completed salad. Dill—lots of it—is a welcome addition.

POACHED EGGS ON ASPARAGUS

For a perfect breakfast or brunch place 2 poached eggs on top of 6 blanched asparagus spears for each helping. Cover with Hollandaise Sauce (page 414) and serve. If you can catch a brook trout and sauté it, you have the ultimate dish!

3. Melt the butter in a heavy saucepan over low heat, and sauté the onion, partially covered, until tender and lightly colored, about 25 minutes. In a second saucepan, bring the milk to a boil.

4. Sprinkle the flour over the onion and butter and, stirring constantly, cook gently for 5 minutes.

5. Shut off the heat and pour in the boiling milk all at once. Beat vigorously with a whisk as the mixture bubbles, and then set the pan over medium heat. Bring the sauce to a boil, stirring constantly, and let it boil for 3 minutes.

6. Remove from the heat. Stir in the egg yolks, one at a time. Then stir in the asparagus purée, ⅓ cup of the Parmigiano-Reggiano, and salt, pepper, and nutmeg. Taste and correct the seasoning. Butter a 1-quart soufflé dish and sprinkle with the remaining cheese. Shake out the excess cheese and reserve it.

7. Beat the egg whites until foamy. Add a pinch of salt and either a pinch of cream of tartar or a few drops of lemon juice and continue to beat until the whites form stiff peaks.

8. Scoop out about a third of the whites and stir them thoroughly into the asparagus-egg mixture. Scrape the remaining beaten whites onto the asparagus mixture and fold in just until incorporated; don't overmix.

9. Pour the soufflé mixture into the prepared dish and rap the dish on a work surface to eliminate any air bubbles. Sprinkle the top with the reserved cheese. Set on the center rack of the oven; reduce the heat to 375°F.

10. Bake for 20 minutes without opening the oven door, then check the soufflé. It should be browning nicely and should have risen 2 inches above the rim of the dish. Let it bake for another 15 or even 20 minutes if you like a very well-done soufflé. Serve immediately.

4 or 5 portions as a first course, 3 portions as a main course

ASPARAGUS EN CROUTE

12 slices of good-quality white sandwich bread
½ pound Jarlsberg or other Swiss cheese
½ cup Dijon mustard
12 asparagus spears, cooked
Approximately 4 tablespoons (½ stick) unsalted butter, melted

1. Preheat the oven to 450°F. Butter a baking sheet.

2. Roll the slices of bread as thin as possible with a rolling pin; trim the crusts. You will have pieces of bread 3 to 3½ inches square.

3. Lay the squares out on a work surface and cover with a damp towel for 10 minutes.

4. Cut the cheese into fingers, more or less the size of the asparagus spears.

5. Spread each bread square evenly with the mustard. Lay an asparagus spear and a strip of cheese on each bread square and roll up. Place, seam side down, on the prepared baking sheet.

6. Brush the rolls with melted butter. Bake in the upper third of the oven until brown, 10 minutes. Serve immediately.

12 rolls, 4 to 6 portions

BEANS

Beans and their leguminous kin, like others of the world's staple foods, are social climbers, their presence on elegant menus and in important kitchens belying their simple origins. Now we are enjoying a renaissance of flavorful heirloom varieties, and cooking them in new and interesting ways. Beans are available, affordable, and high in valuable proteins. In short, the possibilities are limited only if you underestimate the humble bean.

DRIED BEANS AND PEAS

Buy dried beans from a packer whose name you know and trust, or seek out a store that offers its beans loose in bulk. Rinse them in a strainer under cold running water and sort through the beans to remove any pebbles or other foreign matter you may find. Depending on the recipe, the beans may need to be soaked overnight. After they are rinsed, transfer them to a bowl and add enough cold water to cover the beans by at least 3 inches; most dried beans will absorb this much water overnight.

BLACK-EYED PEAS: Small oval legumes (not a true bean), with a black or yellow spot; a favorite in the South.

BLACK (OR BLACK TURTLE) BEANS: Small, mild-flavored, black-skinned; used in Mexican and South American cuisines.

CANNELLINI: Also called white kidney beans; used in salads and soups, particularly in Italy, and are often puréed.

CRANBERRY BEANS: Small oval beans with pink markings; featured in New England cooking —remember succotash?

FAVA BEANS: Known also as broad beans; large, brown, shaped a bit like limas.

FLAGEOLETS: Small, oval, delicately flavored green beans; when found these should be treasured.

GARBANZOS: Also called chickpeas; can be cream-colored or brownish, with a nutlike flavor, round and firm-textured; often used in East Indian, Latin American, and Middle Eastern cuisines.

KIDNEY BEANS: Oval pink or dark-red beans; great in soups, stews, and chilies.

LENTILS: Small, round, and flat legumes—one of our favorites for casseroles and salads; usually greenish tan, brown, or reddish orange.

LIMA BEANS: Mild-flavored, these flat round beans, often called butter beans, are used in soups or in combinations with pork.

PINK BEANS: Small, brownish-red beans; often replace cranberry or pinto beans.

PINTO BEANS: Pale pink and speckled with brown; great in western and Mexican cooking.

RED BEANS: Smaller than kidney, pinto, or pink beans, these are often used in Asian cookery.

SOYBEANS: Small, pea-shaped, and light tan; an Asian staple, used in the East for centuries, and now favorites in the West.

SPLIT PEAS: Both green and yellow; soup standbys.

WHITE BEANS: Beans of varying sizes, delicately flavored; they include Great Northerns, white kidney (cannellini) and marrow beans, and navy beans and white pea beans, both of Boston fame.

COOKING FRESH GREEN BEANS

Buy about ¼ pound beans per person. Snap off the tips of the beans and pull away any strings. (It seems to us that fewer and fewer string beans actually have strings; that feature has been largely bred out. Always check a few, just to make sure, since the strings make for unpleasant eating.)

Bring a large pot of water, to which you have added some salt to taste, to a full rolling boil. Drop in all the beans at once, taking care to leave the heat at its highest since you want the water to return to the boil as quickly as possible. Do not cover the pot. Stir the beans occasionally so they'll cook evenly. The beans may be done in as few as 5 minutes or may take as long as 15. Keep testing until the desired "crunch" is obtained. (Note: Green beans *should* have a crunchy texture; a silent bean is an overcooked bean.)

Have ready a large bowl of ice water. When the beans are cooked to taste, drain them and toss them immediately into the ice water. This will stop the cooking process and set the bright green color. Let the beans stand in the water until completely cool. Drain them and pat dry. Refrigerate the beans, covered, until they are used for crudités or tossed with vinaigrette or rewarmed in butter.

"What is paradise? but a garden, an orchard of trees and herbs, full of pleasure and nothing there but delights."

—WILLIAM LAWSON, 1687

GREEN BEANS WITH TOMATOES

This dish, in which the raw beans are sautéed, calls for the thinnest and tenderest green beans you can find. It is bright, fresh, and crisp, and can be eaten hot or at room temperature.

⅓ cup olive oil
1½ pounds green beans
2 garlic cloves, peeled and chopped
1 medium-size yellow onion, peeled and cut into thin rings
4 small ripe tomatoes, about 1 pound, peeled, seeded, and roughly chopped
¼ cup chopped fresh Italian (flat-leaf) parsley
4½ tablespoons red wine vinegar
1½ teaspoons dried oregano
½ teaspoon salt
½ teaspoon freshly ground black pepper

1. Heat the olive oil in a heavy skillet over medium-low heat, add the beans, and cook, stirring and tossing constantly, until the beans are about half-cooked and become bright green.

2. Reduce the heat and add the garlic and onion. Cook, stirring, for 1 minute.

3. Add the tomatoes, parsley, vinegar, oregano, salt, and pepper, and continue to cook, tossing occasionally, until the sauce is slightly reduced, about another 5 minutes. Serve immediately, or cool and serve at room temperature.

4 to 6 portions

AUTUMN DUCK SALAD WITH GREEN BEANS

This main-course salad is a beauty any time of the year.

2 ducks (4½ to 5 pounds each), defrosted or fresh
Salt
2 cups fresh orange juice
½ cup sugar
½ pound fresh cranberries (about 2 cups)
1½ pounds green beans, trimmed and blanched
1 cup shelled pecans
4 or 5 fresh clementines or tangerines, peeled and sectioned, or 1 cup canned mandarin orange sections, drained
Raspberry Vinaigrette (page 282)
3 scallions (green onions), well rinsed and thinly sliced

1. Reserve the duck giblets for another use. Trim away the wing tips and remove all the fat from the duck cavities. Salt the ducks inside and out and place, breast side up, in a shallow baking dish just large enough to hold them comfortably. Let the ducks come to room temperature, about 45 minutes.

2. Preheat the oven to 450°F.

3. Set the ducks on the center rack of the oven and roast for 15 minutes. Reduce the heat to 375°F and continue to roast, draining the accumulated fat frequently. The ducks will be medium rare after another 20 to 30 minutes, well done after another 35 to 40 minutes.

4. Cool the ducks. Skin them and remove each breast half in one piece. (Save the legs and thighs for the chef's lunch.) Using a thin, very sharp knife, slice the breast meat into long thin pieces. Reserve.

5. Stir together the orange juice, sugar, and cranberries. Set over medium heat and bring to a boil, skimming any foam that accumulates. Remove from the heat as soon as the first berries burst, and let the berries cool in the juice. Drain and reserve the berries. Reserve the cooking syrup for another use (see Note).

6. Divide the duck strips and green beans equally among 6 plates.

7. Combine the cranberries, pecans, and orange sections, and divide equally among the 6 plates.

8. Drizzle the salad with raspberry vinaigrette to taste and sprinkle sliced scallions over all. Serve immediately.

6 portions

Note: The cooking syrup from Step 5 can be frozen into a delightful sorbet.

FRESH BEANS AND PEAS

BEANS:

Black Beluga Beans
Bush Beans
Calypso Beans
Cannellini Beans
Chinese Longbeans
Cranberry Beans
Edamame
French Duet Beans
Great Northern Beans
Haricots Verts
Green Fillet Beans
Ivory White Beans
Lima Beans
Marrow Beans
Mung Beans
Pigeon Beans
Pole Beans
Purple Beans
Rattlesnake Beans
Romano Beans
Runner Beans
Sea Beans
Soy Beans
Spanish Musica Beans
Trout Beans
Wax Beans
White Runner Beans

PEAS:

English Peas
Pea Shoots
Snow Peas
Sugar Snap Peas

BUTTERED GREEN BEANS WITH CASHEWS

The green bean gets a little dressed up for company.

1½ pounds green beans
3 tablespoons unsalted butter, melted
¾ teaspoon salt
½ teaspoon freshly ground black pepper
¼ cup finely chopped fresh parsley
1 cup cashews

1. Blanch the green beans in boiling salted water.

2. While the beans are cooking, melt the butter over low heat and add the salt, pepper, and parsley. Stir to mix.

3. Drain the beans and place in a warm bowl. Sprinkle the cashews on top and then pour the butter mixture over the beans. Toss well. Arrange in a serving dish and serve immediately.

6 portions

Variation: This recipe can be made with pecans, almonds, hazelnuts, pine nuts, or any other favorite nut.

BLACK BEAN SOUP

1 cup olive oil
3 cups diced yellow onions
8 garlic cloves, peeled and crushed
2 pounds black beans, soaked in water overnight
1 meaty ham bone or smoked ham hock
6 quarts water
2 tablespoons plus 1 teaspoon ground cumin
1 tablespoon dried oregano
3 bay leaves
1 tablespoon salt
2 teaspoons freshly ground black pepper
Pinch of cayenne pepper
6 tablespoons chopped fresh Italian (flat-leaf) parsley
1 medium-size red bell pepper, stemmed, seeded, and diced
¼ cup dry sherry
1 tablespoon brown sugar
1 tablespoon fresh lemon juice
1 to 2 cups Crème Fraîche (page 414) or sour cream

from THE SILVER PALATE NOTEBOOK

The dramatic balance you strike between color, texture, flavor, and temperature says much about your style. Make these elements important to the hour, the setting, and the guests.

Strive to make food picture perfect. The effort—and it takes planning, thought, and judgment—is worth it.

"There are terrible temptations that it requires strength, strength and courage to yield to."

—OSCAR WILDE

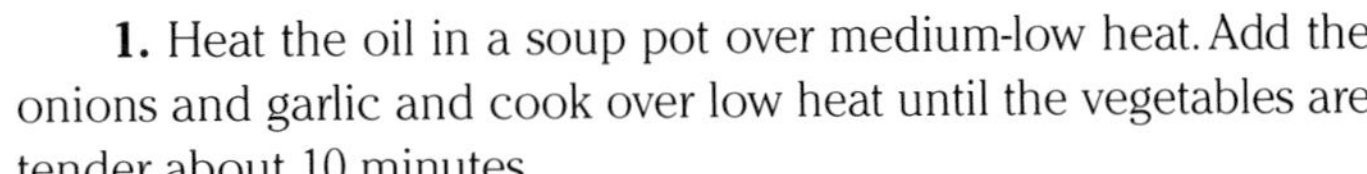

1. Heat the oil in a soup pot over medium-low heat. Add the onions and garlic and cook over low heat until the vegetables are tender, about 10 minutes.

2. Drain the beans and add them, the ham bone or ham hock, and the 6 quarts of water to the pot. Stir in the 2 tablespoons of cumin, the oregano, bay leaves, salt, pepper, cayenne, and 2 tablespoons of the parsley. Bring to a boil, reduce the heat, and cook, uncovered, until the beans are very tender and the liquid is reduced by about three quarters. This will take 1½ to 2 hours.

3. Transfer the ham bone or hock to a plate and cool slightly. Pull off any remaining meat with your fingers and shred finely. Return the meat to the pot.

4. Stir in the remaining parsley, bell pepper, the remaining teaspoon cumin, the sherry, brown sugar, and lemon juice. Simmer for another 30 minutes, stirring frequently. Taste, correct the seasoning, and serve very hot, garnished with a dollop of crème fraîche.

10 to 12 small portions

LENTIL SOUP

¼ pound slab bacon
2 cups finely chopped yellow onions
2 carrots, peeled and finely chopped
3 large garlic cloves, peeled and chopped
7 cups Chicken Stock (page 416) or Beef Stock (page 416)
1 teaspoon dried thyme
¼ teaspoon celery seeds
2 bay leaves
Freshly ground black pepper, to taste
1½ cups brown lentils
Salt, to taste

1. Finely cube the bacon and sauté in a soup pot over medium heat until crisp. Remove the bacon with a slotted spoon and reserve.

2. Add the onions, carrots, and garlic and sauté in the bacon fat over low heat, covered, until tender and golden, about 25 minutes.

3. Add the chicken or beef stock, thyme, celery seeds, bay leaves, a grinding of fresh pepper, and the lentils. Bring to a boil, reduce the heat, and cover. Simmer until the lentils are very tender, about 40 minutes.

4. Discard the bay leaves and purée half of the soup in a food processor or a food mill fitted with a medium disc. Return the puréed soup to the pot.

5. Taste and correct the seasoning, adding salt if necessary. Stir in the reserved crisp bacon and simmer briefly before serving.

6 to 8 portions

THE FRENCH BEAN POT

Cassoulet, like other hearty dishes that come to mind, is peasant fare. It is a specialty of the Languedoc, the southwestern region of France between Spain and Provence. Three towns—Toulouse, Castelnaudary, and Carcassonne—claim to make *le vrai cassoulet* (the true cassoulet). The battle over authenticity can grow very heated, indeed, and to the combatants the distinctions are vast. For our purposes, suffice it to say that cassoulet is a dish of white beans and meats, long simmered together, as rich and fragrant a pot of baked beans as you're ever likely to eat.

To get a taste of the real thing, we suggest some pork, a little lamb, garlic sausages, and, in place of the traditional preserved goose, a duck. Our version is slightly streamlined, but nevertheless authentic. Cassoulet is neither quick nor inexpensive to prepare, but it need not intimidate. The various cooking steps can be spread over 3 or 4 days. Serve it as the centerpiece of an important buffet (it always impresses), or offer it to a group of close, food-loving friends as a hearty midwinter lunch to be followed by a nap. (A story is told of a sign in the door of a shop: "Closed on account of a cassoulet.")

Serve a dry wine—a full-bodied red, white, or even a rosé. Afterward, you'll want to serve a good *digestif,* such as an Armagnac from the neighboring region of Gascony, or a fiery Calvados. And after that, of course, the nap.

CASSOULET

½ pound fresh pork rind
2 pounds dried white beans (Great Northern, or try half Great Northern, half dried flageolets), soaked overnight
1 duckling (4½ to 5 pounds) with neck and giblets
Salt and freshly ground black pepper, to taste
1 pound (more or less) lamb bones
2¼ pounds lamb stew meat, in 1-inch cubes
2 pounds boneless pork shoulder, in 1-inch cubes
1½ tablespoons dried thyme
1 teaspoon ground allspice
1 or 2 tablespoons olive oil, if needed
⅓ cup rendered bacon fat
2 cups chopped yellow onions
3 large carrots, peeled and chopped
2 cups dry white vermouth
6 ounces tomato paste
5 cups Beef Stock (page 416) or canned beef broth
9 large garlic cloves, peeled
5 bay leaves
1½ pounds fresh garlic sausage or kielbasa
1 pound salt pork
4 cups unseasoned dry bread crumbs
1 cup chopped fresh Italian (flat-leaf) parsley

1. Score the fat side of the pork rind, cover it with cold water in a small saucepan, bring to a boil, and simmer for 10 minutes. Drain, cover with cold water again, and repeat the process, this time simmering for 30 minutes. Reserve the pork rind and its second cooking water separately.

2. Preheat the oven to 450°F.

3. Drain the beans and place them in an 8-quart ovenproof pot with a lid. Cover them with water by at least 3 inches and bring to a boil. Reduce the heat and cook briskly, uncovered, for 15 minutes. Remove the pot from the heat and let the beans stand in the cooking liquid.

4. Cut the wing tips off the duck and set them aside, along with the neck, heart, and gizzard. (Save the liver for another use.) Pull all the fat out of the duck, and season the cavity with salt and pepper. Put the duck in a small roasting pan. Put the lamb bones in a second small pan and roast, along with the duck, in the oven for 45 minutes. Drain the accumulated fat frequently. Remove from the oven after the cooking time; the duck should still be slightly underdone; the lamb bones should be well browned; reserve the lamb bones. Drain the juices from the duck cavity into a large bowl and reserve. Cool, cover, and refrigerate the duck.

5. In a heavy skillet, brown the cubed lamb in olive oil in batches over medium heat, seasoning to taste with salt and pepper. Do not crowd the pan. Remove the browned lamb to a large bowl and reserve.

6. Without cleaning the skillet, sauté the pork cubes and the reserved duck giblets, neck, and wing tips in the same fashion, seasoning with salt, pepper, 1 teaspoon of the thyme, and the allspice. You may need to add a tablespoon or two of olive oil if the skillet is particularly dry at this point. Place the browned pork in the same bowl with the lamb. Drain and reserve the meat juices; cover and refrigerate the meat. Add the giblets and wing tips to the beans.

7. Do not clean the skillet. Melt the rendered bacon fat in the skillet over low heat and sauté the onions and carrots, stirring, until tender, about 20 minutes. Add to the pot with the beans.

8. Add the vermouth, along with the duck, lamb, and pork juices, to the skillet. Bring to a boil. Lower the heat slightly and cook briskly, stirring, until the vermouth is slightly reduced and all browned cooking particles remaining in the skillet have dissolved. Pour the vermouth onto the beans.

9. Preheat the oven to 350°F.

10. Stir in the tomato paste, the pork rind cooking liquid, beef stock, remaining thyme, the bay leaves, and the reserved lamb bones. Chop 6 of the garlic cloves and add to the beans. Add additional water if necessary; the liquid should just cover the beans. Put the pork rind, fat side down, on top of the beans, and cover the pot.

11. Bake on the center rack of the oven until the beans are tender, 2 to 2½ hours. Remove and cool to room temperature, uncovered, stirring occasionally. Cover and refrigerate overnight.

12. The next day, prick the garlic sausage all over with a fork and simmer in a pan of water for 30 minutes. Drain and reserve.

13. Put the salt pork in a pan of cold water, bring to a boil, and cook for 10 minutes. Drain, cover with cold water, and repeat, reserving the salt pork in its cooking water.

14. Remove the pot of beans from the refrigerator. Discard the lamb bones, bay leaves, duck neck, and wing tips, and—if you can find them—the heart and gizzard.

15. Drain the salt pork; cut off the rind and discard it. Chop the salt pork into cubes and place them in a food processor. Purée to a paste, dropping the 3 remaining garlic cloves through the feed tube while the motor is running. Stir the paste into the beans.

16. Preheat the oven to 325°F.

17. Skin the duck, pull all the meat from the bones, and cut it into chunks. Stir the duck into the beans along with the lamb and pork cubes. Skin the garlic sausage and cut into rounds; stir into the beans.

18. Before baking the cassoulet, check the beans. If they are too dry (it is preferable that they be too moist), stir in a cup or two of warm water. Smooth the top of the beans, mix the bread crumbs with the parsley, and sprinkle half the mixture over the beans.

19. Bake, uncovered, for 45 minutes. Remove from the oven, stir the top crust into the beans, sprinkle on the remaining bread crumb mixture, and bake until a crust has formed and browned well, another 45 minutes. Serve immediately.

12 portions

"Everything in a pig is good. What ingratitude has permitted his name to become a term of opprobrium?"

—GRIMOD DE LA REYNIÈRE

PECKS OF PEPPERS

From the more than one thousand types of peppers, everyone picks their own favorite peck. They come in an endless variety of colors, shapes, and degrees of heat—from sweet to memorable.

Roasted sweet bell peppers have a velvety texture and a rich, robust flavor. To roast: place on a broiler pan or rack and broil 2 to 3 inches from the heat. Rotate the peppers until the skins are evenly blackened. Using tongs, transfer the peppers to a brown paper bag, foil, or plastic bag and let the peppers sweat for 15 to 20 minutes. The skins will then be easy to peel away and the peppers will be perfectly soft and yielding. Stem, seed, and place them in an airtight container until ready to use. They will keep, refrigerated, for a week.

When it comes to hot chile peppers, you always need to taste your raw pepper before you begin cooking; two peppers from the same plant can have very different heat. Remember, the longer, thinner, and redder the pepper, the hotter it generally is. Be wary. Cutting out the pithy ribs and seeds and just using the outer wall can help you turn down the heat. Then enjoy the fun and flavor chiles can give a dish.

WHITE BEAN AND SAUSAGE SOUP WITH PEPPERS

This soup is a sturdy one-dish meal. Vary the type of sausage as you like—by using pepperoni, knockwurst, or another favorite.

4 tablespoons (½ stick) unsalted butter
2 cups finely chopped yellow onions
2 carrots, peeled and chopped
3 garlic cloves, peeled and minced
6 parsley sprigs
1 teaspoon dried thyme
1 bay leaf
4 cups Chicken Stock (page 416)
1¼ cups dried white beans, soaked overnight
1 red bell pepper
1 green bell pepper
2 tablespoons olive oil
½ pound precooked kielbasa
Salt and freshly ground black pepper, to taste

1. Melt the butter in a large heavy pot over low heat. Add the onions, carrots, and garlic and cook, covered, over low heat until the vegetables are tender and lightly colored, about 25 minutes.

2. Add the parsley, thyme, and bay leaf and pour in the stock. Drain the beans and stir them into the pot. Bring to a boil, reduce the heat, and simmer, partially covered, until the beans are very tender, 45 minutes to 1 hour.

3. Pour the soup through a strainer, reserving the stock; discard the bay leaf, and transfer the solids to a food processor, or use a food mill fitted with a medium disc. Add 1 cup of the cooking stock if using the processor and process until smooth.

4. Return the puréed soup to the pot and stir in additional cooking liquid, 2 to 3 cups, until the soup is of the desired consistency.

5. Cut away the stems and ribs of the peppers and dice them. Heat the olive oil in a small skillet over medium-low heat, add the peppers, and sauté, stirring occasionally, until tender but still crunchy, about 15 minutes. Transfer the peppers to the soup with a slotted spoon.

6. Skin the kielbasa if necessary, dice it, and add it to the soup. Set over medium heat and cook, partially covered, until heated through, about 15 minutes. Season with salt and pepper. Serve immediately.

4 to 6 portions

LENTIL AND WALNUT SALAD

A good lentil salad makes an excellent first course, and this is one of the best we have ever tasted.

2½ cups dried lentils
3 carrots, peeled and quartered
1 medium-size yellow onion, peeled
3 cloves
1½ quarts Chicken Stock (page 416) or canned chicken broth
1 bay leaf
2 teaspoons dried thyme
⅓ cup white wine vinegar
3 garlic cloves, peeled
½ cup walnut oil
Salt and freshly ground black pepper, to taste
1 cup thinly sliced well-rinsed scallions (green onions), with green tops
1 cup shelled walnut halves
Chopped fresh Italian (flat-leaf) parsley, for garnish

1. Rinse the lentils and sort through them carefully, discarding any pebbles you may find.

2. Transfer the lentils to a large pot and add the carrots, the onion stuck with the cloves, chicken stock, bay leaf, and thyme. Set over moderate heat and bring to a boil. Reduce to a simmer, skim any foam that may appear, cover, and cook until the lentils are tender but still hold their shape, about 25 minutes (lentil cooking time varies widely). Do not overcook.

3. While the lentils are cooking, combine the vinegar, garlic, and walnut oil in a blender or a food processor, and process until smooth and creamy.

4. When the lentils are done, drain them, discard the carrots, onion, cloves, and bay leaf, and pour the lentils into a mixing bowl. Rewhisk the dressing and pour it over the still-hot lentils. Toss gently, season generously with salt and pepper, and let the salad cool to room temperature. Toss again, cover, and refrigerate overnight.

5. Just before serving, add the scallions and walnuts. Add an additional tablespoon or two of vinegar or walnut oil if you like, and toss gently. Sprinkle heavily with the chopped parsley and serve, accompanied by a peppermill.

6 to 8 portions as a first course

from THE SILVER PALATE NOTEBOOK

If you love to entertian, it's wise to collect and use recipes that are good cold or at room temperature, or those that taste best prepared a day or two ahead. Avoid last-minute kitchen dramas.

If time is limited, choose a menu that is more assembling than cooking—an antipasto or a charcuterie board, for example.

Always be prepared for an expanded guest list—just in case. And always be gracious about it.

CARROTS

The versatile carrot is a year-round kitchen staple with French, baby, round, and even yellow varieties sparking our interest. Their natural sweetness flavors soups and stocks; they are delicious raw and crunchy for snacking or in salads, or lightly cooked or roasted. Carrots are particularly intriguing when combined with more robust flavors; they add color and texture to any dish and are an especially tasty complement to meats and other root vegetable dishes.

In the English court of the 1700s and early 1800s, carrots were a novelty. They were prized for their delicate green foliage, which was worn like feathers in elegant ladies' hats.

HUNTER'S STYLE CARROTS

A perfect autumn side dish. Serve the carrots with duck, goose, lamb, or any other flavorful meat. As a variation, sprinkle them with Parmigiano-Reggiano cheese just before serving.

½ ounce dried wild mushrooms
½ cup Madeira
3 tablespoons best-quality olive oil
1½ pounds thin carrots, peeled and cut diagonally into ½-inch pieces
Pinch of salt
1 ounce thinly sliced prosciutto, cut into fine julienne
2 large garlic cloves, peeled and finely chopped
3 tablespoons coarsely chopped fresh Italian (flat-leaf) parsley
Freshly ground black pepper, to taste

1. Wash the mushrooms well in a sieve under running water, then soak them in the Madeira for 2 hours. Drain the mushrooms, reserving any liquid, and chop the mushrooms fine. Set aside.

2. Heat the oil in a large skillet over medium-low heat. Add the carrots and cook over medium heat, stirring occasionally, 10 minutes. Season with salt.

3. Add the chopped wild mushrooms and any of the Madeira they have not absorbed. Continue to sauté, stirring and tossing until the carrots begin to brown lightly, another 10 minutes or so.

4. Add the prosciutto and cook until the prosciutto is just heated through, another minute.

5. Stir in the garlic and parsley, grind the black pepper over all, and turn the carrots out into a heated vegetable dish. Serve immediately.

4 to 6 portions

from THE SILVER PALATE NOTEBOOK

Variety and contrast are the spice of a good party arrangement. Don't hesitate to combine your favorite tablecloths, serving pieces, and flower vases, even if they aren't color and pattern coordinated. Contrast antique serving pieces with modern plates and utensils; combine new baskets and old. If you find them attractive, in combination they express your taste in the most direct and personal way possible.

"Nature is pleased with simplicity. . . ."

—SIR ISAAC NEWTON

Warm, fragrant ginger takes candied carrots to new heights.

GINGER CANDIED CARROTS

Sweet and spicy—a good way to prepare carrots any time of the year.

12 medium-size carrots, peeled and cut into 1-inch lengths
4 tablespoons (½ stick) unsalted butter, melted
¼ cup light brown sugar
1½ teaspoons ground ginger
½ teaspoon caraway seeds

1. Place the carrot pieces in a saucepan and add cold water to cover. Cook the carrots over medium heat until tender, 25 to 30 minutes.

2. Melt the butter in a small saucepan over low heat. Add the brown sugar, ginger, and caraway seeds. Mix and set aside.

3. When the carrots are done, drain and return to the pot. Pour the butter mixture over them and cook over low heat, stirring occasionally, 5 minutes.

4. Transfer to a serving dish and serve immediately.

6 portions

WINTER VEGETABLE SALAD

This crisp salad, with its tarragon- and mustard-spiked dressing features a quartet of readily available winter vegetables, including the trusty carrot. The salad keeps well and improves if refrigerated overnight before serving.

1 large bunch of broccoli (about 3½ pounds), trimmed and separated into small florets (see Note)
1 large head of cauliflower (about 3½ pounds), trimmed and separated into florets
3 medium-size carrots, peeled and sliced into ¼-inch rounds
10 ounces frozen green peas
¾ cup Dijon mustard
¾ cup sour cream
¾ cup Homemade Mayonnaise (page 413)
2 teaspoons celery seeds
2 tablespoons dried tarragon, crumbled
½ cup finely chopped fresh Italian (flat-leaf) parsley
Freshly ground black pepper, to taste

1. Bring a large heavy pot of salted water to a boil. Drop the broccoli into the boiling water, let the water return to a boil, and cook for 1 minute. Lift from the water with a slotted spoon and drop immediately into a bowl of ice water. Keep the pot over the heat.

2. Drop the cauliflower into the boiling water, let the water return to a boil, and cook for 2 minutes. Transfer to a bowl of ice water.

3. Repeat the blanching process with the carrots and the peas in turn, using the same pot of water, boiling each 1 minute.

4. Drain all the vegetables thoroughly, making sure they are dry, and toss together in a large mixing bowl.

5. Whisk the remaining ingredients together in another bowl and pour over the vegetables. Toss together gently but thoroughly, cover, and chill until serving time.

6 or more portions

Note: Reserve the stems for another use.

RASPBERRY-MARINATED CARROTS

Tartly sweet and spicy. Serve with pâté or as part of an antipasto.

1½ pounds carrots
⅓ cup raspberry vinegar
Approximately ½ cup best-quality olive oil
Freshly ground black pepper, to taste

1. Peel the carrots and cut them into "coins" ⅛ inch thick. Bring a pot of salted water to a boil and drop in the carrots, cooking them until nearly tender, about 6 minutes. They should retain a slight crunch.

2. Drain the carrots, drop them into a bowl, and sprinkle them with the raspberry vinegar (you must do this while the carrots are still hot). Add enough olive oil to cover the carrots and toss well. Refrigerate at least overnight, although the carrots will keep (and even improve) for several days.

3. To serve, bring the carrots to room temperature and lift them from their marinade with a slotted spoon; it is not necessary to drain them completely; some vinegar and oil should still coat the carrots. Season generously with black pepper.

6 portions

A MEADOW PICNIC

PÂTÉ DE CAMPAGNE WITH WALNUTS

RASPBERRY-MARINATED CARROTS

FRENCH POTATO SALAD WITH BACON

RATATOUILLE

LEMON CHICKEN

APPLE RAISIN CAKE

"Gardening is a very fine thing, because you get such an unmistakable answer as to whether you are making a fool of yourself, or hitting the mark."

—JOHANN WOLFGANG VON GOETHE

CAROTTES RAPEES

A crisp and colorful carrot salad in the French manner.

3 large carrots, trimmed and peeled
½ cup dried currants
Juice of 1 medium-size lemon
Juice of 1 medium-size orange
¼ cup vegetable oil
¼ cup chopped fresh mint
⅛ teaspoon freshly ground black pepper

1. Coarsely shred the carrots, using a food processor or a mandoline.

2. Toss the carrots in a mixing bowl together with the remaining ingredients. Cover and refrigerate. Serve very cold.

4 to 6 portions, as part of an hors d'oeuvre selection

ORANGE ROASTED CARROTS

2½ tablespoons best-quality olive oil
2 pounds carrots (12 to 14 medium-size carrots), peeled and cut into 2-inch lengths
2 tablespoons honey
1 teaspoon Maldon sea salt, or coarse salt
Freshly ground black pepper, to taste
Finely grated zest of 1 orange or tangerine

1. Preheat the oven to 400°F. Oil a baking sheet.

2. Bring a large pot of salted water to a rolling boil. Add the carrots and cook for 5 minutes. Drain well, pat dry, and place in a bowl. Toss the carrots with the oil, honey, salt, and pepper.

3. Place the carrots in a single layer on the prepared baking sheet. Bake until caramelized, shaking the pan and turning the carrots two or three times during baking to prevent sticking, about 40 minutes.

4. Remove the carrots to a bowl and gently stir in the orange zest. Serve immediately.

4 portions

EGGPLANT

Eggplant originated in tropical Asia and was gradually adopted by Indian, Middle Eastern, and Mediterranean cuisines. Now it's very much at home in America as well. That mysterious dark purple egg-shaped orb has recently been upstaged by its white, pale green, violet, black, lime, orange, and striated cousins, with their long, slender lines or round, plump curves. But eggplants of all colors have subtle, elusive flavor and are at their best when accented by garlic and other robust vegetables, spices, and fresh herbs.

COOKING EGGPLANT

Eggplant was a Silver Palate favorite because it is so versatile and is available year-round. Buy only those eggplants that are firm, shiny, and free from wrinkles and blemishes. Store them for no more than a day or two.

Eggplant contains a lot of moisture, which can be bitter. It has a tendency to soak up tremendous amounts of oil or butter when sautéed. Salting, or occasionally blanching, will eliminate both problems. Cut the eggplant as directed in each recipe; there is usually no need to peel it. Layer it in a colander, salting generously as you go. The eggplant should stand for about 1 hour to exude its juices. Rinse off the salt and pat it dry on paper towels before proceeding with the recipe. Blanching for a minute or two in boiling salted water is faster; while more tender eggplant is the result, it can reduce the already subtle flavor.

When sautéing eggplant, use only as much oil as directed in the recipe, or the minimum necessary to coat the skillet, and be sure the skillet is quite hot before the eggplant is added. Toss or turn the eggplant pieces as you add them to coat all sides evenly with oil. *Do not add any more oil!* Even after the salting procedure, eggplant can absorb an amazing amount of oil and the resulting dish could be greasy. If the skillet seems dry, merely stir or turn the eggplant more frequently until properly browned. Drain on paper towels.

BASIL

Basil has long been a symbol of royalty. Legends tell that once only kings using golden sickles were allowed to cut the fragrant herb. To us, basil has always signified the rich warm fertility of summer. This generous plant, pinched back frequently to keep it short and bushy, will give pleasure from midsummer to the first frost.

The number of basil varieties that are available keeps growing. Now the farmers' market is full of Genovese, Napolitano, sweet, Italian large leaf, Thai, lemon, lime, chocolate, lettuce, African blue, Opal, and purple ruffle basil plants—each has its own nuances, each its own staunch supporters.

Fortunately, the season for fresh basil can be extended in several ways. Freshly washed and carefully dried fresh basil leaves can be pounded with enough olive oil to make a smooth purée. We put basil purée in small plastic containers, always with a layer of olive oil over the top. It can be stored in the refrigerator for at least six months, so long as you replace the oil layer after each use. Fresh pesto can be made in batches in the summer and saved this same way (we leave out the cheese until later). This is truly luxurious cooking, year-round.

As a last resort, try this trick: Soak dried basil in a little wine or spirits—vermouth is good, but Strega, vodka, and white wine have also been suggested—for several days. Drain and chop the reconstituted basil together with an equal amount of fresh parsley. Use this in recipes calling for fresh basil. Close your eyes and you can almost hear the crickets.

EGGPLANT SALAD WITH BASIL

A beautiful summer salad.

3 medium-size eggplants (about 4½ pounds in all), cut into 1½-inch cubes (do not peel)
1 cup best-quality olive oil
1 tablespoon coarse salt
4 garlic cloves, peeled and minced
2 large yellow onions, peeled, halved, and thinly sliced
Freshly ground black pepper, to taste
1 cup fresh basil leaves, coarsely chopped
Juice of 2 lemons

1. Preheat the oven to 400°F.

2. Line a roasting pan with aluminum foil and add the eggplants. Toss with half of the olive oil, the coarse salt, and the minced garlic. Bake until the eggplant is soft but not mushy, about 35 minutes. Cool slightly and transfer to a large bowl.

3. Heat the remaining olive oil in a large skillet over medium-low heat. Add the sliced onions and cook, covered, over low heat until tender, about 15 minutes. Add the onions to the eggplant.

4. Season generously with black pepper; add the fresh basil and lemon juice. Toss together. Adjust the seasonings and serve at room temperature.

6 to 8 portions

PEASANT CAVIAR

Serve this well chilled as a first course or as part of an hors d'oeuvre selection, with crisp dry toast or hot triangles of pita bread.

2 small eggplants (about 2 pounds in all)
4 garlic cloves, or more, peeled and slivered
Salt and freshly ground black pepper, to taste
1 teaspoon soy sauce
¼ cup best-quality olive oil
1 medium-size tomato, peeled, seeded, and chopped
¼ cup golden raisins
¼ cup toasted pine nuts (see Sidebar, page 202)
Chopped fresh Italian (flat-leaf) parsley, for garnish

1. Preheat the oven to 350°F.

2. Cut the eggplants lengthwise into halves and make several deep slits in the flesh; be careful not to pierce the skin. Insert the garlic slivers into the cuts. Lightly sprinkle the cut surfaces with salt, and place the halves on a baking sheet. Bake for 1 hour.

3. Remove the eggplants, cool slightly, and invert onto paper towels. As the eggplants finish cooling, squeeze them gently to eliminate any excess liquid. Scrape the eggplant flesh and the cooked garlic out of the skins into a small mixing bowl and mash with a fork.

4. Season with salt and pepper, stir in the soy sauce, olive oil, chopped tomato, and raisins, cover, and refrigerate overnight.

5. Just before serving, stir the peasant caviar well, taste, and correct the seasoning. Stir in the pine nuts and sprinkle generously with the chopped fresh parsley. Serve immediately.

2 cups, 4 portions as a first course

RATATOUILLE

These classic provençal summertime vegetables are ideal for alfresco dining in any season. Sigh!

2 cups best-quality olive oil
4 small eggplants (about 4 pounds in all), cut into 1½-inch cubes
2 teaspoons salt
1½ pounds white onions, peeled and coarsely chopped
7 medium-size zucchini, washed, trimmed, quartered lengthwise, and cut into 2-inch strips
2 medium-size red bell peppers, stemmed, seeded, and cut into ½-inch strips
2 medium-size green bell peppers, stemmed, seeded, and cut into ½-inch strips
2 tablespoons minced garlic
3 cans (16 ounces each) Italian plum tomatoes, drained
1 can (6 ounces) tomato paste
¼ cup chopped fresh Italian (flat-leaf) parsley
¼ cup chopped fresh dill
2 tablespoons dried basil
2 tablespoons dried oregano
Freshly ground black pepper, to taste

1. Preheat the oven to 400°F.

2. Line a large roasting pan with aluminum foil and pour in 1 cup of the olive oil. Add the eggplant, sprinkle it with the salt, and toss well. Cover the pan tightly with foil and bake until the eggplant is done but not mushy, 35 minutes. Uncover and set aside.

3. In a large skillet or in 2 smaller skillets, heat the remaining oil. Sauté the onions, zucchini, red and green peppers, and garlic over medium heat until wilted and lightly colored, about 20 minutes. Add the tomatoes, tomato paste, parsley, dill, basil, oregano, and black pepper. Simmer for 10 minutes, stirring occasionally.

4. Add the eggplant mixture and simmer for another 10 minutes. Taste and correct the seasoning. Serve hot or at room temperature.

12 portions

TOASTING NUTS

To toast nuts and seeds, spread them in a single layer on a baking sheet; place in a preheated 400°F oven for 5 to 7 minutes. Stir once or twice during baking. (Alternatively, brown them in a dry skillet over medium heat, shaking constantly, for about 3 minutes.) Remove immediately when well browned and transfer to a cool plate; otherwise the heat from the baking sheet may cause them to burn. Toasted nuts can be frozen for long-term storage.

MEDITERRANEAN SUMMER LUNCH

PEASANT CAVIAR

PITA BREAD

GREEK LAMB SALAD WITH LEMON-GARLIC MAYONNAISE

RATATOUILLE

CAROTTES RAPÉES WITH BALSAMIC VINAIGRETTE

FRESH FRUIT SALAD

GLAZED LEMON CAKE

EGGPLANT PARMIGIANA

Fresher and lighter than the usual version.

2 small eggplants (about 2 pounds in all)
Salt, for draining the eggplant
2 cups ricotta cheese
2 eggs
¼ cup grated Parmigiano-Reggiano cheese
1 cup chopped fresh Italian (flat-leaf) parsley
Salt and freshly ground black pepper, to taste
Approximately ½ cup olive oil
2 cups Quick Tomato Sauce (page 418)
½ pound whole-milk mozzarella cheese, grated

1. Preheat the oven to 400°F.

2. Slice the eggplants into ½-inch-thick pieces and layer in a colander, salting the slices heavily as you go. Set aside for 30 minutes.

3. Combine the ricotta, eggs, Parmigiano-Reggiano, and chopped parsley. Season with salt and pepper.

4. Rinse the eggplant slices well and pat dry with paper towels. Heat 2 tablespoons olive oil in a large skillet over medium-low heat until it begins to smoke. Add a single layer of eggplant slices with no overlapping. Turn the slices quickly to coat both sides lightly with oil; reduce the heat slightly. Fry the eggplant until lightly browned on both sides. (Do not add more oil after the eggplant is in the skillet.) When the slices are browned, remove to paper towels to drain. Pour 2 tablespoons more oil into the skillet and cook another layer of eggplant. Repeat until all the eggplant pieces are done.

5. Spread ½ cup of the tomato sauce over the bottom of an oval gratin dish measuring 9 x 12 inches. Arrange a layer of eggplant slices over the sauce. Top each eggplant slice with a tablespoon of ricotta mixture and sprinkle about one third of the grated mozzarella over the layer. Repeat, arranging the next layer of eggplant slices to cover the gaps between the slices in the first layer. Add more ricotta mixture and mozzarella. Add a final layer of eggplant, cover it well with the remaining tomato sauce, and spoon the remaining ricotta mixture down the center of the dish. Sprinkle the remaining mozzarella over the exposed tomato sauce.

6. Set the dish on the center rack of the oven and bake until well browned and bubbling, 25 to 30 minutes. Let stand for 10 minutes before serving.

4 to 6 portions

FRESH HERBS

Fresh herbs are a necessity to us, yet others spend a lifetime cooking well without them. If you're one of the former, try growing your own. We have friends, quite unobsessed otherwise, who grow herbs near the bathtub, in window boxes, in large cans, or on the patio.

Be prudent when substituting fresh herbs for dried, and vice versa. The usual formula is to use 2 to 3 times as much fresh as dried, but your taste buds must be the final arbiter.

"If I had to choose just one plant for the whole herb garden, I should be content with basil."

—ELIZABETH DAVID

EGGPLANT WITH HERBS

1 tablespoon minced fresh basil, thyme, rosemary, or oregano
1 tablespoon minced fresh Italian (flat-leaf) parsley
1 large garlic clove, peeled and minced
1 medium-size eggplant (about 1 pound)
Salt and freshly ground black pepper, to taste
2 tablespoons olive oil

1. Preheat the oven to 350°F.

2. Mix together the minced basil, parsley, and garlic.

3. Cut the eggplant lengthwise into halves. Cut several slits in the eggplant flesh, being careful not to cut through the skin. Push the herb and garlic mixture into the slits. Season the eggplant with salt and pepper, and drizzle with the olive oil, about 1 tablespoon per half.

4. Bake the eggplant halves for 30 minutes. Serve hot or, even better, at room temperature, sprinkled with additional fresh herbs.

2 portions

OIL-ROASTED SUMMER VEGETABLES

In this method of cooking vegetables, the oil keeps them from drying out while the salt draws out their natural moisture, concentrating the flavors of the vegetables. Although you can serve this hot, the flavors are even more apparent at room temperature.

6 baby zucchini, about 3 inches long
6 baby eggplants, about 3 inches long
1 pound fresh green beans, cleaned and tipped
6 new potatoes, scrubbed
Approximately ⅓ cup best-quality olive oil
Approximately 2 tablespoons coarse salt

1. Preheat the oven to 375°F.

2. Wash and dry the vegetables, leaving the stems intact, and arrange them in a shallow baking dish just large enough to hold them in a single layer.

3. Drizzle with the olive oil, then sprinkle the coarse salt over all. (While it *is* possible to oversalt the dish, it can stand more salt than you might think; we use about 2 tablespoons.)

4. Set the baking dish in the center of the oven and bake until brown and slightly shriveled. The zucchini and eggplant will be done in 30 minutes or so; potatoes can take an hour. Remove the individual vegetables as they become tender and arrange them on a serving plate.

5. Cool to room temperature and serve at your leisure.

6 portions

When cooking combinations of vegetables, aim for a variety of colors as well as tastes and textures. Our recipe for Oil-Roasted Summer Vegetables calls for eggplant, zucchini, green beans, and new potatoes—try substituting carrots, baby artichokes, and strips of red and green bell peppers.

MUSHROOMS

Mushrooms miraculously appear overnight in the most mysterious places. They have been the subject of legends and folklore for centuries. They were once thought to be the result of thunder, since they appeared after rainstorms, and they still seem to many people as magical as elves, gnomes, fairies, and hobbits. The ancient Greeks thought them "food for the gods." We make a bit of a ceremony about them as well.

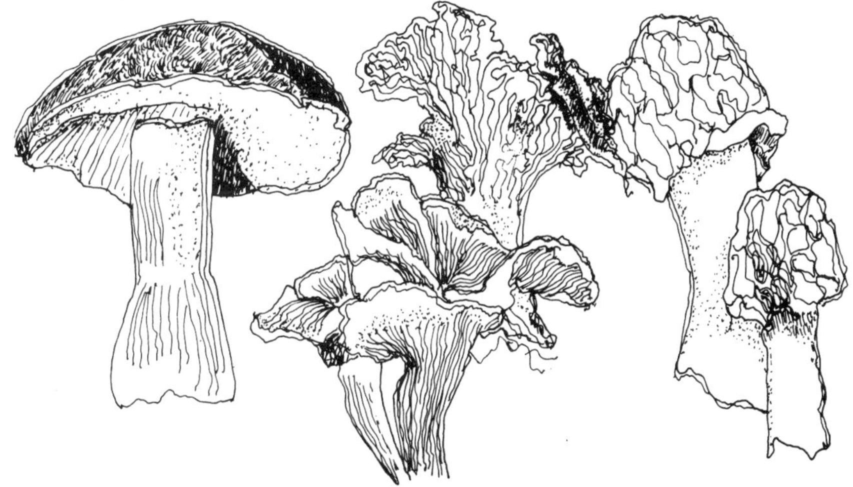

THE DOMESTIC MUSHROOM

Where once we had only one genus of mushroom grown commercially in the United States, today there are many that were formerly found only in the wild and are now tamed and being farmed. A cultivated mushroom often doesn't have as rich a flavor as its wild equivalent, yet it will be delicious and certainly more reliably available. Today many markets stock the button, cremini, enoki, and matsutake, and even more exciting, the morel, portobello, wood ear, and porcini. These farmed mushrooms combine beautifully with those from the wild, either fresh or dried, and allow us to extend those precious morsels more economically.

THE WILD MUSHROOM

Since almost countless species of wild mushroom grow on this earth, hunting them is hardly the esoteric pursuit it is often made out to be. Of course you must know your onions, so to speak, since some mushroom species are poisonous, but courses and guidebooks abound, and the beginning mushroom hunter who learns their lessons and observes their sensible precautions need not fear. Do be cautious and follow the example of the experts: Never eat a mushroom not positively identified as safe.

In certain regions of the United States, spring and fall still signal the start of the mushroom hunt and entire families will happily forage for basketfuls to be rushed home and cooked. Mushrooms often grow under oak and apple trees and all need to be carefully washed. And if you don't have your own secret spots for finding them, the farmers' markets are now filled with foraged wild mushrooms. The names alone capture the imagination: cèpe (porcini), candy cap, golden chanterelle, yellowfoot chanterelle, hen of the woods, bluefoot, abalone, honshimeji, trompettes des morts, french horn, pompom, maitake, nameko, wood ear, hedgehog, lobster, blue oyster, clam shell, matsutake, cauliflower, fried chicken, and mousseron. The flavors make them addictive.

If wandering in the woods is not your thing, however, don't despair. The taste of wild mushrooms can still be yours, captured in dried form. Several kinds of these are available, usually imported from Europe. When they are properly reconstituted by soaking, the flavor and texture are as good as—though different from—those of the fresh.

Buy from a reputable dealer, and preferably one who offers his wares in bulk; dried mushrooms can be invaded by worms and other insects and a wary shopper will examine them closely. Rinse them thoroughly under cold running water and soak them in water, or, more wisely, a liquid that you will be able to incorporate into the recipe, thus saving every bit of elusive flavor. Madeira or Port and chicken stock are the two best choices; lemon juice is good where appropriate.

After soaking, dried mushrooms are usually chopped and sautéed in butter to bring out their full flavor before going into the dish. We have learned to combine an ounce or two of dried with a pound or more of sautéed sliced cultivated mushrooms: the exchange of flavors and textures benefits both, and the result is a generous quantity of wild mushroom flavor with a minimum of expense.

Some of our favorite mushrooms, often available fresh as well as dried, include the following:

CEPES/PORCINI: Thankfully now available fresh in the U.S., for years cèpes were imported dried or canned from France, where they grow in oak, chestnut, and beech forests. Porcini (or "little pigs") is the Italian term for the same mushroom, a kind of boletus. Cèpe and porcini impart rich, deep flavor to game and poultry dishes and to sauces.

CHANTERELLES: Often called "little goblets." They are dainty and reddish yellow, with a cup shape and a slight apricot taste.

GIROLLES: These golden mushrooms sparkle in forests of deciduous trees. They are delicately shaped, reminding us of morning glories; lovely sautéed in an omelet.

MORELS: These are the only fungus to approach the intensity or bouquet of the truffle. After soaking, sauté long and slowly.

ORANGE MUSHROOMS: Also, Caesar's mushroom. Reddish with yellow gills; excellent flavor.

OYSTER MUSHROOMS: White and delicate, these mushrooms are often called "weepers" because of the liquid they produce when sautéed fresh.

TROMPETTES DES MORTS (Horns of Plenty): These black, trumpet-shaped mushrooms traditionally bordered the vineyards of France. Softened in wine and stuffed into meats, dried trompettes give a taste that suggests truffles.

TRUFFLES: The most highly prized of the earth's edible fungi. Their mystery and delicate flavor make grown people a little crazy. They have always been expensive, and must be eaten fresh if all the fuss is to make sense.

Dark, rich truffles are hunted in France, largely in the Périgord, an ancient region where the truffle was once considered a pest. They grow under oak trees and are hunted in the fall with trained hounds or pigs that have been given food mixed with truffles.

In late fall and winter they are available fresh in this country, and, though expensive, their penetrating flavor makes them go a long way. Truffles are also sold whole in cans or jars, infused in oils, in creams, chopped, and puréed. We never tire of them.

Italian white truffles from Piedmont are more pungently flavored than the black and are equally expensive. It is delicious to have one finely shaved over a dish of pasta or scrambled eggs; the truly devoted slice them and warm them briefly in butter.

WILD MUSHROOM SOUP

2 ounces dried cèpes, morels, or chanterelles
¼ cup Madeira
8 tablespoons (1 stick) unsalted butter
2 cups finely chopped yellow onions
2 pounds fresh mushrooms
Salt and freshly ground black pepper, to taste
4 cups Chicken Stock (page 416)
1 pint heavy cream (optional)

1. Rinse the dried mushrooms well in a sieve under cold running water and soak them in the Madeira for 1 hour, stirring occasionally.

2. Melt the butter in a large heavy pot over low heat. Add the onions and cook, covered, over low heat until they are tender and lightly colored, stirring occasionally, about 15 minutes.

3. Trim the stems from the fresh mushrooms and save for another use. Wipe the caps with a damp cloth and slice thin. Add the caps to the soup pot, season with salt and pepper, and cook over low heat, uncovered, stirring frequently, for 15 minutes.

4. Carefully lift the mushrooms from the bowl with a slotted spoon and transfer to the soup pot. Let the Madeira settle a moment and then pour it carefully into the soup pot, leaving the sediment behind.

5. Add the chicken stock and bring to a boil. Reduce the heat, cover, and simmer until the dried mushrooms are very tender, 45 minutes.

6. Strain the soup and transfer the solids to a food processor. Add 1 cup of the liquid and purée until very smooth.

7. Return the purée to the soup pot along with the remaining liquid and set over medium heat. Taste, correct the seasoning, and thin the soup slightly with heavy cream if it seems too thick. Heat until steaming and serve immediately.

6 to 8 portions

CREAMED MUSHROOMS

Creamed mushrooms are perfect folded into crêpes or as an omelet filling, and particularly good spooned over buttered sourdough toast.

2 pounds firm fresh white mushrooms
4 tablespoons (½ stick) unsalted butter
1 teaspoon salt
¼ teaspoon freshly ground black pepper
Pinch of grated nutmeg
⅓ cup heavy cream
2 tablespoons Madeira
1 tablespoon soy sauce
½ cup finely chopped fresh Italian (flat-leaf) parsley

1. Wipe the mushrooms with a damp paper towel and trim the stem ends. Cut the mushrooms into thick slices.

2. Melt the butter in a large skillet over low heat. Add the mushrooms, raise the heat, and toss and stir until the mushrooms render their juices, about 5 minutes.

3. Lower the heat, season the mushrooms with salt, pepper, and nutmeg, and cook, uncovered, for another 5 minutes.

4. With a slotted spoon, transfer the mushrooms to a bowl. Add the cream, Madeira, and soy sauce to the juices in the skillet and bring to a boil. Cook until reduced by about half.

5. Return the mushrooms to the skillet and simmer for another minute or two to heat through. Stir in the parsley and serve immediately.

About 2 cups, serving 4, depending on use

WOODSY WILD MUSHROOM SAUTE

Serve this as an earthy side dish to pork or game.

1 ounce dried cèpes (see Note)
1 ounce dried trompettes des morts (see Note)
4 ounces fresh morels or 1 ounce dried (see Note)
1½ cups Madeira
2 pounds fresh large button mushrooms
6 tablespoons (¾ stick) unsalted butter
¼ cup chopped shallots
4 garlic cloves, very finely minced
½ cup chopped fresh Italian (flat-leaf) parsley
½ teaspoon salt
Freshly ground black pepper, to taste
Juice of 1 lemon

1. Rinse the dried mushrooms under cold running water in a small strainer until they are free of all dirt and grit.

2. Combine the dried mushrooms and Madeira in a small bowl, cover, and let stand for 1 hour, stirring occasionally.

3. Wipe the fresh mushrooms with a damp paper towel. Cut off the stems and save for another use. Slice the mushroom caps in half.

4. Melt half of the butter in a large skillet over low heat and add the halved fresh mushrooms. Cook, stirring, over high heat for 5 minutes.

5. Lift the dried mushrooms carefully from the bowl with a slotted spoon. Coarsely chop the dried mushrooms and add them, the remaining butter, the shallots, garlic, and parsley to the skillet and cook over low heat, stirring occasionally, another 10 minutes. Strain the Madeira into the skillet, leaving any sediment behind.

6. Season with the salt and pepper, turn out into a heated serving dish, and sprinkle with the fresh lemon juice. Serve immediately.

8 to 10 portions

Note: Available at specialty food shops.

"Is there anything more provocative and mysterious than a mushroom?"

—AMY FARGES, *THE MUSHROOM LOVER'S COOKBOOK*

A FRENCH BRUNCH

CROISSANTS WITH UNSALTED BUTTER AND PRESERVES

BLACK FOREST CRÊPE TORTE

WOODSY WILD MUSHROOM SAUTÉ

FRESH FRUIT BASKET

CHÈVRE CHEESES

CAFÉ AU LAIT

"If I can't have too many truffles, I'll do without truffles."

—COLETTE

DUXELLES

This reduced preparation of minced mushrooms is endlessly useful. It can become a stuffing for mushrooms, chicken breasts, or an omelet; it can be stirred into scrambled eggs; a spoonful or two will add intensity to a soup or sauce; a simply roasted piece of chicken can be transformed into something special by a pan deglazing of cream into which a spoonful of *duxelles* is stirred.

Our version includes both cultivated and dried wild mushrooms for extra flavor. The recipe here can easily be halved, but since duxelles freezes well, it is less work to make the larger amount.

1 to 2 ounces dried wild mushrooms (cèpes, morels, trompettes des morts, or a mixture; see Note)
½ cup Madeira
2½ to 3 pounds fresh mushrooms
8 tablespoons (1 stick) unsalted butter
2 large shallots, peeled and finely chopped
1 cup finely chopped yellow onions
1 teaspoon dried thyme
1½ teaspoons salt
Pinch of grated nutmeg
Freshly ground black pepper, to taste
½ cup finely chopped fresh Italian (flat-leaf) parsley

1. Rinse the dried mushrooms under cold running water in a strainer. Drain and place them in a small bowl. Add the Madeira and let stand until the mushrooms are soft, at least 1 hour.

2. Wipe the fresh mushrooms with damp paper towels and trim the stem ends. Mince the mushrooms (a food processor is ideal for this).

3. Melt the butter in a large skillet over low heat. Add the shallots and onions and cook, covered, over low heat until tender and lightly colored, about 25 minutes.

4. Add the minced fresh mushrooms to the skillet, raise the heat, and cook, stirring, until they render their juices, about 5 minutes. Add the thyme, salt, nutmeg, and black pepper.

5. Meanwhile, transfer the reconstituted wild mushrooms to the food processor, lifting them from the Madeira with a slotted spoon. Carefully pour the wine over them, discarding any sediment in the bowl, and purée until very smooth. Add them to the skillet. Reduce the heat and cook, stirring occasionally, until the duxelles is reduced and thickened, about 40 minutes. Near the end of this cooking time the mixture will become dry; stir constantly to prevent scorching.

6. Remove the pan from the heat. Taste the duxelles and correct the seasoning. Stir in the chopped parsley, cool to room temperature, and cover before refrigerating or freezing.

About 1 quart

Note: Available at specialty food shops.

TRUFFLES AND AVOCADOS

Peel and slice an avocado, toss lightly in lemon juice, drain, and cover with olive oil and a shaved raw truffle. Let stand for 1 hour. Serve on a bed of fresh watercress. Luxurious and buttery. Pass the peppermill.

TRUFFLES AND POTATOES

Combine these two wonders from underground: sliced potatoes, sautéed in lots of butter until tender, and tossed when done with shaved raw black truffle—about 1 truffle for every 6 potatoes. Grind pepper liberally over all and live it up.

MARINATED MUSHROOMS WITH RED WINE AND FENNEL

Present the mushrooms in a bowl surrounded by squares of pumpernickel, spread, if you like, with butter and sprinkled with parsley. Scoop the mushrooms onto the bread squares and enjoy.

¼ cup best-quality olive oil
1½ pounds medium-size fresh mushrooms, wiped clean and stems removed (reserve for another use)
Salt and freshly ground black pepper
1 medium yellow onion, peeled and sliced into thin rings
4 to 6 garlic cloves, peeled and chopped
1 tablespoon fennel seeds
1 tablespoon dried basil
2 teaspoons dried marjoram
1 cup canned Italian plum tomatoes, drained and chopped
1 cup hearty red wine
¼ cup balsamic vinegar
Chopped fresh Italian (flat-leaf) parsley, for garnish

1. Heat the oil in a heavy saucepan over medium-low heat. Add the mushrooms and cook, stirring frequently, for 5 minutes. Salt and pepper the mushrooms, and cook further, for 2 to 3 minutes. Remove the mushrooms with a slotted spoon and reserve.

2. Reduce the heat to low and add the onion and garlic to the oil remaining in the pan. Cook until the onions are translucent but still have some crunch, 15 minutes.

3. Add the fennel seeds, basil, and marjoram and cook for another 5 minutes, stirring occasionally.

4. Add the tomatoes, wine, and vinegar to the pan, season with 1 teaspoon salt and pepper to taste, and simmer until slightly reduced, 15 minutes.

5. Return the mushrooms to the pan, simmer for 5 minutes, and remove from the heat. Let cool to room temperature, stirring occasionally, then cover and refrigerate. Marinate for at least 24 hours before serving.

6. Sprinkle heavily with the chopped fresh parsley before serving.

4 to 6 portions

GAZEBO PICNIC

LAYERED VEGETABLE TERRINE WITH TOMATO COULIS

SLICED FILET OF BEEF WITH HORSERADISH SAUCE

MARINATED MUSHROOMS WITH RED WINE AND FENNEL

BULGUR WHEAT SALAD

FRENCH BREAD

PEARS POACHED IN WHITE WINE

BLACK WALNUT COOKIES

POTATOES

The potato, available around the world, is a most comforting vegetable. It has held nations together in times of war and famine, and even today there are places where potatoes are eaten three times a day. The potato used to be considered common by some, but with russets, Idahos, redskins, fingerlings in every color, sweets, yams, Yukon Golds, and Yellow Finns in every size from pea to peewee football, there's nothing boring about the potato any longer. Today potatoes grace the most sophisticated menus in restaurants and homes alike. Common? We don't think so.

DILLED NEW POTATOES

24 tiny new potatoes
8 tablespoons (1 stick) unsalted butter
Salt and freshly ground black pepper, to taste
6 tablespoons chopped fresh dill

1. Scrub and dry the potatoes. Melt the butter in a heavy ovenproof casserole with a tight-fitting cover over low heat Add the potatoes and season with salt and pepper. Coat with the butter.

2. Cover and cook over low heat for 30 to 45 minutes. Shake the casserole occasionally. The potatoes are done when they can be pierced with the tip of a sharp knife.

3. Toss with the dill and serve at once.

4 to 6 portions

THE WELL-DRESSED NEW POTATO

In any season we like to cook the tiny new potato with its jacket on. Scientists tell us the potato retains more vitamins that way. Our eye tells us that the delicate pink or tan of the potato skins makes every dish prettier. Since no one wants to peel the little devils, it saves time, too.

Other potatoes—the larger ones used for slicing or mashing—are peeled, letting the fluffy white insides stand on their own merits.

ORANGE MASHED POTATOES

The earthy neutrality of mashed potatoes makes them compatible with a wide range of partners—herbs, vinegars, cheeses, other vegetables, and even citrus, as here. Use your imagination for these white clouds, as we have done in the following recipe.

"Let the sky rain potatoes."

—WILLIAM SHAKESPEARE, *THE MERRY WIVES OF WINDSOR*

3 pounds potatoes
2 cups finely chopped yellow onions
4 tablespoons (½ stick) unsalted butter
½ cup Crème Fraîche (page 414)
¾ cup fresh orange juice
Grated orange zest, for garnish

1. Peel and quarter the potatoes and drop them into a large pot of cold salted water. Bring to a moderate boil and cook until the potatoes are very tender, 30 minutes or so.

2. Meanwhile, in another pan, cook the onions in the butter, covered, over medium-low heat until very tender and lightly colored, about 25 minutes.

3. Drain and mash the potatoes and stir in the onions and their cooking butter. (Or force the potatoes, onions, and butter through the medium disc of a food mill.)

4. Stir in the crème fraîche and orange juice and beat the potatoes with a wire whisk until fluffy. Turn into a heated serving dish and garnish with orange zest to taste. Serve immediately.

6 portions

SWISS POTATO GRATIN

2 pounds red-skinned boiling potatoes
1 cup ricotta cheese
¾ cup chopped fresh Italian (flat-leaf) parsley
Salt and freshly ground black pepper, to taste
Grated nutmeg, to taste
1 egg
Approximately 1 cup heavy cream
Unsalted butter, for greasing the baking dish
¼ pound Gruyère cheese, grated (about 1 cup)

1. Wash the potatoes well and trim away any discolored spots or eyes. (You may peel the potatoes if you like.) Slice thin and drop into a pot of cold, heavily salted water. Set over high heat and bring to a boil. Boil the potatoes for 1 minute, drain, and rinse with cold water. Drain again and pat dry.

2. Combine the ricotta and parsley and season generously with salt, pepper, and nutmeg.

3. Beat the egg briefly and add enough heavy cream to make 1 cup of liquid. Season with salt, pepper, and nutmeg.

4. Preheat the oven to 350°F.

5. Lightly butter a shallow, oval gratin dish measuring 9 x 12 inches. Arrange a layer of slightly overlapping potato slices in the dish. Dot with about one third of the ricotta mixture; sprinkle with one third of the Gruyère. Repeat, using all of the ingredients and ending with a potato layer.

6. Gently pour the egg and cream mixture into the dish, lifting the potato slices with a fork if necessary to allow the cream to spread evenly among them.

7. Bake on the center rack of the oven until the potatoes are tender and the cheese is browned and bubbling, 35 to 45 minutes. Let sit for about 10 minutes before serving.

4 portions

STUFFED POTATOES

Bake and stuff the largest potato you can find, and you have a savory and elegant luncheon main course or late-night snack that is special and comforting at the same time.

While you can stuff a memorable potato with practically anything you find in the cupboard and refrigerator, here are two of our favorite fillings to get you started.

PIMENTON DE LA VERA

Spain's smoked paprika, *Pimenton de la Vera,* has become one of our cooking "secret ingredients." Its base, ground *Capsicum* pepper, was originally brought from Central America to Spain by Columbus. In the Extremaduran "La Vera" region of Spain, a particularly high-quality smoked paprika is produced. The peppers are dried not in the sun or in ovens before grinding, but by the traditional method of oak smoking. The resulting hot and smoky taste is addictive. We find we like to sprinkle a little over fried or roasted potatoes, in stews, sauces, ratatouilles, pastas, and over beans and sausages. A little goes a long way. The flavor is smoky-spicy and most intriguing—giving a new deep dimension to classic dishes. Our guests are always asking, "What is that intriguing spice I'm tasting?"

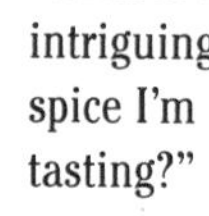

TWICE-BAKED POTATOES WITH CHEESE AND CHILES

4 large baking potatoes
Salt and freshly ground black pepper, to taste
¼ cup chopped imported black olives
½ cup diced canned mild green chile peppers
4 to 6 tablespoons heavy cream
½ cup grated sharp Cheddar cheese, plus additional cheese for topping the potatoes
½ cup sour cream, for garnish
Whole imported black olives, for garnish (optional)

1. Preheat the oven to 375°F.

2. Scrub and dry the potatoes. Cut a small, deep slit in the top of each potato. Set the potatoes on the center rack of the oven and bake until the potatoes are tender when pierced with a fork, about 1 hour. Increase the oven temperature to 400°F.

3. Let the potatoes cool slightly, cut off the tops, and scrape the potato pulp into a bowl. Do not scrape so deeply that you tear the potato skin. Salt and pepper the potato shells; reserve.

4. Mash the potato pulp and stir in the chopped olives, diced green chiles, and enough heavy cream to give the mixture the desired consistency. Season with the salt and pepper and stir in the ½ cup grated cheese.

5. Divide the potato mixture equally among the shells, mounding the filling slightly. Sprinkle with additional grated cheese and place on a baking sheet.

6. Bake again until the potatoes are hot and the cheese is bubbling, 15 to 20 minutes.

7. Top each potato with a generous dollop of sour cream, and add a black olive if you like. Serve immediately.

4 portions

"My idea of heaven is a baked potato and someone to share it with."

—OPRAH WINFREY

TWICE-BAKED POTATOES WITH LOBSTER

4 large baking potatoes
Salt and freshly ground black pepper, to taste
4 tablespoons (½ stick) unsalted butter
½ cup chopped yellow onion
½ cup finely chopped fresh mushrooms
2 cups cooked lobster (or crab) meat
1 cup dry white vermouth
½ cup Crème Fraîche (page 414)
½ cup grated Jarlsberg cheese, plus additional cheese for topping the potatoes
1 to 2 tablespoons heavy cream (optional)

1. Preheat the oven to 375°F.

2. Scrub and dry the potatoes. Cut a small, deep slit in the top of each potato. Set the potatoes on the center rack of the oven and bake until the potatoes are tender when pierced with a fork, about 1 hour.

3. Let the potatoes cool slightly, cut off and discard the tops, and scrape the potato pulp into a bowl. Do not scrape so deeply that you tear the potato skin. Salt and pepper the potato shells; reserve. Mash the potato pulp; reserve.

4. Melt the butter in a small skillet over low heat and sauté the chopped onion, covered, until tender and lightly colored, about 25 minutes. Add the mushrooms and sauté for another 5 minutes. Stir in the lobster or crab. Season with salt and pepper, add the vermouth, then raise the heat to a boil. Stir frequently over high heat until all the liquid has boiled away. Stir in the crème fraîche and remove from the heat.

5. Combine the lobster mixture with the reserved mashed potato pulp and the ½ cup Jarlsberg. Taste and correct the seasoning; add the heavy cream if the mixture seems too dry.

6. Stuff the mixture into the reserved potato skins; mound the filling slightly. Sprinkle additional grated cheese on top and place on a baking sheet.

7. Bake again, at 400°F, until the potatoes are hot and the cheese is bubbling, 15 to 20 minutes. Serve immediately.

4 portions

DILL

Dill was first discovered in England in 1597. Its name is taken from the Saxon "dillan," meaning "to lull," since its reeds were used to soothe babies to sleep.

French Potato Salad with Bacon: picnic perfection.

SOME GOOD EXCUSES FOR A PICNIC

- ♥ bicycling
- ♥ bird watching
- ♥ trout fishing
- ♥ hunting for wild mushrooms
- ♥ watching the autumn foliage turn
- ♥ looking for shooting stars
- ♥ at the beach
- ♥ canoeing
- ♥ skiing cross-country or downhill
- ♥ the Fourth of July
- ♥ istening to the Philharmonic
- ♥ fireworks anytime
- ♥ a birthday
- ♥ after a tennis match
- ♥ halftime of the big game
- ♥ driving cross-country
- ♥ at the summit of the mountain
- ♥ while antique hunting
- ♥ during a James Joyce reading
- ♥ cleaning out closets with a friend
- ♥ organizing photo albums
- ♥ during a day at the zoo
- ♥ studying for finals
- ♥ washing the family car
- ♥ a backgammon tournament
- ♥ a session of constructive criticism
- ♥ annual budget time
- ♥ while working on a Saturday
- ♥ in a hot-air balloon
- ♥ after watching or running the marathon

FRENCH POTATO SALAD WITH BACON

8 or 9 new potatoes (1 pound)
Salt, to taste
¼ pound bacon
¼ cup finely chopped shallots
¼ cup red wine vinegar
2 tablespoons olive oil
Freshly ground black pepper, to taste
¼ cup chopped red onion
½ cup chopped fresh Italian (flat-leaf) parsley

1. Scrub the potatoes under running water with a soft brush. Quarter them and drop them into a large heavy pot of cold, salted water. Bring to a boil and cook until tender but still firm, 8 to 10 minutes after the water reaches a boil.

2. Meanwhile, chop the bacon and sauté in a small skillet over medium-low heat until crisp. Remove the bacon and reserve.

3. In the bacon fat remaining in the skillet, sauté the chopped shallots until tender but not at all browned, 5 minutes or so. Reserve the shallots and fat.

4. When the potatoes are done, drain them and drop them into a mixing bowl.

5. Pour the vinegar, olive oil, shallots, and reserved bacon fat over the still-hot potatoes. Season with salt and pepper and gently toss. Add the red onion and parsley and toss again. Cool to room temperature, cover, and refrigerate.

6. Before serving, bring back to room temperature, toss, correct the seasoning, and add additional oil and vinegar if the salad seems dry. Sprinkle the reserved crisp bacon on top.

4 portions

AMERICAN PICNIC POTATO SALAD

4 pounds boiling potatoes, peeled
Salt, to taste
½ cup white wine vinegar
½ cup olive oil
¼ teaspoon freshly ground black pepper
1 cup thinly sliced red onions
1 cup celery strips, 1 inch long, ¼ inch wide
3 medium-size cucumbers, peeled, seeded, and sliced
2 cups mayonnaise (preferably Hellmann's), plus more if needed
5 tablespoons Dijon or herb mustard (dill, tarragon, or basil)
20 hard-cooked eggs, peeled and quartered
1 cup chopped fresh Italian (flat-leaf) parsley

1. Drop the potatoes as you peel them into a large heavy pot of cold, salted water. Bring to a boil and cook until tender but still firm, 30 minutes or so.

2. When done, drain the potatoes and drop them into a mixing bowl; roughly slice them. Sprinkle the still-hot potatoes with the vinegar, olive oil, 1 teaspoon salt, and pepper.

3. Add the onions, celery, cucumbers, mayonnaise, and mustard; toss gently to combine.

4. Add the quartered eggs and parsley and toss again. Cool to room temperature, cover, and refrigerate overnight. Before serving, toss again, correct the seasoning, and add more mayonnaise if needed.

20 portions

How many potato salads should a cookbook have? We stopped with three, not because we ran out of ideas, but because we ran out of room.

SCANDINAVIAN POTATO SALAD

8 or 9 new potatoes (about 1 pound)
Salt and freshly ground black pepper, to taste
1 cup sour cream
⅓ cup chopped red onion
⅓ cup chopped fresh dill

1. Scrub the potatoes with a soft brush under running water. Quarter them and drop them into a large heavy pot of cold, salted water. Bring to a boil and cook until tender but still firm, for 8 to 10 minutes after the water reaches a boil.

2. When the potatoes are done, drain them and place them in a mixing bowl.

3. Season with salt and pepper, add the sour cream to the still-hot potatoes, and toss gently. Add the chopped onion and dill, toss again, and cool to room temperature before refrigerating for at least 4 hours.

4. Before serving, toss again, correct the seasoning, and add more sour cream if the salad seems dry.

4 portions

"Actually, the true gourmet, like the true artist, is one of the unhappiest creatures existent. His trouble comes from so seldom finding what he constantly seeks: perfection."

—LUDWIG BEMELMANS

SCALLIONS, LEEKS, GARLIC, SHALLOTS, AND ONIONS

These lusty members of the lily family were frowned upon by polite society for centuries. Their taste and smell have been considered common, when in fact, their availability made them the cornerstones of country cooking the world over. Finally, "peasant cooking" from around the world has become the most popular way to cook, and a pantry without the onion and its cousins isn't considered well stocked. Now these aromatic vegetables are seen by wise cooks for what they are—flavor makers in the best sense of the word, adding richness and zest to every dish they meet.

BRAISED SCALLIONS IN MUSTARD SAUCE

The simple scallion, treated with imagination and respect, can become a dressy hot vegetable. Here it is braised with fragrant vegetables and chicken stock and sauced with cream and a bit of mustard. This is rich and is best with simply roasted beef or veal, or as a first course over toast points.

20 to 24 large scallions (green onions)
1 tablespoon unsalted butter
1 celery rib, cleaned and chopped
1 carrot, peeled and chopped
1 teaspoon dried thyme
1 bay leaf
2 parsley sprigs
Freshly ground black pepper, to taste
1½ cups Chicken Stock (page 416) or canned chicken broth
¼ cup Dijon mustard
½ cup heavy cream or Crème Fraîche (page 414)
Salt (optional)

1. Trim and clean the scallions and cut off all but about 1 inch of the green tops. Save the tops for another use if you like.

2. In a skillet large enough to hold the scallions later, melt the butter over low heat and cook the celery and carrot, covered, until tender and lightly colored, about 20 minutes.

3. Add the thyme, bay leaf, parsley, black pepper, and chicken stock. Simmer partially covered, for 15 minutes. Add no salt at this point; you will correct the seasoning as necessary when the dish is completed.

4. Add the scallions to the broth and simmer, uncovered, until barely tender, about 5 minutes. Do not overcook. Remove the scallions with a slotted spoon and reserve.

5. Strain the liquid, discard the solids, measure out ½ cup, and return it to the skillet. Whisk in the mustard and the heavy cream or crème fraîche. Set the skillet over medium heat and simmer, stirring occasionally, until the sauce is reduced by about one third, 10 minutes. Taste and correct the seasoning.

6. Return the scallions to the skillet for 1 minute to warm them through before serving immediately.

4 to 6 portions

TARTE SAINT-GERMAIN

The lowly leek is the star in this glamorous tart.

4 tablespoons (½ stick) unsalted butter
6 leeks, trimmed, well washed, and thinly sliced
2 eggs
2 egg yolks
1 cup half-and-half
1 cup heavy cream
Salt and freshly ground black pepper, to taste
Freshly grated nutmeg (optional)
One 9-inch shell of Pâte Brisée (page 408), partially baked (see Note)
½ cup grated Gruyère cheese

SCALLIONS

Scallions are usually only baby or teenage onions, and they can be sweetly mild or bitingly strong, depending on which onion variety they belong to. They make good if pungent eating just dipped into coarse salt. They add crunch, color, and flavor to soups and salads, and can be used as garnishes in a variety of ways. We love tiny green rings of scallion tops in cool white soups. We sprinkle the chopped white and green scallion bits lavishly over pasta and seafood salads, and are fans of fine scallion julienne, scallion brushes, and whole green scallions as well. Rinse scallions before using them.

CHIVES

Chives are the tenderest and mildest member of the onion family and are a joy to look at and to cook with. We love their bright green tubular leaves and lavender thistlelike flowers on our windowsill.

We always use scissors to snip chives (chopping crushes out the juices) and sprinkle them wherever we need a bit of green or a garnish with more flavor than parsley. We couldn't make vichyssoise without chives. We love to scramble them into eggs; they make that simple dish very special.

Tarte Saint-Germain is rich and deeply satisfying.

1. Melt the butter in a skillet over low heat. Add the sliced leeks and cook, covered, until the leeks are tender and lightly colored, about 30 minutes. Stir frequently or the leeks may scorch. Remove from the heat and cool slightly.

2. Whisk the eggs, yolks, half-and-half, and heavy cream together in a bowl and season with salt and pepper. Add a grating of nutmeg, if you like.

3. Preheat the oven to 300°F.

4. Spoon the cooled leek mixture into the partially baked tart shell. Add the cream and egg mixture to fill the tart to within ½ inch of the top. Sprinkle the Gruyère evenly over the tart.

5. Set the tart on the center rack of the oven and bake until the top is well browned and the filling is completely set, 35 to 45 minutes.

6. Cool for 10 minutes. Cut into wedges and serve warm.

4 main-course portions, or 6 appetizer portions

Note: Use a quiche pan approximately 2 inches deep.

LEEKS NICOISE

Serve these leeks as a sit-down first course, or as part of an alfresco meal.

12 leeks, each 1½ inches in diameter
Salt, to taste
¼ cup best-quality olive oil
1 large garlic clove, peeled and finely minced
3 ripe tomatoes, cut into eighths
½ cup niçoise olives
2 teaspoons dried basil or 1½ tablespoons chopped fresh basil
2 tablespoons chopped fresh Italian (flat-leaf) parsley
Freshly ground black pepper

1. Leave the roots on the leeks for now, but trim away 2 or 3 inches of the toughest tips of the green leaves. Split the leeks down to but not completely through the root end, separate the layers, and wash the leeks carefully under running water; they'll be sandy.

2. Bring a large heavy pot of salted water to a boil and add the leeks. Cook just until the white part is tender. Drain the leeks and reserve.

3. Heat the olive oil in a large skillet over medium-low heat. Add the garlic and cook over low heat for 3 minutes. Pat the leeks dry on paper towels, trim off the roots, and add the leeks to the skillet. Cook over low heat for 5 minutes.

4. Stir in the tomatoes, niçoise olives, basil, parsley, and black pepper to taste and heat together, covered, for 3 to 5 minutes.

5. Transfer the leeks to a serving platter, pour the contents of the skillet over them, and cool to room temperature before serving.

6 portions

LEEKS

Leeks, with their thick white bodies and broad green leaves, grow like and resemble onions, although they have a mild, almost sweet flavor that is all their own. In Europe leeks are plentiful and cheap, and are called "the asparagus of the poor." They were once difficult to find in this country, and though they are more available than they used to be, they are still expensive. Nevertheless, leeks are essential in the stock- or soup pot, adding a depth of flavor not achieved by onions alone. As a vegetable served on their own, leeks can be braised and eaten hot or cold—a favorite first course in French bistros. Sliced and gently sautéed in butter, they become a delicious filling for an omelet or quiche. Like all members of the onion tribe, leeks are pleasantly easy to grow; you'll come to love and rely on this homely vegetable.

Clean leeks carefully, since they often contain a lot of sand. Cut off the root and most, but not all, of the green top. Cut the resulting white part into halves the long way, separate the layers, and wash thoroughly under cold running water. Pat dry before using.

"There is no such thing as a little garlic."

—ARTHUR BAER

BAKED GARLIC

This vegetable side dish is not for garlic lovers only; we hope you'll take our word that after an hour in the oven garlic is soft, sweet, and mellow. We feel certain that you'll become a convert.

In smaller quantities the roasted cloves make a splendid garnish for plain roasted or grilled meats.

6 whole heads of garlic
4 tablespoons (½ stick) unsalted butter
⅓ cup Chicken Stock (page 416)
Coarse salt, to taste
Freshly ground black pepper, to taste

1. Preheat the oven to 350°F.

2. Remove the papery outer skin from the garlic heads, leaving the clusters of cloves intact.

3. Arrange the heads in a baking dish just large enough to hold them comfortably. Add the butter and stock to the pan and set it on a rack in the center of the oven.

4. Bake until the garlic heads are golden brown and tender, 1 hour, basting every 10 minutes or so. Season with coarse salt and freshly ground black pepper. Serve immediately. To eat, separate the cloves and squeeze the soft pulp from its skin.

6 heads, 2 to 6 portions

In our never-ending search for dishes to season with garlic, we discovered that a piece of corned beef, simmered until tender and then cooled to room temperature, is delicious with Aïoli Sauce (page 50). French Potato Salad (page 219) and Ratatouille (page 202) complete this menu for garlic lovers.

DUCK WITH FORTY CLOVES OF GARLIC

Garlic lovers as well as those who are not so sure will be surprised at the mellow sweetness a long, slow baking imparts to these 40 garlic cloves. The duck is perfumed with the heady aroma, and the sauce, finished with sherry vinegar and Cassis, is sweetly tart and nutty. The perfect accompaniments are wild rice, Chestnut and Potato Purée (page 239), and your best Bordeaux.

1 duck, with giblets (4½ to 5 pounds), fresh or thoroughly defrosted
Salt and freshly ground black pepper, to taste
40 large garlic cloves, unpeeled
2 tablespoons vegetable oil
1 cup finely chopped yellow onions
2 carrots, peeled and finely diced
1½ cups Chicken Stock (page 416) or canned chicken broth
1 teaspoon dried thyme
3 parsley sprigs
1 bay leaf
2 tablespoons sherry vinegar
1 tablespoon Crème de Cassis (black currant liqueur)
8 tablespoons (1 stick) unsalted butter, chilled
Chopped fresh parsley, for garnish

1. Remove the neck and giblets from the duck; save the liver for another use. Chop the neck, heart, and gizzard. Cut off the wing tips. Remove all possible fat from the duck's cavity and prick the skin all over with a fork. Salt the inside and outside of the duck and set it in a shallow baking pan just large enough to hold it comfortably. Select 6 of the largest garlic cloves and stuff them into the duck. Arrange the rest of the garlic around the duck. Set aside.

2. Heat the vegetable oil in a small saucepan over medium-low heat, add the chopped giblets and wing tips, and brown over high heat. Season with salt and pepper, reduce the heat to low, and add the onions and carrots. Cover and cook until the vegetables are tender and lightly colored, about 20 minutes.

3. Add the chicken stock, thyme, parsley, and bay leaf, season with salt and pepper, and bring to a boil. Reduce the heat, partially cover, and simmer while the duck roasts.

4. Preheat the oven to 450°F.

5. Set the pan on the center rack of the oven. After 15 minutes turn the temperature down to 375°F and roast the bird for another 35 minutes for medium rare; 5 to 10 minutes more for juicy and still slightly pink. (We do not recommend cooking duck "well done.") Transfer the duck to a platter, cover with aluminum foil, and keep warm.

6. Strain the broth, discard the solids, and measure the broth. You should have ½ cup. If you have less, don't worry. If you have more, return it to the saucepan and cook briskly for 5 minutes or so to reduce it.

7. Lift the garlic cloves from the cooking fat with a slotted spoon and squeeze them from their skins. Puree them in a food processor or force them through a food mill fitted with a medium disc.

8. When the broth is properly reduced, add the vinegar and Cassis, bring to a boil, and reduce the mixture by one third. Whisk in the garlic purée and remove the pan from the heat.

9. Cut the chilled butter into 10 pieces and whisk the butter, piece by piece, into the hot sauce, always adding another piece of butter before the previous one is entirely absorbed. The sauce will

GARLIC

Wild garlic originally sprang up in the Siberian desert, over 5,000 years ago, gradually moving to Egypt by way of Asia Minor, then to India, to Europe, and finally to the New World. It is the strongest-flavored member of the lily family. And over the centuries it has exerted a powerful influence over people around the world. Garlic was once used to ward off evil, Pliny the Elder enumerated sixty-one garlic cures, and today we believe it helps lower cholesterol.

We love garlic and we have loads of company—first and foremost, those who have helped make Italian food the most popular in this country. But many of our favorite cuisines rely on garlic—Greek, Szechuan, French, Spanish, Thai, Vietnamese. It just provides the extra punch that is intoxicating. Where once garlic was frowned upon, it could hardly be more in style. It's celebrated every August at La Fête de l'Air Rose in Lautrec, France, at the Gilroy (California) Garlic Festival, and by garlic connoisseurs at Chez Panisse in Berkeley, California, where it appears in every course of a sold-out garlic dinner.

Young and wild spring garlic is our favorite, because it's less pungent and milder. While we're all most familiar with the white-skinned soft-necked varieties, we urge you to seek out hardneck cloves, which are arranged around a woody core. These have a milder heat and a more complex, rounded flavor. Farmers' markets now abound with dozens of types of organic heirloom garlics. Our favorites include French Red, Red Toch, Spanish Roja, Porcelain, Purple Stripe, Siberian, Persian Star, Romanian Red, Xian, and Asian

Tempest. Each has its own flavor. Taste as many varieties as you can and choose which you like best.

Garlic should always be firm and crisp; the fresher the garlic, the milder the taste. Buy only the quantity you need and store it at room temperature (it mildews in the fridge). The more you mince raw garlic, the more pungent the flavor. Bruised or sliced and added at the last minute to sautéed vegetables, sauces, or pasta dishes, it is milder but still excitingly vibrant. Slivered and inserted into slits in a roast, it permeates the meat with wonder. Whole garlic heads roasted in their skins are a delicious side; chestnut-like, sweet, and buttery, they are perfectly seductive spread on crusty bread.

To grow organic heirloom garlic, contact Filaree Farm, the purveyors of over 100 unique strains of seed garlic, at www.filareefarm.com.

begin to look creamy and thicken slightly. Cover the saucepan and set it in a warm (not hot) place.

10. Carve the duck into 4 serving pieces and divide them between 2 warmed plates. Add the accompaniments you have chosen. Spoon some of the sauce over the duck, and transfer the rest to a sauceboat. Retrieve the garlic cloves remaining inside the carcass and use them to garnish the sauced duck. Sprinkle with the parsley. Serve immediately.

2 portions

RED SNAPPER WITH BUTTER AND SHALLOT SAUCE

In this elegant dish, the hot fillets of red snapper transform the raw spinach into something tender and wonderful. The sauce, a fragile binding of raspberry vinegar, shallots, and butter, is delicately pink and tart. Begin the meal with a pasta dish and serve the main course ungarnished; it is beautiful by itself.

⅓ cup raspberry vinegar (see Note)
2 tablespoons finely minced shallots
2 red snapper fillets (¾ pound each)
⅓ cup Fish Stock (page 417)
⅓ cup dry white wine or vermouth
Salt and freshly ground black pepper, to taste
1 cup (2 sticks) chilled unsalted butter, cut into small pieces
1 tablespoon Crème Fraîche (page 414)
3 cups finely shredded raw spinach

1. Preheat the oven to 400°F.

2. Combine the vinegar and shallots in a small heavy saucepan. Bring to a boil, lower the heat slightly, and simmer until the vinegar is reduced to about 2 tablespoons. Set aside.

3. Arrange the snapper fillets in a shallow baking dish just large enough to hold them without overlapping. Pour the fish stock and the wine over the fillets, season with salt and pepper, and set the dish on the center rack of the oven. Bake for 8 to 10 minutes; the fish should be just slightly underdone since it will continue to cook due to residual heat. Cover with aluminum foil and keep warm.

4. Meanwhile, heat the vinegar and shallot mixture again and, over very low heat, whisk in the chilled butter bit by bit, always

"The sliced onions
give of their essence
after a brew and become
the ambrosia
for gods and men."
—JANE BOTHWELL

SHALLOTS

When we opened The Silver Palate years ago, we had to scramble for shallots. Our sole source was a supplier in New Jersey who made only infrequent trips to the city. What a wonder, then, that now we can find them at our greengrocer as easily as we can celery. In fact, we've spotted them in supermarkets around the country, further evidence of the increasing availability of hard-to-find ingredients.

The delicate but distinctive flavor of shallots falls somewhere between that of garlic and that of onions, and yet is more sophisticated than either. There are three kinds of shallots: red, greenish-white, and purple, which is considered to be the best. They are used most often raw in salads or cooked in dishes where a subtle but emphatic onion touch is needed—the great sauces of the French haute cuisine, for example. They are versatile favorites in our kitchen; we think if you try them, you'll like them too.

adding another piece before the preceding piece is completely absorbed. The sauce will become creamy and glossy. Remove the sauce from the heat, whisk in the crème fraîche, and set the sauce aside, covered.

5. Divide the spinach equally between 2 plates. Using a spatula, transfer a fillet to each plate, centering it on the spinach. Spoon the raspberry butter sauce over the fish and serve immediately.

2 portions

Note: Available at specialty food shops.

SIX-ONION SOUP

The whole array of onions is present in this rich and creamy soup. Float croutons of toasted French bread on the soup and add a sprinkling of chives.

4 tablespoons (½ stick) unsalted butter
2 cups finely chopped yellow onions
4 large leeks, white parts only, well rinsed and thinly sliced
½ cup chopped shallots
4 to 6 garlic cloves, peeled and minced
4 cups Chicken Stock (page 416)
1 teaspoon dried thyme
1 bay leaf
Salt and freshly ground black pepper, to taste
1 cup heavy cream
3 scallions (green onions), trimmed, well rinsed, and diagonally cut into ½-inch pieces
Toasted French bread croutons, for garnish (see page 76)
Snipped fresh chives and scallion greens, for garnish

1. Melt the butter in a large heavy pot over low heat. Add the onions, leeks, shallots, and garlic and cook, covered, over low heat until the vegetables are tender and lightly colored, about 25 minutes.

2. Add the stock, thyme, and bay leaf, and season with salt and pepper. Bring to a boil, reduce the heat, and cook, partially covered, for 20 minutes.

3. Pour the soup through a strainer set over a bowl, transfer the solids and 1 cup of the liquid to a food processor (or use a food mill fitted with a medium disc), and purée.

4. Return the purée and remaining 3 cups of liquid to the pot and set over medium heat. Whisk in the heavy cream and bring to a simmer. Add the scallions and simmer until they are tender, another 5 minutes.

5. Ladle into heated bowls and garnish with croutons of toasted French bread and snipped fresh chives and scallion greens.

4 to 6 portions

PEARLY VEAL AND ONION STEW

This light, herb- and wine-infused stew gains flavor from onions, and is garnished with them as well. Serve it with Parsleyed Rice (page 419) or buttered noodles.

¼ to ½ cup best-quality olive oil
3 pounds boneless veal stew meat, in 1-inch cubes
¼ cup potato starch or flour
10 large garlic cloves, peeled and chopped
3 cups Chicken Stock (page 416)
1½ cups white wine
1 tablespoon fresh or 1 teaspoon dried rosemary
1 teaspoon dried oregano
1 teaspoon salt
½ teaspoon freshly ground black pepper
2 pounds white pearl onions
Chopped fresh parsley, for garnish

1. Heat ¼ cup olive oil in a deep, heavy, ovenproof casserole and brown the veal, a few pieces at a time, adding more oil as necessary. Remove with a slotted spoon and transfer to a bowl. When all the pieces are browned, sprinkle on the potato starch and toss to coat. Reserve.

2. In the same oil cook the garlic over low heat until lightly browned, about 5 minutes.

3. Preheat the oven to 325°F.

4. Return the veal to the casserole, and add the chicken stock, white wine, rosemary, oregano, salt, and pepper. Bring to a simmer on top of the stove. Cover the casserole and set it on the center rack of the oven. Bake, stirring occasionally, for 1 hour.

5. Meanwhile, cut a small X in the root end of each pearl onion, being careful not to cut completely through the root end so the onions will not fall apart in the stew. Bring a pan of salted water to a boil, drop in the onions, and cook until tender, about 15 minutes. Drain them and plunge immediately into cold water. When the onions are cool enough to handle, peel them.

6. Uncover the casserole and taste the stew; correct the seasoning if necessary. Stir in the onions, and cook for another 20 minutes, uncovering the stew for the last 10 minutes of the cooking time. Sprinkle with the chopped parsley and serve immediately.

8 to 10 portions

ONIONS

Teary eyes are a small price to pay for the countless ways that onions enrich our food. The pantry is never without them, and we reach for an onion almost as automatically as we reach for a knife when we begin to cook.

The strength of the onion depends on the variety and its origin; the warmer the climate, the sweeter the onion.

The sweet yellow Spanish, sweeter still the Maui, Walla Walla, and Vidalia, the sharp white, the mild Italian red, the Bermuda, and the Italian cipolline all play their part in the foods we love. Our reliance on this flavorful staple is sincere. Along the way we've learned that chilled onions or those held under cold water cause fewer tears than those at room temperature. Now we hardly ever cry when we cook.

TOMATOES

We've all become a little tomato crazy. When they're good, they're just so darned good! Vine-ripened tomatoes are one of summer's chief garden stars. Most folks we know try to grow at least a few plants of their own, trading varieties and compliments among friends at the harvest. We've all come to cherish that just-ripened rosy treasure, still warm from the sun, eaten out of hand, simply sprinkled with sea salt, or love popping jewel-colored miniatures into our mouths like candy. An assortment of tomatoes with their various hues, thickly sliced and marinated with fresh herbs, balsamic vinegar, and olive oil just long enough to heighten the flavors of all three—pure heaven.

Today, with the renaissance of heirloom tomatoes in all of their colors, shapes, and sizes, tomato time in the garden and at the farmers' market is more of a celebration than ever. Heirlooms are tomatoes that come from a pure strain of seed, never having been crossbred with any other variety. They are the true royals of the tomato family, never compromised to insure long-distance travel, lengthy shelf life, or worst of all, refrigeration that kills the taste of a good tomato.

It's hard to ever get enough of the taste of tomatoes during their short season, so capture the intense flavor of these beauties at their full ripeness every way you can, in chutneys, juices, preserves, sorbets, sauces, and desserts, while you can. Today, there are terrific sun-dried tomatoes available in oil, with spices or herbs in every form you can imagine, and fabulous Italian canned tomatoes picked and preserved at their peak of freshness. We always have oven-roasted tomatoes on hand to brighten a dish. Sometimes we roast them long and slow, sometimes more quickly at a higher temperature (depending on their size and ripeness). Often we allow them to air-dry for one to two days on a warm surface. A stash of sweet roasted tomatoes in the fridge is a luxury we always want. With so many options, it's easy to have the taste of summer all year long!

SOME TOMATO TYPES

ITALIAN PLUM TOMATOES are the essential cooking tomatoes. Canned or fresh, these small chunky tomatoes are full of flavor and low on interior moisture, making them perfect for sauces. At their best, usually sun-ripened and still warm from the garden, they make magnificent eating without adornment.

CHERRY TOMATOES were indispensable at The Silver Palate. As a bright and colorful garnish, a container for delicious fillings, or a hot vegetable, they are unsurpassed. Properly ripened and flavorful cherry tomatoes are available year-round, if you look for them; they are one of the busy cook's best friends.

"BEEFSTEAK" TOMATOES are America's favorite and these big, thick, and meaty tomatoes are truly "American style." Cut them into wedges for a simple salad, stuff and bake them, or just slice them onto a burger. The tomato lover must be wary, however, since these tomatoes are often grown in greenhouses or hydroponically, and can look spectacular but taste like wet cardboard. Shop carefully, or grow your own and don't hesitate to let them ripen a day or two more on a sunny windowsill.

YELLOW TOMATOES are sweeter and less acidic than the red, and can be lovely in salads or in sauces. They are not common, and thus not found in many markets, but seeds are available and they are easy to grow.

GREEN TOMATOES are delicious. If you hate to leave them to rot on the vine after frost, pick them before the frost strikes and utilize them in a dozen ways—in jams, fried and served with brown sugar and cream, or grilled outdoors during a barbecue.

TOMATO COULIS

6 pounds vine-ripened tomatoes (about 12 good-size tomatoes)
2 tablespoons unsalted butter
2 tablespoons best-quality olive oil
2 cups finely chopped yellow onions
Salt and freshly ground black pepper, to taste
1 cup chopped fresh Italian (flat-leaf) parsley

1. Bring a large heavy pot of salted water to a rolling boil. Drop the tomatoes into the boiling water one at a time and leave each for 10 to 15 seconds. Remove with a slotted spoon and drop into a bowl of cold water. Proceed until all the tomatoes have been scalded, then drain them.

2. The tomatoes will now peel easily. Remove the peels and stems, cut the tomatoes horizontally into halves, and use the handle end of a teaspoon to scoop out and discard the seeds and liquid inside the tomatoes. Coarsely chop the tomatoes and reserve.

3. Heat the butter and the oil together in a large heavy pot over low heat. Add the chopped onions, cover, and cook until the onions are tender and lightly colored, about 25 minutes.

4. Stir in the chopped tomatoes and bring to a boil. Season with salt and freshly ground black pepper. Reduce the heat and simmer, uncovered, until the coulis is somewhat reduced and thickened, about 40 minutes.

COULIS

A *coulis* is simply a reduced purée or sauce, often of vegetables. The best-known and most useful is the tomato coulis. It must be made with only the freshest vine-ripened tomatoes. It can be seasoned with herbs, spices, or garlic as required by the recipe it is to be used with.

The coulis can be served hot or cold, as a sauce for dishes such as the Layered Vegetable Terrine (page 37) or Seafood Pâté (page 35).

Spoon a puddle of coulis onto a small plate and set the serving of food in the middle of the pool. Garnish as directed in the recipe.

ELECTION NIGHT CELEBRATION SUPPER

RAW OYSTERS ON THE HALF SHELL WITH *SHALLOT SAUCE*

PASTA WITH LOBSTER AND TARRAGON

FILET OF BEEF

SAUTÉED CHERRY TOMATOES

RASPBERRIES AND *CRÈME FRAÎCHE*

BLACK WALNUT COOKIES

5. Transfer the coulis to a food processor or use a food mill fitted with a medium disc, and purée.

6. Return the coulis to the pot, add the chopped parsley, and simmer for 5 minutes, or longer if you think you would like a thicker purée.

About 2 quarts

Our favorite variation: Add 3 medium-size garlic cloves, minced, to the pot along with the onion. Add ¼ cup Basil Purée (see Note, page 38) to the tomato mixture just before puréeing it.

SAUTEED CHERRY TOMATOES

This is one of the best vegetable side dishes we know. The few minutes of heat accentuate the cherry tomatoes' natural sweetness, a sprinkling of herbs integrates them into the rest of the menu, and the shiny red globes are an attractive garnish.

You can sauté a little garlic in the butter before adding the tomatoes, or sprinkle them with fresh or dried basil, tarragon, or rosemary. Parmigiano-Reggiano cheese is nice, too. Remember, your goal is just to enhance the tomato flavor with heat—they should not cook through and should never burst or become mushy.

6 tablespoons (¾ stick) unsalted butter (or half butter, half olive oil)
3 pints cherry tomatoes, stemmed, rinsed, and dried
Salt and freshly ground black pepper, to taste

1. Melt the butter in a heavy skillet over low heat. Add the tomatoes and raise the heat.

2. Shake and roll the tomatoes around in the butter until they are shiny and heated through, no more than 5 minutes. Do not overcook.

3. Season with salt and freshly ground black pepper. Serve immediately.

6 portions

SPINACH-AND-RICOTTA-STUFFED TOMATOES

8 ripe red tomatoes, the best you can find
Salt, for draining the tomatoes
3 tablespoons best-quality olive oil
1 cup finely chopped yellow onions
10 ounces frozen spinach, defrosted, drained, and squeezed dry
Salt and freshly ground black pepper, to taste
Grated nutmeg, to taste
1 cup ricotta cheese
2 egg yolks
½ cup toasted pine nuts (page 202)
¼ cup grated Parmigiano-Reggiano cheese, plus extra to top the tomatoes
½ cup chopped fresh Italian (flat-leaf) parsley

1. Wash and dry the tomatoes and cut off their tops. With the handle end of a small spoon, scrape out the seeds and partitions, being careful not to pierce the sides of the tomatoes. Salt the cavities and set the tomatoes upside down on a paper towel to drain for 30 minutes.

2. Heat the olive oil in a skillet over medium-low heat, add the onions, and cook, covered, until tender and lightly colored, about 25 minutes.

3. Chop the spinach and add it to the skillet. Combine the onions and spinach thoroughly, season with salt, pepper, and nutmeg, and cover. Cook over low heat, stirring occasionally, for 10 minutes. Do not let the mixture scorch.

4. Preheat the oven to 350°F.

5. Beat the ricotta and egg yolks together thoroughly in a mixing bowl. Add the spinach mixture, pine nuts, ¼ cup of the Parmigiano-Reggiano and the parsley, and season with salt and pepper.

6. Gently blot the tomato cavities dry with a paper towel and spoon an equal share of the spinach mixture into each one. Top each tomato with a sprinkle of additional cheese.

7. Arrange the tomatoes in a shallow baking dish and set in the upper third of the oven. Bake until the tops are well browned and the filling is hot and bubbly, about 20 minutes. Serve immediately.

8 portions

STUFFED TOMATOES

A hollowed-out ripe tomato makes a naturally delicious cup for a salad or other cold food.

The technique is simple. Select large symmetrical tomatoes, the riper the better. Cut off the tops with a serrated knife and reserve the tops. Scoop out the pulp and seeds with a teaspoon, leaving a sturdy wall. Salt the cavities and set the tomatoes upside down on a paper towel for 30 minutes.

Blot the tomato cavities with a paper towel and fill them with your selected stuffing, mounding it slightly. Set the reserved caps back on top at a jaunty angle; refrigerate until serving time.

Depending on the size of the tomatoes, each will hold ½ to ¾ cup stuffing. You can use your imagination endlessly here, but some of our favorite stuffings include Tarragon Chicken Salad (page 250), Shrimp and Grape Salad (page 274), either of the arugula salads (pages 255–258), or Rice and Vegetable Salad (page 262).

Stuffed cherry tomatoes are a bit more work than large ones, but they have the same virtues. Prepare them in the same way as the larger tomatoes. Discard the caps in this case. Salt the tomatoes and drain for 30 minutes, and stuff with the filling of your choice.

Each tomato will hold about 1 tablespoon of filling. Try Salmon Mousse (page 22), Tapenade Dip (page 28), Pesto Mayonnaise (page 413), or Taramasalata (page 20); or mash a bit of soft fresh chèvre cheese such as Montrachet. Chill until serving time.

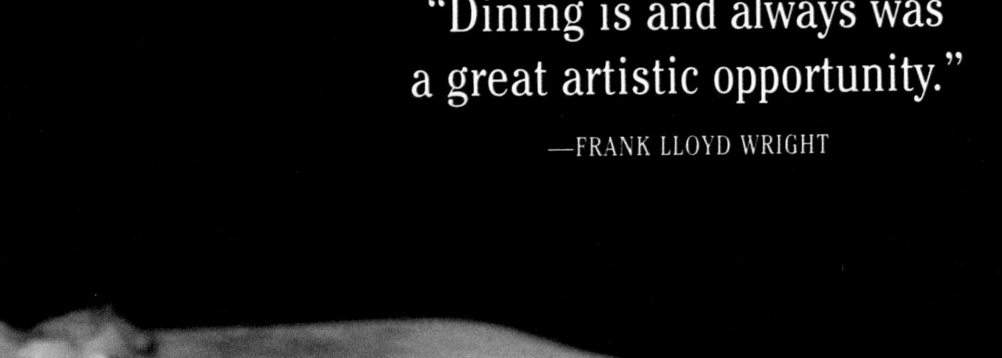

"Dining is and always was
a great artistic opportunity."

—FRANK LLOYD WRIGHT

OVEN ROASTED PLUM TOMATOES

Roasting concentrates tomatoes' natural sweetness.

½ cup best-quality olive oil
12 to 18 ripe plum tomatoes, halved lengthwise and seeded
2 tablespoons sugar
Freshly ground black pepper, to taste
Sea salt, to taste
Small whole Italian (flat-leaf) parsley leaves, or small fresh mint leaves, or finely slivered basil, for garnish

1. Preheat the oven to 250°F.

2. Line a baking sheet with aluminum foil and oil it lightly. Arrange the tomatoes on it in a single layer, cut side up. Drizzle lightly with the remaining olive oil and sprinkle with the sugar and pepper.

3. Bake the tomatoes until they are juicy yet wrinkled a bit, 3 hours.

4. Carefully transfer the tomatoes to a platter. Just before serving, sprinkle them with salt and garnish with the herb leaves.

6 portions

TOMATO DILL SOUP

Our store's most popular soup was based on the rich flavor of the plum tomato. Make it only when you have fresh dill.

8 tablespoons (1 stick) unsalted butter
3 cups sliced yellow onions
2 garlic cloves, peeled and minced
1 bunch of fresh dill, finely chopped, plus dill sprigs for garnish
Salt and freshly ground black pepper, to taste
2 quarts Chicken Stock (page 416)
2 cans (28 ounces each) ripe Italian plum tomatoes, drained and seeded
1 teaspoon ground allspice
Pinch of sugar
Grated zest of 1 small orange
1 cup sour cream, for garnish

We've come a long way since we all complained about winter's pale pink hothouse tomatoes with their cottony textures. Now year-round romas, imported cherry tomatoes on the stem, organics, hydroponics, and new hothouse techniques have made tomatoes a dream come true, most of the time. Of course, refrigeration is anathema to all tomatoes. It simply kills any taste at all. And so, regardless of the season or the source, we always seem to have some ripening on the kitchen windowsill.

But of course our favorites are seasonal, locally grown heirloom tomatoes, those pure strains of tomatoes that have never been compromised. Some may have dazzling good looks, some a blemished exterior that hides brilliantly breathtaking tomato flavor—a perfect example of looks possibly being deceiving. But these are the true glories of the season, worth searching for, even better worth saving seeds and growing in your own garden.

Everyone has their favorites, tiny "gold rush currants" or hefty two-pound "the 1884s," survivors of the Great Ohio Valley Flood. Some prefer pear-shaped and golden, some sweet as candy, others want a little more acidity, or those they remember from childhood. Part of the fun is the quest—so many to taste, so little time. Our favorite "family" heirlooms and their vintages are:

Beanis Yellow Pear
Black Prince
Bonny Best
Burbank
Chocolate
Claudad Vitoria Currant
Deep Purple
Ester Hess Yellow Cherry
Garner's Delight, Germany

Garden Peach, France
Grape
Green Gage
Harman's Yellow Gooseberry
Harbinger, England
Lollipop
Magnus
Mortgage Lifter
Porters Dark Cherry
Principe Borghese, Italy
Riesentraube
Slava, Czech Republic
Snow White
Thai Pink
Yellow Perfection, England

When growing your own tomatoes, remember, if you overwater, you'll get loads of green foliage, but watery tomatoes. Every few days is enough. Tomatoes love sunshine. Heirloom seeds can be found at:

www.johnnyseeds.com
www.rareseeds.com
www.reneesgarden.com
www.seedsavers.com
www.seedsofchange.com
www.tomatobob.com
www.tomatofest.com

1. Melt the butter in a soup pot over low heat. Add the onions and cook, covered, until tender, about 20 minutes. Add the garlic and cook for another 5 minutes.

2. Add half of the dill, season with salt and pepper, and cook, uncovered, for another 15 minutes.

3. Add the chicken stock, tomatoes, allspice, and a pinch of sugar. Bring to a boil, reduce the heat, cover, and simmer for 45 minutes. Add the orange zest, remove from the heat, and cool slightly.

4. Transfer the soup in batches to a food processor or use a food mill fitted with a medium disc. Purée the soup.

5. Return the soup to the pot, add the remaining dill, and simmer for 5 minutes. Serve immediately; or cool and refrigerate, covered, overnight.

6. Taste and correct the seasoning. Garnish the soup, hot or cold, with a dollop of sour cream and a sprig of dill.

8 to 10 portions

LAYERED MOZZARELLA AND TOMATO SALAD

Could any salad be simpler—or better?

4 large ripe tomatoes, cut into ¼-inch slices
2 pounds fresh mozzarella cheese, cut into ¼-inch slices
¼ cup chopped fresh basil
¼ cup chopped fresh Italian (flat-leaf) parsley
½ cup niçoise olives
½ cup Our Favorite Vinaigrette (page 178)
Freshly ground black pepper, to taste

1. On a large serving platter, alternate overlapping slices of tomato and mozzarella cheese.

2. Sprinkle the basil, parsley, and black olives over all.

3. Drizzle the vinaigrette over the salad and grind the black pepper on generously. Serve at room temperature.

6 portions

VEGETABLE PUREES

We've always loved the intense flavor of vegetable purées. They magnify flavors so beautifully. When a vegetable is presented with its texture and sometimes its colors altered, we are forced to focus on its flavor. At the same time purées are rich, comforting, and undemanding, and they often also seem to us to be a bit more stylish, especially at a dinner party. Combinations can be exhilarating, and when two or three purées are presented on the same plate, complementing each other as well as the entrée, the effect is dazzling and often sparks comment. It's time to make a sophisticated statement with your vegetables!

CHESTNUTS

If you've never roasted chestnuts, take a lesson from the street vendors of Paris and New York, who know that crowds will gather whenever the vendors begin to sell their wares. In the kitchen, you'll be pleased with the way their sweet, nutty flavor enhances a menu. Don't wait for Christmas to have them. They're excellent with poultry or game all fall and winter.

Preheat the oven to 400°F. Cut an X in the flat side of each chestnut. Arrange the nuts in a single layer on a baking sheet and bake for 4 or 5 minutes, turning once. Peel with the help of a small, sharp knife, and eat while still very hot; you should burn your fingers just a bit if the chestnuts are to taste their best.

CHESTNUT AND POTATO PUREE

A rich and perfect accompaniment to roast beef, pork, or game.

1¾ cups potatoes, peeled and roughly diced
Salt, to taste
1½ pounds canned unsweetened chestnut purée (see Note)
12 tablespoons (1½ sticks) unsalted butter, at room temperature
⅓ cup Crème Fraîche (page 414)
1 egg
1 egg yolk
¼ cup Calvados
1 teaspoon ground cardamom
Pinch of cayenne pepper

1. Preheat the oven to 350°F.

2. Cover the potatoes with 2 quarts of salted water and cook until tender. Drain well.

3. In a food processor process the chestnut purée until smooth. Transfer to a mixing bowl.

4. Mash the drained potatoes until smooth with 8 tablespoons (1 stick) of the butter. Transfer to the bowl with the chestnut purée.

5. Whisk in the crème fraîche, the whole egg and extra yolk, the Calvados, cardamom, 1½ teaspoons salt, and the cayenne pepper.

6. Smear a 1½-quart soufflé dish with some of the remaining 4 tablespoons of butter and spoon the purée into it. Dot the top with the remaining butter. Bake for 25 minutes before serving.

7. The dish can be made ahead and refrigerated, then baked just before serving.

6 portions

Note: Available at specialty food shops.

BEET AND APPLE PUREE

Serve this delicious, brightly colored purée hot with pork, duck, goose, or ham, or cold with hot grilled sausages.

5 medium-size beets (about 2 pounds)
2 tablespoons salt
8 tablespoons (1 stick) unsalted butter
1 cup finely chopped yellow onions
4 tart apples (about 1½ pounds)
1 tablespoon sugar
½ teaspoon salt
¼ cup raspberry vinegar (see Note)
Chopped fresh dill (optional)

1. Trim away all but 1 inch of the green tops from the beets, leaving the skins and roots; scrub well. Cover the beets with cold water in a large pot, add 2 tablespoons salt, and bring to a boil. Reduce the heat and simmer, partially covered, until the beets are tender, about 40 minutes to 1 hour. Add additional water if necessary to ensure that the beets remain covered. Drain the beets as they are done, cool slightly, and slip off the tops, skins, and roots.

2. Melt the butter in a medium-size saucepan over low heat. Add the onions and cook, covered, until tender and lightly colored, about 25 minutes.

3. Peel, core, and chop the apples and add them to the onions. Add the sugar, salt, and raspberry vinegar, and simmer, uncovered, until the apples and onions are very tender, 15 to 20 minutes.

4. Transfer the apple mixture to a food processor or use a food mill. Chop the beets and add them to the bowl. Process until smooth.

5. Return the purée to the saucepan and reheat, stirring constantly. Taste and correct the seasoning. Serve immediately, garnished with the dill, if you wish, or set aside to cool to room temperature, cover, chill, and serve very cold (again, garnished with the dill, if you like).

6 portions

Note: Available at specialty food shops.

The search for the perfect vegetable drives some of us to walk the city, investigating every farmers' market produce stand and greengrocer we can find (in New York there is at least one per block), and cajoling vendors, large and small. Often the search is spectacularly rewarding, even if it does mean we have a different source for every vegetable on our list.

For others the search can become such a passion that nothing will do but to grow their own. Organically raised vegetables, picked at the peak of perfection in your own backyard, are foods you can trust.

Not all home gardening is done in backyards, however. We know those who use terraces, window boxes, rooftops, and fire escapes. All you need are seeds, sunlight, water, soil with good drainage, and the passionate interest in vegetables to see you through. Watching and watering as your prizes grow will be an astonishingly relaxing and rewarding experience.

NEW YEAR'S EVE MENU

SWEET BLACK CHERRY SOUP

OYSTERS WITH SPINACH AND CAVIAR

FRESH FOIE GRAS AND TOASTS

LAMB WITH PEPPERCORN CRUST

CHESTNUT AND POTATO PURÉE

PURÉED BROCCOLI WITH CRÈME FRAÎCHE

LEEK AND POTATO PURÉE

WATERCRESS, ENDIVE, AND MANDARIN ORANGE SALAD WITH *CHAMPAGNE VINAIGRETTE*

LEMON ICE

DECADENT CHOCOLATE CAKE

PUREED BROCCOLI WITH CREME FRAICHE

A green and hearty purée, good with nearly every entrée in the book.

2 bunches of broccoli (about 5 pounds), trimmed and chopped, including peeled stems
Salt, to taste
1 cup Crème Fraîche (page 414)
¼ cup sour cream
⅔ cup freshly grated Parmigiano-Reggiano cheese
½ teaspoon freshly grated nutmeg
½ teaspoon freshly ground black pepper
2 tablespoons unsalted butter

1. Chop the broccoli, leaving 8 small florets whole, and drop the chopped broccoli and whole florets into 4 quarts of boiling salted water. Cook until just tender, about 8 minutes.

2. Transfer the broccoli, reserving 8 florets, to a food processor. Add the crème fraîche and purée thoroughly.

3. Preheat the oven to 350°F.

4. Scrape the purée into a bowl and stir in the sour cream, Parmigiano-Reggiano, nutmeg, pepper, and salt. Mix well.

5. Mound in an ovenproof serving dish, dot with the butter, and bake until the purée is steaming hot, 25 minutes.

6. Garnish with the reserved florets and serve immediately.

6 portions

LEEK AND POTATO PUREE

Two of our favorite earthy vegetables combined in a rich and soothing purée.

6 large leeks
2 pounds red-skinned potatoes
Salt, to taste
12 tablespoons (1½ sticks) unsalted butter
2 garlic cloves, minced
½ cup heavy cream
Freshly ground black pepper, to taste

1. Trim the roots and most, but not all, of the green leaves from the leeks, leaving each leek about 7 inches long. Split down to but not through the base and wash thoroughly.

2. Bring 3 quarts of salted water to a boil in a pot, add the leeks, and cook until tender, about 15 minutes. Drain and chop.

3. Meanwhile, peel the potatoes. Cover them with cold water in another pot. Add salt and bring to a boil. Reduce the heat and cook until the potatoes are very tender, 20 to 40 minutes, depending on the size. Drain and reserve.

4. Melt 3 tablespoons of the butter in a skillet over low heat. Add the garlic and cook over low heat until lightly colored, about 15 minutes. Add the leeks and an additional 3 tablespoons butter and continue to cook, stirring occasionally, for 15 minutes.

5. Transfer the leeks-and-butter mixture to a food processor and purée until smooth.

6. Mash the potatoes, adding heavy cream as needed. Stir in the leek purée and the remaining 6 tablespoons butter; season with salt and pepper. Reheat gently until steaming. Serve immediately.

6 portions

SWEET POTATO AND CARROT PUREE

4 large sweet potatoes (about 2 pounds), of a moist variety
1 pound carrots
2½ cups water
1 tablespoon sugar
12 tablespoons (1½ sticks) unsalted butter, at room temperature
Salt and freshly ground black pepper, to taste
½ cup Crème Fraîche (page 414)
½ teaspoon freshly grated nutmeg
Dash of cayenne pepper (optional)

1. Preheat the oven to 375°F.

2. Scrub the potatoes and cut a small, deep slit in the top of each. Set on the center rack of the oven and bake until the potatoes are tender when pierced with a fork, about 1 hour.

3. Meanwhile, peel and trim the carrots and cut them into 1-inch lengths. Put them in a saucepan and add the water, sugar, 2 tablespoons of the butter, and salt and pepper. Set over medium heat, bring to a boil, and cook, uncovered, until the water has evaporated and the carrots begin to sizzle in the butter, about 30 minutes. The carrots should be tender. If not, add a little additional water and cook until the carrots are done and all the liquid has evaporated.

4. Scrape out the flesh of the sweet potatoes and combine with the carrots in a food processor. Add the remaining butter and the crème fraîche and process until very smooth.

5. Add the nutmeg, and season with salt and pepper. Add the cayenne, if desired, and process briefly to blend.

6. To reheat, transfer to an ovenproof serving dish and cover with aluminum foil. Heat in a preheated 350°F oven until steaming hot, about 25 minutes.

6 portions

from THE SILVER PALATE NOTEBOOK

When planning a party, take the time to analyze traffic patterns of parties that you've hosted before, or remember other parties you've recently attended. It's important that guests can move freely, knowing where the party boundaries are. It's also always true that if guests can find the kitchen, they'll gather there. Plan for it. Walk through the evening in your mind, looking for snags, loopholes, omissions. Plan the pace of the party, how long cocktail time will last, when the food will be served, and where you might move for dessert.

Always make sure you have provided a room or closet for guests to leave their coats, and make sure it's easy to find so guests can retrieve their coats without fuss. When all is well thought through it allows you time to graciously greet all the guests, introduce them to each other, and ultimately be the life of your own party, because you should be!

SALADS

SIGNIFICANT SALADS

Salads have new importance, yet the key to their success still rests in their simplicity. The salad bowl is no place to mix metaphors or too many good ideas. Stick to a single theme; the best salads are conceived so that the partnerships work together wonderfully while preserving the integrity of the individual ingredients. This can even encompass the use of two dressings, the first to coat the greens, the second to enhance the keynote flavor.

In no other course is there so wide a range of individuality, and there is no single step in the preparation of a salad that is unimportant.

AVOCADO AND HAM SALAD

A colorful, zesty combination.

1 cup fresh lemon juice
¼ cup water
4 ripe avocados, halved and peeled
2 heads of red-leaf lettuce or Boston lettuce, leaves separated, washed, and patted dry
3 pounds baked ham, cut into ¼-inch slices and then into 2-inch strips (make them a bit rough looking)
8 medium-size ripe tomatoes, cut into quarters
1 red onion, peeled and cut into thin rings
1 cup Lemon Vinaigrette (recipe follows)
Salt and freshly ground black pepper, to taste
¼ cup chopped fresh Italian (flat-leaf) parsley
1 bunch of watercress, washed and dried, for garnish

1. Mix the lemon juice and water together in a small bowl. Slice the peeled avocados and dip into the lemon juice mixture. Drain.

2. Line a large serving platter with the lettuce leaves. Arrange the avocados, ham, tomatoes, and onion rings in a decorative spiral on the lettuce leaves.

3. Drizzle the salad with the lemon vinaigrette. Season with salt and pepper and sprinkle with the chopped parsley.

4. Garnish with the watercress and serve immediately.

8 portions

LEMON VINAIGRETTE

1 cup best-quality olive oil
⅔ cup fresh lemon juice
½ cup snipped fresh chives
2 tablespoons finely minced shallots
2 tablespoons Dijon mustard
Salt and freshly ground black pepper, to taste

Combine all the ingredients in a covered container and shake well until blended. Serve immediately.

About 1¾ cups

PERFECT JULIENNE

Preparing a julienne of vegetables can be an exacting exercise. In great chefs' kitchens, "prep" help is expected to spend as much time as necessary at this task so that the chef will have perfect matchstick strips of carrots, leeks, mushrooms, beets, cucumbers, and anything else his heart desires, at his fingertips. While working with some chefs in France we observed a young boy being hit on the hand because the shreds of leek he was making were not of uniform length. The chef was concerned that his clients would return their meals and his reputation would be ruined. For you it needn't be that difficult. These little strips of color serve as a beautiful garnish for many dishes, or combined they make a wonderful vegetable presentation.

CHEF'S SALAD

More than a salad of odds and ends, a chef's salad can be spectacular. Use only the freshest of vegetables and take the time to julienne them beautifully. It's all in the hands of the chef.

1 large head of red-leaf lettuce, leaves separated, washed, and dried
2 medium-size heads of romaine lettuce, leaves separated, washed, and dried
1 bunch of watercress, stems removed, washed, and dried
1 large cucumber, peeled, halved lengthwise, seeded, and sliced into crescents
6 ripe tomatoes, each cut into 6 wedges
½ green bell pepper, stemmed, seeded, and cut into julienne
½ red bell pepper, stemmed, seeded, and cut into julienne
12 ounces bottled marinated artichoke hearts, drained and halved
½ pound Gruyère cheese, cut into julienne
¼ pound thinly sliced prosciutto, cut into julienne
¼ pound thinly sliced hard salami, cut into julienne
½ pound thinly sliced boiled or baked ham, cut into julienne
3 whole cooked boneless, skinless chicken breasts, cut into julienne (3 to 4 cups)
½ cup niçoise or other imported black olive, for garnish
3 hard-cooked eggs, shelled and cut lengthwise into quarters, for garnish
2 cups Our Favorite Vinaigrette (page 178)

1. Line a large salad bowl with whole red-leaf lettuce leaves.

2. Tear the romaine lettuce into medium-size pieces and layer in the lettuce-lined bowl with the watercress, half of the cucumber slices, the tomato wedges, red bell pepper, artichokes, cheese, and two thirds of the meat and chicken.

3. Arrange the remaining vegetables and meats in a decorative spoke fashion around the top of the salad.

4. Garnish with the niçoise olives and hard-cooked eggs. Cover the salad and refrigerate for 1 hour.

5. At table, pour the vinaigrette over the salad and toss.

6 to 8 portions

"Food is the most primitive form of comfort."

—SHEILA GRAHAM

MARINATED BEEF SALAD

This salad originated as a way to utilize leftover London broil, but has long since evolved into a salad so special that we find ourselves making extra London broil so that we can have Marinated Beef Salad. It is a cool solution to the problem of finding salads to please your carnivores. The following recipe is only a suggestion; feel free to improvise with any ingredients you have on hand.

In testing this recipe we marinated a boneless 2-pound sirloin about 2 inches thick in ¼ cup olive oil, ½ cup red wine vinegar, and ¼ cup soy sauce for 3 hours before draining it, patting it dry, and panfrying it over the highest possible heat for about 10 minutes a side.

3 large boiling potatoes
3 to 4 cups cooked beefsteak (preferably medium rare), cut into thick julienne
⅔ cup diced bell pepper, half green and half red
⅓ cup chopped red onion
1 scallion (green onion), well rinsed and thinly sliced
⅔ cup Garlic Dressing (page 268)
⅓ cup chopped fresh Italian (flat-leaf) parsley
Lettuce leaves, washed and patted dry
Grated zest of 1 orange, for garnish

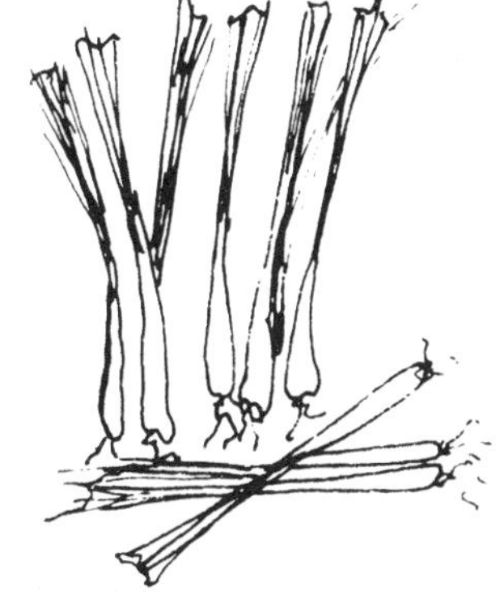

1. Peel the potatoes. Using a melon-baller, scoop the potatoes into small balls; you should have about 2 cups.

2. Transfer the potatoes to a pan of cold, salted water and bring to a boil. Reduce the heat and cook until the balls are tender but not mushy. Drain.

3. Combine the potatoes, beef, green and red bell peppers, onion, and scallion in a mixing bowl.

4. Pour on the garlic dressing and toss thoroughly. Add the parsley and toss again.

5. Arrange the salad on top of the lettuce leaves and garnish with the orange zest. Serve immediately or refrigerate, covered. Let the salad return to room temperature before serving.

4 portions

MEDITERRANEAN CHICKEN SALAD

Not for dieters only, this tart and tasty Riviera-inspired combination is a popular lunch with the getting-ready-to-fit-into-the-summer-wardrobe crowd. Since its creation, it was always a real Silver Palate favorite.

1 medium-size yellow onion, peeled and quartered
2 carrots, peeled and chopped
1 leek, white part only, well rinsed and sliced
1 teaspoon dried thyme
1 bay leaf
6 parsley sprigs
12 black peppercorns
4 whole cloves
Salt, to taste
3 whole chicken breasts (about 3 pounds)
½ cup best-quality olive oil
1½ teaspoons dried oregano
Juice of 1 lemon
¾ cup imported black olives, niçoise preferred
2 tablespoons capers, drained
8 cherry tomatoes, halved, or 2 medium-size ripe tomatoes, cut into wedges
¼ pound green beans, cooked
Freshly ground black pepper, to taste

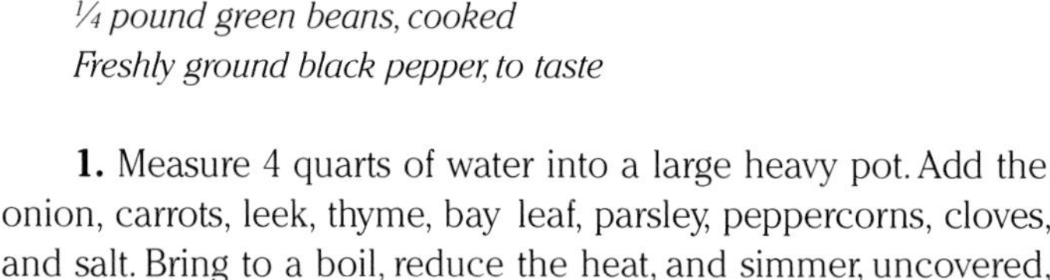

1. Measure 4 quarts of water into a large heavy pot. Add the onion, carrots, leek, thyme, bay leaf, parsley, peppercorns, cloves, and salt. Bring to a boil, reduce the heat, and simmer, uncovered, for 15 minutes.

2. Add the chicken breasts, return to a boil, reduce the heat, and simmer, partially covered, until the chicken is done, about 20 minutes. Remove the pot from the heat and let the chicken cool in the broth.

3. Remove the chicken (saving the broth for soup), discard the skin, and pull the meat from the bones. Tear the meat into large pieces and combine in a bowl with the olive oil and oregano. Cover and let stand at room temperature for 1 hour.

4. Add the remaining ingredients, toss, and season with salt and pepper. Serve immediately.

4 to 6 portions

Note: The salad will keep for several days refrigerated. Reserve the green beans and add them just before serving to prevent discoloration.

from THE SILVER PALATE NOTEBOOK

Flowers have been considered food by many cultures for centuries. In this age of doing what comes naturally, we think flowers make a most appropriate and beautiful garnish. Use your own good sense: some flowers may tend to be too scented and overpowering. We love them when used with a delicate touch: garnishing plates, floating in a glass of Champagne, or scattered in salads.

Some of our favorite flowers include rose petals in salads, tea roses in white wine, and garnishing sprays of pinks, forget-me-nots, wildflowers, chive blossoms, wild thyme and dill flowers, Johnny-jump-ups, yellow bok choy, purple nasturtiums, and borage.

Nasturtiums have a pleasant peppery flavor. They bloom in shades of creamy white to deep crimson, and are great in salads or chopped on a sandwich. Nasturtium seed pods can be pickled for eating by marinating them in equal amounts of vinegar and sugar, along with your favorite herbs. These are very special when sprinkled in salads and sauces, used as you would capers. When you use fresh flowers in your food, be sure to buy organic.

"If you are lazy and dump everything together,
they won't come out as well as if you add
one thing at a time. It's like everything else;
no shortcuts without compromising quality."
—LIONEL POILÂNE

TARRAGON CHICKEN SALAD

We feel this is a chicken salad with style as well as substance. It is dressy enough to serve as a main course, delicious in a sandwich, and so simple to assemble that you'll soon know the recipe by heart. We adore this recipe and think it's pretty safe to say that it wears well—it has for decades now. You can always vary it by using black walnuts, or by tossing in some green grapes or dried cranberries.

About 3 pounds boneless, skinless whole chicken breasts
1 cup Crème Fraîche (page 414) or heavy cream
½ cup sour cream
½ cup mayonnaise, preferably Hellmann's
2 celery ribs, cut into 1-inch-long pencil strips
½ cup shelled walnuts
1 tablespoon crumbled dried tarragon
Salt and freshly ground black pepper, to taste

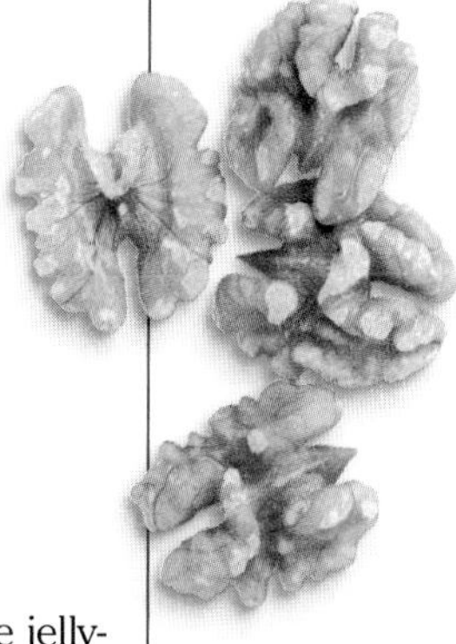

1. Preheat the oven to 350°F.

2. Arrange the chicken breasts in a single layer in a large jelly-roll pan. Spread evenly with the crème fraîche and bake until cooked through, 20 to 25 minutes. Remove from the oven and cool.

3. Shred the meat into bite-size pieces and transfer to a bowl.

4. Whisk the sour cream and mayonnaise together in a small bowl and pour over the chicken mixture.

5. Add the celery, walnuts, tarragon, and salt and pepper, and toss well.

6. Refrigerate, covered, for at least 4 hours. Taste and correct the seasoning before serving.

4 to 6 portions

Note: Use the accumulated juices from the jelly-roll pan to enrich soups or sauces.

MARINATED ITALIAN VEGETABLE SALAD

3 or 4 garlic cloves, peeled and chopped
2 small dried hot red chiles
1 bay leaf
1½ cups peeled carrots, sliced into coins
¾ cup imported white wine vinegar
4 cups cauliflower florets
¾ cup celery, cut into ½-inch pieces
2 tablespoons capers, well drained
1 cup assorted imported olives (Sicilian, alfonso, kalamata)
1 cup best-quality olive oil

"... Poultry is for the cook what canvas is for the painter."

—JEAN ANSELME BRILLAT-SAVARIN

MIDDLE OF THE NIGHT SANDWICHES

Raiding the refrigerator is to some a habit, to others an event. Shared or taken alone, the midnight snack quells the demons of hunger and allows us to relax, the better to sleep. With planning you can insure that there's a little something that, coupled with inspiration, will get you through the night.

- ♥ Fill pita bread with Tarragon Chicken Salad sprinkled with dried currants and sprouts.
- ♥ Put shrimp, cooked peas, and sliced scallions tossed with Chutney Mayonnaise (page 413) on sliced Brioche (page 300). Add red-leaf lettuce for color and crunch.
- ♥ Cut off the top and hollow a French roll. Spread with Hummus bi Tahini (page 420), add sliced chicken breast, diced tomato, and pitted black olives. Sprinkle with lemon juice and toasted sesame seeds, and garnish with shredded raw spinach.
- ♥ Toss cooked bulgur (processed cracked wheat) with olive oil, sliced scallions, grated orange zest, watercress, and dried currants. Stuff into pita bread and dress with mayonnaise.
- ♥ Alternate the thinnest slices of rare roast lamb and charcoal-roasted slices of eggplant on pumpernickel. Dress with lemony Mint and Yogurt Mayonnaise (page 413).
- ♥ Try romaine lettuce on Raisin Pumpernickel (page 297) with avocado slices, tomato, watercress, sliced scallions, a vinaigrette dressing, and cottage cheese.

1. Place the garlic, chiles, and bay leaf in a large bowl.

2. Bring about 3 quarts of salted water to a boil in a pot, drop in the carrot coins, and cook until tender but still crisp. Lift the carrots from the water with a slotted spoon, drain briefly, and drop into the bowl with the garlic mixture. (Keep the water boiling.) Pour the vinegar over the hot carrots and stir.

3. Repeat the blanching procedure with the cauliflower and then the celery, stirring each vegetable into the vinegar, garlic, and herb mixture while hot.

4. Add the capers, olives, and olive oil and let cool to room temperature before covering. Refrigerate for at least 24 hours. Before serving as part of an antipasto, let the salad return to room temperature and adjust the seasoning if necessary.

6 to 10 portions

SMOKED TURKEY SALAD

This meat-cheese-and-fruit salad, with its nutty, sherry-flavored dressing, is a complete meal. Arrange individual servings on lettuce-lined plates, accompanied by pumpernickel or whole-wheat bread and a glass of white wine or beer.

1½ pounds smoked turkey (or lightly smoked ham or chicken), skinned and cut into 2-inch julienne
¾ pound Jarlsberg cheese, cut into 2-inch julienne
2 cups seedless green or red grapes, washed and patted dry
1 cup chopped celery
1½ cups Sherry Mayonnaise (recipe follows)
Salt and freshly ground black pepper, to taste
1 to 2 tablespoons water-packed green peppercorns, drained

1. Combine the turkey, Jarlsberg cheese, grapes, and celery in a mixing bowl.

2. Add the Sherry Mayonnaise and toss gently but well. Season with salt and pepper and toss again. Cover and refrigerate until serving time.

3. Arrange the salad in serving portions and sprinkle with the green peppercorns to taste.

6 portions

SHERRY MAYONNAISE

This complements combinations like the Smoked Turkey Salad but is also delicious on a chicken sandwich or served as a dip for crudités.

1 whole egg
2 egg yolks
1 tablespoon Dijon mustard
¼ cup sherry vinegar
Salt and freshly ground black pepper, to taste
2 cups corn oil

1. Combine the whole egg, egg yolks, mustard, and vinegar in a food processor, and season with salt and pepper. Process for 1 minute.

2. With the motor still running, dribble in the oil in a slow steady stream.

3. When the oil is completely incorporated, shut off the machine, scrape down the sides of the bowl, taste the mayonnaise, and correct the seasoning. Transfer to a storage container, cover, and refrigerate until ready to use.

2½ cups

Always use very fresh, well refrigerated eggs when making mayonnaise from scratch.

DUCK AND PEAR SALAD WITH MANGO CHUTNEY DRESSING

This is a perfect salad for an important luncheon or a cool main course on a hot summer night. We prefer medium-rare duck, roasted at 450°F for 15 minutes and at 375°F for another 20 to 30 minutes. If you prefer duck well done, cook longer, until tender, to your taste. Use wild rice if you can—it makes a spectacular salad—or mix wild and brown rices.

2 ducklings (each 4½ to 5 pounds), cooked and cooled (see Step 1)
3 cups cooked rice, cooled
1 cup chopped celery
4 scallions (green onions), well rinsed and cut diagonally into ½-inch pieces
Grated zest of 1 orange
Salt and freshly ground black pepper, to taste
3 ripe but firm eating pears
1 cup bottled lemon juice
Mango Chutney Dressing (recipe follows)

1. Skin the ducks, remove all the flesh from the bones, and cut the meat into 1-inch cubes.

VERNAL EQUINOX SUPPER

CHILLED SHRIMP AND CUCUMBER SOUP

DUCK AND PEAR SALAD WITH MANGO CHUTNEY DRESSING

FRENCH PEASANT BREAD

BRIE WRAPPED IN PHYLLO

LIME MOUSSE

2. Toss the duck meat and cooked rice together in a mixing bowl. Add the celery, scallions, and orange zest, and season with salt and pepper. Toss again and arrange the salad on a large serving platter.

3. If the skin of the pears seems too thick or spotty, peel the pears. Otherwise quarter, core, and slice them thinly, and drop the slices into a bowl containing the lemon juice. Toss the slices to coat them thoroughly and let them remain in the juice until you have finished slicing all 3 pears.

4. Drain the pear slices and arrange them in a decorative fan across the top of the duck salad. Serve immediately with the mango chutney dressing, offering the peppermill to your guests.

4 to 6 portions

Because the eggs are raw, use very fresh, well refrigerated ones in the Mango Chutney Dressing.

MANGO CHUTNEY DRESSING

1 whole egg
2 egg yolks
1 tablespoon Dijon mustard
¼ cup blueberry vinegar (page 145)
⅓ cup mango chutney
1 tablespoon soy sauce
Salt and freshly ground black pepper, to taste
1 cup peanut oil
1 cup corn oil

1. Combine the whole egg, egg yolks, mustard, vinegar, chutney, and soy sauce in a food processor. Season with salt and pepper and process for 1 minute.

2. With the motor running, dribble in the oils in a slow steady stream. When all the oil has been incorporated, shut off the motor, scrape down the sides of the processor bowl, taste, and correct the seasoning.

3. Transfer the dressing to a storage container, cover, and refrigerate until ready to use.

3 cups

"It's hot!
I can't get cool.
I've drunk a quantity
of lemonade.
I think I'll take
my shoes off and
sit around in
the shade."

—SHEL SILVERSTEIN,
A LIGHT IN THE ATTIC

GREEK LAMB AND EGGPLANT SALAD

Another main-course salad, offering the wonderful flavors of Greece. Of course you can make this with leftover lamb, but it's so good we often roast half a leg of lamb just for this salad.

5 cups 1-inch cubes of peeled eggplant (about 1 large eggplant)
Salt, for draining the eggplant
¼ cup olive oil
¾ pound fresh spinach, washed and dried, with stems removed
4 cups cooked lamb, cut into thick julienne
1 cup imported black olives (kalamata or alfonso)
2 to 3 tablespoons toasted pine nuts (page 202)
Lemon-Garlic Mayonnaise (recipe follows)

1. Layer the eggplant in a colander, salting it generously as you go, and set the colander in the sink or over a plate. Let stand for at least 30 minutes.

2. Preheat the oven to 400°F.

3. Rinse the eggplant, pat the cubes dry with paper towels, and arrange in a single layer in a baking dish. Drizzle the eggplant with the olive oil and bake, turning occasionally, until tender but not mushy, 20 to 30 minutes. Remove from the oven and cool to room temperature. Taste; add salt if needed.

4. Arrange the spinach leaves around the edge of a serving platter.

5. Combine the eggplant and lamb and mound in the center of the platter.

6. Distribute the olives over the lamb and eggplant and sprinkle the pine nuts over all.

7. Serve at room temperature with the lemon-garlic mayonnaise on the side. Offer the peppermill to your guests.

4 portions

LEMON-GARLIC MAYONNAISE

1 whole egg
2 egg yolks
¼ cup fresh lemon juice, plus more if needed
Salt and freshly ground black pepper, to taste
6 to 8 large garlic cloves, peeled and chopped
2¼ cups best-quality olive oil

1. Combine the whole egg, egg yolks, and ¼ cup of the lemon juice in a food processor. Season with salt and pepper and process for 1 minute.

2. Drop the garlic through the feed tube and then begin to pour in the olive oil in a slow steady stream. When all of the oil has been incorporated, shut off the motor, scrape down the sides of the processor bowl, taste, and correct the seasoning. Add additional lemon juice to taste.

3. Transfer the mayonnaise to a storage container, cover, and refrigerate until ready to use.

About 3 cups

REAL LEMONADE

Mix the juice of 12 lemons with ½ cup sugar in a pitcher, stirring until the sugar dissolves. Add the lemon zests—cut into strips—and fill the pitcher with ice. Let the ice melt for about 30 minutes. Presto! Serve the lemonade with crushed ice and garnish with a lemon slice and a sprig of fresh mint.

Always use very fresh, well refrigerated eggs when making mayonnaise from scratch.

"To remember a successful salad is generally to remember a successful dinner; at all events, the perfect dinner necessarily includes the perfect salad."

—GEORGE ELLWANGER, *THE PLEASURES OF THE TABLE*

WHITE BEAN AND HAM SALAD

Serve this charcuterie salad with tart cornichons and whole-wheat bread or pumpernickel. A wonderful autumn or winter lunch, perfect on a picnic. A good dark beer would be especially appropriate here.

1 pound Great Northern or other dried white beans
Salt, to taste
1 to 2 cups Garlic-Mustard Dressing (page 283)
1 medium-size red onion, peeled and sliced paper-thin
1 cup chopped fresh Italian (flat-leaf) parsley
1 pound cooked ham, trimmed and cut into 1-inch cubes
Freshly ground black pepper, to taste
1 cup best-quality imported black olives (kalamata or alfonso), for garnish

1. Rinse and sort through the beans, discarding any pebbles, and soak them overnight in water that covers them by at least 3 inches.

2. Drain the beans and transfer them to a large heavy pot. Add cold water to cover the beans by at least 1 inch. Set over moderate heat. Bring to a boil, skimming any scum that may form, and cook the beans until tender, about 40 minutes, salting to taste after 30 minutes. The cooking times will vary. It is important not to overcook the beans.

3. Drain the beans, transfer them immediately to a mixing bowl, and pour 1 cup of the garlic-mustard dressing over the still-hot beans.

4. Add the onion, parsley, and ham, season with salt and pepper, and toss. Cover and refrigerate.

5. To serve, allow the salad to return to room temperature. Toss again, correct the seasoning (add more dressing if you like), and garnish with the black olives.

6 to 8 portions

AN ALL-ARUGULA SALAD

A salad for arugula lovers. Allow 1 bunch per person.

Bunches of arugula, stems removed
Garlic-Anchovy Dressing (recipe follows)

1. Rinse and dry the arugula leaves thoroughly. Wrap and refrigerate until ready to dress the salad.

2. Toss the arugula in a large bowl with garlic-anchovy dressing to taste. Arrange on plates and serve immediately.

Because the egg is raw, use a very fresh, well refrigerated one in the Garlic-Anchovy Dressing.

ARUGULA

Arugula travels under a variety of names—rugula, roquette, rocket cress, rocket, or garden rocket—but no matter what it's called, this robust leaf has made a distinct impression. Many first tasted it in Italian restaurants, and now most spring salad mixes add it for its distinctive taste. But arugula may be at its best piled high and served on its own with a balsamic vinaigrette, a few heirloom tomatoes, and generous shavings of Parmigiano-Reggiano. Its robust flavor makes it a most satisfying meal. It's also wonderful lightly sautéed with olive oil, or as a chiffonade in salads, frittatas, risotto, or atop seafood. We cross our fingers that arugula on its own will soon be available regularly in your area. Try the farmers' markets first, where it will be sold loose or in big bundles. Nor will you be sorry if you allow a little room in your own garden for a few plants. It grows very quickly, and you'll soon know whether your preference is to snip the tiny milder leaves or wait for the larger ones, packed with more of that peppery punch.

GARLIC-ANCHOVY DRESSING

3 or 4 anchovy fillets
1 to 2 garlic cloves
1 tablespoon Dijon mustard
1 egg yolk
¼ cup red wine vinegar
Salt and freshly ground black pepper, to taste
1 cup best-quality olive oil

1. Coarsely chop the anchovy fillets, then with a fork mash them in a small bowl.

2. Peel and mince the garlic cloves until they are puréed, mashing them against the work surface with the flat of the chopping knife. Add to the anchovies.

3. Whisk in the mustard, then the egg yolk and red wine vinegar, and season with salt and pepper.

4. Dribble the oil into the bowl in a slow steady stream, whisking constantly, until the dressing is creamy and thickened and all the oil has been incorporated.

5. Transfer the dressing to a storage container, cover, and refrigerate until ready to use.

About 1½ cups

ARUGULA AND RED PEPPER SALAD

This colorful salad is perfectly complemented by a dark and sweetly spicy balsamic vinaigrette. The quantities suggested are approximate; adjust the proportions to your own taste. You can even eliminate the lettuce altogether and increase the amount of arugula, especially if you like this green as much as we do!

2 large heads of leafy green lettuce (romaine and others)
2 bunches of arugula
1 pound fresh mushrooms
3 large red bell peppers
Balsamic Vinaigrette (recipe follows)

1. Discard the outer leaves of the lettuce; separate and rinse (if necessary) the inner leaves and dry thoroughly. Wrap and refrigerate.

2. Remove the arugula leaves from their stems, rinse, and dry thoroughly. Wrap and refrigerate.

3. Remove the stems from the mushrooms and reserve for another use. Wipe each mushroom cap with a damp paper towel, wrap, and refrigerate.

4. Cut away the stems and ribs of the red peppers; discard the seeds. Slice the peppers into fine julienne, wrap, and refrigerate.

5. To assemble, tear the lettuce leaves into bite-size pieces and combine with the arugula. Divide among 6 chilled salad plates. Slice the mushrooms and sprinkle evenly over the greens. Arrange the red pepper julienne over the mushrooms. Drizzle each plate with balsamic vinaigrette and serve immediately. (For a more informal presentation, combine all the ingredients in a large salad bowl and toss with the vinaigrette just before serving.)

6 portions

BALSAMIC VINAIGRETTE

1 garlic clove, unpeeled
1 tablespoon Dijon mustard
3 tablespoons balsamic vinegar
Salt and freshly ground black pepper, to taste
1 cup best-quality olive oil

1. Cut the garlic clove into halves and rub the cut sides over the inner surface of a small bowl. Reserve the garlic.

2. Whisk the mustard and vinegar together in the bowl. Season with salt and pepper.

3. Dribble the oil into the bowl in a slow steady stream, whisking constantly, until the dressing is creamy and thickened and all the oil has been incorporated.

4. Taste and correct the seasoning. Add the reserved pieces of garlic; cover the bowl and let the dressing stand at room temperature until you need it. Remove the garlic and rewhisk the dressing if necessary before using.

About 1¼ cups

BALSAMIC VINEGAR

This extraordinary wine-based vinegar is still made in Modena in the Emilia-Romagna region of Italy, as it has been for centuries. It is a mellow, sweet-and-sour vinegar with a heady fragrance. By law, it must be aged for a decade in a variety of kegs made of particular kinds of wood; some batches are aged much longer (and have an even deeper, richer flavor). The vinegar is transferred from red-oak kegs to chestnut, mulberry, and juniper in turn, mellowing at each stage. Eventually, a warm, red-brown color and incredible fragrance are achieved. As a result, the taste is very special.

Balsamic vinegar can be used in salads, sprinkled on cold meats or over hot vegetables, or to deglaze a pan. We love it over berries, atop a prized piece of beef, or luxuriously drizzled over chunks of Parmigiano-Reggiano cheese.

SALADE NICOISE

A salad that never fails to bring the Mediterranean to the table. It's crunchy and fresh-tasting, making a terrific meal in itself. It's also great prepared in advance and layered into a hollowed-out baguette to make a *pan bagnat,* the traditional beach sandwich of Nice. The longer the salad rests on the bread, the more the two become one.

8 new potatoes (about 1 pound), well scrubbed
2 pounds green beans, cooked
10 very ripe Italian plum tomatoes, washed and quartered
1 small purple onion, peeled and thinly sliced
½ cup niçoise olives
¼ cup chopped Italian (flat-leaf) parsley
Pinch of salt
1 teaspoon freshly ground black pepper
¾ cup Our Favorite Dressing (page 178)
6 hard-cooked eggs, shelled and quartered lengthwise
12 ounces canned oil-packed white tuna, well drained
2 ounces anchovy fillets (optional)

A Salade Niçoise always evokes dreams of the Mediterranean.

"Where there is good wine, good vinegar."

—ITALIAN SAYING

1. Cook the potatoes in boiling salted water until tender but not mushy, about 10 minutes. When cool enough to handle, quarter the potatoes and transfer them to a large bowl.

2. Add the green beans, tomatoes, onion, olives, parsley, a pinch of salt, and the pepper. Pour ½ cup of the vinaigrette over the vegetables and toss gently but well.

3. Transfer the mixture to a large serving platter. Arrange the salad informally, or as follows: Place the hard-cooked egg quarters around the edge of the platter. Flake the tuna over the salad and arrange the anchovy fillets, if you use them, over the tuna. Drizzle with additional vinaigrette and serve at room temperature.

6 to 8 portions

SUMMER SALADS

Summer salads are the best salads of all. Now vegetables and fruits are at their freshest, often imported from no farther than your own garden. Such perfect produce needs only a splash of vinaigrette and a sprinkle of herbs to delight the palate and excite the eye. Tomatoes, potatoes, corn—the most ordinary of foods—become works of art. Most summer salads require little or no cooking, and when served at room temperature reveal more of their subtle flavors.

BACKPACKING PICNIC

CHICKEN LIVER PÂTÉ WITH GREEN PEPPERCORNS

ASSORTED SAUSAGES AND MUSTARDS

BRIE CHEESE

TOMATO, MONTRACHET, AND BASIL SALAD

FRENCH BREAD WITH *BASIL-MUSTARD BUTTER*

GREEN GRAPES AND STRAWBERRIES

SHORTBREAD HEARTS

Experiment with serving two salads side by side. Here, we've paired Orange and Onion Salad with Arugula and Red Pepper Salad (page 257).

ORANGE AND ONION SALAD

This unusual salad is as good to eat as it is beautiful to look at, and it's often the answer when you are looking for an offbeat salad that will complement Italian or other Mediterranean menus. It should be chilled briefly but should not sit around, because the oranges will begin tasting like onions and the charm of the whole thing will be lost.

6 large, firm, juicy oranges
3 tablespoons red wine vinegar
6 tablespoons best-quality olive oil
1 teaspoon dried oregano
1 medium-size red onion, peeled and sliced paper-thin
1 cup imported black olives (ideally, tiny black niçoise olives, but kalamata or alfonso olives will do)
¼ cup snipped fresh chives, for garnish
Freshly ground black pepper, to taste

1. Peel the oranges and cut each one into 4 or 5 crosswise slices. Transfer the oranges to a shallow serving dish and sprinkle them with the vinegar, olive oil, and oregano. Toss gently, cover, and refrigerate for 30 minutes.

2. Toss the oranges again, arrange the sliced onion and black olives over them decoratively, sprinkle with the chives, and grind on the pepper.

6 to 8 portions

TOMATO, MONTRACHET, AND BASIL SALAD

This was The Silver Palate's most popular summer salad.

6 large ripe tomatoes
1 medium red onion
¼ cup Basil Purée (see Note, page 38)
¼ cup niçoise or other imported black olives
1 tablespoon chopped Italian (flat-leaf) parsley
¼ cup best-quality olive oil
Dash of red wine vinegar
Salt and freshly ground black pepper, to taste
½ Montrachet cheese, or 6 ounces of other mild creamy chèvre

1. Core the tomatoes, cut into thick slices, then cut the slices into halves. Transfer to a mixing bowl.

2. Peel the onion, slice into thin rings, add to the bowl, and turn gently with a spoon.

3. Add the remaining ingredients except the cheese and again turn gently. Cover and refrigerate for 1 hour.

4. Just before serving transfer the salad to a serving dish and crumble the Montrachet cheese over all.

6 to 8 portions

BULGUR WHEAT SALAD

4 cups water
2 cups bulgur (processed cracked wheat)
1 cup chopped pecans
1 cup dried currants
¼ cup chopped fresh Italian (flat-leaf) parsley
1 tablespoon best-quality olive oil
Grated zest of 1 medium-size orange
Salt and freshly ground black pepper, to taste

1. In a large saucepan combine the water and bulgur. Bring to a boil, reduce the heat, and simmer, covered, until the water is absorbed and the wheat is tender but not mushy, 35 to 40 minutes.

2. Transfer to a bowl and refrigerate, uncovered, until cool.

3. Add the pecans, currants, parsley, olive oil, orange zest, and season with the salt and pepper. Toss thoroughly. Serve cool or at room temperature.

8 portions

RICE AND VEGETABLE SALAD

8 cups hot cooked rice
1½ to 2 cups Our Favorite Vinaigrette (page 178)
1 red bell pepper, stemmed, seeded, and cut into thin julienne
1 green bell pepper, stemmed, seeded, and cut into thin julienne
1 medium-size red onion, peeled and diced
6 scallions (green onions), well rinsed and finely sliced
1 cup dried currants
2 shallots, peeled and finely diced
10 ounces frozen peas, thawed and blanched in boiling salted water for 3 minutes
½ cup pitted black olives (preferably imported), finely chopped
¼ cup chopped fresh Italian (flat-leaf) parsley
½ cup chopped fresh dill
Salt and freshly ground black pepper, to taste

COOKING WITH ZEST

The "zest" of citrus, its colorful outer rind, is full of bright flavors that make so many dishes sparkle. We add citrus zest at every opportunity: Lime zest in Lime Mousse, orange zest in Bulgur Wheat Salad, lemon zest in Gremolata atop Crisply Roasted Asparagus. Citrus zest enhances our cakes, mixed berries, margaritas, mousses, sauces, bruschetta, stews, pasta, and roasted chicken—the uses are endless.

To obtain this citrus essence, first wash the fruit you'll be using. Then remove the thinnest layer of the rind (never the bitter white pith) with a vegetable peeler and mince it with a sharp knife. You can also use a "zester," drawing it over the fruit to yield long, elegant strands of peel, or a Microplane zester, the easiest tool of all. Whichever method you choose, we hope you'll use zest as often as we do. It will make your food sing.

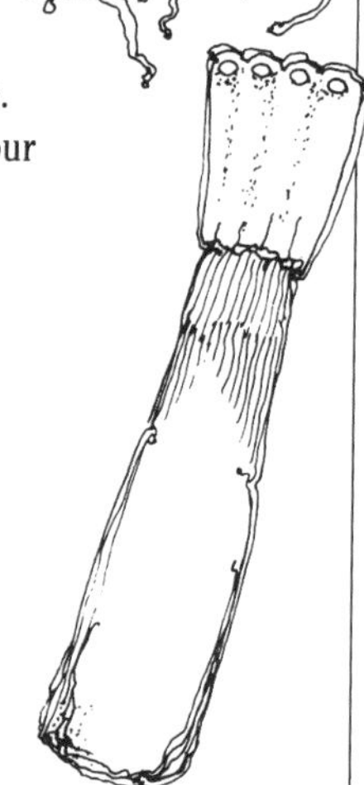

The fruits and nuts in Bulgur Wheat Salad perfectly complement the grain's already nutty flavor.

"Now is the heyday of summer,
The full, warm robust middle age of the year;
The earth, ripe with products as well
as promise."

—DANIEL GRAYSON

1. Transfer the rice to a mixing bowl and pour 1½ cups vinaigrette into the rice. Toss thoroughly. Cool to room temperature.

2. Add the remaining ingredients and toss thoroughly. Taste, correct the seasoning, and add additional vinaigrette if you like.

3. Serve immediately, or cover and refrigerate for up to 4 hours. Return to room temperature before serving.

8 to 10 portions

MINTY CUCUMBER SALAD

This cool salad is good year-round but seems most appropriate during the summer. A favorite menu: butterflied leg of lamb, Bulgur Wheat Salad (page 262), and Minty Cucumber Salad, accompanied by hot pita bread.

3 large cucumbers, peeled, halved, and seeded
½ cup chopped fresh mint leaves
¼ cup chopped fresh Italian (flat-leaf) parsley
Grated zest of 1 orange
½ cup best-quality olive oil
1 cup red wine vinegar
¼ cup sugar

1. Cut the cucumber halves crosswise into crescents. Toss them in a bowl with the mint, parsley, and orange zest.

2. Whisk the oil, vinegar, and sugar together in a small bowl and pour over the salad. Cover the salad and refrigerate for at least 4 hours.

3. Toss again before serving very cold.

6 to 8 portions

"To see cucumbers in a dream denotes that you will speedily fall in love."

—RICHARD FOLKARD

MARINATED GARBANZO SALAD

This slightly Middle Eastern concoction makes a good first course arranged on lettuce leaves, or a good accompaniment to simple grilled lamb, chicken, or pork.

½ cup best-quality olive oil
1 cup finely minced yellow onions
1 tablespoon dried thyme
½ cup coarsely chopped red bell pepper
½ cup dark raisins
2 cans (16 ounces each) garbanzos (chickpeas), drained and rinsed (about 3½ cups)
½ teaspoon salt
½ cup white wine vinegar

SIMPLE SUMMER PLEASURES

- ♥ Make photo scrapbooks
- ♥ Watch the clouds
- ♥ Make lemonade from scratch
- ♥ Spend the whole day in a hammock
- ♥ Plant an herb garden
- ♥ Press flowers
- ♥ Wear only white for a week
- ♥ Read romantic Russian novels
- ♥ Skinny dip in the moonlight
- ♥ Play all of your old records
- ♥ Spend a silent day
- ♥ Fast on fruit juices and water
- ♥ Write a letter and many postcards
- ♥ Read poetry
- ♥ Polish the silver
- ♥ Visit the library
- ♥ Wander in the museum
- ♥ Do crossword puzzles
- ♥ Go clamming
- ♥ Go antiquing
- ♥ Ride horseback around a lake
- ♥ Make a kite
- ♥ Go to a country fair
- ♥ Fill the house with flowers
- ♥ Make ice cream
- ♥ Sleep outdoors
- ♥ Put flowers on a floppy hat
- ♥ Walk barefoot
- ♥ Pick the morning glories
- ♥ Toast marshmallows on the beach
- ♥ Ride a roller coaster
- ♥ Have lunch in your bathing suit
- ♥ Ride in a convertible
- ♥ Watch shooting stars
- ♥ Listen to classical music
- ♥ Hum
- ♥ Play cribbage
- ♥ Smell fresh mint
- ♥ Meander among wildflowers
- ♥ Give someone a rub with coconut oil
- ♥ Snooze in the sun

1. Heat the olive oil in a saucepan over low heat. Add the onions and thyme and cook over low heat, covered, until the onions are tender and lightly colored, about 25 minutes.

2. Add the chopped red pepper and cook for another 5 minutes.

3. Add the raisins and garbanzos and cook, stirring occasionally, for another 5 minutes. Do not overcook the garbanzos or they will become mushy.

4. Season with the salt, transfer to a bowl, and pour the vinegar over the hot mixture.

5. Let the vegetables cool to room temperature, then cover and refrigerate for at least 24 hours before serving. Allow to return to room temperature before serving.

6 to 8 portions

BASQUE SALAD

A hearty main-course salad of rice, meats, and seafood.

¼ cup best-quality olive oil
12 scallions, green tops included, well rinsed and thinly sliced
1 scant teaspoon whole saffron
2 cups converted rice
1½ teaspoons salt, plus more to taste
4 cups Chicken Stock (page 416)
1 pound medium-size raw shrimp, shelled and deveined
¼ pound hard sausage (salami, pepperoni, or other), cut into julienne
½ pound prosciutto, thinly sliced
1 green bell pepper, stemmed, seeded, and cut into thin julienne
1 red bell pepper, stemmed, seeded, and cut into thin julienne
½ cup chopped fresh Italian (flat-leaf) parsley
¾ teaspoon freshly ground black pepper

1. Heat the oil in a heavy pot. Add the scallions and sauté over medium heat, stirring, until wilted, 5 minutes. Add the saffron and cook for 2 minutes longer.

2. Add the rice and stir, coating the grains well with oil. Season with the 1½ teaspoons salt, pour in the chicken stock, and stir. Bring to a simmer, cover, and cook over low heat until the rice is just done and all the liquid has been absorbed, 20 minutes. Fluff with a fork and let cool somewhat.

3. Meanwhile, bring 2 quarts of water to a boil, then add the shrimp. Immediately remove from the heat, cover, and let stand for 2 minutes. Drain the shrimp and reserve.

4. Transfer the cooked rice to a large bowl. Add the shrimp, sausage, prosciutto, green and red peppers, and parsley. Season with salt and the black pepper. Toss thoroughly. Arrange on a large platter and serve at room temperature.

8 portions

ALL-AMERICAN SALADS

Some salads seem particularly all-American to us. These are the kind that turn up at church suppers, on the menus of rustic inns and restaurants off the beaten track, and in our grandmothers' handwritten "receipt" books. They are simple and good, and deserve, in these sophisticated times, not to be forgotten.

"What is literature compared with cooking? One is shadow, the other is substance."

—E. V. LUCAS

BEET AND ROQUEFORT SALAD WITH WALNUTS

This hearty salad is especially welcome in winter. It goes perfectly with a ham, grilled sausages, or the like, and the color combination is striking on a buffet table.

As a variation you may omit the Roquefort and sprinkle the salad generously with chopped fresh dill.

8 to 10 medium-size beets
3 tablespoons red wine vinegar
3 tablespoons walnut oil
½ cup shelled walnut halves
¼ pound imported Roquefort cheese
Freshly ground black pepper, to taste

1. Wash the beets well, and trim the stems and roots without piercing the skin. Drop the beets into a large heavy pot of boiling salted water and cook until tender, 20 to 40 minutes, depending on the beets. Drain, cool, and peel the beets, and cut into julienne.

2. In a mixing bowl, toss the beets gently with the vinegar and walnut oil. Taste and add more of either if you like; there should be just enough to coat the beets. Cover and chill until serving time.

3. To serve, toss the walnuts with the chilled beets and arrange in a shallow serving bowl. Allow to return to room temperature. Crumble the Roquefort evenly over the top and grind on black pepper. Serve immediately.

6 to 8 portions

TAILGATE PICNIC

CREAMY COLESLAW

COLD LEMON CHICKEN

PEASANT CAVIAR

PITA BREAD

BLACKBERRY ICE

A showstopper—Beet and Roquefort Salad with Walnuts.

CREAMY COLESLAW

Sheila's version of the delicatessen regular. A fresh taste, perfect with your favorite sandwich.

1 small head of green cabbage, cleaned, cored, and cut into slivers
1 large carrot, trimmed, peeled, and grated
1 medium-size green bell pepper, stemmed, seeded, and grated
1 cup prepared mayonnaise, preferably Hellmann's
½ cup corn oil
½ cup sour cream
2 tablespoons heavy cream
1 teaspoon caraway seeds
Salt and freshly ground black pepper, to taste

1. Put the cabbage slivers, grated carrot, and green pepper together in a large bowl.

2. Combine the remaining ingredients with salt and pepper in a small bowl and whisk together well. Pour over the cabbage mixture, stir, cover, and chill for at least 4 hours before serving.

3. Allow the slaw to return to room temperature before serving.

6 to 8 portions

TECHNICOLOR BEAN SALAD

Three-bean salad always seems so limiting, so we've gone a bit further.

1 can (16 ounces) each of garbanzos (chickpeas), white kidney beans, red kidney beans, baby lima beans, and black-eyed peas
1 pound fresh green beans, or half green and half yellow wax beans, cooked
Garlic Dressing (recipe follows)
1 cup chopped well-rinsed scallions (green onions)
½ cup chopped fresh Italian (flat-leaf) parsley, for garnish

1. Drain the canned beans, rinse thoroughly with water, and drain again.

2. Cut the green beans into 2-inch lengths.

3. Toss the canned and fresh beans together in a large bowl. Pour in the dressing, sprinkle on the scallions, and toss again.

4. Cover and refrigerate overnight before serving. Garnish with the chopped parsley. Serve at room temperature.

10 to 12 portions

GARLIC DRESSING

1 egg yolk
⅓ cup red wine vinegar
1 tablespoon sugar
1 tablespoon chopped garlic
Salt and freshly ground black pepper, to taste
1 cup best-quality olive oil

1. Combine the egg yolk, vinegar, sugar, garlic, and salt and pepper in a food processor. Process briefly.

2. With the motor running, slowly dribble in the olive oil.

3. Taste, correct the seasoning if necessary, and transfer to a storage container.

About 1½ cups

PARK BENCH PICNIC

GAZPACHO

ASSORTED QUICHES

TECHNICOLOR BEAN SALAD

BRIOCHE

CHOCOLATE MOUSSE

STRAWBERRIES

"Red beans and ricely yours"

—LOUIS ARMSTRONG, SIGNING HIS LETTERS

Because the egg is raw, use a very fresh, well refrigerated one in the Garlic Dressing.

This apple and walnut salad is as crisp and bright as a fall afternoon.

AUTUMN APPLE AND WALNUT SALAD

This crisp salad is rich with the special taste of sherry vinegar.

2 Granny Smith apples, chilled
2 Red Delicious apples, chilled
½ cup sherry vinegar, or more if needed
1 cup chopped celery
3 scallions (green onions), well rinsed and cut diagonally into ½-inch pieces
½ cup shelled walnut halves
4 to 5 tablespoons walnut oil
Salt and freshly ground black pepper, to taste

1. Wash the apples and dry them well. Core and chop, but do not peel them, and toss them in a bowl with the sherry vinegar.

2. Add the celery, scallions, and walnut halves, and drizzle with 4 tablespoons of the walnut oil. Toss again.

3. Taste and correct the seasoning, adding more vinegar and up to 1 tablespoon more oil as necessary, and serve immediately.

4 to 6 portions

MARDI-GRAS SLAW

2 cups shredded red cabbage
2 cups shredded green cabbage
2 cups grated peeled carrots
½ cup finely minced yellow onion
⅓ cup red wine vinegar
¼ cup sugar
1 tablespoon Dijon mustard
Salt and freshly ground black pepper, to taste
⅔ cup best-quality olive oil
1 tablespoon caraway seeds

1. Toss both kinds of cabbage, the grated carrots, and minced onion together in a large bowl. Reserve.

2. In a small bowl, whisk together the vinegar, sugar, and mustard; season with salt and pepper. Slowly whisk in the oil to form a fairly thick and creamy dressing. Taste and correct the seasoning as necessary.

3. Pour half of the dressing over the vegetables in the bowl. Sprinkle on the caraway seeds and toss well. Taste; add additional dressing as you like. Cover and refrigerate for up to 4 hours. Allow to return to room temperature before serving.

6 to 8 portions

EGG SALAD WITH DILL

There is nothing revolutionary about this recipe, but when we reflected on all the bad egg salads we have tasted, it seemed a good idea to include this version. It makes a zesty sandwich, especially when served on pumpernickel. Although the dill is optional, it makes the salad special.

8 hard-cooked eggs
½ cup finely chopped red onion
⅓ cup chopped fresh dill
½ cup prepared mayonnaise, preferably Hellmann's
¼ cup sour cream
¼ cup Dijon mustard
Salt and freshly ground black pepper, to taste

1. Peel the eggs and very coarsely chop them. Place in a mixing bowl with the onion and dill.

2. In another bowl, whisk together the mayonnaise, sour cream, and mustard and pour over the egg mixture.

3. Toss gently, season with salt and pepper, and toss again. Cover and refrigerate if you must, but the salad is at its best eaten immediately.

6 portions

A PICNIC CHECKLIST

One of the most important elements for successful picnicking is complete planning. Love your menu; leave nothing out! Once you're done watching the sun set into the lagoon, it's rough to have forgotten the corkscrew. Make lists of essentials and accessories, and bear in mind that people tend to eat more when they're outdoors. Also, picnics tend to last a long time, and your group may grow in number quite spontaneously along the way.

- ❑ tablecloth, napkins, and paper towels
- ❑ flatware, plates, and glasses
- ❑ corkscrew and bottle opener
- ❑ thermos or ice for cold drinks
- ❑ thermos for hot drinks
- ❑ good sharp knife
- ❑ light cutting board/platter
- ❑ matches
- ❑ charcoal, if necessary
- ❑ extra leakproof containers
- ❑ garbage bag
- ❑ spatula
- ❑ candles or flashlight
- ❑ small first-aid kit
- ❑ insect repellent, sunscreen, zinc oxide

Because the eggs are raw, use very fresh, well refrigerated ones in the French Dressing and Poppy-Seed Dressing.

"The French approach to food is characteristic; they bring to their consideration of the table the same appreciation, respect, intelligence and lively interest that they have for the other arts, for painting, for literature, and for the theatre. We foreigners living in France respect and appreciate this point of view but deplore their too strict observance of a tradition which will not admit the slightest deviation in a seasoning or the suppression of a single ingredient. Restrictions aroused our American ingenuity, we found combinations and replacements which pointed in new directions and created a fresh and absorbing interest in everything pertaining to the kitchen."

—ALICE B. TOKLAS, 1954

FRENCH DRESSING

From an American family cookbook comes this alternative to the orange horror available on your grocer's shelf today. We've reduced the sugar, and the result is a sweet-tart golden beauty of a dressing that is perfect on a chef's salad or a Reuben sandwich.

2 eggs
½ cup red wine vinegar
⅓ cup sugar
1 tablespoon Dijon mustard
½ teaspoon salt
1 teaspoon imported sweet paprika
1 cup vegetable oil

1. Combine the eggs, vinegar, sugar, mustard, salt, and paprika in a food processor. Process until the sugar is dissolved, about 2 minutes.

2. With the motor running, dribble in the oil in a slow steady stream. When all the oil is incorporated, shut off the motor, scrape down the sides of the processor bowl, taste, and correct the seasoning if necessary.

3. Transfer to a storage container, cover, and refrigerate.

About 2 cups

POPPY-SEED DRESSING

Tart dressings are more stylish now, but this one still seems good to us, particularly on a spinach salad with rings of red onion, sliced hard-cooked egg, crumbled crisp bacon, and homemade croutons sautéed in butter with garlic (see page 76).

1 egg
¼ cup sugar
1 tablespoon Dijon mustard
⅔ cup red wine vinegar
½ teaspoon salt
3 tablespoons grated yellow onion, plus any juice from the grating
2 cups corn oil
3 tablespoons poppy seeds

1. Combine the egg, sugar, mustard, vinegar, salt, and grated onion and juice in a food processor. Process for 1 minute.

2. With the motor running, pour in the oil in a slow steady stream. When all the oil is incorporated, shut off the motor, taste, and correct the seasoning.

3. Transfer the mixture to a bowl, stir in the poppy seeds, and refrigerate, covered, until ready to use.

About 1 quart

SALADS OF THE SEA

A combination of seafood and vegetables in a main-course salad is light eating at its best, with no lack of flavor or simple enjoyment. Such dining is one of the best ways we know to remain cool, healthy, and trim.

SEAFOOD SALAD WITH CREAMY TARRAGON-MUSTARD DRESSING

This salad can be made with any combination of seafood you like—lump crabmeat, octopus, squid, or conch are all appropriate, although using more than three kinds results in a bit of a jumble. In any case, try to make the salad and serve it immediately, without refrigeration. If you must chill it, be sure to let it return to room temperature before serving.

Salt, to taste
1 pound medium-size raw shrimp, shelled and deveined
1 pound fresh bay scallops, rinsed thoroughly
½ pound cooked lobster meat (about 1½ cups meat, the equivalent of a 3¼- to 4-pound lobster), or a similar amount of frozen lobster meat, defrosted overnight in the refrigerator
1 cup uncooked tiny peas, fresh or frozen
2 scallions (green onions), trimmed, well rinsed, and cut diagonally into ½-inch pieces
Freshly ground black pepper, to taste
1 cup Creamy Tarragon-Mustard Dressing (recipe follows)
2 cups coarsely shredded raw spinach leaves, thoroughly rinsed and dried

1. Bring 4 quarts of salted water to a boil in a pot. Drop in the shrimp, wait 1 minute, and drop in the scallops. Just before the water returns to a full boil, pour the contents of the pot through a strainer set in the sink. Cool the seafood to room temperature.

2. Drain the lobster (if frozen) and sort through it carefully to remove any bits of shell. Reserve several large pieces of lobster meat (particularly claw meat) for garnish and cut the rest into chunks.

3. Reserve 3 or 4 shrimp and scallops for garnish and combine the rest with the lobster meat in a mixing bowl.

4. Add the peas and scallions, season lightly with salt and pepper, and pour in the tarragon-mustard dressing. Toss the salad gently and add more dressing if you like.

5. Arrange the spinach in a border around a shallow serving bowl. Spoon the seafood salad into the center of the bowl and arrange the reserved seafood garnish on top.

6. Serve immediately, offering additional dressing on the side if you like.

6 portions as a first course, 4 portions as a main course

CREAMY TARRAGON-MUSTARD DRESSING

This light, savory dressing calls for raw eggs, so be sure to use very fresh, well refrigerated ones.

1 whole egg
2 egg yolks
⅓ cup tarragon mustard or Dijon mustard
¼ cup tarragon vinegar
1 teaspoon crumbled dried tarragon
Salt and freshly ground black pepper, to taste
1 cup best-quality olive oil
1 cup light vegetable oil

1. In a blender or a food processor, combine the whole egg, egg yolks, mustard, vinegar, and tarragon. Season with salt and pepper and process for 1 minute.

2. Measure out the oil and with the motor still running, dribble the oil into the processor or blender in a slow steady stream. Shut off the motor, scrape down the sides, taste, and correct the seasoning.

3. Transfer to a storage container, cover, and refrigerate until ready to use.

About 3 cups

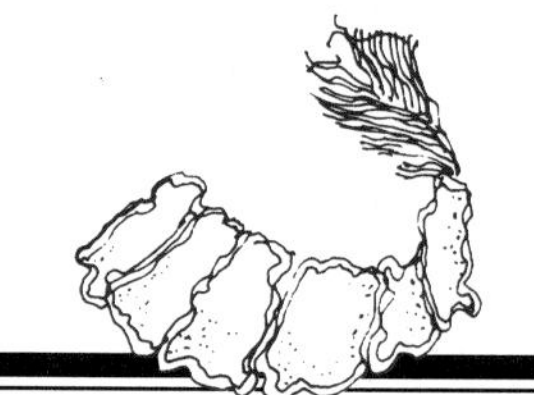

SHRIMP AND GRAPE SALAD WITH DILL

This light salad is a beautiful luncheon offering.

A SEASIDE LUNCH

FRESH RASPBERRIES AND STRAWBERRIES WITH SUGAR AND *CRÈME FRAÎCHE*

SEAFOOD SALAD WITH CREAMY TARRAGON-MUSTARD DRESSING

FRESH OYSTERS WITH *SHALLOT SAUCE*

BULGUR WHEAT SALAD

CHOCOLATE MOUSSE

BLACK WALNUT COOKIES

Salt, to taste
2 pounds medium-size raw shrimp, shelled and deveined
1 cup sour cream
1 cup prepared mayonnaise, preferably Hellmann's
2 cups seedless green grapes, washed and patted dry
½ cup chopped fresh dill, or more to taste
Freshly ground black pepper, to taste
Lettuce leaves, for serving

1. Bring 4 quarts of salted water to a boil and drop in the shrimp. Wait 1 minute; empty the pot into a colander set in the sink. Let the shrimp cool in the colander.

2. Transfer the cooled shrimp to a bowl.

3. In a separate small bowl, whisk the sour cream and mayonnaise together well.

4. Pour the dressing over the shrimp and toss gently. Add the grapes and toss again. Finally, sprinkle on the chopped dill, add salt and pepper, and toss once more and refrigerate, covered, for at least 4 hours.

5. Just before serving, taste, correct the seasoning, and toss again. Arrange on the lettuce leaves and serve immediately.

6 portions as a main course, 8 portions as a first course

"Life's a beach. Go play in the sand."

—JOHN BANKS

SHRIMP AND ARTICHOKE SALAD

Salt, to taste
2 pounds medium-size raw shrimp, shelled and deveined
2 cups broccoli florets
2 cans (8 ounces each) water-packed artichoke hearts, drained
8 scallions (green onions), well rinsed, trimmed, and cut diagonally into ½-inch pieces
2 cups Sherry Mayonnaise (page 251)
Freshly ground black pepper, to taste

1. Bring 4 quarts of salted water to a boil and drop in the shrimp. Wait 1 minute; empty the pot into a colander set in the sink. Let the shrimp cool in the colander.

2. Bring a second pot of salted water to a boil and drop in the broccoli florets. Cook until the stems are just tender, 3 to 5 minutes; do not overcook. Remove the florets from the water with a slotted spoon or skimmer and drop into a bowl of ice water. This will stop the cooking process and set the brilliant green color. When the broccoli is cool, drain well and reserve.

3. Cut the artichokes into halves or quarters, depending on their size, and combine in a mixing bowl with the shrimp, broccoli, and scallions.

4. Add the sherry mayonnaise, toss, season with salt and pepper, and toss again. Cover and refrigerate until ready to serve.

6 portions

SALADS ON THE GREEN

Mesclun, mâche, mibuna, mizuna, poc choi, tatsoi, shiso, baby bok choi, shungihu, purslane, dandelion, red oak, rapini, amaranth, frisée, arugula, lolla rossa, rapini, treviso, miner's lettuce, radicchio, Boston, tango, limestone, loose leaf, baby lettuces, microgreens, red and green mustards, pea shoots, sprouts, chards, and cresses, and flowers galore from Johnny jump-ups to lavender wands. The names are hypnotic, melodic. They are greens in every shade imaginable, with heritages from around the globe, now available in markets across the country, in cities large and small. It's a far cry from the days of only iceberg.

Salads made from fresh, crisp, small-leafed greens are now a part of most Americans' daily menu—at least once, often twice. And nowhere in cooking does freshness and seasonality play a more important role than in greens. Cooks want their greens as crisp and vibrant as possible, and backyard gardens, foraging, local farmers' markets, and specialty stores all play a role in meeting this goal. Once home, greens are treated with imagination and respect. The simple green salad has become one of the glories of the American table.

A GREEN SAMPLER

Salad greens vary dramatically in taste, texture, and color. When combined with other summer foods and endless vinaigrettes they can match every mood and occasion.

Be certain to rinse the greens carefully and dry them thoroughly. Keep them crisp in the refrigerator, wrapped in a towel, or stored in a covered bowl until serving time.

ARUGULA: Intense in color and pungent in flavor, it is an ideal companion to softer and sweeter leaves and wonderful on its own. Toss with a strong vinaigrette and sprinkle with sieved hard-cooked egg.

BELGIAN ENDIVE: Crisp and opalescent, it is so special it makes a great first course combined with thinly sliced prosciutto and red wine basil vinaigrette.

BIBB LETTUCE: Delectably small, tight leaves with a crunchy sweetness. Bibb leaves are best on their own with a light vinaigrette.

BOSTON LETTUCE: Pale green, loosely packed, and tender, this fragile green has a pleasing hearty flavor.

CHICORY: Tart and crunchy, it combines well with other vegetables for a salad or entrée course.

CRESS ALBISEOIS: The most delicate of cresses, it deserves a delicate vinaigrette. Watch for it in the market.

DANDELION GREENS: Wild or cultivated, they have a refreshing tart taste alone or in combination with other greens. Be certain they're young and fresh.

ESCAROLE: Yellow-white leaves with a pleasantly tart flavor that can take stronger dressings than other leaves.

FENNEL GREENS: Snip the feathery tips of anise-flavored fennel into mixed green salads as a seasoning.

FIELD LETTUCE or **LAMB'S TONGUE (MACHE):** A lovely fall and winter green that comes in small bunches. Combine with other greens.

FRISEE: Sweetest of the chicory family with pale green slender but curly leaves, mildly bitter.

ICEBERG LETTUCE: Used on occasion, seems new again.

LEAF LETTUCE: Curly, green- or red-tipped, the tasty, tender leaves of the various leaf lettuces are rather soft in texture. Especially delicious when young.

MIXING GREENS

We have some very favorite green salad combinations. Tossed with complementary vinaigrettes, the possibilities are endless. Allow ⅓ to ½ cup of vinaigrette for every 6 servings. The dressing should gently coat the greens, not smother them.

- ♥ Watercress, Belgian endive cut into julienne, and walnut halves. Serve with Walnut Oil Vinaigrette (page 283).
- ♥ Fresh dark green arugula and delicate Bibb lettuce leaves. Serve with Garlic Dressing (page 268).
- ♥ Romaine lettuce (outer leaves removed), watercress, and chicory. Serve with a red wine vinaigrette.
- ♥ Whole baby Bibb lettuce. Serve with Blueberry Vinaigrette (page 178).
- ♥ Tender young fresh spinach leaves, ruby-red lettuce, and seeded sliced cucumbers. Serve with Sesame Mayonnaise (page 177).
- ♥ Belgian endive (separated whole leaves) and slivered white mushrooms. Serve with Champagne Shallot Dressing (page 282) and garnish with freshly snipped chives.
- ♥ Boston lettuce and baby nasturtium leaves. Serve with Green Peppercorn Vinaigrette (page 282).

MESCLUN: A mixture of tiny, very delicate greens that may include arugula, chervil, dandelion, and oak-leaf lettuce.

NASTURTIUM LEAVES: Use sparingly with milder greens. They give a surprising peppery flavor.

PURSLANE: Vinegary flavor, crisp texture that complements milder greens.

RADICCHIO: A ruby-red miniature leaf with a slightly bitter flavor. This mixes color and flavor with other greens and can stand a hearty vinaigrette.

RED LEAF LETTUCE: Purple-red, it is a soft crinkly lettuce that is good to eat as well as aesthetically pleasing. Use it combined with other sturdier greens.

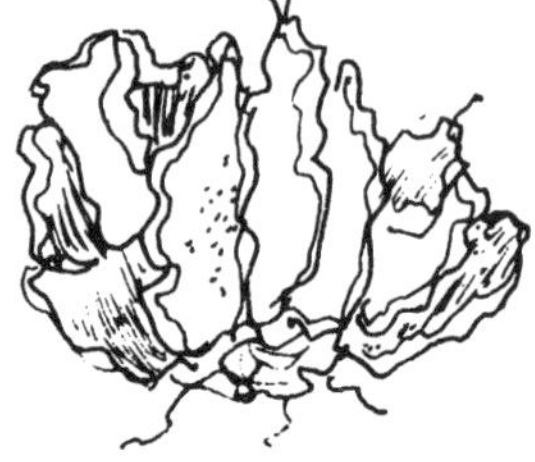

ROMAINE: Firm tight leaves with a robust nutty flavor. This green can be dressed with a strong vinaigrette.

SORREL: The taste of lemons and light vinegar. This bright green leaf is tart, and should be mixed sparingly with milder leaves.

SPINACH: Dense, dark green, small, rounded leaves, and the crinkliest. Don't limit its complements to bacon bits and hard-cooked eggs; its flavor blends well in many combinations.

WATERCRESS: Dark green and spicy with cloverlike leaves, it has become a staple. Alone or mixed with others, cress has a beautiful color and is a good taste balancer.

THE OIL OF THE OLIVE

We adore olive oil. It is the only oil of culinary importance pressed from the flesh of a ripe fruit (not a seed or a nut), and we think that's why it's one of the most delicious and versatile food products in creation. Having access to great olive oil has been one of the most significant improvements in the quality of our cooking in recent decades. We're not alone in our enthusiasm; more and more cooks are telling us they can't live without it.

Today, olive oil is made anywhere olive trees grow (of course!) and that list stretches to include Spain, Italy, France, Portugal, Greece, Australia, Africa, California, New Zealand, South America, Syria, Turkey, and Israel. Olives, like wine grapes, require a warm climate and particularly sandy soil. The best come from Italy and the south of France. Like most good things, olive trees improve with age; interestingly, an olive tree must be 35 years old before it bears fruit.

Italian olive oil has a more pronounced olive flavor, giving it a deep nutty or leafy taste, or a peppery spiciness. Exceptional olive oils are from Tuscany, Liguria, and Puglia. French oil from Provence is fruitier with just a subtle hint of spice. Spanish oil has a more intense flavor with good ones from Catalonia, Sierra de Gata, and Andalusia. Greek oil has a lighter olive taste, but is rich and rather thick in consistency. And today California has its own very good olive oil producers. Each olive grower creates his own unique-tasting oil.

There are a number of qualities of oil on the market today, though we don't think the variety needs to be confusing.

EXTRA EXTRA OR EXTRA VIRGIN OLIVE OIL is the oil made from the very first pressing of the olives. It is usually green, sometimes bordering on greenish black, depending on the filtering the oil has undergone. Its intense flavor and aroma is that of green olives. The later the harvest, the riper the olives, the greener the oil. But the yields are quite low and consequently the prices are quite high. Extra virgin oil is best for use in salads or marinades, or tossed with just-cooked vegetables.

VIRGIN OLIVE OIL is also a direct product of the olive fruit, though it may be the result of a second pressing. It should have a sweetish, nutty flavor.

PURE OLIVE OIL is made up of oils extracted by treating the previously pressed olive pulp with solvents.

FINE OLIVE OIL is oil that has also been extracted from olive pulp, to which water has been added. It is perfect for cooking or frying.

There's no reason to feel intimidated when buying olive oil. The basic rule remains: You get the quality you pay for. The better the taste of the ingredient, the better the taste of the prepared dish.

As important as your choice of oil is the care you take of it. Even good oil can go stale or turn rancid if not stored carefully. After 2 weeks, opened oil should be stored in a refrigerator, especially in summer. It may become cloudy, but it will clear rapidly upon returning to room temperature.

OTHER OILS

A host of seeds and nuts also produce flavorful oils suitable for cooking.

ALMOND OIL, HAZELNUT OIL, PISTACHIO OIL, PECAN OIL, PINE NUT OIL: These are sweet, light, delicate oils that are indeed nutty in taste. They are splendid in salads, or tossed with hot vegetables as a change from butter.

PEPPER OILS: The best of these delicately flavored oils balance the richness of grapeseed oil and the spiciness of the pepper.

WALNUT OIL: A very light and delicate oil. It must be used quickly after opening, as its fresh flavor is short-lived. Refrigerate.

HERB-FLAVORED AND FUNGI-FLAVORED OILS: These are usually olive or grapeseed oils that have been flavored with any number of herbs, spices, mushrooms, or white and black truffles. We couldn't do without them for our favorite vinaigrettes and marinades or just drizzling them over crostini, frittatas, fish or meat carpaccio, cured meats, or salads. Basil, citrus, tarragon, bay leaf, sage, rosemary, pumpkin seed, garlic, and peppercorns, alone or mixed, are among the flavorings used.

VINEGAR

We think of vinegar as a very practical natural product. Basically it is fermented fruit juice that has become acidic, though there's a bit of poetry involved as well.

The Chinese made vinegar from rice wine over 3,000 years ago, while the Romans refreshed themselves with a mixture of vinegar and water flavored with mint leaves.

The same soldiers of Caesar's army who filled the hills of Dijon, France, with mustard seeds also helped name vinegar—quite by accident. The conquered French peasants called the Roman wine that had fermented *vinaigre,* or sour wine. It was in the Middle Ages that vinegar, seasoned with spices and herbs, first made its appearance in French cuisine.

The bases for vinegar are countless: wine, including sherry and Champagne; malted grain; apples, pears, other fruits and berries, and even sugar and honey.

Americans have become interested in lighter eating habits and in the subtleties of wonderful oils and vinegars. Vinegars have never been more in demand as a creative cooking ingredient.

DISTILLED VINEGARS: These are made by distilling alcohol from grain such as corn, rye, malt, or barley. They are the most acidic and lend themselves best to pickling.

WINE VINEGARS: These are made by fermenting wine. Red and white wine, sherry, and even Champagne create mild vinegars (balsamic vinegar also is made from wine). These flavors enhance marinades, salads, and sauces in a special manner. Herbs may also be added for additional flavor.

FRUIT VINEGARS: These are being used by modern cooks in any number of dishes for their light fresh flavor. Their flavorings include raspberries, blueberries, blackberries, peaches, quince, Golden Delicious apples, figs, and elderberries. Even vegetables are being used, red peppers and cucumbers to name a couple. The flavor these vinegars lend to recipes is inimitable. (We even know one woman who splashes fruit vinegar in her Daiquiris.)

HERB VINEGARS: These are prepared by infusing herbs in a broad range of traditional vinegars. Flavorings include red or green basil, tarragon, oregano, wild thyme, peppercorns, mint, rosemary, dill, chervil, chive blossoms, and savory, or combinations of several of these and others. Herb vinegars offer any number of possibilities for the creative cook.

CIDER VINEGAR: This is a mild vinegar tasting of the apples from which it is made.

MALT VINEGAR: An English favorite, this is made from ale and is milder than wine vinegar. It has a yeasty flavor and is good on/in salad dressings and is traditional with fish and chips.

HERB VINEGARS

Herb vinegars are beautiful and useful in cooking and in salad making. Pour good-quality white or red wine vinegar over a generous handful of fresh herbs in a jar and let stand, covered, for 2 weeks. To speed the process, heat the vinegar slightly first. Strain the vinegar or not, as you like. Particularly good are: tarragon in cider vinegar; green and red basil in red wine vinegar; dill flowers, chive blossoms, lemon peel, garlic, oregano, mint, rosemary, or wild thyme in white wine vinegar. A great treat for giving and getting.

"Show me another pleasure like dinner which comes every day and lasts an hour."

—CHARLES MAURICE DE TALLYRAND

RASPBERRY VINAIGRETTE

½ cup best-quality olive oil
½ cup raspberry vinegar (see Note)
½ teaspoon salt
Freshly ground black pepper, to taste
1 tablespoon Crème Fraîche (page 414)

Combine all the ingredients and shake well.
About 1 cup
Note: Available at specialty food shops.

GREEN PEPPERCORN VINAIGRETTE

1 tablespoon Homemade Mayonnaise (page 413)
¼ cup white wine herb vinegar
½ teaspoon crushed green peppercorns
¼ cup green peppercorn oil
2 tablespoons chopped fresh parsley

Combine all the ingredients and shake well.
1 cup

CHAMPAGNE SHALLOT DRESSING

⅓ cup Champagne or white wine vinegar
1 tablespoon finely minced shallots
2 teaspoons Dijon mustard
1 teaspoon sugar
Salt and freshly ground black pepper, to taste
½ cup best-quality olive oil or grapeseed oil

Whisk the vinegar, shallots, mustard, sugar, and salt and pepper together in a small bowl. Slowly drizzle in the oil, whisking constantly, until thickened. Adjust the seasonings to taste. Store, covered, in the refrigerator for up to 3 days.
¾ cup

THE MUSTARD MAZE

Mustards have been prepared through the centuries. The Chinese cultivated the pods over 3,000 years ago, Hippocrates praised mustard for its alleged medicinal value, Caesar's conquering troops sowed mustard seeds in the hills of Dijon, France, and Thomas Jefferson introduced the mustard plant to Monticello in 1780.

Prepared mustard is made from the seeds of several species of the mustard plant, dried, ground, and then mixed with a liquid—from Champagne to milk to vinegar—and often with salt, spices, or herbs, until the desired flavor and consistency are reached. In recent years, poetic license has been taken and the interesting mustard flavors that have been developed have made mustard one of the world's most popular condiments.

Traditional mustards are available in a wide variety, and innovative versions have recently become hotter, spicier, sweeter, and more colorful than ever before.

GRAINY MUSTARDS are blends made with whole or coarsely chopped mustard seeds. Use with ham, corned beef, smoked meats, cold cuts, or to coat meats.

DIJON MUSTARD is made from husked and ground mustard seeds, white wine, vinegar, and spice. It has a smooth texture and is easily the most versatile mustard for cooking and eating. ("Dijon" is a general term for this style of mustard produced in Dijon, France, and only mustard made there may label itself as such. An exception to this is Grey Poupon mustard, which has been licensed and is produced in the United States.)

HOT MUSTARD is usually an English or German condiment. This is great with roast beef, sausages, or Chinese food. It is easily made at home, by mixing ground mustard with enough water, gin, vodka, dry wine, beer, or milk to make a smooth paste. Set aside for 1 hour before using, and watch out!

SWEET MUSTARD is especially appealing to Americans. It is great on ham, pork, or chicken. To make one, mix together 4 ounces ground mustard and 4 cups cider vinegar and let them sit for 2 to 8 hours (the longer the better). Then add 2 beaten eggs and 1 cup sugar and cook in a double boiler, stirring frequently, until thick. Keep refrigerated between uses.

PEPPERCORN MUSTARD, made with red or green peppercorns, is wonderful used in a vinaigrette or as a bond in beef and chicken sauces.

HERB MUSTARDS include tarragon, dill, basil, or multicolored mixtures of herbs, a natural combination with mustard. They often include a touch of garlic as well, and are delicious in vinaigrettes and on poultry.

FRUIT MUSTARDS can be made with orange, lemon, lime, and tomato.

WINE MUSTARDS are flavored with sherry, red wine, and Champagne. Taste and experiment; let your creativity wander.

Because the egg is raw, use a very fresh, well refrigerated one in the Garlic-Mustard Dressing.

SHERRY VINAIGRETTE

1 tablespoon Dijon mustard
¼ cup sherry vinegar
¼ teaspoon salt
Freshly ground black pepper, to taste
1½ cups best-quality olive oil

1. Whisk the mustard and sherry vinegar together in a small bowl.

2. Stir in the salt and black pepper.

3. Whisking constantly, dribble the olive oil into the vinegar mixture in a slow, steady stream.

4. Taste, correct the seasoning, and reserve, covered, until ready to use.

1¾ cups

WALNUT OIL VINAIGRETTE

2 tablespoons Dijon mustard
3 tablespoons red wine vinegar
7 tablespoons walnut oil
½ tablespoon minced fresh parsley
Salt and freshly ground black pepper, to taste

Whisk together the mustard and vinegar. Gradually add the oil in a slow steady stream. Whisk in the parsley and season with salt and pepper.

¾ cup

GARLIC-MUSTARD DRESSING

1 egg
⅓ cup Dijon mustard
⅔ cup red wine vinegar
Salt and freshly ground black pepper, to taste
6 garlic cloves, peeled and chopped
2 cups best-quality olive oil

1. Combine the egg, mustard, and vinegar in a food processor. Season with the salt and pepper and process for 1 minute.

2. With the motor still running, drop the garlic cloves through the feed tube. Then begin dribbling in the olive oil in a slow steady stream.

3. When all the oil is incorporated, shut off the motor, taste, and correct the seasoning (the dressing should be very garlicky).

4. Transfer to a storage container and refrigerate until ready to use.

3 cups

BASIL-WALNUT VINAIGRETTE

This is a perfect summer vinaigrette—tart, slightly crunchy, and full of fresh basil flavor. Try it on sliced, vine-ripened tomatoes; thinly sliced zucchini and chopped red onion; or our favorite—a cool plateful of crisp-cooked garden-fresh green beans, garnished generously with walnut halves.

1 tablespoon Dijon mustard
⅓ cup red wine vinegar
¾ cup coarsely chopped fresh basil leaves
Salt and freshly ground black pepper, to taste
1 cup best-quality olive oil
½ cup shelled walnut pieces

1. Combine the mustard, vinegar, and basil in a food processor and season with salt and pepper. Process for 1 minute, shut off the motor, scrape down the sides of the bowl, and process for 30 seconds longer.

2. Leave the motor running and dribble in the oil in a slow steady stream. When the oil is incorporated, drop the walnuts through the feed tube and shut the machine off immediately. Check the texture of the walnuts; they should be chopped evenly and fairly finely, but should still be discernible in the dressing. Process with short bursts of power until you achieve the desired texture. Do not overprocess.

3. Cover and refrigerate until ready to use.

About 1½ cups

HOW TO DRESS A SALAD

Making homemade salad dressing should be a matter of pride, not fear. It is easy to figure out the balance between oil and more piquant seasonings once you've experimented with dressing recipes for a while. Practice with the recipes in this book and you'll soon get the knack.

Once you've prepared a dressing, carefully taste the results before and after you dress the salad. You'll know instinctively whether the greens need more of this or less of that.

When it's time to dress your salad, remember the three cardinal rules: Don't dress it too far in advance, don't drown it, and toss the greens very well. We generally keep our rinsed and dried greens in a wooden salad bowl in the fridge until about 30 minutes before we're ready to serve. Then we drizzle a little dressing at a time on the greens and toss, toss, toss until every leaf is coated evenly. Serve and enjoy without delay.

CHEESES
AND BREADS

ARTISANAL CHEESES

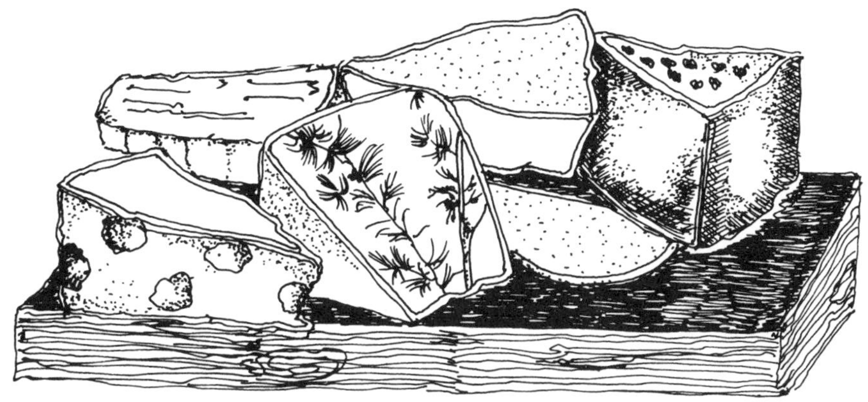

A great cheese is like a great wine. If made by artisans it can be a memorable experience. While artisanal cheese making has long been a tradition around the world, the craft has exploded in America in the past two decades. Across the country, passionate cheese lovers, unable to find the kinds of cheese they enjoyed while traveling, have begun to study the art of authentic cheese making, investing in cheese rooms or small herds of heirloom goats, sheep, or cows. Flavor comes first in these often organic, sometimes seasonal cheeses that reflect their "terroir"—the character of their environment—and the creativity of their makers.

Serious importers, distributors, and cheese makers sell to serious cheese shops. These merchants respect the craft of cheese making and know how to care for the cheese to showcase its flavor at its peak, and they're all too willing to share their knowledge with their customers. Good cheese merchants can be found at local farmers' markets, specialty cheese shops, gourmet shops, upscale grocers, and greengrocers; often their wares are available by mail order or on the Internet.

Of course, the prices of these cheeses reflect the care with which they are made. But once you taste the difference between handmade and commercial factory cheeses, you'll have started out on a mind- and taste bud–expanding adventure. The famous motto of cheese makers around the world is, "If it smells bad, it will probably taste good, very, very good." So be adventurous—a restaurant's cheese tasting course is a great way to sample some new cheeses.

Here are some of our favorites. Due to the small size of many of the suppliers, availability may vary. If you can't find a particular cheese on this list, ask your local cheesemonger for help finding something similar. Our guess is he won't have much trouble coming up with suggestions!

BLUE-VEINED CHEESES

Legend has it that the first blue was discovered by a shepherdess, after she accidentally left her bread-and-cheese lunch in a cave overgrown with the blue-green mold *Penicillium roqueforti.* When she returned to the cave some days later, she discovered that the cheese had become marbled with blue veins, and had taken on a distinctive pungent flavor. Today the blue cheese family includes cheeses made from many different types of milk, and all share the characteristic veiny mold; members include Gorgonzola, Stilton, Maytag, and Roquefort.

1. Shropshire Blue
2. St. Maure, Jacquin
3. Edel de Cleron
4. Red Hawk
5. Mimolette
6. Tomme de Brebis
7. Stravecchio
8. Humboldt Fog

In Vermont, Green Mountain Farm's GORE-DAWN-ZOLA is a memorable gorgonzola-style blue with tangy sharpness and a crumbly texture. For a British hue, try a COLSTON BASSET STILTON, a creamy, highly veined cow's milk cheese that is aged four months and handmade using traditional rennet. Massachusetts' BERKSHIRE BLUE, crafted from unpasteurized cow's milk, is one of the best blue cheeses in America today—raw, high butterfat, and very sweet, with a mushroomy flavor to the vein. Roquefort, the quintessential historic blue, comes from the eponymous region in France; try one from the artisan cheese maker Carles, whose piquant, crumbly sheep's milk cheese melts in your mouth. FireFly Farms makes the interesting MOUNTAIN TOP BLUE—a pyramid-shaped goat cheese that is peppered inside with blue mold and aged five to eight weeks. The result is a rich and creamy goat cheese with a delicate blue flavor. Quite lovely.

CHEVRES
(GOAT CHEESES)

Initially known to Americans as an accessory of the 1980s haute cuisine craze, goat cheese has become so ubiquitous you'd be hard pressed to find a sandwich menu without it. But there's much more to goat cheese than the mass-produced versions would lead you to believe.

Cypress Grove's HUMBOLDT FOG comes from the mists of Northern California; a very thin, wavy horizontal line of ash adds a slight blue flavor to the

creamy, lemony taste. THE O'BANON chèvre, wrapped in chestnut leaves and macerated with Kentucky Bourbon, and WABASH CANNONBALLS, creamy one-ounce balls with a fluffy ash finish, both come from the Indiana-based Capriole Farm. The famed CHAROLLAIS is a soft and nutty cheese from Burgundy; its dense, rich texture is perfect on a thick slice of crusty bread. A tangier raw goat's milk can be found in CHABICHOU DU POITOU, whose crinkly white skin belies an interior that literally melts in your mouth. Sweetly heart-shaped, fresh-tasting LUMIERE is semi-ripened, its pure white interior crossed with a thin line

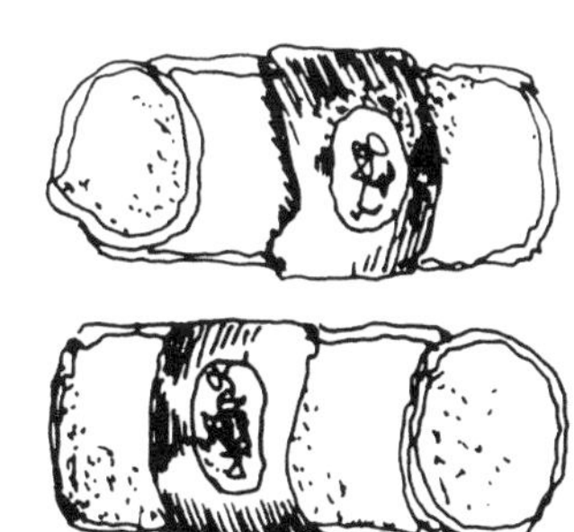

of grapevine ash. With the largest goat herd in the country, New York's Coach Farm Dairy was one of the earliest American pioneers in the genre; try their GREEN PEPPERCORN PYRAMID—aged creaminess cut with an occasional bit of heat.

FRESH CHEESES

Fresh cheeses are those that have not been aged. They are soft, white, and creamy, many of them with an uncomplicated taste calling to mind milk or butter. Others may be pungent with herbs or garlic. Fresh cheeses are rushed to stores by air and by land from the rural farmhouses where they are made.

MOZZARELLA DI BUFALA is the real deal—made from the milk of water buffalo, soft, creamy, and not stringy in the least. Freshness is key, so this Italian cheese should be enjoyed as quickly as possible. The Vermont Butter & Cheese Company makes one of the best versions of MASCARPONE you'll find in this country; their line is quite well distributed, so you shouldn't have a problem finding this luxurious, smooth, and very thick dessert cheese (the key ingredient in tiramisù). The owner of California's South El Monte cheese brought the recipe for his magical GIOIA CHEESE from Italy nine years ago; his effort was well worth it. Louisiana's Bittersweet Dairy makes FELICIANA NEVAT, a domed, soft-ripened Guernsey cow and goat's milk cheese that tastes like a triple crème cheese with a slight tang. ROBIOLA LA ROSSA is a spectacular leaf-wrapped cheese made from raw cow's and goat's milk and wrapped and aged in cherry leaves; the Piedmontese blend is both earthy and fruity, and very, very buttery. Last but not least, Capriole Farm's devilishly good FROMAGE A TROIS features luscious layers of chèvre, basil pesto, toasted pine nuts, and sun-dried tomatoes.

It's ALL ABOUT THE COW

We have a friend, a cheesemaker with a small dairy in Washington State, who has been making some marvelous cheeses. She makes wonderful goat's, cow's, and sheep's-milk cheeses in a variety of styles, some with washed rinds and some wrapped in leaves. One we especially liked was a Guernsey cheese wrapped in chestnut leaves—a lovely addition to our cheese board. And then one day, it was no longer available. We called only to discover her cow had died!

Now, we're quite certain there will be an outcry from customers around the country and she'll get another Guernsey or two, but we tell this story only to emphasize just how small and exacting some of the artisanal cheese makers are. Many want to stay small. By remaining independent, they feel they can do what they love and devote the care for their animals and their product that is required. We admire their integrity—and their cheeses.

HARD CHEESES

Hard pressed cheeses account for many of the most popular varieties in America, including Cheddar, Parmigiano-Reggiano, and Swiss. The cheese curd is either heated or left uncooked and then pressed to drain out the whey and make the cheese firm and smooth. Cheeses such as Cheddar and Manchego contain cooked curds; Gouda and Gruyère, among others, do not.

PENNSYLVANIA NOBLE, from Green Valley Dairy, is a pale yellow, natural-rind Cheddar made in small batches from organically fed cows; it has that wonderful, traditional English Cheddar flavor. Though GOUDA BOERE KAAS is of Dutch origin, a particularly delicious variety is made in the United States by Winchester Cheese in California. Slightly granular, nutty, and salty with butterscotch tones, its trademark tiny holes result from what's known as the "crumbling process." Spain's most famous cheese, EL TOBOSO MANCHEGO, is made from sheep's milk in the La Mancha region; aged six months for a firmer texture, it boasts a sweet, nutty, and complex taste. Whenever we can find it, we stock up on CRAVERO PARMIGIANO-REGGIANO for snacking and cooking. There's no substitute for the intense flavor of Parmigiano carefully aged for five years in the Italian mountains of Piedmont. FIORE SARDO, a sheep's milk pecorino of Sardinia, has a smoky, sharp flavor that works as well for nibbling as it does grated over pasta.

MOUNTAIN CHEESES

The monastery or mountain cheeses are a legacy from monks who had the time, patience, and instinct for preserving knowledge. The results of their experiments comprise a group of similar cheeses that are soft and buttery with a pungency that comes from fullness rather than strength.

A semi-hard raw goat cheese, MONT ST. FRANCIS is an aged

monastery-style cheese from Indiana's Capriole Farm. An intriguing and delicate cheese, TUMALO TOMME is aged and rubbed on pine planks for a woodsy flavor; the alfalfa-fed goats from Juniper Grove in Oregon might have something to do with it, too. ROLF BEELER'S GRUYERE from Switzerland is nutty and slightly sweet with underlying mushroom flavors; it's aged in caves for sixteen months to fully develop. A homegrown taste of the French Alps by way of Vermont, Thistle Hill Farm's TARENTAISE ALPINE CHEESE is a wonderful organic Gruyère made in the tradition of Savoie; pale and granular, it's a true "terroir" cheese reflective of the farm's soil, climate, and flora. A raw goat's milk cheese rolled out in ten-pound wheels, Sweet Grass Dairy's HOLLY SPRINGS is sweet and nutty, with a semi-soft, creamy texture.

SOFT-RIPENED CHEESES

Also known as "bloomy rind" cheeses, these semi-soft varieties—including Brie and Camembert—are ripened from the outside in. The cheese's thin rind is deliberately exposed to or sprayed with molds that develop the cheese from the crust inward, leaving a velvety white "bloom" on the cheese's exterior and a creamy texture within.

Old Chatham Sheepherding Company's HUDSON VALLEY CAMEMBERT, unlike the traditional cow's milk version, is made from a mixture of sheep and cow's milk. Its sweet, grassy flavor is a perfect complement to a glass of chilled white wine. The color of fresh-churned butter, COULOMMIERS is a heartier cousin of Brie, made in a smaller and thicker round. It can be hard to find, but it's worth seeking out. VACHERIN MONT D'OR is so runny you'll need to serve it from its cedar box with a spoon—apt treatment for a cheese made in the spring, when the cows are fed from the first cutting of the grasses. For special occasions, the decadent triple-crème PIERRE ROBERT is aged in caves until it attains a buttery richness that would put a Brillat-Savarin to shame. Sweet Hill

Farm's double-cream cow's milk GREEN HILL cheese shines with the herbaceous flavors of the clover, cow peas, millet, and sunflowers that cover the farm's acres. It is a lovely cheese—clean, semi-firm, and buttery. Vermont's Lazy Lady produces the organic BUCK HILL SUNSHINE, a cow's milk cheese in a thin round that's meltingly brie-like, dense, smooth, with a tiny bit of sharpness. CHESTNUT LEAF AGED SHEEP CHEESE from Washington's Sally Jackson Cheeses is not something to pass up—if you can get your hands on it. This semi-firm, raw cheese is sweet, complex, and beautiful to look at. An aesthete's cheese if there ever was one, CONSTANT BLISS is a compact, creamy, and earthy raw cow's milk cylinder from Jasper Hill Farm in Vermont. What could be more poetic than a cheese made exclusively of "evening milk," from cows weaned on jazz and classical music?

WASHED-RIND CHEESES

These powerfully scented "stinky" cheeses are often much more mildly flavored than their stench would lead you to believe. Their rind is usually a muted orange color, the result of being rubbed or washed in beer, brine, brandy, wine, or a combination, which promotes the growth of flavor-enhancing molds.

A true Frenchman's cheese, EPOISSES is a pungent and addictive cow's milk cheese from Burgundy. It is washed with brine and finished with brandy, and we just love it. DESPEARADO is a "hooligan" cheese from Cato Corner Farm in Connecticut. It is washed with fermented pear mash and Poire Williams eau de vie; the family-run business is known for its singularly brined offerings. WINNEMERE is another semi-soft cheese from the eclectic Jasper Hill Farm; wrapped in spruce bark and washed with lambic beer, it's only available the first six months of the year. Often compared to an Epoisses, Cowgirl Creamery's triple-cream RED HAWK is aged six weeks to fully develop its very special flavor. VERO ARRIGONI TALEGGIO is a slightly stinky, semi-soft cow's milk cheese from Valtaleggio in Lombardy; melt-in-your-mouth gooey with a thin stripe of blue, it's one of Italy's favorites.

BRIE PINWHEEL

Here is a spectacular treatment when a simple wheel of Brie doesn't seem festive enough.

1 whole ripe Brie (about 5 pounds)
1 cup dried currants
1 cup finely chopped walnuts
1 cup chopped fresh dill
½ cup poppy seeds
1 cup slivered blanched almonds

1. Carefully cut away the rind from the top of the Brie. Using the back of the knife, lightly score the top of the Brie into 10 equal wedge-shape areas.

2. Sprinkle half of the currants onto one of the wedge-shape areas and press gently into the surface of the Brie. Repeat the procedure with half of the walnuts, dill, poppy seeds, and almonds, patting each garnish into a wedge-shape area as you proceed around the top of the Brie. Use the remaining garnishes on the remaining wedges.

3. Wrap and refrigerate for no more than 4 hours. Allow to stand at room temperature for 30 minutes before serving.

At least 20 portions

BRIE WRAPPED IN PHYLLO

12 sheets of phyllo pastry (see "Working with Phyllo," page 10)
1 pound (4 sticks) unsalted butter, melted
1 whole Brie, not fully ripe (about 5 pounds)

1. Butter a baking sheet large enough to hold the Brie.

2. Lay 5 sheets of phyllo on the baking sheet, brushing melted butter on each layer as you go. Set the Brie on top of the phyllo and fold the edges of the phyllo up around the cheese.

3. Cover the top of the cheese with 6 sheets of phyllo, brushing melted butter on each layer. Tuck the ends of the pastry under the cheese. Brush the top and sides with the melted butter.

4. Preheat the oven to 350°F.

5. Fold the last sheet of phyllo in a 1-inch-wide strip. Brush it with butter and form a flower shape. Center the flower on top of the Brie and again brush with the butter.

6. Bake until golden brown, 20 to 30 minutes. Let stand for at least 30 minutes before serving.

20 portions

AFTER THE THEATER BUFFET

BLANCHED FRESH ASPARAGUS

SESAME MAYONNAISE IN A HOLLOWED PURPLE CABBAGE

GRAVLAX WITH DILL MUSTARD SAUCE

BRIE WRAPPED IN PHYLLO

GARDEN SALAD OF SNOW PEAS, ROMAINE LETTUCE, SHELLED PEAS, ASPARAGUS TIPS, AND WATERCRESS WITH *LEMON VINAIGRETTE*

FRESH HERB BUTTER

ASSORTED BREADS AND BISCUITS

FRESH STRAWBERRIES

PROFITEROLES

VANILLA ICE CREAM

CHOCOLATE FUDGE SAUCE AND WHIPPED CREAM

When you want to impress, serve Brie Wrapped in Phyllo.

"You two can be what you like, but since I am the big fromage in this family, I prefer to think of myself as Gorgon Zola."

—OGDEN NASH

BRIE SOUFFLE

A most luxurious brunch dish, served with Champagne and fresh fruit.

8 tablespoons (1 stick) unsalted butter, at room temperature
6 slices of good-quality white sandwich bread, crusts removed
1½ cups milk
1 teaspoon salt
Dash of Tabasco
3 eggs
1 pound slightly underripe Brie, rind removed

1. Preheat the oven to 350°F. Butter a 1½-quart soufflé dish.

2. Butter one side of the bread slices and cut each slice into thirds. Whisk together the milk, salt, Tabasco, and eggs. Coarsely grate the Brie.

3. Arrange half of the bread, buttered side up, on the bottom of the dish. Sprinkle evenly with half of the Brie and then repeat, using the remaining bread and Brie. Carefully pour the egg mixture over the bread. Let stand at room temperature for 30 minutes.

4. Bake until bubbling and golden, 25 to 30 minutes.

4 to 6 portions

BAKED BANONS

Icy cold salad greens and hot and tangy goat cheese combined on the same plate are a perfect ending to a rustic French meal.

6 tablespoons (¾ stick) unsalted butter
6 Banon cheeses, leaves removed, or 6 slices, each 2 inches thick, Montrachet (about ¾ pound)
½ cup mixed dried peppercorns (equal amounts, more or less, of black, white, and green)

1. Preheat the oven to 350°F.

2. Butter a baking sheet with 3 tablespoons of the butter and arrange the Banons on the sheet.

3. Crush the peppercorns with a rolling pin, or load them into a peppermill and sprinkle or grind the mixture onto the Banons to taste. Top each cheese with ½ tablespoon butter.

4. Bake the cheeses until heated through, 10 to 12 minutes. Serve immediately.

6 portions

We are often asked if the crust of Brie cheese is edible. It is, but you may remove it after serving if you wish; many do.

PORT

On the first crisp day of fall we inevitably know that we'll take a break to enjoy a glass of Port, some Stilton, and crusty bread with unsalted butter—our autumn tradition.

Port is not as well known in America as it is in Europe, where it is known as an Englishman's drink. The French drink it too, and we wish more people would investigate the rich, heady taste of a good vintage Port.

Port is made by adding a bit of brandy to wine during the fermentation. This stops the process before all the natural sugar has been converted into alcohol. The result is a fruity, slightly sweet wine, with the additional alcoholic boost of the brandy. Vintage Ports lose some of this sweetness as they age.

The British make a ritual of after-dinner Port. The host must always pass the decanter to his left, and even today women are often excluded from the company while the men linger over Port and cigars.

Because Port is too often thought of as a dessert wine, many hesitate to serve it. We urge you to taste, experiment, and come to your own conclusions. This is an enjoyment that you may have been missing.

"... cheese, milk's leap toward immortality."

—CLIFTON FADIMAN

MARINATED CHEVRES

1 cup best-quality olive oil
2 bay leaves
6 black peppercorns, slightly crushed
1 tablespoon dried thyme
4 Crottin or other small hard goat cheeses
1 cup coarsely chopped fresh basil leaves
4 garlic cloves, peeled and halved
Lettuce leaves, for serving

1. Combine the olive oil, bay leaves, peppercorns, and thyme in a small heavy saucepan. Set over moderate heat and cook, stirring occasionally, until the oil is very hot, about 5 minutes.

2. Arrange the cheeses in a single layer in a small heatproof bowl or pan. Sprinkle the chopped basil and garlic over the cheeses and then pour the hot oil and seasonings over them.

3. Let the cheeses cool to room temperature, cover, and refrigerate for at least 4 hours before serving. (The cheeses can be stored in their oil marinade for up to 1 week, if kept refrigerated.)

4. To serve, arrange the cheeses on lettuce leaves on individual plates and drizzle with a few spoonfuls of marinade. Or broil the cheeses, basting with the marinade, until brown and bubbling.

4 portions

SO MANY CHEESES, SO LITTLE TIME

There are hundreds of cheeses—and once you consider all of the variables that go into cheese making, it becomes clear why there are so many. Each element of the age-old process contributes to the unique character of the finished product.

THE MILK

It all begins with the milk, the flavor and quality of which impact every fine cheese. Milk is so much more than that familiar beverage we enjoy with cookies—it has depth and body, and depending on where it comes from, its own distinct flavor. The rich, buttery milk from a Jersey cow is quite different from that of a Brown Swiss or Ayrshire; the singular flavor of water buffalo milk stands apart from the thinner, less fatty milk of a goat or a sheep. And just as these differences exist in milk, so they appear later on down the line, in cheese.

Like wine, milk is also affected by "terroir," or the land and other natural influences. The mineral content of the terrain impacts what types of grasses and flowers grow to become the animals' diet, and the flavor of these plants affects the flavor of the animals' milk. Whether the plants are very green, or dry and haylike, or heavy with pollen, the milk will reflect the characteristics of the landscape.

The land influences the cheese maker as well—if the area is rocky, the dairyman will most likely raise goats or sheep and thus make goat's or sheep's milk cheeses. Lush meadowland is ideal for pasturing cows, so you'll tend to find a concentration of cow's milk cheeses in such fertile areas.

THE SEASON

Traditional cheese is a seasonal product. There are times when certain cheeses are at their best, times when they are at their worst, and times when they're unavailable altogether. Thus, a dairy's winter cheese will probably taste different than its spring cheese (milk is young and rich in the spring and fall, less so in the summer and winter).

THE CHEESE MAKER

The skill of the cheese maker, and all of the dozens of choices he or she makes, greatly influence the taste of a cheese. The selection of rennet or starter cultures, the aging techniques used, the finishing and storage—all of these elements reflect the cheese maker's experience, intellect, and whim, and in turn, all are reflected in the cheese.

BUYING AND STORING CHEESE

Ideally you should purchase cheese at or near its peak from a merchant you trust. Don't be afraid to ask questions or request a taste of this or that as you shop—most cheesemongers are truly passionate about their product, and will be eager to share their knowledge and enthusiasm with you. When you select a cheese, bring it home and consume it within 48 hours—cheese continues to ripen and can start to deteriorate if you wait any longer.

> "Buying cheese is an art. Express yourself."
>
> —PIERRE ANDROUET, CELEBRATED PARISIAN CHEESE EXPERT

It's best to store cheeses in a dark, cool place, avoiding frequent temperature changes. A cellar or the refrigerator's vegetable bin both work well. Always wrap cheeses individually, covering only the cut edges with lightly waxed parchment or cheese paper; let the rind breath. Be sure to remove cheese from cold storage at least several hours before serving, to present it at its fullest and most glorious.

SERVING CHEESE

A cheese course during a dinner is a lovely way to prolong good wine and conversation while preparing the palate for the next course. We like to offer at least three cheeses at once, though depending on the number of guests, we might present five or seven (estimate about two ounces of cheese per person).

Balance the cheese course with the rest of the meal: Serve more extravagant cheeses with a light meal, and simpler cheeses with a hearty meal. Try to choose cheeses with flavors that are compatible with the other foods you'll be serving, and mix it up a bit in terms of taste, texture, and color. Select several types of cheese, perhaps one that will challenge the palate and at least two familiar friends such as Brie or Cheddar. Or try a "vertical" tasting: all goat cheeses, all blue, all mountain cheeses.

Crusty breads, focaccia, flatbreads, and crackers are all excellent cheese companions. We love to serve other delights as well: some nuts such as almonds, brazil nuts, hazelnuts, or walnuts; some fruit, perhaps apples, peaches, grapes, or pears; and often some chutney, olives, capers, medjool dates, or dried figs. Wines should provide balance and harmony. In reds, we like Zinfandel, Syrah, Pinot Noir, Barbaresco/Nebbiolo, or Cabernet Sauvignon. In whites, try Rieslings, Sauvignon Blanc, Champagne, Pinot Blanc, Pinot Gris, and Viognier.

BEST BREADS

These are good times for bread in America. The intoxicating smell of baking bread is everywhere! Pass by a bakery in almost any town, big or small, and you'll want to follow the aroma. It will bring to mind all the meaningful things in life: your grandma lovingly kneading bread for Sunday supper; your own first, perhaps clumsy, attempts at making a loaf or two; ample stone ovens serving as the center of small villages around the world; those amber waves of grain. Just one whiff, and a flurry of images.

Not so long ago, "American bread" seemed an oxymoron—it meant bread that was soft, white, and squishy, bearing very little resemblance to the light, airy, crackly-crusted breads anyone with a passport had sampled overseas. We'd hear the cries for "real bread" and plead for patience; if you want good bread, it will come. And eventually it did.

A few savvy American food pioneers did their homework and figured out how to make bread worthy of the butter spread upon it. They set the bar high, and as other bakers mastered the techniques and found a deep passion for "real bread," so our daily bread got better and better. Now American bread is something to be proud of—tangy sourdoughs, hearty pumpernickels, and dense wholegrain loaves, even perfect baguettes and boules. Yet while American markets today offer breads of a higher quality than ever before, there's still nothing like homemade. Baked in your very own oven, the aromas scenting your kitchen for an hour or so, those first warm slices with a smear of sweet farmstand butter . . . well, it just doesn't get much better.

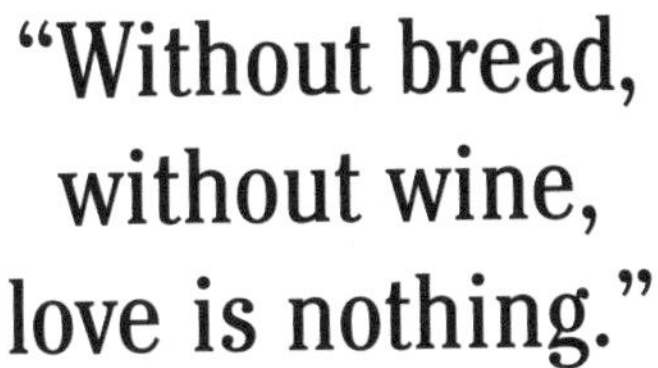

RAISIN PUMPERNICKEL

This uniquely New York bread, reputedly invented in a venerable Manhattan bakery, is now widely copied and available throughout the city. "Black Russian," as it is also called, is delicious and more versatile than you might imagine. Try it with a ripe piece of Brie, turn it into a tuna sandwich, or transform it into fabulous French toast. We offer this recipe for those who have never tasted "raisin pump" and for those transplanted New Yorkers who have despaired of ever tasting it again.

1½ cups lukewarm water (105° to 115°F)
½ cup molasses
1 package active dry yeast
1 tablespoon instant coffee granules
1 tablespoon salt
2 cups medium rye flour
1½ tablespoons unsweetened powdered cocoa
2 cups whole-wheat flour
2 cups bread flour or unbleached all-purpose flour
2 tablespoons vegetable oil
1 cup raisins
3 to 4 tablespoons cornmeal
1 tablespoon cold water
1 egg white

1. Stir together the lukewarm water and molasses in a large mixing bowl. Sprinkle in the yeast and stir to dissolve. Let stand for 10 minutes, or until slightly foamy.

2. Stir in the instant coffee, salt, and rye flour. Sprinkle in the cocoa and stir well to combine. Add the whole-wheat flour and 1 cup of the bread flour, or enough to make a sticky dough.

3. Turn the bread out onto a lightly floured work surface and let it rest. Wash and dry the bowl.

4. Sprinkle additional bread flour over the dough and begin to knead. Continue until most of the remaining bread flour is incorporated and you have a smooth elastic ball. (Breads with rye flour will always be slightly sticky.)

5. Pour the vegetable oil into the mixing bowl, turn the ball of dough to coat well, cover the bowl with a towel, and set aside to rise until the dough is tripled in bulk, 3 to 4 hours.

6. Lightly flour the work surface with bread flour or all-purpose flour and turn the dough out onto it. Flatten it into a large rectangle and sprinkle with the raisins. Roll up the dough and knead it, to distribute the raisins evenly, for about 5 minutes. Return the dough to the bowl, cover, and let rise until doubled, about 2 hours.

7. Sprinkle a large baking sheet with 3 to 4 tablespoons cornmeal. Turn the dough out, cut it into 3 pieces, and shape each piece into a small round loaf. Set the loaves on the baking sheet, leaving as much room as possible between them, cover, and let rise until doubled, about 2 hours.

8. Preheat the oven to 375°F.

9. Beat the egg white together with the 1 tablespoon cold water in a small bowl. When the loaves have risen sufficiently, brush the tops with the egg white mixture.

10. Bake the loaves on the center rack of the oven until they are dark brown and sound hollow when the bottoms are rapped, 25 to 35 minutes. Cool completely on racks before cutting or wrapping.

3 loaves

Up to the last two hundred years, only white flour was used in baking for the nobility. It's ironic how much we all now prefer rough cut, dark, and mixed whole grains.

PATIO PICNIC MENU

CHICKEN MARBELLA

BULGUR WHEAT SALAD

BRIE CHEESE

SEMOLINA BREAD

LEMON MOUSSE

FRESH STRAWBERRIES

BREAD FLOUR

Major millers market a flour especially formulated to duplicate professional bakers' flour. While not always available in all markets, this bread flour is worth seeking out. It makes bread with superior flavor and texture. If you do not find it in your supermarket, ask the manager to begin stocking it.

SEMOLINA BREAD

Because of its high gluten content and golden color, this makes a spectacular loaf that, while delicious any way you serve it, seems best when dunked into the tomato sauce at the end of an Italian meal. Semolina (or durum, hard winter wheat, or pasta flour) is available in health-food stores and Italian groceries.

We have found that while a 100-percent semolina loaf is too heavy, a mixture of half semolina and half bread flour (or unbleached all-purpose flour) perfectly duplicates the crisp, light, and flavorful loaves available in high-quality bread shops. Since this bread always seems to come sprinkled with sesame seeds we have included them in the recipe, but you can substitute poppy or other seeds, or eliminate them altogether.

2 cups lukewarm water (105° to 115°F)
1 package active dry yeast
3 cups semolina flour
1 tablespoon salt
2 to 3 cups bread flour or unbleached all-purpose flour
2 tablespoons olive oil
3 to 4 tablespoons cornmeal
1 egg
Sesame seeds (optional)

1. Pour the water into a mixing bowl, stir in the yeast, and let stand for 10 minutes. Stir again to be certain all the yeast is dissolved.

2. Add the semolina flour and salt and stir well.

3. Add 2 cups of the bread flour and stir to make a sticky dough. Turn the dough out onto a floured work surface and let rest while you wash and dry the bowl.

4. Begin kneading the dough, sprinkling it with the remaining cup of bread flour as necessary to keep it from sticking to your hands. After about 10 minutes the dough will be smooth and elastic and will have absorbed more or less the last cup of flour.

5. Shape the dough into a ball and place it in the bowl. Pour the olive oil over the dough and turn it several times to coat with the oil. Cover the bowl with a towel and set aside until the dough has tripled in bulk. (The increase in volume is more important than the time it takes; depending on room temperature this may be 2 or more hours. Do not try to force the dough to rise more rapidly by setting it on radiators, etc. This can sour the bread. Patience is a virtue.)

6. Punch down the dough, turn it out onto a lightly floured work surface, knead briefly (5 minutes or less), and return it to the bowl. Cover and let rise again until doubled.

7. Punch down the dough, cut it into thirds, and shape each third into a thin loaf about 24 inches long. Sprinkle a baking sheet with 3 to 4 tablespoons cornmeal and arrange the loaves on the sheet, leaving as much room between the loaves as possible. Cover and let rise until not quite doubled, about 30 minutes.

8. Preheat the oven to 425°F.

9. Beat together the egg and the 1 tablespoon water. When the loaves have risen, brush them well with this egg wash. Sprinkle the sesame seeds to taste, and slash the loaves decoratively on top with a sharp knife, making diagonal cuts.

10. Slide the baking sheet onto the center rack of the oven and reduce the heat to 375°F. Bake until the loaves are brown and sound hollow when the bottoms are thumped, 30 to 40 minutes. (For a crisper bottom crust, remove the loaves from the baking sheet and place them directly on the oven rack for the last 5 to 10 minutes of baking time.)

11. Remove the loaves from the oven and cool on a rack. Wrap when cool.

3 loaves, about 18 inches long

BRIOCHE

This recipe is slightly less complex than the traditional French brioche method, but it produces a rich, firm, and buttery bread that is completely satisfying. It can be baked in regular loaf pans, yielding a spectacular sandwich and toasting bread. It is perfect for enclosing roasts and other meat to be baked *en brioche,* and of course it can be formed into the traditional round brioche shape, delicious served warm from the oven with butter and preserves.

2 cups milk
1 cup (2 sticks) unsalted butter, plus extra for greasing the pans
¼ cup sugar
2 packages active dry yeast
4 teaspoons salt
3 eggs, at room temperature
8 cups unbleached all-purpose flour
2 to 3 tablespoons vegetable oil

1. Combine the milk, butter, and sugar in a medium-size saucepan and bring to a boil. Remove from the heat and pour into a large mixing bowl. Cool to lukewarm (105° to 115°F).

2. Stir in the yeast and let stand for 10 minutes. Stir in the salt. Beat the eggs thoroughly in a small bowl and add to the milk mixture. Stir in 7 cups of the flour, 1 cup at a time, until you achieve a sticky dough. Flour a work surface and turn the dough out onto it. Wash and dry the bowl.

3. Sprinkle additional flour over the dough and begin to knead it, adding more flour as necessary until you achieve a smooth, elastic dough, about 10 minutes.

4. Pour 2 to 3 tablespoons vegetable oil into the bowl. Turn the ball of dough in the oil to coat well. Set the dough aside, covered with a towel, to rise until tripled in bulk, about 2 hours.

5. Punch down the dough, turn out onto a lightly floured work surface, and knead for about 2 minutes. Return the dough to the bowl, cover, and let rise again until doubled.

"Bread deals with living things, with giving life, with growth, with the seed, the grain that nurtures. It is not coincidence that we say bread is the staff of life."

—LIONEL POILÂNE

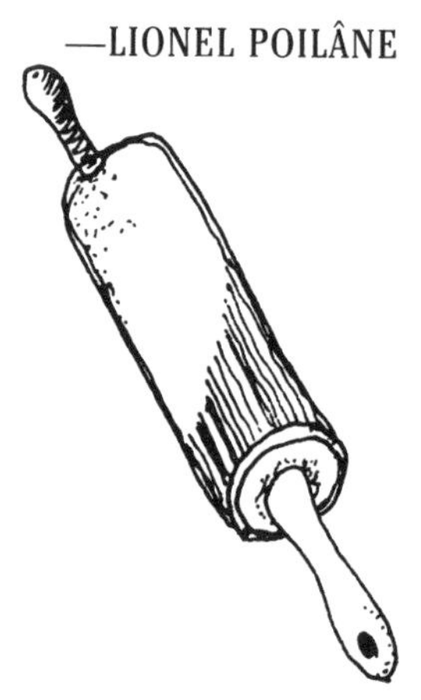

It seems to us that Brioche must be the most cheerful of breads.

6. Preheat the oven to 375°F.

7. The dough is now ready to be formed. If you are baking it in loaf pans, use 2 pans (5 x 9 x 3 inches), lightly buttered. For traditional brioche, use buttered muffin tins or imported brioche molds, available in varying sizes from cookware shops. If you are enclosing a roast or other food in brioche, proceed according to that recipe. Let the formed loaves rise until nearly doubled.

8. Bake until golden brown, 30 to 40 minutes (slightly less for small brioches). The loaves will sound hollow when thumped on the bottom. Cool slightly before unmolding; cool completely before wrapping.

2 loaves, or about 2 dozen 3-inch brioches

CHALLAH

This splendid loaf makes wonderful eating straight from the oven and spread with butter and honey. We love French toast made with it. If any of this bread manages to last long enough to become stale, it makes excellent bread crumbs.

2 cups milk
8 tablespoons (1 stick) unsalted butter
⅓ cup sugar
2 packages active dry yeast
4 eggs, at room temperature
2 teaspoons salt
6 cups unbleached all-purpose flour
⅓ cup cornmeal
1 tablespoon cold water
Poppy seeds

1. Bring the milk, 6 tablespoons of the butter, and the sugar to a boil together in a medium-size saucepan. Remove from the heat, pour into a large mixing bowl, and let cool to lukewarm (105° to 115°F).

2. Stir the yeast into the milk mixture and let stand for 10 minutes.

3. Beat 3 of the eggs well in a small bowl, and stir them and the salt into the milk-and-yeast mixture.

4. Stir in 5 cups of the flour, 1 cup at a time, until you achieve a sticky dough. Flour a work surface lightly and turn the dough out onto it. Wash and dry the bowl.

5. Sprinkle additional flour over the dough and begin kneading, adding more flour as necessary, until you have a smooth elastic dough.

6. Smear the reserved 2 tablespoons butter around the inside of the bowl and add the ball of dough to the bowl, turning to coat it lightly with the butter. Cover the bowl with a towel and set aside to let the dough rise until tripled in bulk, 1½ to 2 hours.

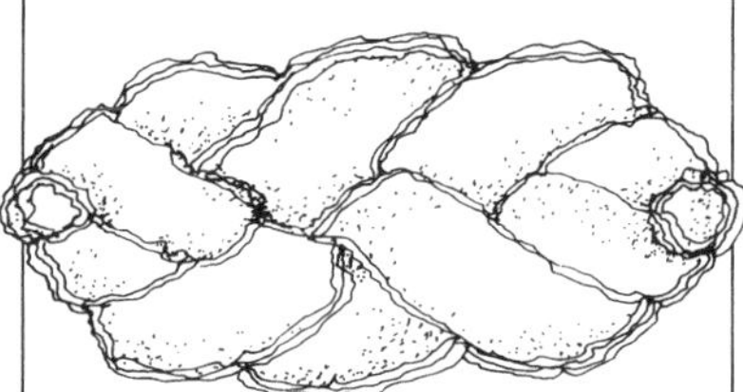

Challah represents the ceremonial show bread that was placed on the table by the priest in the ancient Temple of Jerusalem. There were twelve such breads, each representing one of the Israelite tribes. Challah was always braided to invest it with special beauty. Each family traditionally places two challahs on the table for the Sabbath meal, representing double portions of manna from heaven that fell on the sixth day so that the Israelites would not have to collect manna on the seventh day, the day of rest.

"I do like a little bit of butter to my bread."

—A. A. MILNE, *WHEN WE WERE VERY YOUNG*

7. Turn the dough out onto a lightly floured work surface and cut into halves. Cut each half into 3 pieces. Roll the pieces out into long "snakes" about 18 inches long. Braid three of the snakes together into a loaf and tuck the ends under. Repeat with the remaining snakes.

8. Sprinkle a large baking sheet with the cornmeal and transfer the loaves to the sheet. Leave room between the loaves for them to rise. Cover the loaves with the towel and let rise until nearly doubled, about 1 hour.

9. Preheat the oven to 350°F.

10. Beat the remaining egg and the 1 tablespoon cold water together well in a small bowl. Brush this egg wash evenly over the loaves. Sprinkle immediately with poppy seeds to taste.

11. Set the baking sheet on the center rack of the oven. Bake until the loaves are golden brown and sound hollow when their bottoms are thumped, 30 to 35 minutes. Cool completely on racks before wrapping.

2 large loaves

CRACKLING CORN BREAD

Southern-style goodness. Serve this comforting bread warm with lots of butter and honey.

Butter, for greasing the pan
1 cup stone-ground cornmeal
1 cup unbleached all-purpose flour
1⁄3 cup sugar
2 1⁄2 teaspoons baking powder
1⁄4 teaspoon salt
1 cup buttermilk
1 cup diced, crisp-cooked bacon
6 tablespoons (3⁄4 stick) unsalted butter, melted
1 egg, slightly beaten

1. Preheat the oven to 400°F. Grease a 9-inch square baking pan.

2. Stir the dry ingredients together in a bowl. Then stir in the buttermilk, bacon, melted butter, and egg and mix gently.

3. Pour the batter into the prepared pan, set on the center rack of the oven, and bake for 25 minutes. The corn bread is done when the edges are lightly browned and a knife inserted in the center comes out clean. Cut into 3-inch squares to serve.

9 squares

Variation: Spoon the batter into 10 greased muffin cups and bake for about 20 minutes.

SILVER PALATE GENESIS BRUNCH

CHAMPAGNE

FRESH OYSTERS WITH *SHALLOT SAUCE*

FIGS AND PROSCIUTTO

RASPBERRY MOUSSE

BLACKBERRY MOUSSE

LEMON MOUSSE

CROISSANTS WITH *STRAWBERRY BUTTER*

GRANDMA CLARK'S SODA BREAD WITH BUTTER

ASSORTED CHEESES

CAPPUCCINO

GRANDMA CLARK'S SODA BREAD

An authentic gift from the very Irish Clark family of County Mayo, Ireland, and Saugatuck, Michigan. This was Grandma Sarah's own creation for teatime. It's sassy, just like her. We love it for breakfast as well, toasted slices with a smear of unsalted butter. Yummy.

6 tablespoons (¾ stick) unsalted butter
3 cups unbleached all-purpose flour
1½ teaspoons salt
1 tablespoon baking powder
1 teaspoon baking soda
¾ cup sugar
1½ cups dried currants
1¾ cups buttermilk
2 eggs, well beaten
1 tablespoon caraway seeds (optional)

1. Smear 2 tablespoons of the butter evenly in a 10-inch cast-iron skillet. Line the buttered skillet with a circle of wax paper. Melt 2 more tablespoons butter in a separate small saucepan and set aside.

2. Preheat the oven to 350°F.

3. Sift the dry ingredients together. Add the currants to the dry ingredients and toss well to coat.

4. Whisk together the buttermilk, eggs, and melted butter. Add to the dry ingredients, along with the caraway seeds if desired, and mix just until blended. Do not overmix.

5. Spoon the batter into the prepared skillet and smooth the top gently with a spatula. Dot the top with the remaining 2 tablespoons butter.

6. Bake on the center rack of the oven until golden brown and puffed, about 60 minutes. Cool slightly, remove from the skillet, and cool on a rack. Or serve warm from the skillet. Cut into wedges.

1 loaf, 6 portions

Toasted and slathered with butter, this fruit-studded soda bread is hard to resist.

BANANA BREAD

8 tablespoons (1 stick) unsalted butter, at room temperature, plus extra for greasing the pan
¾ cup sugar
2 eggs
1 cup unbleached all-purpose flour
1 teaspoon baking soda
½ teaspoon salt
1 cup whole-wheat flour
3 large, ripe bananas, mashed
1 teaspoon vanilla extract
½ cup shelled walnuts, coarsely chopped

1. Preheat the oven to 350°F. Grease a 9 x 5 x 3-inch loaf pan.

2. Cream the butter and sugar until light and fluffy. Add the eggs, one at a time, beating well after each addition.

3. Sift the all-purpose flour, baking soda, and salt together, stir in the whole-wheat flour, and add to the creamed mixture, mixing well.

4. Fold in the mashed bananas, vanilla, and walnuts.

5. Pour the mixture into the prepared pan. Bake on the center rack of the oven until a cake tester inserted in the center comes out clean, 50 to 60 minutes. Cool in the pan for 10 minutes, then on a rack.

1 loaf

DATE-NUT BREAD

4 tablespoons (½ stick) unsalted butter, cut into 6 chunks, plus extra for greasing the pan
1 cup pitted dates, coarsely chopped
¼ cup dark brown sugar
¼ cup sugar
¾ cup boiling water
1 egg, beaten
2 cups unbleached all-purpose flour, sifted
2 teaspoons baking powder
½ teaspoon salt
½ cup shelled black walnuts, coarsely chopped
½ teaspoon vanilla extract
1½ tablespoons rum

1. Preheat the oven to 350°F. Grease a 5 x 9 x 3-inch loaf pan.

2. Place the butter in a large mixing bowl, place the dates on top, and pour both sugars over. Pour the boiling water over the ingredients in the bowl. Let sit for 7 minutes. Stir well.

3. When the mixture is cool, add the egg and mix well.

4. Sift the flour, baking powder, and salt together. Add to the date mixture, beating for 30 seconds. Stir in the walnuts, vanilla, and rum.

5. Pour the mixture into the prepared pan. Bake on the center rack of the oven for 45 to 50 minutes.

1 loaf

"And the best bread was of my mother's own making—the best in all the land!"

—SIR HENRY JAMES, *OLD MEMORIES*

ORANGE PECAN BREAD

8 tablespoons (1 stick) unsalted butter, at room temperature, plus extra for greasing the pan
¾ cup sugar
2 eggs, separated
Grated zest of 1 large or 2 small oranges
1½ cups unbleached all-purpose flour
1½ teaspoons baking powder
¼ teaspoon baking soda

FRUIT BUTTERS

Fruit butters are an especially delicious way to sweeten tea breads. We like Orange Butter on Orange Pecan, Banana, or Apricot Raisin Breads. Strawberry Butter is a wonderful addition to Orange Pecan Bread, croissants, brioches, or crisp waffles. Cream the ingredients together, transfer to a small crock, and chill. The butters keep several days in the refrigerator or many weeks in the freezer. Let the butter return to room temperature before serving. Even morning toast seems like a treat with a pat of fruit butter melting on it.

♥ Orange Butter: 8 tablespoons (1 stick) unsalted butter, ⅓ cup orange marmalade, ½ teaspoon confectioners' sugar, grated zest of 1 orange.

♥ Strawberry Butter: 8 tablespoons (1 stick) unsalted butter, ⅓ cup strawberry jam, ½ teaspoon fresh lemon juice, and ½ teaspoon confectioners' sugar.

Pinch of salt
½ cup fresh orange juice
1 cup shelled pecans, chopped
Orange Glaze (page 359)

1. Preheat the oven to 350°F. Grease an 8½ x 4½-inch loaf pan.

2. Cream the butter. Add the sugar gradually, beating with an electric mixer until light. Beat in the egg yolks, one at a time, and the grated orange zest.

3. Sift the flour with the baking powder, baking soda, and salt, and add the dry mixture to the batter alternately with the orange juice, beginning and ending with the flour. Gently mix in the pecans.

4. Beat the egg whites until stiff and fold them carefully into the batter.

5. Pour the batter into the prepared pan, set on the center rack of the oven, and bake for 50 to 60 minutes.

6. Spoon the hot glaze over the bread as soon as the bread is removed from the oven. Cool in the pan on a wire rack.

1 loaf

ZUCCHINI BREAD

For the best flavor, wrap the bread when cool and let it stand overnight before serving. With its sugar, spices, and nuts, this tea bread is almost cakelike.

1½ tablespoons unsalted butter, plus extra for greasing the pan
3 eggs
¾ cup vegetable oil
1½ cups sugar
1 teaspoon vanilla extract
2 cups grated unpeeled raw zucchini
2½ cups unbleached all-purpose flour
2 teaspoons baking soda
1 teaspoon baking powder
1 teaspoon salt
1 teaspoon ground cinnamon
1 teaspoon ground cloves
1 cup shelled walnuts, chopped

1. Preheat the oven to 350°F. Butter a 9 x 5 x 3-inch loaf pan.

2. Beat the eggs, oil, sugar, and vanilla until light and thick. Fold the grated zucchini into the egg mixture.

3. Sift the dry ingredients together. Stir into the zucchini mixture until just blended. Fold in the walnuts.

4. Pour the batter into the buttered loaf pan. Bake on the center rack of the oven until a cake tester inserted in the center comes out clean, about 1 hour and 15 minutes.

5. Cool slightly, remove from the pan, and cool completely on a rack.

1 loaf

CRANBERRY BREAD

This bread is especially good toasted and buttered.

Butter, for greasing the pan
2 cups unbleached all-purpose flour
½ cup sugar
1 tablespoon baking powder
½ teaspoon salt
⅔ cup fresh orange juice
2 eggs, beaten slightly
3 tablespoons unsalted butter, melted
½ cup shelled walnuts, coarsely chopped
1¼ cups cranberries
2 teaspoons grated orange zest

1. Preheat the oven to 350°F. Grease an 8 x 4½ x 3-inch loaf pan.

2. Sift the flour, sugar, baking powder, and salt into a mixing bowl.

3. Make a well in the middle of the sifted mixture and pour in the orange juice, eggs, and melted butter. Mix well without overmixing. Fold in the walnuts, cranberries, and orange zest.

4. Pour the batter into the prepared pan and set on the center rack of the oven. Bake until a knife inserted in the center comes out clean, 45 to 50 minutes.

5. Remove the bread from the oven and cool in the pan for 10 minutes. Remove the bread from the pan and allow to cool completely on a rack. Wrap and put away for 1 to 2 days before serving.

1 loaf

APRICOT RAISIN BREAD

Butter or oil, for greasing the pan
Approximately 1 cup boiling water
¾ cup coarsely chopped dried apricots
½ cup raisins
3 tablespoons plus ½ cup sugar
⅓ cup vegetable oil
2 eggs, beaten
2¼ cups unbleached all-purpose flour
1 tablespoon baking powder
½ teaspoon salt
⅔ cup milk
¾ cup unprocessed bran

1. Preheat the oven to 350°F. Grease a 9 x 5 x 3-inch loaf pan.

2. Pour the boiling water over the apricots and raisins just to cover. Let sit for 10 minutes. Drain well and add 3 tablespoons sugar. Mix well.

Just the names of these tea breads bring the harvest to mind: Orange Pecan, Cranberry, and Date Nut.

3. Meanwhile, add the remaining ½ cup sugar to the oil and beat well. Add the eggs, one at a time, beating until well mixed.

4. Sift the flour, baking powder, and salt together and add alternately with the milk and bran to the oil mixture. Fold in the fruits.

5. Pour the mixture into the prepared pan. Bake on the center rack of the oven until a cake tester inserted in the center comes out clean, 1 hour.

6. Remove from the oven and cool for 10 minutes. Remove from the pan and cool on a cake rack.

1 loaf

LEMON–BLACK WALNUT BREAD

Our favorite loaf for tea; serve with lots of unsalted butter.

1 cup (2 sticks) unsalted butter, plus extra for greasing the pans
1½ cups sugar
4 eggs, separated
⅔ cup fresh lemon juice
2 tablespoons grated lemon zest
3 cups cake flour
2 teaspoons baking powder
1 cup milk
Pinch of salt
1 cup shelled black walnuts, chopped
¼ cup water

1. Preheat the oven to 350°F. Butter two 9 x 5 x 3-inch loaf pans with 3 tablespoons of the butter.

2. In a mixing bowl cream together the remaining butter and 1 cup of the sugar. Beat in the egg yolks, one at a time, then stir in ⅓ cup of the lemon juice and the grated lemon zest.

3. Combine the cake flour with the baking powder. Add one third of the flour mixture to the creamed butter and sugar. Then add half of the milk, another third of the flour mixture, the remaining milk, and the remaining flour mixture. Do not overmix.

4. In another bowl beat the egg whites and pinch of salt together until stiff but not dry. Fold the beaten egg whites and black walnuts gently into the batter.

5. Pour the batter into the prepared pans. Bake on the center rack of the oven until a cake tester inserted in the center of a loaf comes out clean, 45 to 50 minutes.

6. Cool the bread slightly, remove from the pans, and cool completely on a rack.

7. Boil the remaining ⅓ cup of the lemon juice, the water, and the remaining ½ cup sugar together in a small saucepan for 2 minutes.

8. Drizzle the lemon syrup over the tops of the cooled loaves and let them set until completely cool before wrapping.

2 loaves

"'Take some more tea,' the March Hare said to Alice very earnestly.

'I've had nothing yet,' Alice replied in an offended tone, 'so I can't take more.'

'You mean you can't take less,' said the Hatter, 'it's very easy to take more than nothing.'"

—LEWIS CARROLL,
ALICE IN WONDERLAND

BLACK WALNUTS

Different species of black walnut are found throughout the United States. The tree or shrub has dark brown furrowed bark. It grows fifteen to thirty-five feet in height; its alternating leaves have tapered points and serrated edges. The nut is round, thick-shelled, and found inside a greenish-brown husk. It is indeed "a hard nut to crack."

SWEETS

THE COOKIE BASKET

Everyone has a special fondness for cookies. They make children out of us at any age. Some like them snappy, others soft and chewy. Our philosophy is the more the merrier, and to us a ribbon-trimmed basket—filled with all shapes, sizes, and styles of cookies—seems like an invitation for fun! On a party buffet table, as a gift, or just on the sideboard when friends come to call, it's the nicest way we know to present cookies. If you are making batches of different kinds of cookie for a basket, remember that the most dazzling statement is made by clustering the same kinds of cookie together—lushly and abundantly. This gives the basket a sense of style and importance. But you certainly don't have to wait to make these cookies all at once. Each of the following recipes, on its own, will satisfy even the most discerning sweet tooth and bring smiles all around.

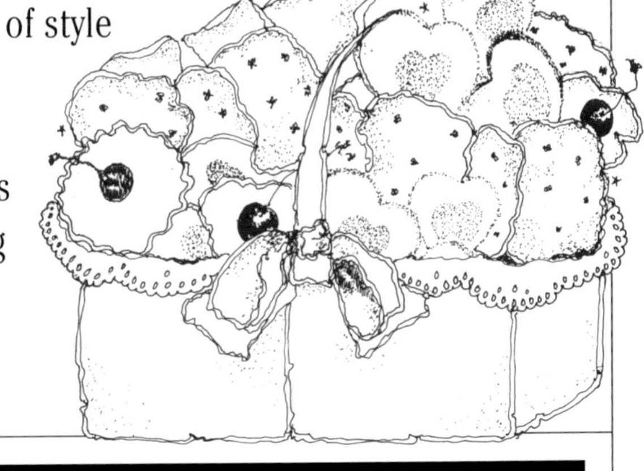

"Almost every person has something secret he likes to eat."

—M.F.K. FISHER

PECAN SQUARES

CRUST

Butter, for greasing the pan
⅔ cup confectioners' sugar
2 cups unbleached all-purpose flour
½ pound (2 sticks) unsalted butter, at room temperature

TOPPING

⅔ cup (approximately 11 tablespoons) unsalted butter, melted
½ cup honey
3 tablespoons heavy cream
½ cup light brown sugar
3½ cups shelled pecans, coarsely chopped

1. Preheat the oven to 350°F. Grease a 9 x 12-inch baking pan.

2. Make the crust: Sift the sugar and flour together. Cut in the butter, using two knives or a pastry blender, until fine crumbs form. Pat the crust into the prepared baking pan. Bake until golden brown, 20 minutes; remove from the oven. Leave the oven on.

3. Prepare the topping: Mix the melted butter, honey, cream, and brown sugar together. Stir in the pecans, coating them thoroughly. Spread over the crust.

4. Return the pan to the oven and bake for 25 minutes more. Cool completely before cutting into squares.

36 squares

COCONUT MACAROONS

Butter, for greasing the cookie sheet
⅓ cup unbleached all-purpose flour
2½ cups shredded coconut
⅛ teaspoon salt
⅔ cup sweetened condensed milk
1 teaspoon vanilla extract

1. Preheat the oven to 350°F. Grease a cookie sheet well.

2. Mix the flour, coconut, and salt together in a bowl. Pour in the condensed milk and vanilla and stir well to make a thick batter.

3. Drop the batter by quarter-cupfuls onto the well-greased cookie sheet, allowing an inch of space between the cookies. Bake until golden brown, 20 minutes. Remove from the pan at once and cool on racks.

About 1½ dozen macaroons

TOFFEE BARS

Light, crisp, and chocolaty.

1 cup (2 sticks) unsalted butter, plus extra for greasing the pan
1 cup light brown sugar
1 egg yolk
2 cups unbleached all-purpose flour
1 teaspoon vanilla extract
12 ounces semisweet chocolate chips
1 cup shelled walnuts or pecans, coarsely chopped

"*Epicure:* One who gets nothing better than the cream of everything, but cheerfully makes the best of it."

—OLIVER HEREFORD

ACADEMY AWARD BUFFET

PHYLLO TRIANGLES FILLED WITH BRIE

CAVIAR ECLAIRS

SALMON MOUSSE WITH TOASTS

CARPACCIO WITH *ANCHOVY MAYONNAISE*

CHICKEN LIVER PÂTÉ WITH GREEN PEPPERCORNS

CHAMPAGNE

A COOKIE BASKET

1. Preheat the oven to 350°F. Grease a 9 x 12-inch baking pan.

2. Cream the butter and sugar. Add the egg yolk; beat well.

3. Sift in the flour, mixing well, then stir in the vanilla. Spread the batter in the prepared pan. Bake until golden brown, 25 minutes.

4. Remove the pan from the oven, cover the cake layer with the chocolate chips, and return to the oven for 3 to 4 minutes.

5. Remove the pan from the oven and spread the melted chocolate evenly. Sprinkle with the nuts. Cool completely in the pan before cutting.

About 30 bars

BUTTERBALLS

While there are many versions of this cookie, often called "wedding cookies," this one has long been a Rosso family Christmas tradition. Quite objectively, we think it's the best we've ever tasted. The secret is the honey, even though you hardly know it's there. That, and baking the cookies to an ever so slight golden brown so they take on a nutty flavor. There's little reason to save them for just one season of the year. Store in a tin and they'll keep for several weeks, if they don't "call to you" too often.

8 tablespoons (1 stick) unsalted butter, at room temperature, plus extra for greasing the cookie sheets
3 tablespoons honey
1 cup unbleached all-purpose flour
½ teaspoon salt
1 tablespoon vanilla extract
1 cup shelled pecans, chopped moderately fine
¾ cup confectioners' sugar

1. Preheat the oven to 300°F. Grease one or two cookie sheets.

2. Cream the butter. Beat in the honey; gradually mix in the flour and salt, then the vanilla. Add the pecans. Wrap the dough in plastic and chill for 1 hour.

3. Form the balls by hand, the size of quarters. Place 2 inches apart on the prepared cookie sheets. Bake until golden brown, 35 to 40 minutes.

4. Remove the cookie sheet from the oven; as soon as the cookies are cool enough to touch, roll in the confectioners' sugar. Allow to cool and roll again in the sugar.

About 36 cookies

LINZER HEARTS

These tiny hearts melt in your mouth.

1½ cups (3 sticks) unsalted butter, at room temperature
1¾ cups confectioners' sugar
1 egg
2 cups unbleached all-purpose flour, sifted
1 cup cornstarch
2 cups shelled walnuts, very finely chopped
½ cup red raspberry preserves

1. Cream the butter and 1 cup of the sugar until light and fluffy. Add the egg and mix well.

2. Sift together the flour and cornstarch; add to the creamed mixture and blend well. Mix the walnuts in thoroughly.

3. Gather the dough into a ball, wrap in wax paper, and chill for 4 to 6 hours.

4. Roll the dough out to ¼-inch thickness. Using a small heart-shaped cookie cutter about 1½ inches long, cut out the cookies and place on an ungreased cookie sheet. (If you like, use a smaller cookie cutter to make a "window" in half of the cookies.) Chill the cookies for 45 minutes.

5. Preheat the oven to 325°F.

6. Bake the cookies until they are evenly and lightly browned, 10 to 15 minutes. Remove and cool on a rack.

7. While they are still warm, spread the whole cookies with raspberry preserves, using ¼ teaspoon of jam for each. Top each with one of the "window" cookies.

8. Sift the remaining ¾ cup confectioners' sugar into a bowl and press the tops and bottoms of the cookies into the sugar to coat.

4 dozen cookies

"The rule is jam tomorrow and jam yesterday, but never jam today."

—LEWIS CARROLL, *ALICE IN WONDERLAND*

Something for everyone: Butterballs, Linzer Hearts, and Oatmeal Raisin Cookies.

OATMEAL RAISIN COOKIES

Use the Giant Cookies method on page 321 for these crisp cookies.

12 tablespoons (1½ sticks) unsalted butter, plus extra for greasing the cookie sheets
½ cup granulated sugar
1 cup light brown sugar
1 egg
2 tablespoons water
1 teaspoon vanilla extract
⅔ cup unbleached all-purpose flour
1 teaspoon ground cinnamon
½ teaspoon salt
½ teaspoon baking soda
3 cups quick-cooking oats
1 cup raisins

1. Preheat the oven to 350°F. Grease two cookie sheets.

2. Cream the butter and both sugars until fluffy. Add the egg and beat thoroughly. Mix in the water and vanilla.

3. Sift together the flour, cinnamon, salt, and baking soda; add to the egg mixture and mix well. Add the oats and raisins, and mix.

4. Form the cookies on the prepared cookie sheets, following the method for giant cookies. Bake until the edges are done but the centers are still soft, 15 to 17 minutes. Remove to a rack and cool.

25 to 30 large cookies

"You have to eat oatmeal or you'll dry up. Anybody knows that."

—KAY THOMPSON, *ELOISE*

BLACK WALNUT COOKIES

A butter cookie with a special difference; we think you'll agree that the black walnuts are worth their price.

1½ cups (3 sticks) unsalted butter, at room temperature
⅔ cup sugar
3 eggs
½ teaspoon vanilla extract
3 cups unbleached all-purpose flour
¼ teaspoon salt
⅔ cup shelled black walnuts, finely chopped

1. Cream the butter and sugar until light and fluffy. Mix in the eggs, one at a time, beating well after each addition; add the vanilla.

2. Sift the flour with the salt and add to the creamed mixture. Mix well.

3. Wrap the dough in wax paper and refrigerate for 4 to 6 hours. When thoroughly chilled, roll out to ⅛-inch thickness and cut with a 1-inch-diameter cookie cutter. Place 1½ inches apart on ungreased cookie sheets. Sprinkle the cookies with the black walnuts and chill again for 45 minutes.

4. Preheat the oven to 325°F.

5. Bake until the cookies are evenly and lightly browned, 15 minutes. Remove from the sheets and cool on a rack.

5 dozen cookies

GIFT OF FOOD

One tradition we love and keep is the gift of food. This is something special that comes from the heart. A gift will remind the recipient of the giver as it is enjoyed. An especially nice gift is a tiny loaf of bread or a fruit tart, wrapped with a pretty ribbon and accompanied by a copy of the recipe. Or you might fill an antique basket with homemade cookies, candies, or a jam, chutney, or other preserve put up in your own kitchen.

BROWNIES

Dark, fudgy, and wonderful—what could be better?

1 cup (2 sticks) unsalted butter, plus extra for greasing the pan
¾ cup unbleached all-purpose flour, plus extra for flouring the pan
4 ounces unsweetened chocolate
4 eggs
1½ cups sugar
1 teaspoon vanilla extract
⅔ cup shelled walnuts, coarsely chopped

1. Preheat the oven to 350°F. Grease and flour a 9 x 13-inch baking pan.

2. Melt the butter and chocolate in the top part of a double boiler over boiling water. When melted, set aside to cool to room temperature.

3. Meanwhile, beat the eggs and sugar until thick and lemon-colored; add the vanilla. Fold the chocolate mixture into the eggs and sugar. Mix thoroughly.

4. Sift the flour and fold gently into the batter, mixing just until blended. Fold in the walnuts.

5. Pour into the prepared pan. Bake until the center is just set, 25 minutes. Do not overbake.

6. Allow the brownies to cool in the pan for 30 minutes before cutting into bars.

28 large brownies

> **"Cooking is like love—it should be entered into with abandon or not at all."**
>
> —HARRIET VAN HORNE

SWEETMEATS

These are rich little treasures, great with coffee.

CRUST

1 cup (2 sticks) unsalted butter, at room temperature, plus extra for greasing the pan
1⅔ cups brown sugar
1⅔ cups unbleached all-purpose flour

TOPPING

1 cup brown sugar
4 eggs, slightly beaten
2 tablespoons unbleached all-purpose flour
2 cups shelled walnuts, coarsely chopped
1 cup shredded coconut

1. Preheat the oven to 350°F. Grease a 9 x 12-inch baking pan.

2. Prepare the crust: Cream the butter and brown sugar together. Add the flour and mix well. Pat the mixture into the prepared baking pan. Bake for 15 to 20 minutes. Remove from the oven.

3. Prepare the topping: Beat the sugar and eggs together. Add the 2 tablespoons flour; stir well. Fold in the walnuts and coconut. Pour the topping onto the crust.

4. Bake until the topping is set, 20 to 25 minutes longer. Cool in the pan and cut into squares.

30 squares

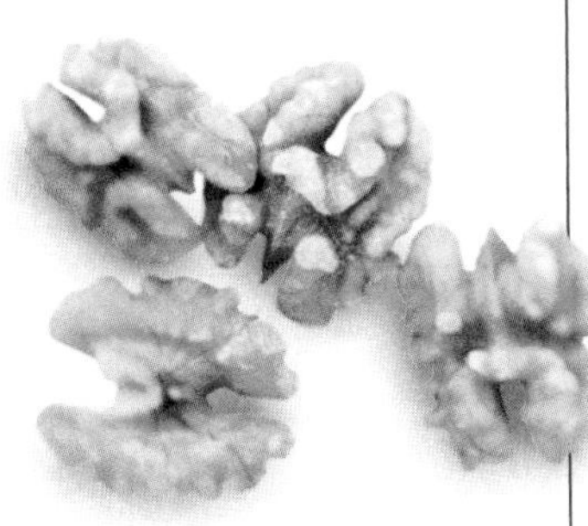

SHORTBREAD HEARTS

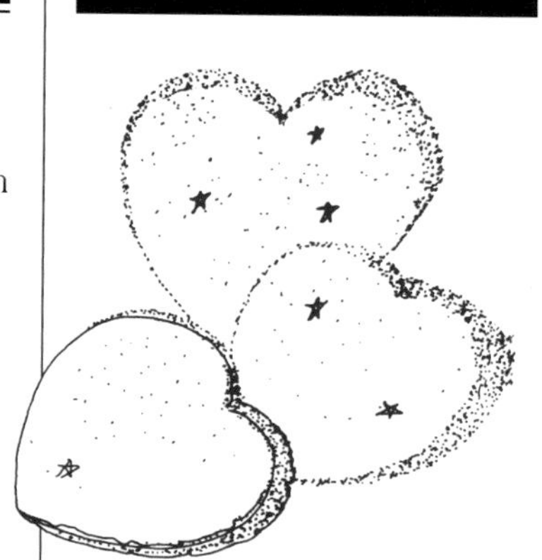

Another Silver Palate favorite, good year round, but essential on Valentine's Day.

1½ cups (3 sticks) unsalted butter, at room temperature
1 cup confectioners' sugar
3 cups unbleached all-purpose flour, sifted
½ teaspoon salt
½ teaspoon vanilla extract
¼ cup granulated sugar

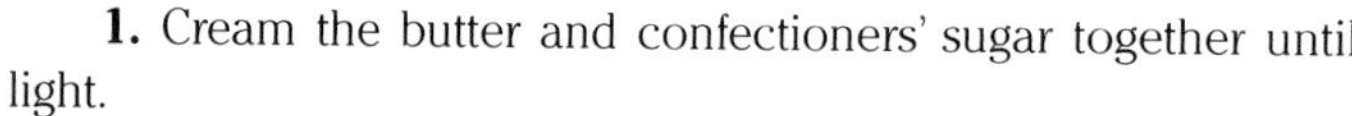

1. Cream the butter and confectioners' sugar together until light.

2. Sift the flour and salt together and add to the creamed mixture. Add the vanilla and blend thoroughly.

3. Gather the dough into a ball, wrap in wax paper, and chill for 4 to 6 hours.

4. Roll out the chilled dough to ⅝-inch thickness. Using a 3-inch-long heart-shaped cookie cutter, cut out cookies. Sprinkle the tops with granulated sugar. Place the cut-out cookies on ungreased cookie sheets and refrigerate for 45 minutes before baking.

5. Preheat the oven to 325°F.

6. Bake until just starting to color lightly, 20 minutes; the cookies should not brown at all. Cool on a rack.

20 cookies

MOLASSES COOKIES

These soft, chewy, spicy cookies were one of the store's most popular. Don't expect them to be crisp; they are not gingersnaps. They stay moist, in an airtight tin, for at least a week.

12 tablespoons (1½ sticks) unsalted butter
1 cup sugar
¼ cup molasses
1 egg
1¾ cups unbleached all-purpose flour
½ teaspoon ground cloves
½ teaspoon ground ginger
1 teaspoon ground cinnamon
½ teaspoon salt
½ teaspoon baking soda

1. Preheat the oven to 350°F.

2. Melt the butter in a saucepan over low heat. Remove from the heat, add the sugar and molasses, and mix. Lightly beat the egg and add to the butter mixture; blend well.

"Life is uncertain. Eat dessert first."

—ANONYMOUS

GIANT COOKIES

Chocolate chip cookies have always been one of our passions. The day before we opened our shop we even sponsored a contest to pick the best cookie maker, and were the first on our block to sell giant chocolate chip cookies. The technique for making these extra-large cookies couldn't be simpler. Apply it to your own favorite recipe, or use our prizewinner at right.

After you've made the basic batter, use an average-size ice-cream scoop for portioning the dough. Drop the ball onto a greased cookie sheet, wet your hand with water, and SPLAT the dough ball out into a 5-inch round. Repeat with the remaining dough and bake according to directions.

The resulting cookie is spectacular—a real handful!

3. Sift the flour with the cloves, ginger, cinnamon, salt, and baking soda and add to the first mixture; mix. The batter will be wet.

4. Lay a sheet of aluminum foil on a cookie sheet. Drop tablespoons of cookie batter on the foil, leaving 3 inches between the cookies. These will spread during the baking.

5. Bake until the cookies start to darken, 8 to 10 minutes. Remove from the oven while still soft. Let cool on the foil.

24 very large flat cookies

CHOCOLATE CHIP COOKIES

Our favorite chocolate chip cookie.

1 cup (2 sticks) unsalted butter, at room temperature, plus extra for greasing the cookie sheet
1 cup light brown sugar
¾ cup granulated sugar
2 eggs
1 teaspoon vanilla extract
2 cups unbleached all-purpose flour
1 teaspoon baking soda
1 teaspoon salt
1½ cups semisweet chocolate chips

1. Preheat the oven to 325°F for giant cookies, 350°F for regular cookies. Grease a cookie sheet.

2. Cream the butter and both sugars together until light and fluffy. Add the eggs and vanilla and mix well.

3. Sift the dry ingredients together and stir in, mixing thoroughly. Add the chocolate chips to the batter, and form the cookies according to the method for giant cookies (see sidebar).

4. Bake on the prepared cookie sheet, on the center rack of the oven, for 15 to 17 minutes for giant cookies; 8 to 10 minutes for regular cookies. Remove from the oven while the centers are slightly soft. Cool on the baking sheet for 5 minutes before transferring the cookies to a rack to cool completely.

25 giant cookies (about 5 inches across), or about 80 regular cookies

Variations:
♥ Add 1 cup chopped walnuts.
♥ Add 1 cup unsalted peanuts.
♥ Add 1 cup shredded coconut.
♥ Substitute 1 teaspoon mint extract for the vanilla extract.

AMERICAN AS APPLE . . .

"As American as apple pie" has become a familiar phrase, probably because we produce more apples than any other nation. We owe much to the legendary John Chapman—fondly known as Johnny Appleseed—who spent half a century encouraging apple production by planting apple seeds and selling and donating apple trees to early American settlers. The apple, its lore, and the good things made from it have been beloved by generations of Americans ever since.

Today many of Johnny's apples are experiencing a renaissance, growing in orchards across the country. Seed savers—conservers of heirloom seeds—and organic growers have nurtured this rebirth and we thank them for it. We marvel at the nuances in taste from one apple to another, and everyone seems to have their favorites. Thousands of heirloom varieties have been revitalized in seeds found from around the world—Ananas Reinette of the Netherlands, circa 1821; Coe's Golden Drop from England, 1842; the Black Twig from Arkansas, 1868; the Api Etoile of Switzerland, 1600s; Matsu from Japan, 1948; Nehou from France, 1920; Mother from Massachusetts, 1840; Orleans Reinette from France, 1776; Lady or Christmas Apple from France, 1600; Duchess of Oldenburg from Russia, 1700; and the Court Pendu Plat from France, 1613—just the names and dates make us dream.

APPLE CHART

NAME	SEASON	COLOR	FLAVOR/ TEXTURE	EATING	PIE
Astrachan	July–Aug	Yellow/ Greenish red	Sweet	Good	Good
Baldwin	Oct–Jan	Red/Yellowish	Mellow	Fair	Fair
Cortland	Oct–Jan	Green/Purple	Mild, tender	Excel.	Excel.
Delicious, Red	Sept–June	Scarlet	Sweet, crunchy	Excel.	Good
Delicious, Golden	Sept–May	Yellow	Sweet, semifirm	Excel.	Excel.
Empire	Sept–Nov	Red	Sweet, crisp	Excel.	Good
Gala	Sept–June	Yellow w/red stripes	Sweet, semifirm	Excel.	V. Good
Granny Smith	Apr–July	Green	Tart, crisp	V. Good	V. Good
Gravenstein	July–Sept	Green w/red stripes	Tart, crisp	Good	Good
Ida Red	Oct	Red	Rich	Good	Good
Jonathan	Sept–Jan	Brilliant red	Tart, tender, crisp	V. Good	V. Good
Macoun	Oct–Nov	Dark red	Tart, juicy, crisp	Excel.	Good
McIntosh	Sept–June	Green to red	Slightly tart, tender, juicy	Excel.	Excel.
Newtown Pippin	Sept–June	Green to red	Slightly tart, firm	V. Good	Excel.
Northern Spy	Oct	Red	Crisp, tart	V. Good	V. Good
Rhode Island Greening	Sept–Nov	Green	Very tart, firm	Poor	Excel.
Rome Beauty	Oct–June	Red	Tart, firm, slightly dry	Good	V. Good
Stayman-Winesap	Oct–Mar	Red	Semifirm, sweet, spicy	V. Good	Good
Winesap	Oct–June	Red	Slightly tart, firm, spicy	Excel.	Good
Yellow Transparent	July–Aug	Yellow	Tart, soft	Poor	Excel.
York Imperial	Oct–Apr	Greenish yellow	Mild, firm	Fair	Good

"Don't sit under
the apple tree
with anyone else
but me."

—THE ANDREWS SISTERS, 1940

We've made a tradition of this Medieval Apple Tart, taught to us by a Frenchwoman, Madame Bouchard of Villeneuve-sur-Lot. Whenever we bake it, we are reminded of that afternoon in Madame Bouchard's country kitchen. She stretched and rolled her fresh strudel dough by hand while her husband peeled the apples. Later, while the tart baked, we shared an Armagnac. We've substituted phyllo pastry for the strudel, but the result is just as delicious.

AN APPLE ORCHARD

We've planted our own small orchard of heirloom apple trees and it doesn't take much room. It's exciting to watch those first tiny buds awaken in spring, emerge as soft white blossoms, and gradually become tiny green apples. By fall the branches start swooping to the ground, heavy with balls of vibrant color. Then we like to keep daily tabs on our upcoming harvest by sampling the fruits as they ripen—from when they're face-scrunching sour until they bring a smile and it's time to harvest. In some small way, it makes us feel a part of history.

Quality heirloom apple root stocks can be found at the following sources:
www.californiararefruitgrowers.com
www.raintreenursery.com
www.seedsofchange.com
www.treesofantiquity.com
www.westonsantiqueapples.com

MEDIEVAL APPLE TART

This light, tender, and flaky version of a regional French *croustade* is made with thinly sliced apples and Grand Marnier. Serve it warm with a dollop of Crème Fraîche (page 414).

12 phyllo leaves, fresh or thoroughly defrosted
2 cups (4 sticks) unsalted butter, plus extra for greasing the pan
1 cup sugar
Approximately 6 tablespoons Grand Marnier or Calvados
6 medium-size tart apples, peeled, cored, and thinly sliced

1. Unwrap the phyllo sheets and cover them with a damp towel for 10 minutes. Melt the butter in a saucepan over low heat.

2. Preheat the oven to 425°F.

3. Using a pastry brush, lightly butter a 14-inch baking pan. Lay a phyllo sheet on the pan. Remember to re-cover the unused phyllo with the damp towel each time. Brush the phyllo with some of the melted butter, and sprinkle with 1 tablespoon of the sugar and 1 teaspoon of the Grand Marnier. Repeat, using 5 more phyllo leaves.

4. Arrange the apples in the center of the top sheet of phyllo in a circular mound about 6 inches in diameter. Brush them with butter and sprinkle with some sugar and Grand Marnier.

5. Stack 6 more phyllo sheets on top of the apples, repeating the buttering and sprinkling with sugar and Grand Marnier. The top (twelfth) sheet of phyllo should only be buttered.

6. Trim off the corners of the phyllo sheets so you have a large round, about 8 inches in diameter. Turn up the edges of the phyllo and pinch lightly to seal. Be tidy, but don't work too long on this; the tart should look rustic.

7. Set the pan on the center rack of the oven and bake until golden, 30 to 40 minutes. If the pastry becomes too brown before this time, cover it loosely with aluminum foil.

8. Serve the tart immediately, or reheat gently before serving.

4 to 6 portions

JOHNNY APPLESAUCE

This fresh and chunky apple compote is named in honor of the man who became a legend. It is delicious hot or cold, and is equally at home as dessert or as a tart accompaniment to pork and game entrées.

2½ cups water
4 tablespoons strained fresh lemon juice
7 medium-size Granny Smith or other firm, tart apples
½ cup sugar
⅔ cup good French Sauternes
6 tablespoons red currant jelly
2 cinnamon sticks
Grated zest of 2 lemons
½ cup shelled walnuts, coarsely chopped (optional)
⅓ cup raisins (optional)

1. Mix half of the water and half of the lemon juice together in a bowl.

2. Peel and core the apples and cut them into 1½-inch irregular chunks. As you cut each apple, drop the pieces into the water to prevent discoloration.

3. In a medium-size saucepan with a heavy bottom, combine the remaining water and lemon juice, the sugar, and the Sauternes. Bring to a boil, reduce to a simmer, and add the apple chunks. Partially cover and cook gently until the apples are just tender; the apple chunks should remain whole.

4. With a slotted spoon, transfer the apples to a bowl. Add the currant jelly and cinnamon sticks to the syrup remaining in the pan. Set over medium heat, bring to a boil, reduce to a simmer, and cook until the syrup is reduced by one third. Stir in the lemon zest.

5. Pour the syrup over the apples. Stir in the walnuts and raisins if you use them. Serve warm; or cool, cover, and refrigerate.

6 portions

CINNAMONY BAKED APPLES

Served still warm and drizzled with their syrupy juices, these apples are enhanced by a dollop of Crème Fraîche (page 414) or softly whipped cream.

2 cups water
2¼ cups brown sugar
1½ tablespoons ground cinnamon
1½ tablespoons fresh lemon juice
6 medium-large tart baking apples, washed (do not peel)
¾ cup raisins
½ cup shelled pecans, chopped
1 tablespoon grated lemon zest
3 tablespoons Calvados or applejack
3 tablespoons unsalted butter

1. Preheat the oven to 375°F.

PRESERVING

The art of preserving food by sealing it hermetically in containers was devised only in the early nineteenth century, unlike some of the more traditional methods of food preservation (e.g., salting, freezing, curing, drying, smoking, and pickling) that have been with mankind almost since the days of the caveman.

The credit for first developing the process goes to Nicolas-François Appert, a Parisian confectioner and distiller; the discovery won him a 12,000-franc prize from the French government in 1810. His discovery allowed the French army to carry more varied supplies for greater distances without risking spoilage. He used his prize money to found the House of Appert, the first commercial business venture in canning and preserving.

PRESERVES are made from perfect fruits, either whole or in large pieces, cooked with sugar (often a smaller portion of sugar than jams) only long enough for the syrup to thicken while the fruit still holds its shape.

JAMS are made from fruit, usually a single kind, that has been chopped or crushed, then cooked with sugar (or, less usually, honey) until the mixture is thick.

JELLY is sweetened and jellied fruit juice. It contains no pieces of fruit, but is sparkling, clear, and tender and can be unmolded from the jar in which it is preserved.

MARMALADES are halfway between jelly and jam; small pieces of fruit, usually citrus, and peel are suspended in a transparent jelly.

Served warm, Cinnamony Baked Apples say "home."

CONSERVES are jamlike combinations of fruits, nuts, and sugar, cooked until thick.

CHUTNEYS are relishes made by combining fruits and vegetables with tart or sweet ingredients such as honey, sugar, spices, and vinegar. They capture the best of the sweet and the sour.

FRUIT SPREADS are made from sieved or long-cooked fruit pulp, cooked with "sweetening" and usually spices, to a spreadable (but not jelled) consistency.

2. Mix the water, ¾ cup of the brown sugar, ½ tablespoon of the cinnamon, and the lemon juice in a saucepan. Bring to a boil and cook for 3 minutes. Remove the syrup from the heat and reserve.

3. Remove the apple cores, but do not cut all the way through the bottoms.

4. In a bowl, mix the remaining 1½ cups brown sugar, the raisins, pecans, lemon zest, and remaining 1 tablespoon cinnamon. Fill each apple to within ¼ inch of the top. Pour 1 teaspoon of Calvados over the filling in each apple and top with ½ tablespoon butter.

5. Transfer the apples to a 9 x 13-inch baking dish and pour the the syrup over the apples. Sprinkle the remaining tablespoon of Calvados into the syrup.

6. Bake the apples until tender, basting them occasionally with the syrup in the pan, 1 hour.

7. When the apples are done, transfer them with a slotted spoon to a serving dish. Pour the syrup from the pan into a small saucepan, bring to a boil, and cook until slightly reduced, about 5 minutes. Cool slightly, pour a tablespoon of syrup over each apple, and serve the remaining syrup on the side.

6 portions

SAUTEED APPLES WITH CALVADOS

Serve these apple brandy–spiked apples as an accompaniment to pork or ham. They are also delicious folded into omelets or crêpes.

6 cooking apples (Golden Delicious are a good choice)
8 tablespoons (1 stick) unsalted butter
½ cup firmly packed brown sugar
⅔ cup Calvados

1. Core the apples, and peel them if you like. (We prefer the added texture of the peels, but peeled apples look more sophisticated.) Cut the apples crosswise into ¼-inch-thick slices.

2. Melt about 2 tablespoons of the butter in a skillet over low heat and add a single layer of apple slices. Raise the heat to medium and sauté the slices, turning occasionally, until browned, 5 minutes. With a slotted spoon, transfer the apples to a bowl. Repeat with more butter and another batch of apples until all have been cooked.

3. Add the brown sugar to the butter remaining in the skillet and stir over low heat until it dissolves. Add the Calvados and bring to a boil. Boil for 5 minutes, stirring constantly.

4. Return the apples to the skillet, reduce the heat, and simmer until the apples are heated through, another 5 minutes. Do not overcook. Transfer the apples to a heated dish and serve immediately.

6 to 8 portions

CALVADOS

Normandy, on the northern coast of France, has long been famous for its apples and for Calvados, the fiery apple brandy that has been made there since the sixteenth century. It is traditionally served much younger than other brandies, although the best is that which has aged in oak for 12 years and is a potent drink indeed. In cooking it imparts a special fruity tang and complexity. Although the taste of Calvados is unique, you can substitute American apple brandy (applejack) in most recipes.

APPLESAUCE RAISIN CAKE

1 cup (2 sticks) unsalted butter, plus extra for greasing the pan
3 cups unbleached all-purpose flour, plus extra for flouring the pan
2 cups sugar
2 eggs
2 cups applesauce (see Note)
1 teaspoon vanilla extract
1 teaspoon ground cinnamon
1 teaspoon freshly grated nutmeg
2 teaspoons baking soda
1 cup raisins
Lemon-Orange Icing (recipe follows)

1. Preheat the oven to 325°F. Butter and flour a 10-inch tube pan.

“No mean woman can cook well, for it calls for a light head, a generous spirit, and a large heart.”

—PAUL GAUGUIN

2. In a mixing bowl, cream together the butter and sugar until light and fluffy. Add the eggs, one at a time, beating well after each addition. Stir in the applesauce and vanilla.

3. Sift the flour, cinnamon, nutmeg, and baking soda together; then sift the dry ingredients over the applesauce mixture, sprinkle in the raisins, and blend gently but thoroughly.

4. Pour the batter into the tube pan and set on a rack in the center of the oven. Bake until a cake tester inserted into the cake comes out clean, 1 hour and 10 to 15 minutes.

5. Cool in the pan for 15 minutes. Turn out onto a cake rack and cool completely.

6. When cool, drizzle with the lemon-orange icing.

8 to 10 portions

Note: Or make Johnny Applesauce (page 325), omitting the walnuts and raisins. Purée until smooth and use 2 cups.

LEMON-ORANGE ICING

1 cup confectioners' sugar
½ teaspoon ground cinnamon
1½ tablespoons fresh lemon juice
1½ tablespoons fresh orange juice

1. Sift the confectioners' sugar and cinnamon into a small bowl.

2. Dribble in the juices, stirring constantly until the icing is smooth. Drizzle over the cooled cake.

Enough icing for 1 Applesauce Raisin Cake

CHUNKY APPLE WALNUT CAKE

Dark, moist, and chunky, with a dream of a glaze.

1½ cups vegetable oil, plus extra for greasing the pan
2 cups sugar
3 eggs
2 cups unbleached all-purpose flour, sifted
⅛ teaspoon ground cloves
1¼ teaspoons ground cinnamon
¼ teaspoon ground mace
1 teaspoon baking soda
¾ teaspoon salt
1 cup whole-wheat flour, sifted
1¼ cups shelled walnuts, coarsely chopped
3¼ cups coarse chunks of peeled and cored Rome Beauty apples
3 tablespoons Calvados or applejack
Apple Cider Glaze (recipe follows)

1. Preheat the oven to 325°F. Grease a 10-inch round cake pan.

2. In a large bowl, beat the vegetable oil and sugar until thick and opaque. Add the eggs, one at a time, beating well after each addition.

3. Sift together the all-purpose flour, cloves, cinnamon, mace, baking soda, and salt, then stir in the whole-wheat flour. Add to the oil and egg mixture and mix until well blended.

4. Add the walnuts, apple chunks, and Calvados all at once and stir the batter until the pieces are evenly distributed.

5. Pour the batter into the prepared pan. Bake until a cake tester inserted in the center comes out clean, 1 hour and 15 minutes.

6. Let the cake rest for 10 minutes, then unmold and pour the glaze over the warm cake, or cut the cake and pour the glaze over the slices.

One 10-inch cake, 10 to 12 portions

"He that plants trees loves others besides himself."

—ENGLISH PROVERB

APPLE CIDER GLAZE

4 tablespoons (½ stick) unsalted butter
2 tablespoons brown sugar
6 tablespoons granulated sugar
3 tablespoons Calvados or applejack
4 tablespoons sweet cider
2 tablespoons fresh orange juice
2 tablespoons heavy cream

1. Melt the butter in a small saucepan over low heat and stir in both sugars.

2. Add the remaining ingredients, stir, raise the heat, and bring to a boil. Reduce the heat slightly and cook for 4 minutes.

3. Remove from the heat and cool slightly. Pour while still warm over the warm cake.

1½ cups

SOUR CREAM APPLE PIE

A little slice goes a long way. Serve it with whipped cream or vanilla ice cream on top.

CRUST

2½ cups unbleached all-purpose flour
5 tablespoons sugar
¾ teaspoon salt
¾ teaspoon ground cinnamon
6 tablespoons (¾ stick) unsalted butter, chilled
6 tablespoons solid vegetable shortening, chilled
4 to 6 tablespoons apple cider or juice, chilled
Butter or shortening, for greasing the pan

FILLING

5 to 7 tart apples
⅔ cup sour cream
⅓ cup sugar
1 egg, lightly beaten
¼ teaspoon salt
1 teaspoon vanilla extract
3 tablespoons unbleached all-purpose flour

TOPPING

3 tablespoons brown sugar
3 tablespoons sugar
1 teaspoon ground cinnamon
1 cup shelled walnuts, chopped

1. Prepare the crust: Sift the flour, sugar, salt, and cinnamon into a bowl. Cut in the butter and shortening with a fork or pastry cutter until the mixture resembles rolled oats.

2. Moisten with just enough cider, tossing the ingredients lightly with a fork, to permit the dough to be formed into a ball. Wrap and refrigerate for 2 hours.

3. Cut off one third of the dough and return it to the refrigerator. Roll out the remaining dough between sheets of wax paper. Grease a 9-inch pie pan and line it with the dough. Trim the overhang and crimp the edge decoratively.

4. Preheat the oven to 350°F.

5. Prepare the filling: Peel, core, and thinly slice the apples; drop the slices into a mixing bowl.

6. Whisk together the sour cream, sugar, egg, salt, vanilla, and flour in a small bowl. Pour the mixture over the apples and toss well to coat. Spoon the apples into the pastry-lined pie pan.

7. For the topping: Mix the sugars, cinnamon, and walnuts together and sprinkle evenly over the apple filling.

8. Roll out the remaining pastry between sheets of wax paper to form a 10-inch circle. Cut the dough into ½-inch strips and arrange these lattice fashion over the apples; trim the ends of the strips and crimp the edge of the crust decoratively.

9. Set the pie on the center rack of the oven and bake until the juices are bubbling and the apples are tender, 55 to 65 minutes. If the crust browns too quickly, cover loosely with aluminum foil.

10. Serve warm or cool.

6 portions

"All millionaires love a baked apple."

—RONALD FIRBANK

SUNDAY LUNCH MENU

CHICKEN LIVER PÂTÉ WITH GREEN PEPPERCORNS

PÂTÉ DE CAMPAGNE WITH WALNUTS

LAYERED VEGETABLE TERRINE

CORNICHONS AND PICKLED WILD CHERRIES

BOUILLABAISSE

AN ALL-ARUGULA SALAD WITH BALSAMIC VINAIGRETTE

ELLEN'S APPLE TART

ELLEN'S APPLE TART

Ravishingly caramelized apples on a circle of flaky puff pastry; the best apple tart we have ever eaten.

4 medium-to-large tart cooking apples, peeled, cored, and halved
¾ cup sugar
3 tablespoons water
2 tablespoons unsalted butter
1 tablespoon fresh lemon juice
1 teaspoon freshly grated nutmeg
2 tablespoons Calvados or applejack
1 pound Puff Pastry (page 409)

1. Poach the apples according to the method described in Poached Fruit (see page 381), removing them from the syrup while they are still slightly firm; omit the cooling period in the syrup. Transfer the apples to a strainer set over a bowl and allow them to cool completely.

2. Meanwhile, pour the sugar and water into a 10-inch cast-iron frying pan and stir to combine. Set over medium heat and cook, watching carefully, until the sugar syrup reaches a golden brown. Remove immediately from the heat and set the pan on a cool surface. The caramelized sugar will harden.

3. Place 1 apple half, rounded side down, on the caramelized sugar in the center of the pan. Surround with 6 of the remaining halves, placing them close together. Slice the last half into 6 slices and place them in the spaces between the apples in the ring, with their rounded edges outward.

4. Melt the butter in a saucepan. Whisk in the lemon juice, nutmeg, and Calvados, and drizzle over the apples.

5. Preheat the oven to 425°F.

6. Roll out the puff pastry to ¼-inch thickness, and cut out a round 12 inches in diameter. Place over the apples and roll the edges of the pastry back 1 inch all around to give the edges a finished look.

7. Place the tart in the oven (make sure it has reached 425°; preheating is very important to ensure the puff pastry rises). Bake until the pastry is a deep golden brown and the syrup is bubbling around the edges, 30 to 35 minutes. If the pastry browns too quickly, cover it with a piece of aluminum foil.

8. When the tart is done, remove it from the oven and let it sit for 15 minutes. Invert onto a serving platter. Serve warm or at room temperature.

8 to 10 portions

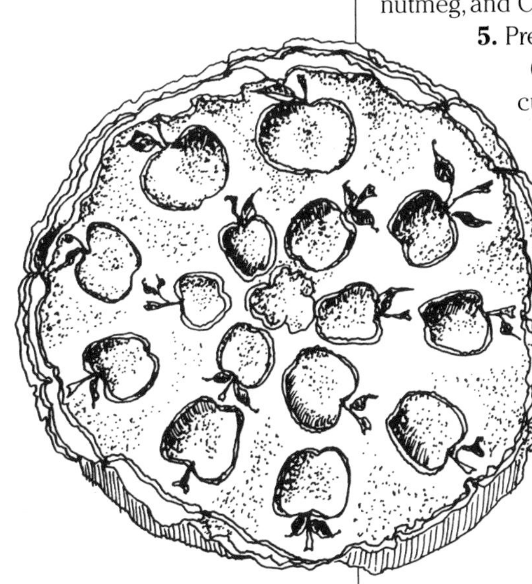

IT'S THE BERRIES

The berry season is one that comes and goes all too fast. As soon as berries appear in the market, they vanish into the baskets of urban berry pickers. Of our favorites, strawberries, raspberries, and blackberries are delicate and must be treated with care; blueberries are sturdier and keep longer. All should be stored in a dark but cool and airy place, preferably not the refrigerator, since it encourages mold. If you must refrigerate them, don't wash them first. It's best to eat berries as quickly as possible after picking or purchasing them.

Berries are wonderful to eat as they are, or with just a little crème fraîche or whipped cream flavored with a fruit liqueur. Eat one kind alone or combined with others in dozens of ways. Make the most of them this season. It's the berries!

ZABAGLIONE

This dessert is wonderfully versatile, since it can be served hot or cold, is good by itself, and is even better as a topping for a combination of berries. We like equal parts of blueberries, raspberries, and strawberries.

8 egg yolks
¾ cup sugar
⅓ cup Marsala

1. Mix the ingredients together in the top of a double boiler and cook over rapidly boiling water, whisking constantly until the mixture doubles in bulk and thickens.

2. Remove from the heat and whisk for another minute.

3. Pour the mixture warm over fresh berries, serve it in a tall glass by itself, or chill it and serve as a sauce for berries.

6 portions

You can't go wrong with the beloved strawberry. The French discovered an ancestor of this large, lush berry in Chile in the eighteenth century, and eventually produced the forerunners of today's varieties by crossing it with the tiny wild berries of North America. Today wild berries are scarce, but the cultivated version grows in all but the hottest desert. Americans have made it their national berry.

SUMMER SAIL PICNIC

CRUDITÉS WITH
SESAME MAYONNAISE

GLAZED BLUEBERRY CHICKEN

SCANDINAVIAN POTATO SALAD

FRESH SPINACH SALAD WITH
POPPY-SEED DRESSING

STRAWBERRY ICE CREAM

"The only emperor is the emperor of ice cream."

—WALLACE STEVENS

CHAMPAGNE SABAYON

A simple and elegant cousin of zabaglione. Spoon it over fresh berries in stemmed glasses.

4 egg yolks
⅓ cup sugar
¾ cup Champagne
2 tablespoons Kirsch
4 cups favorite berries

1. Whisk the egg yolks and the sugar together in the top of a double boiler over boiling water until foamy.

2. Add the Champagne and whisk constantly until thick and creamy, about 10 minutes.

3. Remove from the heat, add the Kirsch, stir, and serve immediately over your favorite berries.

2½ cups, sauce for about 4 cups berries, 4 to 6 portions

STRAWBERRY ICE CREAM

Churning homemade ice cream is traditionally one of the great American pastimes. It's even better when the ice cream being churned is flavored with the all-American strawberry.

1⅓ cups milk
2⅔ cups heavy cream
½ vanilla bean, split
8 egg yolks
1¼ cups sugar
1 pint ripe strawberries

1. Combine the milk and heavy cream in a large heavy saucepan. Add the vanilla bean and bring almost to a boil. Reduce the heat and simmer for 5 minutes.

2. Whisk the egg yolks together with 1 cup of the sugar until smooth and all the sugar is dissolved. Remove the milk mixture from the heat, remove the vanilla bean, and whisk 1 cup of the hot milk thoroughly into the eggs. Stir well, then whisk the egg mixture back into the milk.

3. Return the saucepan to the stove and cook over low heat, whisking constantly, just until the custard thickens; do not let it boil. Strain the custard, cool, and chill well.

4. Meanwhile, rinse, drain, and stem the strawberries. Crush them and stir in the remaining sugar. Let stand for 30 minutes.

5. Combine the strawberries with the chilled custard. Transfer to an ice cream maker and freeze according to the manufacturer's instructions.

1½ quarts

PAVLOVA

Created in honor of the great ballerina.

Butter, for greasing the pan
Flour, for flouring the pan
4 egg whites, at room temperature
¼ teaspoon salt
¼ teaspoon cream of tartar
1 cup superfine sugar
4 teaspoons cornstarch
2 teaspoons white wine vinegar
1 teaspoon vanilla extract
1 cup heavy cream, chilled
2 to 3 cups strawberries, sliced and sprinkled with sugar and Grand Marnier

Pavlova is light, airy, and elegant—like its namesake.

Strawberries are so called from the old English word "straw," meaning to cover the ground with scattered things. It is a fruit full of summer.

AUTUMN DINNER PARTY

ZUCCHINI-WATERCRESS SOUP

FRUIT-STUFFED CORNISH HENS

GINGER CANDIED CARROTS

NUTTED WILD RICE

PAVLOVA

1. Preheat the oven to 275°F. Butter and lightly flour an 8-inch springform pan.

2. Beat the egg whites, salt, and cream of tartar together in a bowl until the whites hold a stiff peak. Add the sugar, a few tablespoons at a time, beating until the mixture is stiff and glossy. Beat in the cornstarch, then the vinegar and the vanilla.

3. Gently fill the pan with the meringue mixture, spreading it higher around the edges than in the center of the pan to form a depression.

4. Bake the cake until the meringue is firm and lightly browned, 1 to 1½ hours. Pavlova will remain moist inside. Cool slightly, unmold, slide onto a serving plate, and cool completely.

5. Lightly whip the cream. Just before serving, spread the pavlova with whipped cream and then with the strawberries. Serve immediately.

4 to 6 portions

STRAWBERRY SHORTCAKE

One of our mothers long ago showed her spirit by announcing a dinner of only strawberry shortcake. Though we promised to keep it secret, we were typical elementary school students and couldn't wait for "Show and Tell" the next day.

We've been making strawberry shortcake for ages, but it's even better now that Sheila's pal Sally McArthur, from Seattle, has generously shared her biscuit recipe with us. Here, we share it with you.

Unsalted butter, at room temperature, for greasing the baking sheet and topping the biscuits
2 cups self-rising flour
2½ tablespoons sugar
⅛ teaspoon salt
8 tablespoons (1 stick) cold unsalted butter, cut into small pieces
¾ cup milk
2 tablespoons plus 1½ cups heavy cream, chilled
6 cups strawberries, sliced and sugared to taste
6 perfect strawberries, for garnish

1. Preheat the oven to 400°F. Grease a baking sheet.

2. Combine the flour, sugar, and salt in a bowl.

3. Add the 8 tablespoons butter and using a pastry blender or your fingers, rub it into the dry ingredients until the mixture resembles coarse meal. Pour in the milk and mix gently until a very soft dough is formed. Do not overwork.

4. Drop the dough in 6 equal portions onto the prepared baking sheet. Lightly pat the dough into rounds 3 to 3½ inches in diameter and lightly brush the tops with the 2 tablespoons cream.

5. Bake the biscuits on the center rack of the oven until golden brown, 15 to 20 minutes.

6. Cool the biscuits slightly on a wire rack, split them, and spread the room temperature butter lightly over the cut surfaces. Set the bottoms on dessert plates; spoon on the sliced strawberries and crown with the tops of the biscuits. Whip the 1½ cups chilled cream and spoon a dollop onto each shortcake, then garnish with a single perfect strawberry. Serve immediately.

6 shortcakes

STRAWBERRY CHOCOLATE TART

A pretty way to serve strawberries.

Chocolate Filling (recipe follows)
9-inch prebaked Sweet Buttery Tart Crust (page 411)
1½ pints strawberries, washed, stemmed, and dried
½ cup Red Currant Glaze (page 421)
Fresh mint sprig, for garnish

1. While the chocolate filling is still warm, spread it in the tart shell. The filling should be about ⅛ inch thick.

2. Place the berries, tips up, over the warm chocolate filling in a circular pattern, working from the outside in until the surface is covered.

3. Warm the glaze in a small saucepan over low heat until thin enough to brush easily, then coat the berries evenly.

4. Refrigerate the tart for 2 hours; remove from the refrigerator 45 minutes before serving. Garnish with the mint sprig.

8 portions

CHOCOLATE FILLING

1 cup semisweet chocolate pieces
2 tablespoons unsalted butter, melted
3 tablespoons Kirsch
¼ cup confectioners' sugar, sifted
1 tablespoon water

1. Melt the chocolate in a bowl placed over simmering water; this will take about 20 minutes. When the chocolate has reached 110°F, add the melted butter and Kirsch. Whisk quickly and thoroughly until smooth.

2. Add the confectioners' sugar and water, continuing to whisk until smooth.

3. Remove from the heat and keep warm.

STRAWBERRY WAYS

- ♥ Top Crème Brulée (page 375) with crushed fresh strawberries.
- ♥ Steep strawberries in a goblet of red wine; add a bit of honey if you like. Serve with a spoon.
- ♥ Toss sliced strawberries with sugar and Grand Marnier to taste; leave at room temperature for a few hours. Serve in small bowls, or spoon over vanilla ice cream.
- ♥ Sweeten ripe berries with fresh orange juice to taste. A sprinkle of dark rum is nice, too.

"Doubtless God could have made a better berry, but doubtless God never did."

—DR. WILLIAM BUTLER, 1535–1618

The ingredients for Fig and Raspberry Tart are as inviting as the tart itself.

If we had to choose just one favorite berry, it would be the raspberry, the most elegant of all. Raspberries have been cherished for centuries, and they never seem to be abundant or affordable enough to be taken for granted. When the season is at its peak, eat them plain or with a bit of cream. Pure pleasure!

FIG AND RASPBERRY TART

12 figs, green or purple
½ cup Kirsch
9-inch prebaked Sweet Buttery Tart Crust (page 411)
1 cup Pastry Cream (page 410)
½ pint raspberries, picked over
Red Currant Glaze (page 421)

1. If using green figs, carefully peel them and leave them whole. If using purple figs, cut them lengthwise into halves but do not peel. Pour the Kirsch over the figs in a bowl, cover, and refrigerate for 12 hours, stirring occasionally.

2. To assemble the tart, spread the pastry cream in the baked tart shell. Remove the figs from the Kirsch and drain them. If using green figs, cut them lengthwise into quarters, but do not cut completely through the base. Fan the quarters out like flower petals, and arrange close together over the surface of the pastry cream. If using purple figs, arrange the halves cut side down. Fill in the spaces between the figs with raspberries.

3. Warm the currant glaze and brush over the tart to glaze all the fruit. Serve within 3 hours of assembling.

6 to 8 portions

RED RASPBERRY PIE

4 cups raspberries, picked over
1 cup sugar
⅓ cup Crème de Cassis (black currant liqueur)
¼ cup cornstarch
1 tablespoon fresh lemon juice
Pinch of salt
1 recipe Piecrust (page 411)
2 tablespoons unsalted butter
3 paper-thin slices of lemon

1. Preheat the oven to 425°F.

2. Toss the raspberries and sugar together in a mixing bowl. Whisk the Cassis and cornstarch together in a small bowl until smooth. Stir the Cassis mixture, lemon juice, and salt gently into the berries.

3. Roll out two thirds of the pastry and line a 9-inch pie pan; leave the edges untrimmed. Spoon in the berries, dot with the butter, and arrange the lemon slices overlapping slightly in the center of the berries.

4. Roll out the remaining pastry into a 10-inch round and cut into ½-inch strips. Arrange over the berries in a lattice pattern. Trim the overhanging pastry; bring the edge of the lower crust over the lattice and crimp the edge decoratively.

5. Set on the center rack of the oven and bake for 15 minutes. Lower the heat to 350°F and bake until the crust is golden brown and the filling is bubbling, another 30 to 40 minutes.

6 to 8 portions

RASPBERRY-SAUTERNES DESSERT SOUP

On the hottest day of the hottest summer we can remember, we found ourselves expecting some Very Important People for dinner. When all was ready except a dessert, we had time for an elaborate finale or a run to the beach, but not both. Inspiration, in the form of a well-iced bottle of Sauternes in the back of the refrigerator, led to this creation—quick, easy, and elegant. (Our tan looked great at dinner, too!)

1 bottle of good, but not great, French Sauternes, chilled
3 cups fresh raspberries
½ cup Crème Fraîche (page 414)
Fresh mint leaves, for garnish

1. Pour the Sauternes into a mixing bowl.

2. Sort through the raspberries, discarding any less-than-

"One third of a tumbler filled with raspberry vinegar— add ice, a teaspoon of sugar and top with carbonated water. Garnish with fresh berries and a mint leaf."

—MARY RANDOLPH, *THE VIRGINIA HOUSEWIFE,* 1824

perfect berries. Crush about half of the berries with the back of a spoon and stir all of them into the Sauternes. Cover and refrigerate for at least 4 hours.

3. Just before serving, measure the crème fraîche into a small bowl. Ladle out 2 cups of the chilled Sauternes and whisk it gradually into the crème fraîche. Now whisk this mixture back into the remaining Sauternes in the mixing bowl. Ladle into chilled soup bowls or Champagne glasses, dividing the raspberries fairly. Garnish each serving with the fresh mint leaves. Serve immediately.

4 to 6 portions

RASPBERRY CORDIAL

For the fullest flavor let this steep until Christmastime; then give it as a gift or enjoy it yourself.

2 cups sugar
2 pints ripe raspberries, picked over
1 quart vodka

1. Place the sugar in a 3-quart glass jar with a lid. Add the raspberries and the vodka, and cover.

2. Place in a dark, cool place. Each week for about 2 months open the jar and stir the cordial.

3. Strain the finished cordial through a very fine sieve into a lovely decanter. Its color is vibrant.

1½ quarts

DAMSON PLUM BRANDY

Pierce the skin of each plum several times with a fork. Follow the recipe for Raspberry Cordial substituting damson plums at their peak. Stir each week, letting the brandy mature for at least 4 months. If you time it right, the brandy will be ready by Christmas Eve. Serve the fruit over ice cream and serve the brandy around the fire afterward.

BLUEBERRY LEMON TART

Other fruits can be used in place of the blueberries. Try combining green and red seedless grapes, blueberries, and thinly sliced peaches, or lightly sautéed apple slices sprinkled with plumped raisins. Use your imagination and enjoy!

1 cup fresh lemon juice (about 6 lemons)
5 tablespoons grated lemon zest
8 tablespoons (1 stick) unsalted butter, melted
6 eggs, lightly beaten
1 cup granulated sugar
9-inch partially baked Sweet Buttery Tart Crust, 1 inch deep (page 411)
1½ cups blueberries, rinsed, sorted, and dried
Confectioners' sugar

1. Preheat the oven to 400°F.

2. Whisk the lemon juice, grated zest, and melted butter in a medium-size bowl. Beat in the eggs and granulated sugar; mix well.

Robert Frost called these dewy bunches of blue "a vision of thieves," though they needn't be stolen to be enjoyed. These are blueberries, and we're thankful that cultivators have made them readily available. Today's blues are generously grand and as popular as Fats Domino when he sang "Blueberry Hill."

3. Pour into the partially baked tart shell and bake until golden brown, about 20 minutes.

4. Arrange the blueberries (or other fresh fruit) over the warm filling, pressing lightly. When cool, dust with confectioners' sugar.

8 portions

BLACKBERRY ICE

This ice makes the most of the blackberry's tart, intense flavor. Delicious on a summer's day, especially if you've spent the afternoon picking the berries in a hot thicket.

3 pints ripe blackberries
½ cup sugar
Juice of 2 lemons
¾ cup Crème de Cassis (black currant liqueur)

1. Combine all the ingredients in a heavy saucepan and set over medium heat. Cook, stirring frequently, until all the berries have burst, 20 minutes.

2. Cool the mixture slightly and force through a sieve or through the fine disc of a food mill. Cool the resulting purée completely.

3. Pour the cooled mixture into a shallow metal pan (a cake tin is ideal), and set it in your freezer.

4. When the mixture is about half frozen, in 2 to 3 hours, remove the pan from the freezer, scrape the blackberry ice out of the pan into a bowl, and beat with a wire whisk until the soft parts and icy parts are completely mixed. Return the ice to the pan, set it back in the freezer, and freeze completely.

5. The ice will be very solid. To serve, temper it in the refrigerator for 15 to 30 minutes before attempting to dish it up.

6 portions

The scarcest of all American berries is the blackberry. Count yourself lucky if you happen to have a thicket on your property or in your neighborhood. The wild blackberry is very tart; the cultivated varieties tend to be less so. All members of the blackberry tribe lend themselves to superb jams and pies. Some people dislike the large seeds the berries hide; that means more blackberries are left for us!

BLACKBERRY MOUSSE

Search the field or market for these black wonders; they're worth it. The flavor and color of the mousse are gorgeous.

1 tablespoon unflavored gelatin
2 tablespoons cold water
Juice and grated zest of 1 orange
2 pints blackberries, or 2 bags (10 ounces each) frozen berries without sugar; reserve several for garnish
2 egg yolks
½ cup sugar
2 tablespoons Cointreau
2 cups heavy cream
2 kiwis, peeled and sliced, for garnish (optional)
8 to 10 whole berries, for garnish

"Whenever I get married I start buying *Gourmet* magazine."

—NORA EPHRON

Show off Blackberry Mousse by spooning it into fancy water goblets.

Blackberries are found throughout the United States. In the west, the berries grow in mountainous country, mostly at higher altitudes. The blackberry is a shrub with thorns. The stems are flowering and clustered; the flower is white and five-petaled. The leaflets are 3 to 5 in number and the fruit is black or dark purple. The blackberry is sometimes called bramblebush.

1. Soak the gelatin in the cold water in a saucepan for 5 minutes. Add the orange juice, grated orange zest, and berries, and bring just to a boil, stirring. Cool to room temperature.

2. Beat the egg yolks and sugar in a bowl until pale yellow. Add the Cointreau and beat for another minute.

3. Put the egg yolk mixture in the top of a double boiler over simmering water. Stir until slightly thickened and hot to the touch. Cool to room temperature.

4. Add the egg yolk mixture to the blackberry mixture and stir until well blended. Whip the heavy cream to soft peaks and fold gently into the blackberry and egg yolk mixture. Divide among serving dishes and chill until ready to serve.

5. Garnish with sliced kiwis, each topped with a whole berry, or with the berries alone.

8 to 10 portions

MOUSSE MAGIC

After a heavy meal, when guilt pangs are running high and yet you want just a little something sweet, a cool, smooth mousse is the perfect dessert. The Silver Palate shop was never without row after row of these lovely light treats in individual portions. You can present your dessert mousses in the same way—spooned into chilled stemmed balloon glasses and garnished with berries, a slice of citrus, chocolate curls, or mint. Or, more simply, chill the mousse in your favorite clear bowl and then divide it among dessert plates at table and serve with your best cookies. Either way, your guests will love it as an elegant grand finale.

LIME MOUSSE

Our tart and buttery Lime Mousse was one of the store's most popular desserts for years. Team it with our chocolate brownies for a sensational dessert. For variations, substitute fresh lemon or orange for the lime.

8 tablespoons (1 stick) unsalted butter
5 eggs
1 cup sugar
¾ cup fresh lime juice (6 or 7 limes)
Grated zest of 5 limes
2 cups heavy cream, chilled

1. Melt the butter in the top of a double boiler over simmering water.

2. Beat the eggs and sugar in a bowl until light and foamy. Add the mixture to the melted butter. Cook gently, stirring constantly, until the mixture becomes a custard, about 8 minutes. Do not overcook or the eggs will scramble.

3. Remove the custard from the heat and stir in the lime juice and grated zest. Cool to room temperature.

4. This step is unorthodox but crucial. Using an electric mixer, whip the chilled cream until very stiff—almost, but not quite, to the point where it would become butter.

5. Stir the lime custard into the whipped cream until just incorporated. Pour into 8 individual serving glasses or a serving bowl. Chill for at least 4 hours.

8 portions

from THE SILVER PALATE NOTEBOOK

Catch the first violets when the snow is melting and add their mild flavor to spring greens. Surprise your guests by floating violets in great goblets of white wine, or topping a mousse with violet leaves and blossoms. For an elegant garnish for ice cream, sorbet, or chocolate cake, dip violets into superfine sugar and let them dry until they are brittle, usually about 2 days.

USING RAW EGGS

As a general rule, you'll always want to purchase very fresh, high-quality eggs. Eggs should always be well refrigerated, clean, and have their shells intact. This is especially important when the eggs will be eaten raw, or only gently cooked, as they are in some of our mousse recipes. While the risks are slight, it's best to err on the side of caution.

PEACH MELBA MOUSSE

3 ripe peaches, peeled, pitted, and quartered
⅔ cup raspberries, picked over
3 tablespoons peach brandy, plus a little more for garnish
1 tablespoon unflavored gelatin
3 tablespoons fresh lemon juice
⅓ cup sugar
⅛ teaspoon almond extract
Pinch of salt
½ cup heavy cream, chilled
2 egg whites

1. Purée the peaches and raspberries with the brandy in a blender or a food processor.

2. In a saucepan, soak the gelatin in lemon juice for 5 minutes. Add the puréed fruits, sugar, almond extract, and salt. Bring just to a boil, stirring. Remove from the heat, transfer to a bowl, and cool to room temperature.

3. Whip the cream to soft peaks and gently fold into fruit mixture. Refrigerate until the mixture just begins to set, 1 hour.

4. Beat the egg whites until stiff. Gently fold half the egg whites into the mousse. Fold in the remaining egg whites, making sure there are no lumps.

5. Spoon into dessert glasses or a serving bowl. Chill for 4 hours. To serve, drizzle a few drops of peach brandy over each portion.

4 portions

GINGER PUMPKIN MOUSSE

4 eggs
7 tablespoons sugar
1 tablespoon unflavored gelatin
1½ cups pumpkin purée or canned pumpkin
¾ teaspoon ground cinnamon
½ teaspoon freshly grated ginger
¼ teaspoon grated nutmeg
1 cup heavy cream, chilled
Minced crystallized ginger, for garnish

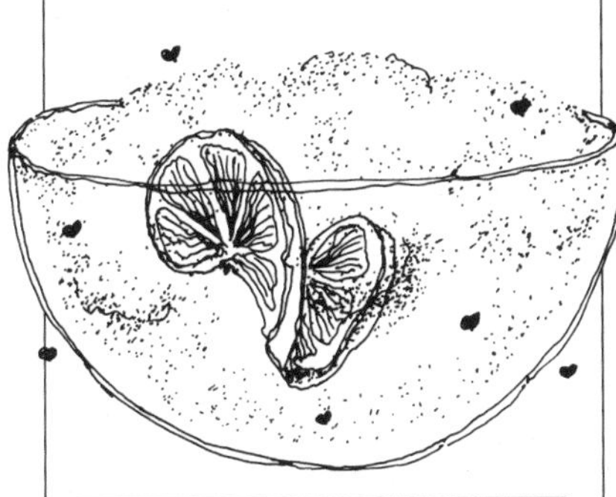

1. Beat the eggs with the sugar until the mixture is light colored and thick. Add the gelatin and beat to blend well. Mix in the pumpkin purée and spices and chill the mixture until it begins to set.

2. Whip the cream into soft peaks; fold into the pumpkin mixture. Pour into 4 to 6 dessert dishes or a large serving bowl.

3. Chill for 4 hours. Before serving, decorate with the crystallized ginger.

4 to 6 portions

STRAWBERRY MOUSSE

2½ pints strawberries, stemmed, washed, and drained
2 tablespoons fresh lemon juice
1 tablespoon unflavored gelatin
6 tablespoons boiling water
2 egg yolks
⅔ cup sugar
2 tablespoons Cointreau
2 cups heavy cream, chilled
Additional whole strawberries, for garnish

1. Combine the strawberries, lemon juice, and gelatin in a food processor. Purée until smooth. Carefully pour in the boiling water and process again, briefly. Let the mixture cool to room temperature.

2. Beat the egg yolks and sugar together until pale yellow and thick. Whisk in the Cointreau and beat for another minute. Pour the egg mixture into the top of a double boiler set over simmering water and stir until slightly thickened and hot to the touch. Cool to room temperature.

3. Combine the strawberry and egg mixtures and chill until just beginning to set.

4. Whip the cream to soft peaks and fold gently into the chilled mousse mixture. Spoon into 8 to 10 individual dessert glasses or a serving bowl. Chill for at least 4 hours. Garnish with the whole strawberries before serving.

8 to 10 portions

MOCHA MOUSSE

⅓ cup sugar
6 tablespoons prepared espresso or strong coffee
6 ounces semisweet chocolate
4 tablespoons light cream
3 egg whites
1½ cups heavy cream, chilled

1. In a heavy saucepan, dissolve the sugar in the coffee over medium heat. Set aside.

2. In the top of a double boiler set over simmering water, slowly melt the chocolate. When melted, whisk in the light cream and the coffee mixture, stirring until smooth. Cool.

3. Beat the egg whites to soft peaks. Gently fold in ½ cup of the chocolate mixture. Pour this mixture back into the chocolate mixture, folding gently. Beat the chilled cream to soft peaks and fold in gently until totally mixed.

4. Pour into 8 individual dessert glasses or a large serving dish, and chill for 4 hours.

8 portions

Three luscious mousses: Strawberry, Lime, and Mocha.

AMARETTO MOUSSE

4 tablespoons (½ stick) unsalted butter
5 eggs
1 cup sugar
1½ teaspoons unflavored gelatin
¾ cup amaretti (tiny macaroons), crushed
1½ tablespoons amaretto liqueur
1½ cups heavy cream, chilled

1. Melt the butter in the top part of a double boiler over simmering water.

2. In a bowl, beat the eggs with the sugar and add the gelatin. Add to the melted butter and cook, stirring constantly, until thickened, 6 to 8 minutes. Remove from the heat.

3. Add ½ cup of the crushed amaretti and the amaretto. Blend well. Cool, then refrigerate until the mixture just begins to set.

4. Whip the cream to soft peaks. Gently fold into the amaretto mixture. Spoon into 8 to 10 individual serving glasses or a serving bowl. Chill until set, about 4 hours.

5. Just before serving, sprinkle with the reserved amaretti.

8 to 10 portions

FLOWER CUPS

Crisp cookie cups to fill with your favorite mousse or sorbet.

1⅓ cups unbleached all-purpose flour
¾ cup confectioners' sugar
3 egg whites, lightly beaten
2 egg yolks, lightly beaten
1 teaspoon grated orange zest
1 tablespoon Cointreau
Butter, for greasing the baking sheet
1 large orange

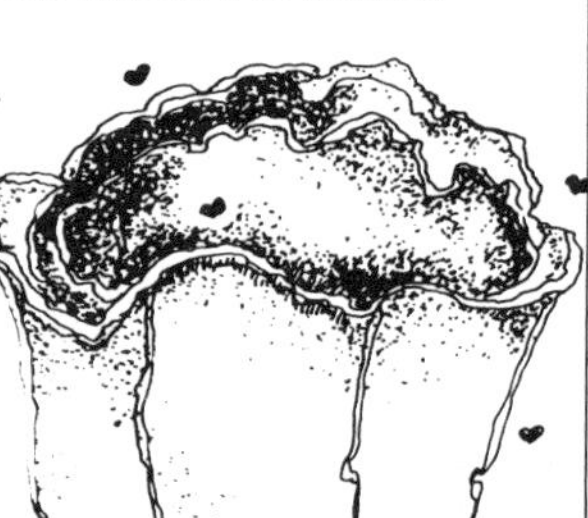

1. Preheat the oven to 350°F.

2. Sift the flour and sugar together. Add the egg whites, egg yolks, orange zest, and Cointreau. Mix well. Let the batter sit for 20 minutes.

3. Grease a baking sheet and mark 5-inch circles on the surface (use a saucer as a guide), placing them well apart. Using a tablespoon, drop 1 spoonful of batter in the center of each circle, spreading the batter to cover the area evenly and neatly.

4. Bake the cookies until the edges are browning but the center is still soft, 5 to 6 minutes. Working quickly, remove the cookies with a spatula and form cupped shapes, using the orange as a mold. Set the shaped cookies on a rack to cool.

5. Let the sheet cool, wipe clean, grease again, and make, bake, and cool another batch; repeat until all the batter has been used.

15 to 20 cookie cups

EUROPEAN SEND-OFF BUFFET

SALMON MOUSSE
WITH
DABS OF BLACK CAVIAR
AND SPRIGS OF
FRESH DILL

PUMPERNICKEL
ROUNDS

PÂTÉ MAISON

CHICKEN MARBELLA,
CUT INTO
BITE-SIZE PIECES

RICE AND VEGETABLE SALAD
WITH CREAMY
TARRAGON-MUSTARD
DRESSING

COLD BLANCHED
ASPARAGUS

RED WINE
VINAIGRETTE

SLICED
HARD-COOKED EGGS

L'EXPLORATEUR,
MONTRACHET, AND BASIL
TORTA CHEESES

BLACKBERRY MOUSSE

LIME MOUSSE

A COOKIE BASKET

ESSENTIALLY CHOCOLATE

We have a passion for chocolate. It's smooth, sweet, rich, and sophisticated—all qualities we love. For those who crave it as much as we do, here are a few of the most delicious chocolate desserts we know.

SUMMER SATURDAY LUNCHEON

CONSOMMÉ WITH ASPARAGUS AND DILL

SEAFOOD SALAD WITH CREAMY TARRAGON-MUSTARD DRESSING

BULGUR WHEAT SALAD

CHOCOLATE MOUSSE

FRESH RASPBERRIES

CHOCOLATE MOUSSE

The deepest, darkest, richest chocolate mousse we've ever met—filled with secrets.

1½ pounds semisweet chocolate chips
½ cup prepared espresso coffee
½ cup Grand Marnier
4 egg yolks
2 cups heavy cream, chilled
¼ cup sugar
8 egg whites
Pinch of salt
½ teaspoon vanilla extract
Candied rosebuds, for garnish (optional)

1. Melt the chocolate chips in a heavy saucepan over very low heat, stirring; add the espresso coffee, then stir in the Grand Marnier. Let cool to room temperature.

2. Add the egg yolks, one at a time, beating thoroughly after each addition.

3. Whip 1 cup of the cream until thickened, then gradually beat in the sugar, beating until stiff. Beat the egg whites with salt until stiff. Gently fold the egg whites into the cream.

4. Stir about one third of the cream and egg mixture thoroughly into the chocolate mixture. Then scrape the remaining cream and egg mixture over the lightened chocolate base and fold together gently. Pour into 8 individual dessert cups or a serving bowl. Refrigerate for 2 hours, or until set.

5. At serving time, whip the remaining cup of cream until thickened, add the vanilla, and whip to soft peaks. Top each portion of the mousse with a share of the cream and the optional rosebuds.

8 portions

CHOCOLATE HAZELNUT CAKE

The best chocolate cake in the universe.

4 eggs, separated
1 cup sugar
4 ounces unsweetened chocolate
12 tablespoons (1½ sticks) unsalted butter, plus extra for greasing the pan
1 cup plus 1 tablespoon cake flour, plus extra for flouring the pan
¼ teaspoon salt
3 tablespoons very finely ground skinned hazelnuts
Hazelnut Buttercream (recipe follows)
Chocolate Icing (recipe follows)
8 whole hazelnuts, for garnish

1. Beat the egg yolks and sugar together until the mixture is thick and pale yellow.

2. Meanwhile, in the top of a double boiler set over simmering water, melt the chocolate with the 12 tablespoons butter, whisking constantly until smooth; cool slightly.

3. Preheat the oven to 350°F. Grease an 8-inch springform pan. Line the bottom with a circle of wax paper. Grease the paper and lightly flour the lining and sides of the pan.

4. Pour the chocolate-butter mixture into the egg mixture and stir just to blend. Fold in the 1 cup plus 1 tablespoon flour, salt, and ground hazelnuts.

5. Whip the egg whites until stiff and fold gently into the batter.

6. Pour the cake batter into the prepared pan and rap the pan lightly on the work surface to eliminate any air bubbles.

HAZELNUTS

Hazelnuts (also called filberts—the terms are used interchangeably) have long been regarded by European pastry makers as one of the supreme dessert nuts. Their delicious flavor appears alone and in combination, especially with chocolate, in dozens of desserts. They are usually expensive and quite perishable—two reasons that have deterred Americans from appreciating hazelnuts as fully as they might. This is especially unfortunate since hazelnuts are grown in the northwest United States and thus are quite available.

Buy hazelnuts from a reputable dealer with a good turnover to ensure freshness. Store them in the freezer, well wrapped, if you must keep them for any length of time. Their skins can be tough and are often removed before cooking with the nuts. Spread the hazelnuts in a single layer on a baking sheet and toast at 350°F for 10 to 15 minutes. Cool slightly and rub them between your fingers or in a kitchen towel. Their skins will flake off easily.

7. Set the pan on the center rack of the oven and bake until the edges are firm and the inside is set but still somewhat soft, 35 to 40 minutes. Do not worry if the top cracks slightly. Cool in the pan, set on a rack, for 1 hour. Remove the sides of the pan and cool the cake to room temperature.

8. When the cake is cool, invert it onto a serving plate and spread the top and sides with the hazelnut buttercream. Refrigerate the cake for 30 minutes.

9. Remove the cake from the refrigerator and spread the top and sides with warm chocolate icing. Work quickly, as the icing sets.

10. Decorate the top of the cake with the 8 whole hazelnuts. Refrigerate the cake for at least 1 hour before cutting and serving.

8 portions

HAZELNUT BUTTERCREAM

1¼ cups shelled hazelnuts
5 tablespoons corn syrup
2 tablespoons brandy
1 cup confectioners' sugar, sifted
4 tablespoons (½ stick) unsalted butter, at room temperature

1. Preheat the oven to 350°F.

2. Roast the hazelnuts on a baking sheet oven until their skins have loosened, 10 to 15 minutes. Remove from the oven and rub between towels to remove the skins.

3. Transfer to a food processor and run the machine until the nuts begin to form a paste, like peanut butter in texture.

4. Scrape the paste into a bowl and stir in the corn syrup and brandy. Let sit for 20 minutes. (The hazelnut paste can be prepared in advance and refrigerated. Let it return to room temperature before proceeding with the recipe.)

5. Cream the confectioners' sugar and butter together until light and fluffy. Add the hazelnut paste and mix thoroughly.

Enough for the top and sides of one 8-inch layer

"Life without chocolate is too terrible to contemplate."

—ANONYMOUS

CHOCOLATE ICING

4 tablespoons (½ stick) unsalted butter
4 ounces semisweet chocolate
3 tablespoons heavy cream
Approximately ⅔ cup sifted confectioners' sugar
1 teaspoon vanilla extract

1. Melt the butter and chocolate together in the top of a double boiler over simmering water, whisking constantly.

2. Remove the pan from the heat and beat in the cream. Sift in the confectioners' sugar and vanilla. The icing should be very smooth. Spread while warm.

Enough for the top and sides of one 8-inch cake layer

DECADENT CHOCOLATE CAKE

8 tablespoons (1 stick) unsalted butter, plus extra for greasing the pan
2 cups less 2 tablespoons unbleached all-purpose flour, sifted, plus extra for flouring the pan
1 cup boiling water
3 ounces unsweetened chocolate
1 teaspoon vanilla extract
2 cups sugar
2 eggs, separated
1 teaspoon baking soda
½ cup sour cream
1 teaspoon baking powder
Chocolate Frosting (recipe follows)

1. Preheat the oven to 350°F. Grease and flour a 10-inch tube pan. Knock out the excess flour.

2. Pour the boiling water over the chocolate and the butter; let stand until melted. Stir in the vanilla and sugar, then whisk in the egg yolks, one at a time, blending well after each addition.

3. Mix the baking soda and sour cream and whisk into the chocolate mixture.

4. Sift the flour and baking powder together and add to the batter, mixing thoroughly.

5. Beat the egg whites until stiff but not dry. Stir a quarter of the egg whites thoroughly into the batter. Scoop the remaining egg whites on top of the batter and gently fold together.

6. Pour the batter into the prepared pan. Set on the center rack of the oven and bake until the edges have pulled away from the sides of the pan and a cake tester inserted into the center comes out clean, 40 to 50 minutes. Cool in the pan for 10 minutes; unmold and cool completely before frosting.

12 portions

CHOCOLATE FROSTING

2 tablespoons unsalted butter
¾ cup semisweet chocolate chips
6 tablespoons heavy cream
1¼ cups sifted confectioners' sugar, or as needed
1 teaspoon vanilla extract

Place all the ingredients in a heavy saucepan over low heat and whisk until smooth. Cool slightly; add more sugar if necessary to achieve a spreading consistency. Spread on the cake while the frosting is still warm.

Enough frosting for 1 cake

COCKTAIL BUFFET MENU

BRIE, BRILLAT-SAVARIN, AND BOUCHERON CHEESES WITH RED, GREEN, AND PURPLE GRAPE CLUSTERS

WALNUTS IN BOWLS

LINZERTORTE

DECADENT CHOCOLATE CAKE WITH WHIPPED CREAM

COFFEE SPICED WITH CINNAMON STICKS

CHOCOLATE LOVERS FOREVER!

We're mad for dark, rich chocolate. It seems just about everyone is. Chocolate shops and new artisanal chocolate makers have blossomed across the country and around the world to meet this passion for chocolate. There are clubs, societies, and cookbooks extolling the virtues and complexities of chocolate. The amount of liquor in a chocolate has become a debate; the percentage of cocoa content you crave, a measure of sophistication. Once again it all amounts to adventurously tasting and eventually selecting your own favorites. Your own taste, that's all that's important.

We prefer dark chocolate, the darker the better. We generally use dark chocolate in the 62 to 65 percent range in our cooking, but the percentages soar to 70, 82, and even 90 percent. For melting on our tongues we prefer dark chocolate in the 70 to 80 percent range (or, if we're feeling daring, even the 99 percent range). The higher the percentage of cocoa beans, the stronger and more intense the chocolate flavor. Our favorite are Valrhona and Barry Callebaut from Europe, Scharffen Berger and Guittard from San Francisco, and El Rey from Venezuela. We also adore the finely crafted chocolates of Debauve & Gallais, Michel Cluizel, and Maison du Chocolate in France; Jacques Torres in New York; and Michael Recchiutti in San Francisco. And there are loads of premium American, Swiss, French, German, and Dutch bittersweet, semisweet, white, and milk chocolates on the market today. Taste them all. You'll soon find your own favorites.

BITTERSWEET CHOCOLATE CAKE

1½ cups plus 4 tablespoons (3½ sticks) unsalted butter, at room temperature, plus extra for greasing the pan
2 cups granulated sugar, plus extra for coating the pan
14 ounces bittersweet chocolate (the darkest you can find)
3 tablespoons cold water
12 eggs, separated
1 cup unbleached all-purpose flour, sifted
Confectioners' sugar

1. Preheat the oven to 325°F. Grease and sugar a 10-inch springform pan and tap out any extra sugar.

2. Grate or break the chocolate into small pieces. Place in the top of a double boiler with the cold water. Melt over simmering water, whisking until smooth. Let the chocolate cool slightly.

3. Beat the egg yolks with the granulated sugar until they are thick and pale yellow and form a ribbon when they fall from the beater. Fold in the warm chocolate. Stir in the very soft butter and then fold in the sifted flour. Mix thoroughly but gently.

4. Beat the egg whites until stiff. Stir a large spoonful of the chocolate mixture into the beaten egg whites. Mix well. Pour this mixture into the chocolate mixture; fold together gently, incorporating the whites completely. Be very careful at this stage not to overmix.

5. Turn the batter into the prepared pan. It will come close to the top of the pan. Set the pan on the center rack of the oven and bake until a cake tester inserted in the center comes out clean, 1 hour and 20 minutes. Cool on a rack for 15 minutes, then remove the rim of the pan. Allow the cake to cool completely before removing the bottom of the pan. Refrigerate.

6. When ready to serve, using a paper doily as a stencil, sprinkle with confectioners' sugar to make a design. Serve cold.

20 small but sweet portions

CHOCOLATE-GLAZED PEARS

A perfectly elegant dessert.

Fruit Poaching Syrup (page 381)
6 large pears
⅓ cup dried apricots, coarsely chopped
⅓ cup raisins
⅓ cup shelled black walnuts, coarsely chopped
Chocolate Glaze (recipe follows)
Dried apricots and walnut halves, for garnish

1. Prepare the poaching syrup and simmer for 10 minutes.

2. Peel the pears and core them from the bottom, leaving the stems in place. Reserve the cores.

3. Poach the pears in the syrup, standing them upright, until tender but not mushy, about 12 minutes. Let the pears cool in the poaching syrup.

4. Meanwhile, combine the apricots and raisins in a small bowl. Measure out 1 cup of hot syrup from the pot of pears, pour over the fruit, and let stand for 1 hour.

5. Drain the pears and gently pat very dry. Drain the soaked dried fruits and combine with the black walnuts. Stuff some of the mixture into each pear, leaving ½ inch of space at the bottom. Trim a piece ½ inch thick from the end of each reserved pear core and plug the pear cavities. Arrange the pears, standing upright, well apart on a baking sheet.

6. Using a large spoon, gently and slowly pour the chocolate glaze over each pear. Be careful to coat them completely without being overly generous. Let the chocolate set completely, about 45 minutes.

7. To serve, gently transfer the pears to individual serving plates.

6 portions

CHOCOLATE GLAZE

10 ounces semisweet chocolate, in pieces
3 tablespoons solid vegetable shortening

Melt the chocolate and shortening in a stainless-steel bowl over simmering water, whisking until smooth. Cool slightly before using.

Enough glaze for 6 pears

CHOCOLATE-DIPPED FRUITS

Strawberries, raspberries, cherries, orange sections, bananas, and apple and pear slices—all taste just a little bit better when dipped in chocolate. And making these confections couldn't be easier.

Simply gather your fruits together and choose your favorite eating chocolate—dark, milk, or white. We prefer dark. Melt two thirds of the amount of chocolate you are using, broken into pieces, in the top of a double boiler over simmering water (judging this amount is always a bit of a guessing game and depends on the quantity of fruit you plan to dip—for reference, 8 ounces of chocolate will coat about 12 to 14 large strawberries). Once the chocolate is melted, remove it from the heat and add the remaining chocolate, incorporating it well, to temper it. (You're cooling the chocolate so that it's right for dipping and will harden fairly quickly.) Let it cool for 10 to 15 minutes while you turn your attention to the fruit.

Whenever possible leave the stems and leaves on whole fruits; be sure the surface of the fruit is dry and use a toothpick to hold the fruit. Dip the fruit into the chocolate and cover it halfway. If you can, poke the other end of the toothpick into a piece of Styrofoam, letting the fruit dry upside down. Otherwise place it on a baking sheet covered with aluminum foil or parchment paper. Work quickly so that the chocolate doesn't start to thicken too much. If it does, simply set it over low heat for a moment or two and temper it again. Allow the fruit to dry in a cool, dry place. Chocolate-dipped fruit is best eaten within twenty-four hours.

PROFITEROLES

4 tablespoons (½ stick) unsalted butter, plus extra for greasing the cookie sheet
⅔ cup water
1 tablespoon sugar
½ teaspoon salt
1 cup unbleached all-purpose flour, sifted
4 eggs, at room temperature
Approximately 1 pint vanilla or coffee ice cream
Chocolate Fudge Sauce (recipe follows)
1 cup heavy cream, chilled

1. Preheat the oven to 450°F. Grease a cookie sheet.

2. In a heavy saucepan, combine the water, butter, sugar, and salt. Bring to a boil. Remove from the heat and add the flour all at once. Stir hard until the mixture forms a ball in the middle of the saucepan. Cool slightly.

3. Add the eggs, one at a time, beating after each addition until the dough shines.

4. Drop rounded teaspoons of dough onto the cookie sheet. Set the cookie sheet on the center rack of the oven and bake for 5 minutes, then reduce the heat to 350°F. Continue baking until the sides of the puffs are completely firm and the color is golden, about 15 minutes. Cool the puffs on a cake rack.

5. At serving time, cut off the tops of the puffs and set the lids aside. Whip the cream until stiff. Fill the puffs with vanilla or coffee ice cream. Replace the tops and arrange the puffs in a large bowl.

6. Cover with the hot fudge sauce and lots of whipped cream, and serve at once.

4 to 6 portions

Profiteroles are tender pastry puffs filled with ice cream and drizzled with chocolate fudge sauce. They are one of the easiest and most delicious desserts we know.

If you wish, the puffs can be filled with ice cream and frozen 1 to 2 hours in advance of serving time.

CHOCOLATE FUDGE SAUCE

This is a deep, dark, fudgy sauce that hardens on ice cream to a thick, delicious glaze.

4 ounces unsweetened chocolate
3 tablespoons unsalted butter
⅔ cup water
1⅔ cups sugar
6 tablespoons corn syrup
1 tablespoon rum

1. Melt the chocolate and butter very slowly in a heavy saucepan over low heat. Meanwhile, heat the water to boiling. When the chocolate and butter have melted, add the water and stir well.

2. Add the sugar and corn syrup and mix until smooth. Turn the heat up and stir until the mixture starts to boil; adjust the heat so that the sauce is just maintained at the boiling point. Allow the sauce to boil, without stirring, for 9 minutes.

A RUSSIAN BRUNCH

LEMON VODKA

BLINI WITH SOUR CREAM AND CAVIAR

SCOTCH SALMON

RUSSIAN PUMPERNICKEL

CHOCOLATE-DIPPED STRAWBERRIES

3. Remove the sauce from the heat and cool for 15 minutes. Stir in the rum. Serve the sauce warm over ice cream or profiteroles.

2½ cups

from THE SILVER PALATE NOTEBOOK

There are many ways to give a party. Just make sure yours is never dull. You're the life of it! Plan your party to one of three natural progressions:

♥ Serve from one table, beginning the evening with finger food, which is then refreshed with a spread of more substantial food; later clear the table to serve dessert and coffee.

♥ Have waiters serve finger food from trays while entrées and salads are served buffet style. Coffee and dessert may be served either way or not at all.

♥ Serve different courses in various rooms to create the element of surprise and encourage people to circulate.

" 'How long does getting thin take?' Pooh asked anxiously."

—A. A. MILNE, *WINNIE THE POOH*

CHOCOLATE PEANUT BUTTER BITES

¾ cup brown sugar
1 pound confectioners' sugar
8 tablespoons (1 stick) unsalted butter
2 cups peanut butter
1 cup unsalted peanuts
12 ounces semisweet chocolate chips
1 tablespoon unsalted butter

1. Mix the first 5 ingredients together. Pat into an ungreased jelly-roll pan, about 10 x 15 inches and 1 inch deep. Flatten the top with a rolling pin.

2. Melt the chocolate chips and butter in the top of a double boiler over simmering water. Spread the chocolate on the peanut butter mixture.

3. Chill for 15 to 20 minutes. Cut into bite-size squares. Remove from the pan. Serve chilled.

50 or more bites

CHOCOLATE TRUFFLES

¼ cup heavy cream
2 tablespoons Grand Marnier
6 ounces German's sweet chocolate, broken up
4 tablespoons (½ stick) unsalted butter, at room temperature
Powdered unsweetened cocoa

1. Boil the cream in a small heavy pan over medium heat until reduced to 2 tablespoons, about 5 minutes. Remove from the heat, stir in the Grand Marnier and chocolate, and return to low heat; stir until the chocolate melts.

2. Whisk in the butter. When the mixture is smooth, pour into a shallow bowl and refrigerate until firm, 40 minutes.

3. Scoop the chocolate up with a teaspoon and shape into 1-inch balls. Roll the truffle balls in the unsweetened cocoa.

4. Store the truffles, covered, in the refrigerator. Let the truffles stand at room temperature for 30 minutes before serving.

24 truffles

Variations: Substitute dark rum, Cognac, Kahlúa, framboise, or amaretto for the Grand Marnier.

HOT FROM THE OVEN

We all have memories of cakes, tarts, or pies cooling on the windowsills of our childhood or our dreams. The tradition of warm, freshly baked goods is one that we treasured at The Silver Palate. Our favorites in this category changed continually, but standards always remained high—cakes should be moist, pies fruit-filled and flaky, and fruit tarts and tortes as picture perfect as can be.

BISHOP'S CAKE

Our search for a truly moist pound cake ended here. Delicious, especially when served with a scoop of not-too-sweet sorbet.

1 cup (2 sticks) unsalted butter, plus extra for greasing the pan
2 cups unbleached all-purpose flour, plus extra for flouring the pan
2 cups sugar
1 tablespoon fresh lemon juice
1 teaspoon pure vanilla extract
5 eggs

1. Preheat the oven to 350°F. Grease and flour a 10-inch bundt pan.

2. Cream the butter in a mixing bowl and add the sugar gradually; beat until light and fluffy.

3. Sift the flour and add to the butter mixture. Stir just enough to blend.

4. Add the lemon juice and vanilla; stir well. Add the eggs, one at a time, mixing well after each addition.

5. Pour the batter into the prepared Bundt pan. Bake until a cake tester inserted into the center of the cake comes out clean, 1 hour. (After 30 minutes, cover the cake closely with aluminum foil.)

6. When the cake is done, cool in its pan on a cake rack for 20 minutes. Remove from the pan and cool completely.

8 to 10 portions

"A gourmet who looks at calories is like a tart who looks at her watch."

—JAMES BEARD

A DANISH BRUNCH

GRAVLAX WITH LEMON WEDGES

DILL MUSTARD SAUCE

PICKLED HERRING IN SOUR CREAM WITH CHOPPED FRESH DILL

BEET AND ROQUEFORT SALAD WITH WALNUTS

MINTY CUCUMBER SALAD

PÂTÉ MAISON

CRACKERS AND RYE BREAD WITH UNSALTED BUTTER

ORANGE CAKE

DANISH BLUE AND HAVARTI CHEESES

ORANGE CAKE

8 tablespoons (1 stick) unsalted butter, at room temperature, plus extra for greasing the pan
¾ cup sugar
2 eggs, separated
Grated zest of 2 oranges
1½ cups unbleached all-purpose flour
1½ teaspoons baking powder
¼ teaspoon baking soda
¼ teaspoon salt
½ cup fresh orange juice
Orange Glaze (recipe follows)

1. Preheat the oven to 350°F. Grease a 10-inch bundt pan.

2. Cream the butter in a mixing bowl and gradually add the sugar, beating until light and fluffy. Beat in the egg yolks, one at a time, and the orange zest.

3. Sift the flour with the baking powder, baking soda, and salt. Add the dry ingredients alternately with the orange juice to the batter.

4. Beat the egg whites until stiff and fold them into the batter.

5. Pour the batter into the prepared Bundt pan. Bake until the sides of the cake shrink away from the edges of the pan and a cake tester inserted in the center comes out clean, 30 to 35 minutes.

6. Cool for 10 minutes in the pan, unmold onto a rack, and drizzle with the orange glaze while warm. Cool before serving.

8 to 10 portions

ORANGE GLAZE

¼ cup fresh orange juice
¼ cup sugar

Combine the orange juice and sugar in a small saucepan and simmer gently for 5 minutes, stirring occasionally, until a light syrup forms. Remove from the heat and keep warm until using.

Enough glaze for 1 cake

ORANGE-POPPY SEED BUNDT CAKE

8 tablespoons (1 stick) unsalted butter, at room temperature, plus extra for greasing the pan
1½ cups sugar
4 eggs
2 cups unbleached all-purpose flour
2½ teaspoons baking powder
½ teaspoon salt
¾ cup milk
½ cup poppy seeds
1 teaspoon vanilla extract
Grated zest of 2 oranges
Double recipe of Orange Glaze (page 359)

1. Preheat the oven to 325°F. Grease a 10-inch bundt pan.

2. Cream the butter and sugar together in a mixing bowl until light and fluffy. Add the eggs, one at a time, beating well after each addition.

3. Sift the flour, baking powder, and salt together. Add to the creamed mixture alternately with the milk. Mix well after each addition.

4. Fold in the poppy seeds, vanilla, and grated orange zest. Pour the batter into the prepared Bundt pan.

5. Set on the center rack of the oven and bake until the edges shrink away slightly from the sides of the pan and a cake tester inserted into the center comes out clean, 50 to 60 minutes. Let the cake cool in the pan for 30 minutes before turning it out onto a cake rack.

6. When the cake has cooled, prick holes in it 1½ inches apart with a long toothpick and pour the orange glaze evenly over the top. Serve warm with ice cream on the side.

12 portions

GLAZED LEMON CAKE

1 cup (2 sticks) unsalted butter, at room temperature, plus extra for greasing the pan
2 cups sugar
3 eggs
3 cups unbleached all-purpose flour, sifted
½ teaspoon baking soda
½ teaspoon salt
1 cup buttermilk
2 tightly packed tablespoons grated lemon zest
2 tablespoons fresh lemon juice
Lemon Icing (recipe follows)

from THE SILVER PALATE NOTEBOOK

Have dinner in an unlikely place—the living room, in front of the fireplace; the kitchen, with all hands helping final assembly; the library; outdoors anytime it's comfortable. Transform a basement, a garage, or a poolroom into another world with fabrics, plants, flowers, or candlelight.

If you're lucky enough to have a pretty kitchen, use it as much as possible for entertaining. Involve your guests; serve from it at informal parties.

The perfect teatime: a cup of English Breakfast and a warm slice of Orange-Poppy Seed Bundt Cake.

1. Preheat the oven to 325°F. Grease a 10-inch tube pan.

2. Cream the butter and sugar together in a mixing bowl until light and fluffy. Beat in the eggs, one at a time, blending well after each addition.

3. Sift together the flour, baking soda, and salt. Stir the dry ingredients into the egg mixture alternately with the buttermilk, beginning and ending with the dry ingredients. Add the lemon zest and juice.

4. Pour the batter into the prepared tube pan. Set the pan on the center rack of the oven and bake until the cake pulls away from the sides of the pan and a tester inserted in the center comes out clean, 1 hour and 5 minutes.

5. Cool the cake in the pan, set on a rack, for 10 minutes. Remove the cake from the pan and spread on the icing at once, while the cake is still hot.

8 to 10 portions

"Looks can be deceiving—it's eating that's believing."

—JAMES THURBER

LEMON ICING

1 pound confectioners' sugar
8 tablespoons (1 stick) unsalted butter, at room temperature
3 tightly packed tablespoons grated lemon zest
½ cup fresh lemon juice

Cream the sugar and butter together in a mixing bowl. Mix in the lemon zest and juice; spread on the warm cake.

Enough icing for 1 cake

CHESTNUT CAKE

Chestnut Cake is light and moist, our favorite yellow cake.

Butter, for greasing the pans
2½ cups unbleached all-purpose flour, plus extra for flouring the pans
2 cups sugar
4 eggs
1 cup vegetable oil
1 cup dry white wine
½ teaspoon salt
2¼ teaspoons baking powder
1 teaspoon vanilla extract
Chocolate Icing (page 351), warm
¾ cup sweetened chestnut purée (see Note)
Whole chestnuts preserved in syrup, for garnish (optional; see Note)

1. Preheat the oven to 350°F. Grease and flour two 9-inch round layer cake pans.

2. Beat the sugar and eggs together in a mixing bowl, using an electric mixer, for 30 seconds on medium speed. Add the oil, wine, flour, salt, baking powder, and vanilla; beat for 1 minute.

3. Pour the batter into the prepared pans. Set on the center rack of the oven and bake until the cake has pulled away from the sides of the pan and a knife inserted in the center comes out clean, 30 minutes.

4. Let the cakes cool in the pans for 5 minutes. Turn them out on a rack and let cool for at least 2 hours before frosting.

5. Arrange 1 cake layer on a serving plate. Spread with the warm chocolate icing. Set the second layer on top of the first and spread with the chestnut purée. Cover the sides of the cake with the remaining icing. Decorate the top with well-drained preserved chestnuts if desired. Chill the cake for 45 minutes before serving.

8 or more portions

Note: Available at specialty food shops.

BANANA CAKE

½ cup (1 stick) unsalted butter, plus extra for greasing the pans
2 cups unbleached all-purpose flour, plus extra for flouring the pans
1 cup granulated sugar
3 eggs, separated
1 cup mashed ripe bananas
1 teaspoon baking powder
1 teaspoon baking soda
½ teaspoon salt
½ cup buttermilk
1 teaspoon vanilla extract
Cream Cheese Frosting (page 365)
1½ to 2 medium-size, firm but ripe bananas, sliced
1½ cups shelled chopped walnuts
Confectioners' sugar, for dusting the top

1. Preheat the oven to 350°F. Grease and flour two 9-inch layer cake pans.

2. Cream the butter and granulated sugar together in a mixing bowl. Add the egg yolks and beat well. Add the mashed bananas.

3. Sift the baking powder, baking soda, and salt together and add them to the butter mixture. Stir until just combined. Add the buttermilk and vanilla. Beat the egg whites to soft peaks. Fold gently into the batter.

4. Pour the batter into the prepared pans. Set on the center rack of the oven and bake until a cake tester inserted into the center comes out clean, 25 to 30 minutes. Cool in the pans on a rack for 10 minutes. Unmold and cool on a rack for 2 hours.

5. When cooled, place one layer on a serving plate and frost with the cream cheese frosting. Arrange slices of banana over the frosting; cover with the second layer and frost the top and sides of the cake.

6. Cover the sides of the cake with the chopped nuts, holding the nuts in your palm and pressing them firmly to the sides of the cake. Dust the top of the cake with confectioners' sugar.

8 or more portions

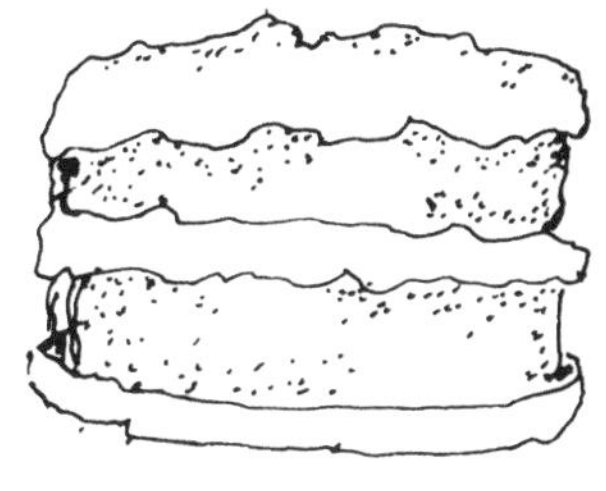

"Let them eat cake."
—MARIE ANTOINETTE

CARROT CAKE

In the beginning, Sheila's mother drove her famous carrot cakes down to Manhattan daily from her Connecticut kitchen. The cake became a Silver Palate classic; it may now become yours as well.

Butter, for greasing the pan
3 cups unbleached all-purpose flour
3 cups sugar
1 teaspoon salt
1 tablespoon baking soda
1 tablespoon ground cinnamon
1½ cups corn oil
4 large eggs, lightly beaten
1 tablespoon vanilla extract
1½ cups shelled walnuts, chopped
1½ cups shredded coconut
1⅓ cups puréed cooked carrots
¾ cup drained crushed pineapple
Cream Cheese Frosting (recipe follows)

1. Preheat the oven to 350°F. Grease two 9-inch springform pans.

2. Sift the dry ingredients into a bowl. Add the oil, eggs, and vanilla. Beat well. Fold in the walnuts, coconut, carrots, and pineapple.

3. Pour the batter into the prepared pans. Set on the center rack of the oven and bake until the edges have pulled away from the sides and a cake tester inserted in the center comes out clean, 50 minutes.

4. Cool on a cake rack for 3 hours. Fill and frost the cake with the cream cheese frosting.

10 to 12 portions

CREAM CHEESE FROSTING

8 ounces cream cheese, at room temperature
6 tablespoons (¾ stick) unsalted butter, at room temperature
3 cups confectioners' sugar
1 teaspoon vanilla extract
Juice of ½ lemon (optional)

1. Cream together the cream cheese and butter in a mixing bowl.

2. Slowly sift in the confectioners' sugar and continue beating until fully incorporated. The mixture should be free of lumps.

3. Stir in the vanilla, and lemon juice if desired.

Frosting for a 2-layer cake

PEACH CAKE

CAKE

4 tablespoons (½ stick) unsalted butter, plus extra for greasing the skillet
¼ cup sugar
1 egg
1 cup unbleached all-purpose flour
1½ teaspoons baking powder
½ teaspoon salt
¼ cup milk
3 ripe peaches, peeled and sliced

TOPPING

½ cup sugar
½ teaspoon ground cinnamon
¼ teaspoon grated nutmeg
4 tablespoons (½ stick) unsalted butter

Heavy cream, for serving

1. Preheat the oven to 350°F. Grease a heavy 9-inch skillet well.

2. Prepare the cake: Cream the butter and sugar in a mixing bowl until light and fluffy. Beat in the egg.

3. Sift the dry ingredients together. Beat half into the creamed mixture; beat in half of the milk. Repeat, beating well.

4. Pour the batter into the prepared skillet. Arrange the peach slices on top of the batter. Bake for 25 minutes.

5. Meanwhile, cut the ingredients for the topping together in a small bowl with a fork. After the cake has baked for 25 minutes, open the oven and quickly crumble the topping over the peaches.

6. Close the oven and bake until the cake is firm and has pulled away from the edges of the skillet, another 8 minutes. Serve warm, accompanied by a pitcher of heavy cream.

8 portions

MAY DAY PICNIC

ASSORTED CRUDITÉS WITH *TAPENADE DIP AND PESTO MAYONNAISE*

COLD ROAST VEAL

BEET AND ROQUEFORT SALAD WITH WALNUTS

FRENCH BREAD AND BUTTER

PEACH CAKE

VANILLA ICE CREAM

ICED ESPRESSO

COCONUT CAKE

2 layers of yellow cake, baked and cooled (see Chestnut Cake, page 362)
2 cups sour cream
1 teaspoon vanilla extract
5 cups shredded coconut
1 cup sifted confectioners' sugar

1. Prepare the chestnut cake through Step 4. Mix the sour cream, vanilla, and coconut in a mixing bowl. Blend well. Add the sugar to the coconut mixture and mix thoroughly.

2. Place one cake layer on a cake platter and spread the top with half of the coconut mixture. Place the second layer on top of the first and spread with the remaining coconut mixture, leaving the sides of the cake unfrosted.

8 or more portions

LINZERTORTE

1 cup plus 4 tablespoons (2½ sticks) unsalted butter, at room temperature
1 cup granulated sugar
1½ teaspoons grated lemon zest
2 eggs
1¼ cups unbleached all-purpose flour
½ teaspoon ground cinnamon
¼ teaspoon ground cloves
¼ teaspoon salt
1¼ cups blanched almonds, finely ground
⅔ cup raspberry preserves
Confectioners' sugar, for dusting the top

1. Preheat the oven to 325°F.

2. Cream the butter and sugar together in a mixing bowl until light and fluffy. Add the grated zest and eggs and mix well.

3. Sift the flour, cinnamon, cloves, and salt together. Add the flour mixture and almonds to the butter mixture and blend thoroughly.

4. Pat half of this mixture evenly into the bottom of a 9-inch removable-bottom tart pan. Spread the preserves to within ½ inch of the sides.

5. Transfer the remaining dough to a pastry bag and form a ring of dough around the edge of the tart, then squeeze out a lattice crust on top.

6. Set the tart pan on the center rack of the oven and bake until the lattice is evenly browned and the preserves are bubbling, 50 minutes. Sprinkle the top lightly with confectioners' sugar. Serve warm or cold.

6 to 8 portions

"I'm glad I was not born before tea."

—SYDNEY SMITH

PECAN PIE

Golden and lush, but not too sweet, our Pecan Pie is a taste of the Old South.

9-inch unbaked Piecrust (page 411)
4 eggs
1 cup dark brown sugar
¾ cup light corn syrup
½ teaspoon salt
¼ cup (½ stick) unsalted butter, melted
1 teaspoon vanilla extract
2 cups shelled pecans, chopped
⅓ cup shelled pecan halves

1. Preheat the oven to 400°F. Line a 9-inch pie pan with the pastry.

2. Beat the eggs well in a large bowl. Add the brown sugar, corn syrup, salt, melted butter, and vanilla, and mix thoroughly.

3. Sprinkle the chopped pecans in the pastry-lined pan. Pour the egg mixture over the pecans. Arrange the pecan halves around the edge of the filling next to the crust for decoration.

4. Set the pan on the center rack of the oven and bake for 10 minutes. Reduce the heat to 325°F and bake until set, 25 to 30 minutes longer.

5. Remove from the oven and let cool to room temperature before serving.

8 portions

PUMPKIN PIE

Save room for a piece of this one.

3 eggs
⅓ cup granulated sugar
⅓ cup light brown sugar
2 cups canned puréed pumpkin
1 teaspoon ground ginger
1½ teaspoons ground cinnamon
½ teaspoon ground cloves
½ teaspoon ground allspice
¼ teaspoon ground cardamom
Pinch of salt
¾ cup heavy cream
¾ cup half-and-half
½ recipe Piecrust (page 411)
Pecan halves, for garnish

1. Preheat the oven to 450°F.

2. Beat the eggs and both sugars together in a mixing bowl until light and fluffy. Stir in the pumpkin purée, spices, and salt and mix thoroughly. Stir in the cream and half-and-half.

3. Roll out the pastry on a lightly floured work surface and line a 9-inch pie pan with it; trim and crimp the edges. Pour in the filling.

4. Bake the pie for 8 minutes, then reduce the heat to 325°F and bake until the filling is set (a knife inserted in the center will come out clean), another 40 to 45 minutes.

5. Arrange the pecan halves decoratively around the edge, pressing them lightly into the warm filling. Arrange another 5 pecans in a flower pattern in the center of the pie. Cool completely before cutting.

6 portions

AFTER-DINNER COFFEES

Try these delicious combinations after special dinners, when something more festive than regular coffee is called for.

- Kahlúa Coffee: Add 1 ounce of Kahlúa to a cup of rich coffee; top with whipped cream and sprinkle with grated orange zest.
- Almond Coffee: Add 1 ounce of amaretto liqueur to a cup of hot coffee, and top with a dollop of whipped cream and toasted almond slivers.
- Brandy Coffee: Combine 2 tablespoons sugar and 1 ounce of brandy with a cup of hot coffee; stir in 1 teaspoon unsalted butter and garnish with a cinnamon stick.

"I prefer the errors of enthusiasm to the indifference of wisdom."

—ANATOLE FRANCE

Featuring the best of fall flavors, Pumpkin Pie.

OLD-FASHIONED LEMON PIE

This one is even better than the one you remember your grandmother making.

9-inch unbaked Piecrust (page 411)
1¼ cups milk
1⅛ cups sugar
3 tablespoons cornstarch
3 egg yolks, slightly beaten
Juice of 3 lemons
Grated zest of 2 lemons
1 teaspoon vanilla extract
1 cup lemon marmalade
3 kiwis, peeled and thinly sliced

1. Preheat the oven to 325°F. Line a 9-inch pie pan with the pastry.

2. Heat the milk in the top of a double boiler over simmering water. Mix the sugar with the cornstarch and whisk into the milk. Add the beaten egg yolks. Stir well and cook for 3 minutes. Pour in the lemon juice, zest, and vanilla. Blend thoroughly.

3. Pour the filling into the pastry-lined pan. Set on the center rack of the oven and bake until set, 25 minutes.

4. Cool the pie 10 minutes. Melt the lemon marmalade over low heat and brush a thin layer of it over the surface of the pie. Arrange the sliced kiwis in an overlapping layer to cover the top of the pie completely. Brush again, generously, with the remaining marmalade. Cool completely before cutting.

6 to 8 portions

KITE-FLYING PICNIC

PÂTÉ DE CAMPAGNE WITH WALNUTS

SALADE NIÇOISE

MARINATED CHÈVRES

FRENCH BREAD AND *RAVIGOTE BUTTER*

OLD FASHIONED LEMON PIE

FRESH STRAWBERRIES

HARVEST TART

1 cup pitted prunes
1 cup dried apricots
1 cup chopped peeled apples
½ cup golden raisins
⅓ cup sugar
½ cup shelled walnut halves
4 tablespoons (½ stick) unsalted butter, melted
⅔ cup Grand Marnier
Double recipe of Sweet Buttery Tart Crust (page 411)
1 egg, beaten

1. Preheat the oven to 350°F.

2. Combine the prunes, apricots, apples, and raisins in a heavy saucepan. Add water just to cover, set over moderate heat, and simmer until the fruit is tender, about 20 minutes. Drain the fruit thoroughly and chop.

3. Return the fruit to the saucepan, add the sugar, walnuts, melted butter, and Grand Marnier, and simmer for 5 minutes, stirring occasionally. Cool to room temperature.

4. Roll out half of the pastry dough on a lightly floured board and use it to line a 9-inch pie pan. Spoon the filling into the pastry-lined pan, mounding it slightly. Trim the excess crust, leaving about 1 inch all around.

5. Roll out the remaining dough to a 10½-inch round and cut into ½-inch strips. Arrange the strips lattice fashion over the filling, trim the ends, and turn up the edge of the bottom crust over the ends of the strips; crimp decoratively. Brush the lattice top lightly with the beaten egg.

6. Bake the tart until the top is golden brown and the filling is bubbling, 30 to 35 minutes. Serve warm or cool.

6 to 8 portions

"It is, in my view, the duty of an apple to be crisp and crunchable, but a pear should have such a texture as leads to silent consumption."

—EDWARD BUNYARD, *THE ANATOMY OF DESSERT*

ALMOND TART

CRUST

¾ cup unbleached all-purpose flour, sifted
1 tablespoon sugar
5 tablespoons unsalted butter, cold
½ teaspoon vanilla extract
2 to 3 teaspoons water, or as needed

FILLING

½ cup sugar
3 tablespoons apricot preserves
¾ cup sliced blanched almonds
½ cup heavy cream
2 tablespoons amaretto liqueur
¼ teaspoon salt

1. Prepare the crust: Mix the flour and sugar together. Working quickly, cut in the cold butter with 2 knives or a pastry blender until the mixture resembles oatmeal. Add the vanilla and 2 teaspoons of the water and toss with a fork until the dough just holds together. (Add more water, a few drops at a time, if necessary.) Do not overwork.

2. Press the dough evenly into an 8-inch removable-bottom tart pan. Chill in the refrigerator for 45 minutes.

3. Preheat the oven to 400°F.

4. Line the chilled dough with aluminum foil and fill with dried beans. Bake in the lower part of the oven for 8 minutes. Remove the foil and beans and bake 5 minutes longer. Remove from the oven.

5. Make the filling: Stir the sugar and apricot preserves together in a bowl, mixing well. Add the remaining ingredients, blending thoroughly. Pour into the partially baked shell.

6. Set on the center rack of the oven and bake until the filling top is golden brown, 25 to 30 minutes. Cool and serve.

10 to 12 portions

"He may do it with a better grace but I do it more natural."

—WILLIAM SHAKESPEARE, *TWELFTH NIGHT*

PINWHEEL FRUIT TART

4 kiwis
1½ cups Pastry Cream (page 410)
9-inch prebaked Sweet Buttery Tart Crust (page 411)
1 pint raspberries, picked over
1 pint strawberries, rinsed, stemmed, patted dry, and halved lengthwise
Red Currant Glaze (page 421), warmed

1. Peel the kiwis and slice thin.

2. Spread the pastry cream in the cooled tart shell.

3. Make a pinwheel design over the cream, arranging each fruit in patches, first using the raspberries, then the strawberries (cut sides down), then layered slices of kiwis. Repeat with the remaining fruit.

4. Brush the fruit with the red currant glaze. Serve within 2 to 3 hours.

8 to 10 portions

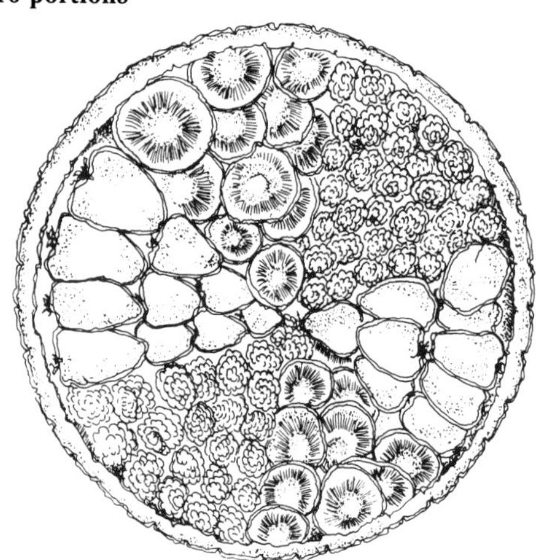

COMFORTING CONCLUSIONS

These are the sweets that soothe the soul. The ones that we crave when the grown-up world's become particularly grumpy or it's a rainy Saturday and we're dreaming of a cozy afternoon by the fireplace. These are sweets to eat with a spoon. Each always brings back wonderful memories.

"[The kitchen] will be, as it should be, the most comforting and comfortable room in the house."

—ELIZABETH DAVID

BREAD PUDDING

A childhood favorite, with a very adult sauce. This is an adaptation of a recipe given to us by Alzina Pierce of the Bon Ton Restaurant in New Orleans, more proof that a recipe is certainly a living thing.

1 loaf of stale French bread
1 quart milk
10 tablespoons (1¼ sticks) unsalted butter, at room temperature, plus extra for greasing the baking dish
4 eggs
1½ cups granulated sugar
2 tablespoons vanilla extract
1 cup raisins
1 cup confectioners' sugar
¼ cup whiskey

1. Crumble the bread into a bowl. Pour the milk over it and let stand for 1 hour.

2. Preheat the oven to 325°F. Grease a 9 x 13 x 2-inch baking dish with 1 to 2 tablespoons of the butter.

3. In another bowl, beat together 3 eggs, the granulated sugar, and the vanilla extract. Stir this mixture into the bread mixture. Stir in the raisins.

4. Pour into the prepared baking dish, place on the center rack of the oven, and bake until browned and set, about 1 hour and 10 minutes. Cool to room temperature.

TODAY'S TIMES

When we reflect on life in the city, we're often reminded of Russell Baker's column in the May 30, 1980, issue of *The New York Times.* Entitled "Elephant's Eye High," the article asks, "Do you ever wish you had it to do over again, folks? Do you wish you'd have taken up the kind of work where you could call people 'folks,' instead of 'Sir' and 'Deadbeat' and 'Big Shot' and 'Meathead'? The kind of life where you say 'By golly!' and 'There's a heap of goodness in this old world of ours'? Remember where your granddaddy was sitting when he was advising you not to go off to the city? In a rocking chair. Remember where the rocking chair was situated? On the front porch. You don't have a rocking chair, do you? Don't have a porch either, I bet."

Well, for all the things we hanker after—sitting on the porch swing at sunset, smelling the honeysuckle, whistling down the lane—think of all the things we've gained. The trick is holding on to a little of each.

Crème Brulée, with its candylike topping, always seems special.

5. To make the sauce, stir 8 tablespoons butter and the confectioners' sugar together in the top of a double boiler over simmering water until the sugar is dissolved and the mixture is very hot. Remove from the heat. Beat the remaining egg well and whisk it into the sugar mixture. Remove the pan from the base and continue beating until the sauce has cooled to room temperature. Add the whiskey to taste.

6. Preheat the broiler. To serve, cut the pudding into squares and transfer each square to a heatproof serving dish. In batches, set the dishes on a baking sheet. Spoon the whiskey sauce over the pudding and run under the broiler until bubbling.

8 to 10 portions

CREME BRULEE

Long a favorite at The Silver Palate, this is a dessert that, while comforting, can also end a dinner party elegantly.

2⅔ cups heavy cream
⅔ cup milk
¼ cup sugar
3 whole eggs
3 egg yolks
1 teaspoon vanilla extract
¾ cup light brown sugar

1. Preheat the oven to 300°F.

2. Heat the cream, milk, and sugar in a heavy saucepan to almost boiling. In a separate bowl, beat the whole eggs and the egg yolks together well.

3. Gradually whisk the heated mixture into the eggs, then return the mixture to the saucepan. Cook over medium heat, stirring constantly with a wooden spoon, until the custard coats the back of the spoon, 3 to 4 minutes; remove from the heat. Stir in the vanilla.

4. Pour the custard into 6 individual custard dishes or into 1 shallow baking dish about 9 inches across. Set the dishes or dish in a large pan and place on the center rack of the oven. Carefully pour hot water into the outer pan to come level with the custard.

5. Bake until the center of the custard is set, 35 to 45 minutes. When done, remove the custard from the water bath and cool. Cover and chill.

6. A few hours before serving, preheat the broiler.

7. Sift the brown sugar evenly over the top of the custards, spreading it to the edges. Set the custards on a baking sheet and place under the broiler as close to the heat as possible. Broil until browned but not burned, about 1½ minutes. Watch closely. Remove and chill.

6 portions

PEACH COBBLER

A dessert that brings memories of summer or that celebrates it in the moment—a perfect sweet to cozy up to after beachcombing on an unseasonably cool day.

You can use yellow or white peaches for this dish, or a combination. The almond extract heightens the flavor of either.

4 cups peeled and sliced ripe peaches
⅔ cup plus 3 tablespoons sugar
1 teaspoon grated lemon zest
1 tablespoon fresh lemon juice
¼ teaspoon almond extract
1½ cups unbleached all-purpose flour
1 tablespoon baking powder
½ teaspoon salt
⅓ cup vegetable shortening
1 egg, lightly beaten
¼ cup milk
1 cup heavy cream, chilled
3 to 4 tablespoons peach brandy or peach cordial

1. Preheat the oven to 400°F. Butter a 2-quart baking dish.

2. Arrange the peaches in the baking dish. Sprinkle with the ⅔ cup sugar, the lemon zest and juice, and the almond extract.

3. Bake for 20 minutes.

4. While the peaches are baking, sift the flour, 1 tablespoon of the remaining sugar, the baking powder, and salt together into a bowl. Cut in the shortening until the mixture resembles cornmeal. Combine the beaten egg and milk and mix into the dry ingredients until just combined.

5. Remove the peaches from the oven and quickly drop the dough by large spoonfuls over the surface. Sprinkle with the remaining 2 tablespoons sugar. Return to the oven until the top is firm and golden brown, 15 to 20 minutes.

6. Whip the cream to soft peaks. Flavor with the peach brandy to taste.

7. Serve the cobbler warm, accompanied by the whipped cream.

4 to 6 portions

"I remember his showing me how to eat a peach by building a little white mountain of sugar and then dipping the peach into it."

—MARY McCARTHY

GINGERBREAD

Warmly aromatic and inviting yet not too sweet, gingerbread just might have inspired the term "comfort food."

Butter, for greasing the pan
1⅔ cups unbleached all-purpose flour, plus extra for flouring the pan
1¼ teaspoons baking soda
1½ teaspoons ground ginger
¾ teaspoon ground cinnamon
¾ teaspoon salt
1 egg, lightly beaten
½ cup sugar
½ cup molasses
½ cup boiling water
½ cup vegetable oil
Lemon Glaze (recipe follows)

1. Preheat the oven to 350°F. Grease and flour a 9-inch square baking pan.

2. Sift the dry ingredients together into a mixing bowl. Add the egg, sugar, and molasses. Mix well.

3. Pour the boiling water and the oil over the mixture. Stir thoroughly until smooth.

4. Pour the batter into the prepared pan. Set on the center rack of the oven and bake until the top springs back when touched and the edges have pulled away slightly from the sides of the pan, 35 to 40 minutes.

5. While the gingerbread is still hot, pour the glaze over the top and cool in the pan, set on a rack.

12 portions

"Had I but one penny in the world, thou shouldst have it for gingerbread."

—WILLIAM SHAKESPEARE, *LOVE'S LABOR'S LOST*

LEMON GLAZE

⅔ cup confectioners' sugar
3 tablespoons fresh lemon juice

Sift the sugar into a bowl; add the lemon juice and mix well.
Enough for 1 gingerbread

CAPPUCCINO ICE

A mellower variation on the classic Italian espresso ice.

3 cups prepared strong coffee, made at least partially with espresso coffee
1 cup half-and-half
1 cup sugar

1. Combine the ingredients in a saucepan and set over medium heat. Stir constantly until the mixture is about to boil and all the sugar is dissolved.

2. Cool to room temperature, pour into a shallow pan (an 8-inch square cake pan is ideal), and freeze.

3. The mixture will take from 3 to 6 hours to freeze and, because of its relatively low sugar content, will be very solid. Before serving, set it in the refrigerator for 30 minutes to temper the texture slightly.

1 quart, at least 6 portions

SUMMER SUPPER BY THE POOL

ASPARAGUS SPEARS WITH *SESAME MAYONNAISE, GREEN HERB DIPPING SAUCE, AND AÏOLI SAUCE*

GREEK LAMB AND EGGPLANT SALAD

LINGUINE WITH TOMATOES AND BASIL

AN ALL-ARUGULA SALAD WITH OUR FAVORITE VINAIGRETTE

PUMPERNICKEL BREAD

CAMPARI ORANGE, LEMON, AND CAPPUCCINO ICES

LEMON ICE

2 cups strained fresh lemon juice
2 cups water
2 cups sugar

1. Combine the lemon juice with the water in a small saucepan. Stir in the sugar.

2. Set the saucepan over medium heat. Bring to a boil, stirring constantly, then remove from the heat and cool to room temperature.

3. Pour the lemon mixture into a shallow pan (an 8-inch square cake tin is ideal) and set it in the freezer.

4. The ice will be ready in 3 to 6 hours, depending on the efficiency of the freezer. Because of the high sugar content, this ice will usually be soft enough to serve, so you may as well make it in advance of the day you'll be needing it.

1 quart of very intense ice, at least 6 portions

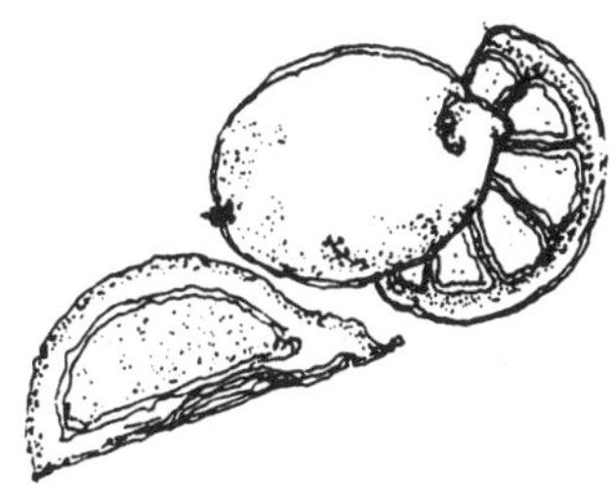

CAMPARI ORANGE ICE

Another afternoon cooler, this one with the special taste of Campari, Italy's bright red, bitter apéritif.

3 cups strained fresh orange juice
1 cup Campari
Juice of 1 lemon
1 cup sugar

1. Combine all the ingredients in a heavy saucepan and set over medium heat. Stir constantly until the mixture is about to boil and all the sugar is dissolved.

2. Cool to room temperature. Pour into a shallow pan (an 8-inch square cake pan is ideal), and set in the freezer.

3. The mixture will take from 3 to 6 hours to freeze and, because of its relatively low sugar content, will be very solid. To serve, set in the refrigerator for 30 minutes to temper the texture slightly.

1 quart, at least 6 portions

DATE-NUT PUDDING

Traditionally served at your family's winter holiday dinners, this pudding will warm your heart.

8 tablespoons (1 stick) unsalted butter, plus extra for greasing the baking dish
1 cup sugar
2 eggs, beaten
1 cup milk
1½ tablespoons unbleached all-purpose flour
1½ teaspoons baking powder
1 cup pitted dates, coarsely chopped
1 cup shelled walnuts, coarsely chopped
1 cup heavy cream, chilled

1. Preheat the oven to 325°F. Grease well a 9 x 13 x 2-inch glass or ceramic baking dish.

2. Cream the butter in a mixing bowl, gradually adding the sugar, until light and fluffy.

3. Add the eggs, milk, flour, and baking powder; mix well. Fold in the dates and walnuts.

4. Turn into the prepared baking dish and place on the center rack of the oven. Bake until set, 50 to 60 minutes.

5. Serve slightly warm or at room temperature with a spoonful of the cream, whipped to soft peaks.

8 portions

"The proof of the pudding is in the eating."

—MIGUEL DE CERVANTES, *DON QUIXOTE*

POACHED FRUIT

Fruits poached in a syrup gain flavor and sophistication, as well as easing the pressure on a busy cook. Light and beautiful, they may wait in your refrigerator for 3 or 4 days until you are ready to serve them.

1½ cups sugar
Piece of a cinnamon stick
6 whole cloves
½ vanilla bean
Zest of 1 lemon, cut into fine julienne
1 pound fruit of your choice

1. Combine the sugar, cinnamon stick, cloves, vanilla bean, and lemon zest in 1 quart of water.

2. Simmer for 10 minutes.

3. Add 1 pound fruit of your choice (apples and pears should be peeled, cored, and quartered; peaches and apricots should be poached whole and peeled only after they are cool). Bring the syrup back to a simmer and cook the fruit gently until the fruit is tender but not mushy, about 12 minutes. Do not overcook!

4. Remove the pan from the heat and let the fruit cool in the syrup.

5. The fruit is now ready to be served, but can be stored in the poaching liquid in the refrigerator.

4 portions

Variations:

♥ Substitute a fruity red wine such as Beaujolais or Zinfandel for half of the water when poaching pears. Serve in small bowls with a spoonful or two of chilled syrup, and sprinkle with crumbled amaretti.

♥ Substitute dry white wine for half of the water when poaching apricots or peaches. Top with chilled raspberry sauce and garnish with whole raspberries and fresh mint.

♥ Prepare the syrup using apple cider instead of water. Soak a handful of raisins in dark rum for 1 hour. Poach apples in the syrup, add the raisins to the syrup while it is still warm, and spoon over the warm apples. Sprinkle with pecans to taste.

♥ A secret of many French chefs is to add 6 to 10 whole black peppercorns to the poaching syrup for extra flavor and spiciness.

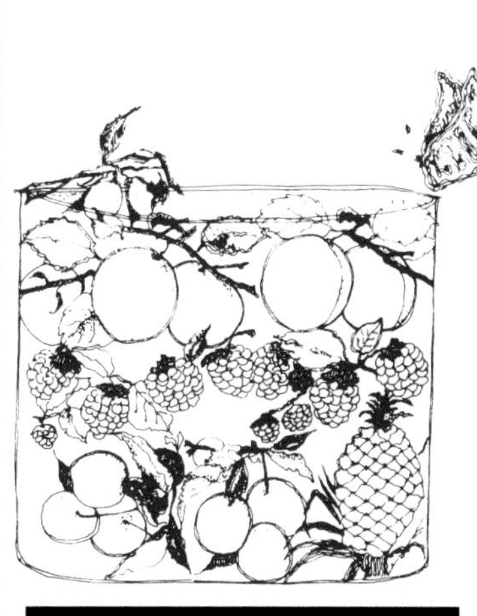

THE GRAND FINALE

After-dinner drinks have always been popular in America. Now, with our new desire to end a meal less heavily, Cognac, Armagnac, fruit brandies, or eaux-de-vie brandies made from grape pomace such as marc and grappa are replacing fruit liqueurs in popularity.

A true fruit brandy, or eau-de-vie, must be distilled entirely from the fruit itself; the result is a dry, often colorless liquid whose aroma bursts forth from the uncorked bottle. It's almost as if you've been transported to an orchard or a berry field.

Some prefer these brandies served ice cold. We like them at room temperature, but in any case, offer them in your finest tiny glasses. They are expensive, since they are the pure essence of the fruit, but worth experiencing.

ESSENCE	FRUIT	ORIGIN	NOTES
Armagnac	Saint-Emilion, Meslier, and Picpoule grapes	Gers and Landes, France	Armagnac is amber to brown in color, depending on its age. The smoother and more richly flavored are aged five years or longer in oak.
Applejack	Apple	United States	An American favorite, but without the rich body of Calvados.
California Brandy	Thompson Seedless grape	California	These pale gold brandies are not yet the equal of the European, but are pleasant to sip and excellent for cooking.
Calvados	Apple	Normandy, France	Rich in color and crisp apple flavor, it reflects the sophistication of aging.
Cognac	Saint-Emilion, Folle Blanche, and Colombard grapes	France	Cognacs are brandies; not all brandies are Cognacs. A true Cognac is made only in the Cognac region, by a lengthy aging process. The resulting amber liquid is worth the price.
Grappa	Grape pomace	Piedmont and Friuli, Italy	A by-product of the wine-making process. It has a fiery and biting flavor.
Fraise	Strawberry	France	An eau-de-vie that is not sweet, but fully fruit-flavored.
Framboise	Raspberry	France	Made from the essence of 40 pounds of fruit per bottle, it fairly explodes with the smell and flavor of raspberries.
Marc de Bourgogne	Grape pomace	Burgundy, France	Another by-product of the wine-making process; it is often considered harsh and "plebeian," but in France it is the favorite of the rural gentry.
Mirabelle	Yellow plum	Lorraine and Alsace, France	Clear and delicate—this is a spectacular sipping brandy.
Pear Brandy or Poire Williams	Williams pear	France, Switzerland, Germany	An eau-de-vie with the full, elegant flavor of pears. An experience.

THE BRUNCH BUNCH

RISE AND SHINE

Brunch has become many Americans' favorite way to fill a weekend day with special people. Whether you're a late sleeper or an avid early morning jogger, whether you've traveled to church or just out to get the great thick Sunday paper, whether you're in the mood for a football game or chamber music, brunch is just the thing for that unstructured day called Sunday. (And we think Saturdays are deserving of some special treatment, too.) Brunch can be for any number, but make it light, informal, and pretty. A buffet allows people to come and go comfortably as they please, indoors or out. For two or twenty, brunch should be light and lingering, allowing the day to drift where it may. Make sure you have enough copies of the paper to keep everyone happy!

HOW TO MAKE AN OMELET

While it's true that the simplest dishes are often the most difficult to make, we think there is an unnecessary amount of fuss made concerning omelet making. At the bottom line, an omelet is nothing more than eggs, butter, and body English. Fillings, toppings, and garnishes can enhance the finished product, but won't disguise an overbeaten, overcooked, or poorly formed disaster. In other words, it all begins with the egg and ends with technique. Once you have managed to turn out a perfectly cooked, golden-brown oval of an omelet, the rest will take care of itself.

There are as many omelet techniques as there are cooks; after a failure or two, you will arrive at your own. Our advice is to make an omelet a day for a week; like getting to Carnegie Hall, omelet making requires practice. Sooner or later the particular combination of timing, wrist action, and intuition that works for you will produce a perfect omelet. Here, as a guideline, is our no-nonsense approach to omelet making.

THE PAN

A lot of mystique is attached to the omelet pan. Many cooks require a certain kind or weight of pan, some swearing that it must be steel, or cast iron, or aluminum, or coated with a nonstick surface. And more than one professional we know insists that the pan used for omelets must never be washed.

In our experience, however, the size of the pan is the only critical factor. For a 2- or 3-egg omelet, sufficient for 1 portion, we recommend a 5- to 6-inch skillet. Small pans give a thick and often undercooked omelet, while too large a pan gives a thin omelet that is easily overcooked.

As far as the actual construction of the pan is concerned, some of the best omelets we ever made were cooked in a heavy, black, straight-sided cast-iron skillet over an open fire. Other favorites include a #24 iron French chef's crepe pan and an inexpensive nonstick department-store skillet. We wash them when they need it, we try not to scratch their cooking surfaces, and we oil the chef's pan occasionally to keep it from rusting. The rest is hoopla.

THE EGGS

Use the freshest eggs possible. If you have access to new-laid eggs, by all means use them. City dwellers, however, will usually have to rely on the nearest high-volume supermarket, where a steady turnover of dated eggs is some assurance of freshness.

Crack the eggs into a small bowl. Cold eggs are harder to overcook; room-temperature eggs make a slightly fluffier omelet—take your choice. Sprinkle in a pinch of salt and beat the eggs briefly with a fork. Do not overbeat; your goal here is to mingle the whites and yolks so lightly that the finished omelet will have striations of both. Homogenizing the texture of the eggs produces a tougher omelet. Grind in a little black pepper and set the eggs aside.

A SUREFIRE WAY TO COOK BACON

Place thick slices of bacon on an aluminum foil-covered baking sheet (the foil makes cleaning up easier). Bake in a 350°F oven for about 6 minutes. Turn and bake for another 2 or 3 minutes. No spatters, and the bacon is flat and perfect every time.

THE OMELET TECHNIQUE

1. Set the pan on the burner. Have at hand a tablespoon of softened butter, a fork, the prepared eggs, and the plate you plan to serve the omelet on.

2. Turn the heat under the skillet to medium-high and drop in the butter. It's worth noting that from here on out it will probably take you longer to read the rest of this recipe than to make the omelet. The butter will melt, begin to foam, and then the foam will subside. The pan is ready for the eggs.

3. Pour the eggs in all at once, take the skillet handle with one hand and the fork with the other, and begin gently stirring the eggs with the flat of the fork as if you were scrambling them. Raise and lower the skillet from the burner to control the heat.

4. As the bottom of the omelet begins to set, lift it with the fork to allow the uncooked egg to run underneath. When the eggs are almost done to your liking, return the skillet to the burner, shut off the heat, and arrange any filling you like across the center of the omelet at a right angle to the handle of the pan.

5. Now grip the skillet handle with your palm upward, raise the handle, and bring the far edge of the skillet over the edge of the serving plate. With the fork, start rolling the upper edge of the omelet at the same time you bring the handle of the skillet farther over the plate. You have just tipped and rolled the omelet out of the pan at the same time.

Wet omelet fillings and sauces are better added after the omelet has been rolled. Cut a short, deep slit in the top of

the omelet, spread it open slightly, and spoon in the filling or sauce; pour some over the top of the omelet.

6. Don't worry if the omelet is untidy—it will still taste good and you'll gain control as you practice. One professional chef's trick we like is to place a paper towel over the rolled omelet and use the palms of both hands gently to shape the omelet into the classic oval. This also blots up excess butter. Garnish the omelet and serve immediately.

FILLING THE PERFECT OMELET

The possibilities are endless, and improvisation is the name of the game. An omelet should be generously filled but not grossly overstuffed; about ¼ to ⅓ cup of filling is ample for each 3-egg omelet. Here are some of our favorites to get you started.

♥ *Apple and Cheddar Omelet:* Dice unpeeled tart apples, sauté in butter until golden, fold into the omelet together with diced Vermont or other sharp Cheddar cheese.

♥ *Creamed Mushroom Omelet:* Prepare and roll the omelet; cut a short, deep slit in the top and spoon in hot Creamed Mushrooms (page 209).

♥ *Ratatouille Omelet:* Roll hot Ratatouille (page 202) into the omelet.

♥ *Omelet Grandmère:* Fill the omelet with crisp-cooked bacon, and sautéed diced potatoes and sweet onion. Lavish with chopped fresh parsley.

♥ *Ricotta-Tomato Omelet:* Flavor fresh ricotta cheese to taste with basil, minced garlic, and grated Parmigiano-Reggiano cheese; fold into the omelet and top with hot Tomato Coulis (page 232).

♥ *Sausage Ragoût Omelet:* For a hearty suppertime omelet, fold hot Sausage Ragoût (page 163) into the omelet. Sprinkle with grated Parmigiano-Reggiano cheese before serving.

♥ *Omelet Normandy:* Fold hot Sautéed Apples with Calvados (page 328) into the omelet; top with a dollop of Crème Fraîche (page 414).

♥ *Watercress Omelet:* Wilt fresh watercress briefly in hot butter. Lift with a slotted spoon and roll into the omelet.

♥ *SoHo Omelet:* Combine crisp-cooked bacon, grated sharp Cheddar cheese, and tender leaves of raw spinach and roll the mixture into the omelet. The heat of the eggs will gently cook the spinach while leaving its fresh taste intact.

♥ *Southwest Omelet:* Lay avocado slices or guacamole or Avocado Dip (page 26) in the omelet and cover with a spoonful of salsa before rolling.

♥ *Dinner Omelet:* Fold sautéed bacon and diced tomatoes, red onions, baked ham, and red bell peppers into the omelet. Top with a dollop of sour cream and a sprinkling of snipped fresh chives.

♥ *Deli Omelet:* Fill the omelet with diced ripe tomatoes and lightly browned kosher salami.

♥ *Springtime Omelet:* For a delicate brunch, fill the omelet with coarsely chopped roasted tomatoes and 1-inch pieces of steamed or roasted asparagus. Sprinkle with grated fresh mozzarella.

♥ *Jam Omelet:* Dollop in a spoonful of your favorite jam or preserve and another of fresh ricotta cheese before serving.

Danish Mary Ice is a refreshing way to begin a lazy day.

DANISH MARY ICE

This icy sorbet with its kick of aquavit is a perfect way to start a summer brunch.

2 cups tomato juice
6 ounces aquavit
½ cup fresh lemon juice, more or less
2 egg whites
1 teaspoon salt
Freshly ground black pepper, to taste
Fresh dill, for garnish

1. Process all the ingredients except the fresh dill together in a food processor. Taste and correct the seasonings.

AQUAVIT

Aquavit is distilled from grain or potatoes. Like gin, it is a flavored alcohol; herbs, spices, and seeds (most commonly caraway, fennel, or dill) contribute flavor. It is best ice cold from the freezer and traditionally is served in small glasses alongside large glasses of cold beer.

CREPE FILLINGS

- Apples, walnuts, and raisins sautéed in butter and sprinkled with cinnamon, sugar, and lemon juice.
- Ratatouille (page 202) and sausage.
- Curried mushrooms: Sauté sliced mushrooms and onions in butter, season to taste with curry powder, and simmer with heavy cream until thickened.
- Goat cheese and honey: Spread fresh mild goat cheese on a crêpe; sprinkle with walnuts if you like, roll up, and warm briefly in a low oven. Drizzle with honey.
- Jam crêpes: Roll your favorite jam or preserve into a crêpe, and sprinkle it with confectioners' sugar.
- Santa Fe: Spread hot Chili for a Crowd (page 158) on a crêpe, sprinkle with grated Cheddar cheese, chopped scallion, and chopped black olives, roll, and bake at 350°F until bubbling.

"I am one who eats his breakfast gazing at morning glories."

—BASHO

2. Pour into an ice cube tray or freezer container and freeze at least overnight.

3. If time allows, let the ice freeze completely, then remove it from the container, process briefly to break up the ice crystals, and refreeze. The ice will be slushy.

4. Spoon into stemmed wineglasses and garnish with fresh dill.

4 portions

Variation: This ice can also be made with vodka. Garnish with a fresh basil leaf.

BUCKWHEAT CREPES

2½ cups milk
4 tablespoons (½ stick) unsalted butter, cut up
1 cup buckwheat flour, sifted (see Note)
1 cup unbleached all-purpose flour, sifted (see Note)
¼ teaspoon salt
4 eggs
Vegetable oil, for frying

1. Warm the milk in a small saucepan with the butter over low heat. When the butter has melted, set aside to cool slightly.

2. Pour both flours into a food processor. Add the salt and process for an instant to blend.

3. With the motor running, pour in the milk and butter mixture and then drop in the eggs; process just until blended. Let the batter stand for 30 minutes.

4. Brush a 7-inch crêpe pan with a paper towel dipped into vegetable oil. Set over medium heat and heat until smoking. Pour ¼ cup batter into the pan and immediately tilt and turn the pan so that the batter will cover the surface evenly. The crêpe may have a few holes; this is fine. Turn the crêpe when the underside is well browned, 3 or 4 minutes, and cook the other side for 2 or 3 minutes. Slide the crêpe out onto a kitchen towel to cool. Repeat with the remaining batter, stacking the finished crêpes; add additional milk if the batter seems too thick, and re-oil the skillet after each crêpe.

5. When the crêpes are cool, use immediately, or layer with wax paper and refrigerate or freeze.

16 crêpes, 7-inch size

Note: Sift the flours into dry-measure cups and sweep level with a knife.

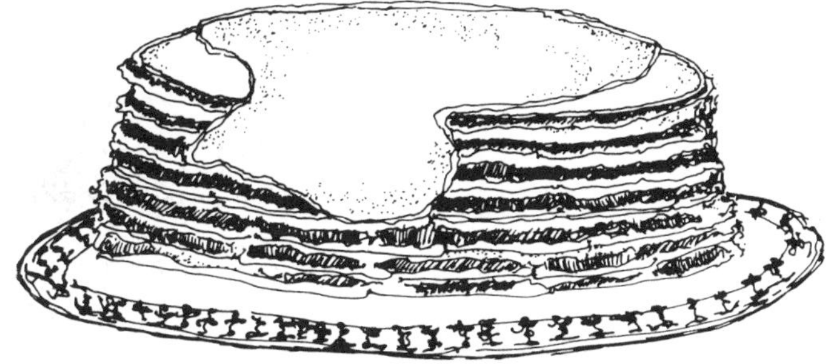

BISMARCKS

This light and wonderful pancake was the way we began every Sunday morning at the Lewises' weekend house in Quogue in the late 60s. Robin's mother had learned it from the historic Bismarck Hotel in Chicago's Loop twenty years before. We all quickly adopted it as our own weekly regimen.

8 tablespoons (1 stick) unsalted butter
½ cup milk
½ cup unbleached all-purpose flour
2 eggs
Fresh lemon juice, to taste
Confectioners' sugar, for dusting

1. Preheat the oven to 475°F.

2. Put the butter in a heavy ovenproof frying pan or a shallow casserole and place it in the oven.

3. Meanwhile, mix together the milk, flour, and eggs lightly to make a batter.

4. When the butter has melted, add the batter to the pan and bake until nicely browned and puffy, 12 minutes. Remove from the oven and place the bismarck on a plate.

5. Pour a little of the melted butter from the pan onto the pancake, and squeeze on a little lemon juice to taste. Roll it up like a loose jelly roll and sprinkle with confectioners' sugar.

Variations:

♥ Sprinkle with brown sugar.

♥ Omit the confectioners' sugar and use a fruit- or maple-flavored syrup.

♥ Spread with a favorite fruit preserve or fill with fresh berries.

♥ Lightly sprinkle with Grand Marnier.

♥ Fill with chestnut cream.

♥ Top with cooked link sausages after 4 minutes of cooking time.

A SUNDAY IN NEW YORK BRUNCH

DANISH MARY ICE

GRAVLAX

CREAM CHEESE

BAGELS OR ENGLISH MUFFINS

BISMARCKS

ORANGE JUICE

COFFEE

FRESH BERRIES WITH SUGAR

SAINT-ANDRÉ, ROBBIOLA DEL BEK, LOU PERALOU CHEESES

"My wife and I tried to breakfast together, but we had to stop or our marriage would have been wrecked."

—WINSTON CHURCHILL

BLACK FOREST CREPE TORTE

This is a wonderfully comforting brunch dish that also manages to look elegant and complex. If you have the tricky components prepared in advance and refrigerated, the torte will go together in a matter of minutes. Pass the crème fraîche and let the guests help themselves.

2 cups Béchamel Sauce (page 415)
1½ cups Gruyère cheese, grated
Freshly ground black pepper, to taste
16 Buckwheat Crêpes (page 389)
32 very thin slices of Black Forest ham (look for the round shape)
8 tablespoons (1 stick) unsalted butter
8 ounces Crème Fraîche (page 414)

1. Preheat the oven to 400°F.

2. Warm the béchamel sauce in a heavy saucepan over low heat until just hot. Add the cheese and whisk until smooth. Season with black pepper.

3. On a round ovenproof platter spread 4 tablespoons of the béchamel and cheese in a crepe-size circle. Place a crepe on the sauce and cover with 2 slices of ham. Dot with bits of butter. Continue this sequence of layers (crepe, ham, butter) until all the crepes and ham are used, ending with a crepe.

4. Pour the remaining béchamel sauce over the torte. Bake until browned and bubbling, 20 minutes. To serve, cut into 6 wedges. Accompany with crème fraîche.

6 portions

SAUTEED CHICKEN LIVERS WITH BLUEBERRY VINEGAR

The tart fruity sauce is a perfect complement to the rich chicken livers. Serve them at brunch with fried potatoes; at dinner with wild rice.

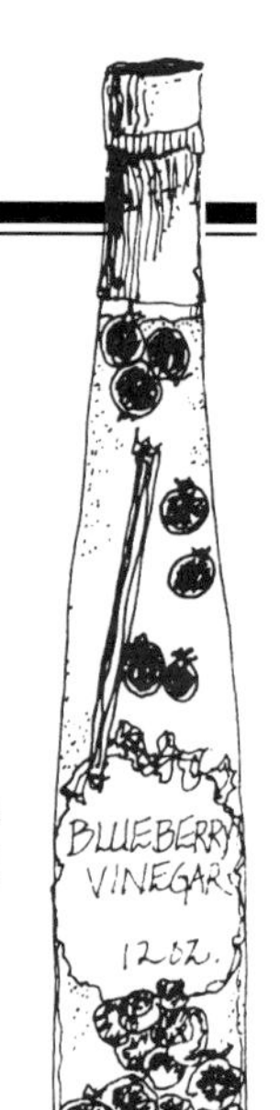

"We plan, we toil, we suffer—in hope of what? A trip to the moon? No, no, no. Simply to wake just in time to smell coffee and bacon and eggs. How rarely it happens! But when it does—then what a moment, what a morning, what a delight."

—J. B. PRIESTLEY

WATERS RUN DEEP

These days everyone seems to have their favorite water. But when you're the host, it's up to you to provide an assortment—still, with bubbles, flavored, chilled, and unchilled. Water may be served to lighten a cocktail, sparkle a wine spritzer, soften fruit juice, or "straight up" with a twist or a berry. Bottoms Up!

AN ENGLISH GRILL BREAKFAST

FRESH APRICOT NECTAR

BISCUITS AND BREADS WITH PRESERVES, MARMALADE, AND UNSALTED BUTTER

SMOKED TROUT WITH *APPLE HORSERADISH MAYONNAISE*

BAKED HAM WITH GLAZED APRICOTS

SAUTÉED CHICKEN LIVERS WITH BLUEBERRY VINEGAR

DANISH BACON

BOILED, POACHED, FRIED, SCRAMBLED, OR SHIRRED EGGS

AMERICAN COFFEE

ENGLISH TEA

HOT CHOCOLATE

4 tablespoons (½ sticks) unsalted butter
4 scallions (green onions), including the green tops, well rinsed and chopped
1 cup unbleached all-purpose flour
Generous pinch each of ground ginger, mace, allspice, nutmeg, and cloves
Salt and freshly ground black pepper, to taste
1 pound chicken livers halved, trimmed, and patted dry
⅓ cup blueberry vinegar (page 145)
⅓ cup Crème Fraîche (page 414) or heavy cream
½ cup fresh blueberries, for garnish (optional)

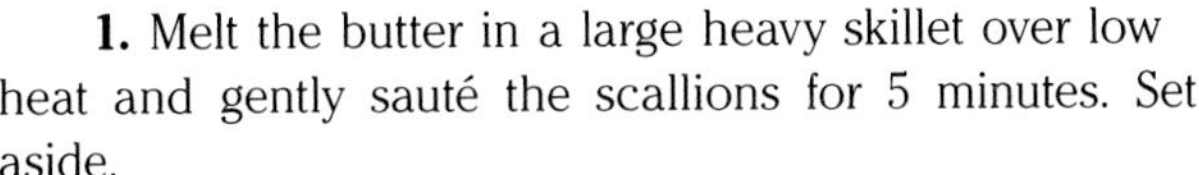

1. Melt the butter in a large heavy skillet over low heat and gently sauté the scallions for 5 minutes. Set aside.

2. Shake the flour in a plastic bag with the spices, salt, and pepper. Drop the livers into the bag with the flour, shake them to coat well, and empty the bag into a strainer set over a bowl. Shake the strainer to remove any excess flour.

3. Return the skillet with the scallions to the stove, raise the heat to medium, and when hot add the livers and cook, turning occasionally, until the livers are browned and slightly stiffened, about 5 minutes. Remove them with a spoon and keep warm.

4. Add the vinegar to the skillet and deglaze over high heat, scraping up any browned bits and reducing the vinegar to a few syrupy spoonfuls.

5. Whisk in the crème fraîche and boil for 1 minute. If you are using fresh blueberries, add them to the sauce and simmer gently just long enough to heat the berries through without overcooking them, 2 or 3 minutes.

6. Arrange the livers on serving plates and spoon the sauce over them. Serve immediately.

4 portions as an appetizer, 2 or 3 portions as a main course

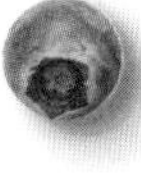

ANGIE'S COFFEE CAKE

1 package active dry yeast
1 cup lukewarm milk (105° to 115°F)
3 tablespoons granulated sugar
4 cups unbleached all-purpose flour
1 teaspoon salt
1¼ cups solid vegetable shortening
2 whole eggs
1 egg, separated
2 cups (4 sticks) unsalted butter, at room temperature, plus extra for greasing the pans
2 cups brown sugar
2 cups shelled pecans, coarsely chopped
3 cups coarsely chopped dates
1 tablespoon ground cinnamon
2¼ cups confectioners' sugar
2 tablespoons warm honey
½ cup fresh lemon juice (2 or 3 lemons)

1. Dissolve the yeast in the lukewarm milk in a small bowl. Stir in the granulated sugar and let stand for 10 minutes.

2. Sift the flour and salt together. Cut in the vegetable shortening until the mixture resembles rolled oats. Stir in the milk and yeast mixture. Beat the whole eggs and the egg yolk together and stir gently but thoroughly into the dough. Cover with a towel and set aside to rise until tripled, about 3 hours.

3. Grease 3 jelly-roll pans, 9 x 13 inches. Divide the risen dough into thirds, and roll out 1 piece of dough thinly into a rectangle about 3 times the size of the jelly-roll pan. Slide a pan under the center third of the dough.

4. Set aside one third of the butter (a little more than 10 tablespoons). Divide the remaining butter into thirds and spread half of one portion over the center portion of the dough on the pan. Sprinkle ⅓ cup of the brown sugar, ⅓ cup of the chopped pecans, and ½ cup of the chopped dates evenly over the buttered center section of dough. Sprinkle with ½ teaspoon of the cinnamon. Fold one side of the dough over the center section. Again spread with softened butter and sprinkle with the same amounts of brown sugar, pecans, and dates. Fold the final third of the dough over the center section. Repeat with the remaining dough and ingredients. Set aside to rise for 2½ to 3 hours.

5. Preheat the oven to 400°F.

6. Mix together the reserved butter, 1 cup of the confectioners' sugar, the reserved egg white, and the warmed honey. Cut 3 deep, decorative slits in the risen coffee cakes, being careful not to cut through to the bottom layer. Spread the honey mixture evenly over the tops of the cakes.

7. Set the pans on the center rack of the oven and bake until puffed, brown, and firm, 25 to 30 minutes. Cool slightly.

Angie's Coffee Cake was a gift to us from a good neighbor in Kalamazoo; we pass it along to you. While it appears to be an all-day project, it is not, and you'll find it is well worth the effort. Because it makes three cakes, it's perfect to bring to a fund-raiser as well as an open-house brunch.

BRUNCH FOR TWO

Brunch for two can be a joint kitchen affair, shared in front of a fire, on the terrace, or in the garden. You can also take it, and yourselves, back to bed. However you celebrate the late-morning meal, here are some ideas to increase your pleasure:

- ♥ For a special breakfast treat, scramble eggs slowly in butter to the desired doneness, season with freshly ground black pepper, and top the eggs with black caviar.
- ♥ Celebrate the morning with Champagne, fresh raspberries and cream, croissants with butter and Brie cheese, eggs any way you like them, and café au lait.
- ♥ Stock a small bedside refrigerator with fresh orange juice, vodka, Scotch salmon, cream cheese with chives, fresh lemon, and bagels. If you want hot coffee, you'll have to get out of bed. Sorry!

HOUSEGUESTS

It has been said that there are two kinds of people in the world: hosts and guests. Happily, most people are a combination of both. When people who don't usually live together gather under one roof to spend a weekend, or a week, it's not really fair for either hosts or guests to have to conform to their archetypal roles. The greatest hosts are those who treat their guests as warmly as family. And the best guests are those who know instinctively that they have been invited to amuse themselves by day and their hosts by night.

8. Mix together the remaining confectioners' sugar and the lemon juice and drizzle over the warm coffee cakes. To serve, cut into narrow strips and serve warm.

9. The coffee cakes can be wrapped in aluminum foil and frozen. Defrost and rewarm slightly in the foil before serving.

3 coffee cakes, each 9 x 13 inches

JULEE'S ORIGINAL SOUR CREAM COFFEE CAKE

A renaissance worth celebrating. This elegant cake is just scrumptious served to a large brunch party, and it's perfect, too, with late-afternoon coffee and a good book. For brunch, it's worth timing so you can serve it thirty minutes out of the oven.

1 cup (2 sticks) unsalted butter, plus extra for greasing the pan
2 cups unbleached all-purpose flour, plus extra for flouring the pan
2½ cups sugar
2 eggs, beaten
2 cups sour cream
1 tablespoon vanilla extract
1 tablespoon baking powder
¼ teaspoon salt
1½ cups shelled pecans, coarsely chopped
1 tablespoon ground cinnamon

1. Preheat the oven to 350°F. Butter and flour a 10-inch Bundt pan.

2. Cream together the butter and 2 cups of sugar. Add the eggs, blending well, then the sour cream and vanilla.

3. Sift together the flour, baking powder, and salt.

4. Fold the dry ingredients into the creamed mixture and beat until just blended. Do not overbeat.

5. In a separate bowl, mix the remaining ½ cup sugar with the pecans and cinnamon.

6. Scrape half of the batter into the prepared pan. Sprinkle with half of the pecan and sugar mixture. Spread the remaining batter and top with the rest of the pecan mixture.

7. Set the pan on the center rack of the oven and bake until a cake tester inserted in the center comes out clean, 50 to 55 minutes. Let rest 20 to 30 minutes. Invert on a serving plate. Serve warm.

10 portions

BLACK FRUIT SALAD

1 cup black cherries, pitted
1 cup black grapes
½ cup blueberries or black currants
⅓ cup light brown sugar
Juice of 1 lemon
1 cup sour cream
Fresh mint sprigs

1. Combine the fruits and sprinkle with the brown sugar and lemon juice. Let stand for 2 hours, tossing several times.

2. Lift out the fruit with a slotted spoon and divide equally among 4 balloon wineglasses.

3. Stir the sour cream into the collected juices in the bowl.

4. Serve the fruits topped with a dollop of the sour cream sauce and a sprig of fresh mint.

4 portions

Variations: We also like a combination of green grapes, kiwis, and green apples, or a mixture of just grapes.

MINTED FRUIT SALAD

A perfect summer brunch salad, but you can substitute other seasonal fresh fruits as you please.

1 pint strawberries
3 kiwis
1 medium-size ripe cantaloupe
1 medium-size ripe honeydew melon
Handful of fresh mint leaves
½ cup fresh orange juice
¼ cup fresh lemon juice
3 tablespoons sugar

1. Wash, drain, and hull the strawberries.

2. Peel the kiwis and slice thin, reserving 1 sliced kiwi for garnish.

3. With a melon-baller, cut balls from the cantaloupe and honeydew melons.

4. Mix all the fruits together except for the reserved kiwi.

5. Chop the mint leaves and tender stems very fine and sprinkle on the fruits.

6. Mix the orange and lemon juices with the sugar and pour over all. Toss the salad gently and thoroughly.

7. Arrange the reserved kiwi slices on top and garnish with a fresh mint leaf. Chill for 2 to 3 hours and serve cold.

12 portions

FRUIT SALADS

It's not really necessary to have a recipe for a fruit salad; almost any combination of fresh seasonal fruits can begin or end a meal on a satisfactory note. You may add a light touch of sugar or honey, some lemon juice, finely chopped mint or liqueur, according to the sweetness of the fruit and your own taste.

Add such sweetening just before serving, as sugars tend to draw the natural juices out of fruit. We have also learned that melon combined with other fruits becomes soft unless added at the very last moment.

- ♥ Combine peeled and sliced kiwis with strawberries. Steep in red wine, and serve a glass of the same wine with the fruit.
- ♥ Mix 3 kinds of melon with orange and lemon juices. Sprinkle with lots of chopped fresh mint.
- ♥ Combine seedless green grapes, blueberries, and honeydew balls. Sprinkle with dark rum and grated fresh orange zest.
- ♥ Toss chilled grapefruit sections with honey, lime juice, and chopped fresh mint leaves.

THE BIG BREAD SANDWICH

This special sandwich seems, more and more often, to be the answer for almost every entertaining occasion—from brunch to picnics to late-night suppers. The Big Bread can easily serve any number of people, and makes a spectacular-looking, edible centerpiece for a buffet. It is self-contained, portable, and may be served indoors or out.

You can make your own bread or buy good bakery bread if time is short. The loaf should be 12 to 14 inches wide, about the same in length, and at least 4 inches high, either round or rectangular. Any type of bread will make perfectly delicious Big Bread Sandwiches.

A BREAD BOX

A giant brioche or loaf of bread, hollowed and filled with miniature sandwiches decoratively shaped and imaginatively filled, makes a splendid centerpiece for any kind of buffet.

Cut off the top of the loaf with a serrated knife and reserve the top. Pull out the soft interior crumb of the bread, being careful to leave the crust intact, and save the crumb for another use or discard.

With a rolling pin, flatten slices of thin sandwich bread and then cut into shapes using cookie cutters. Make sandwiches with your choice of fillings, spreads, or flavored butters, and arrange inside the hollow loaf. Set the top back on, wrap, and refrigerate until serving.

THE BIG BREAD

4 cups lukewarm water (105° to 115°F)
2 tablespoons molasses
2 packages active dry yeast
11 to 12 cups unbleached all-purpose flour, plus more if needed
2½ tablespoons salt
3 tablespoons olive oil
Cornmeal, to cover the baking sheet

1. Stir the lukewarm water and the molasses together in a very large bowl. Sprinkle in the yeast, stirring to dissolve all the particles, and let stand for 10 minutes.

2. Begin adding the flour, 1 cup at a time, stirring as you go. Add the salt and beat well after 5 cups of flour have been incorporated, then stir in 5 more cups of flour.

3. Turn the dough out onto a heavily floured work surface. Wash and dry the bowl.

4. Sprinkle 1 cup of the remaining flour over the dough and begin to knead it; the dough will be very sticky at this point. Keep kneading and adding more of the remaining flour as needed to keep the dough from sticking to your hands or to the board. It's a big loaf and will need a lot of kneading, about 15 minutes. The dough is ready when it is smooth and elastic.

5. Pour the olive oil into the dried bowl and turn the dough in

"Too few people
understand
a really good
sandwich."
—JAMES BEARD

it to coat it with oil. Cover the dough with a towel and let it stand until tripled in bulk; this will take between 1½ and 3 hours. The volume is what to watch here, not the time it takes.

6. Turn the risen dough out onto the floured work surface and knead again, for about 5 minutes. Shape into a ball, turn again in the bowl, cover, and let rise until doubled in volume.

7. Sprinkle a large baking sheet evenly with cornmeal. Turn the dough out onto the work surface and shape it into a large oval loaf. Transfer to the baking sheet, cover, and let rise until doubled, about 1 hour.

8. Preheat the oven to 450°F.

9. Rub the risen loaf generously with flour. Slash it shallowly across the top with a sharp knife. Set the baking sheet on the center rack of the oven and bake for 15 minutes. Reduce the heat to 375°F and bake until the loaf is well browned and sounds hollow when tapped on the bottom crust, another 30 minutes. Let cool.

MARINATED EGGPLANT LIVIA

This is excellent not only in the Big Bread Sandwich, but also in salads or as part of an antipasto.

1 eggplant (about 1 pound), stem end trimmed
1 tablespoon coarse salt
1 cup best-quality olive oil
2 small dried red chiles
2 whole garlic cloves, crushed
¼ cup red wine vinegar
2 tablespoons dried oregano
1 tablespoon dried basil
1 cup olive oil, for frying

1. Cut the unpeeled eggplant into ¼-inch crosswise slices. Place in a colander in layers and sprinkle all over with the salt. Let rest for 1 to 1½ hours.

2. Meanwhile, make the marinade. Whisk together the olive oil, chiles, garlic, vinegar, oregano, and basil in a medium-size bowl.

3. After 1½ hours, pat the eggplant dry with paper towels and line a baking sheet with paper towels.

4. Working in batches, heat ¼ cup of the frying oil in a large nonstick skillet and brown the eggplant over medium heat, turning once, until golden brown on each side, 3 to 4 minutes per side. (Add more oil if necessary.) Drain on paper towels.

5. Remove the eggplant to a container with a lid and pour the marinade over the eggplant. Cool to room temperature, cover with the lid, and refrigerate overnight.

6. Remove the eggplant from the refrigerator 1 hour before use.

4 portions or enough for 1 Big Bread Sandwich

The Big Bread Sandwich.

THE BIG BREAD SANDWICH

1 loaf of Big Bread (page 397)
3 green bell peppers, cored, seeded, and cut into thin strips
4 red bell peppers, cored and cut into thin strips
Approximately 2 tablespoons olive oil
6 sweet Italian sausages, cut lengthwise into halves
6 hot Italian sausages, cut lengthwise into halves
¼ teaspoon salt, plus additional to taste
½ teaspoon ground black pepper, plus additional to taste
1 cup sliced pitted black olives
Approximately 5 tablespoons chopped fresh Italian (flat-leaf) parsley
Dried oregano, to taste
1 cup Garlic-Anchovy Dressing (page 257)
16 very thin slices of prosciutto
10 plum tomatoes, cut horizontally into 1-inch slices
8 thin slices of fontina cheese
2 bunches of arugula (about 2 cups), rinsed, dried, and stemmed
1 cup ricotta cheese
¼ cup grated Romano cheese
1 recipe Marinated Eggplant Livia (page 399)

1. Slice the bread horizontally into 4 slices 1 inch thick.

2. Sauté the green and red peppers in about 2 tablespoons olive oil, together with the sweet and hot sausages, until the peppers and sausages are browned. Add salt and pepper to taste. With a slotted spoon transfer the sausages and peppers to the bottom layer of bread, topping with sliced black olives, 2 tablespoons parsley and oregano. Drizzle the cooking oil over the next layer of bread and set the layer in place.

3. Pour some of the Garlic-Anchovy Dressing over the bread. Cover with layers of prosciutto, tomatoes, fontina cheese, arugula, salt, pepper, and oregano to taste, 1 tablespoon parsley, and more vinaigrette. Cover with the third slice of bread.

4. Combine the ricotta cheese, Romano cheese, 2 tablespoons chopped parsley, the ½ teaspoon ground black pepper, and the ¼ teaspoon salt in a small bowl. Spread the cheese mixture on the bottom bread layer. Arrange the Eggplant Livia over the cheese and pour on a bit of the marinade from the eggplant. Top with the fourth slice of bread.

5. Wrap the sandwich in clear plastic. Place between 2 cookie sheets, put something heavy on top to weight the sandwich, and refrigerate for 3 hours.

6. To serve: Place on a large cutting board and cut into wedges with a serrated knife.

10 to 12 portions

BUFFET SANDWICHES

The best brunches are the laziest, stretching into the afternoon and beyond, with guests that come and go. They call for casual but substantial food, and we love to offer an array of interestingly shaped and flavored sandwiches. Add a pitcher of lemonade (page 254), chill bottles of wine or beer, and toss a salad. The rest of the day will take care of itself.

- ♥ Put thinly sliced roast veal, spread with Anchovy Mayonnaise (page 413), on pumpernickel. Sprinkle with capers.
- ♥ Try Filet of Beef (page 118), equal parts of Roquefort and cream cheese, and sprigs of watercress on pumpernickel rolls.
- ♥ Spread Pâté de Campagne with Walnuts (page 34) on a French roll. Layer on a green apple slice and some Brie cheese.
- ♥ Butter pumpernickel with Anchovy Butter (page 145); pile high with thinly sliced radishes and watercress.
- ♥ Stack Steak Tartare (page 30) and thinly sliced red onion on a pumpernickel roll. Add lots of black pepper.
- ♥ Layer carpaccio with Ravigote Butter (page 145) on pumpernickel. Sprinkle with chopped fresh parsley.
- ♥ Purée equal parts of cooked shrimp and softened butter; season to taste with salt, pepper, and lemon juice; spread on whole-wheat bread and top with a slice of cherry tomato.
- ♥ Make Egg Salad with Dill (page 270) and top with asparagus tips.
- ♥ Combine smoked red caviar, onions, lemon juice, cream cheese, and dill. Spread on pumpernickel.
- ♥ Arrange thinly sliced chicken breast, tarragon mayonnaise, walnuts, and watercress on pumpernickel.
- ♥ Try lobster with Tomato-Basil Mayonnaise (page 413) and arugula on white bread.
- ♥ Spread Pecan Cream Cheese (page 421) on Banana Bread (page 305).

BRUNCH DRINKS

Brunch drinks fall into several categories; the strength you choose is up to you and may have something to do with your whereabouts and temperance of the previous evening. They range from morning wake-up potions, for medicinal purposes only, to mellow sipping drinks that pace you through the afternoon.

A VIRGINIA HUNT BREAKFAST

BLOODY MARYS

BAKED HAM WITH GLAZED APRICOTS

BARBECUED BEANS

MIXED GREEN SALAD *WITH CHAMPAGNE SHALLOT DRESSING*

BISCUITS AND HONEY

FRESH LADY APPLES AND BLACK CHERRIES WITH VIRGINIA GOUDA CHEESE AND BRILLAT-SAVARIN CHEESE

CRACKLING CORN BREAD

A GOOD SPICY BLOODY MARY

The Bloody Mary has become an American weekend wake-up call, with variations substituting aquavit for the vodka, or adding consommé (for a Bull Shot). Garnish with fresh basil, dill, oregano, or black peppercorns. While delicious chilled, in the traditional way, it is also good hot, served in a mug on the top of a mountain anywhere.

1 quart tomato juice
½ cup fresh lemon juice
2 tablespoons prepared horseradish
Freshly ground black pepper, to taste
Several hefty dashes of Worcestershire sauce, to taste
Several hefty dashes of Tabasco, to taste
1½ cups vodka
Chopped basil leaves, for garnish

1. Combine all the ingredients except the vodka and basil in a large saucepan over medium heat. Simmer for 5 to 6 minutes. Let cool.

2. Pour a jigger of vodka into an ice-filled red-wine goblet or tall thin glass. Add the Bloody Mary mixture, stir, and top with chopped basil. Let chill.

6 to 8 portions

Variations:

♥ Mexican: substitute tequila for vodka.
♥ Texan: add 2 tablespoons barbecue sauce.
♥ Asian: add soy sauce and grated fresh ginger.
♥ Sea Style: use canned mixed clam-and-tomato juice instead of tomato juice.

BLACK SANGRIA

1½ cups mixed cherries, blackberries, and black grapes
1 strip of peel from a whole lemon
½ cup strongly brewed black tea, warm
1 bottle dry red wine
Chilled club soda, to taste

1. Place the fruits and lemon peel in a 2½-quart pitcher.

2. Add the tea and enough wine to cover the fruits. Chill the remaining wine.

3. Before serving, pour the remaining wine in the pitcher. Stir, and add ice and club soda to taste.

4 to 6 portions

WHITE SANGRIA

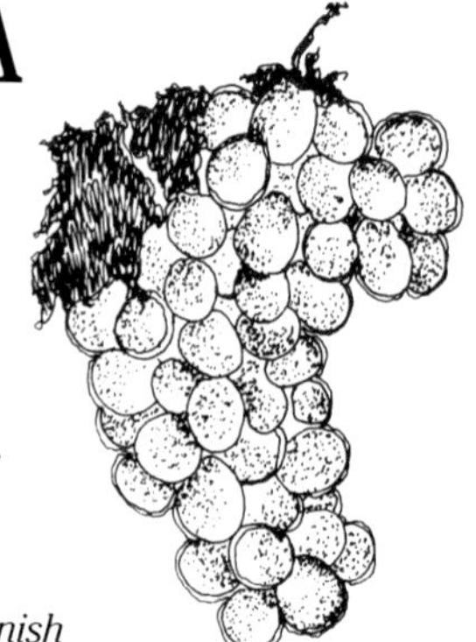

1 bottle of dry white wine
2 kiwis, peeled and sliced
1 large pear, sliced very thin
1 cup seedless green grapes
2 tablespoons superfine sugar
2 tablespoons Calvados or Armagnac
3 tablespoons Cointreau
1½ cups bottled sparkling water
Sprigs of mint or fresh flowers, for garnish

1. Pour the wine into a large glass pitcher. Add the kiwis, pear, grapes, sugar, Calvados, and Cointreau to the pitcher and stir. Cover and refrigerate for 4 to 5 hours.

2. To serve, stir well, add the sparkling water, and pour over ice in tall glasses. Garnish with a sprig of mint or a flower.

6 portions

FRESH FRUIT DAIQUIRI

Fresh fruit and white rum to combine to bring an island mood any time of the year. The proportions are flexible.

Vanilla or fruit-flavored ice cream
White rum
Fresh strawberries, peaches, raspberries, blueberries, or a combination, plus extra for garnish
Fresh mint sprigs, for garnish

Whip the ice cream, rum, and fruit in a blender until smooth and serve over ice; garnish each glass with fruit and a sprig of mint.

BEER

Beer has become more intriguing. Many say it is the drink of the moment. Microbreweries and brew pubs across the country have given beer new dimension and are we ever glad. Even if you haven't sipped a beer since your last college football game, you owe it to yourself to try again with gusto. Who among us doesn't crave a frosty mug of brew from time to time? Our British friends clearly relish their pints, half pints, and nips.

Serious beer drinkers always order by brand, and though the array of available ales, stouts, lights, imports, and microbrews grows daily, a good host can be content with offering at most two or three beers—a domestic light, a domestic premium, and one of the imports with a national reputation. We have been to beer-tasting parties, however, where a dozen or more varieties were presented, along with the appropriate fare. In some circles, they've replaced wine tastings. Whatever beer you serve, be sure it is properly chilled and that you offer a tall, well-designed beer glass, also chilled. It does not take much effort to make a beer drinker happy.

Fruity and fragrant, White Sangria is always a bit unexpected.

CHAMPAGNE COCKTAIL

Champagne is one thing we can never get enough of. Every bottle is the memory of a party, an indulgence after a Sunday morning jogging workout, or the accompaniment to a soliloquy delivered under the midnight stars. Do serve it in a tulip glass or Champagne flute; the bubbles last longer and it's so pretty.

1 ounce Cognac
½ ounce Grand Marnier
6 ounces Champagne, chilled
3 raspberries

Mix together the Cognac and Grand Marnier in a goblet, fill with Champagne, and garnish with the raspberries.

1 portion

KIR ROYALE

2 ounces framboise
1 bottle of the best crème de cassis (black currant liqueur)
Champagne

Add the framboise to the crème de cassis and keep on hand as a mixer. For each portion, put 1 demitasse spoonful of the mixture into a glass of Champagne so that the wine becomes lightly pink, and serve as an aperitif.

MIMOSA

Champagne
Fresh orange juice
Fresh mint leaves, for garnish

For each portion, fill each glass two thirds full with Champagne. Top each off with fresh orange juice and garnish with a mint leaf.

CHAMPAGNE IN THE MORNING!

To begin the day effervescently, there is nothing like Champagne. In fact, if the truth be told, we like Champagne just about anytime—before, after, or during lunch or dinner.

The drier the Champagne, the more we like it. Some people find sweeter Champagnes cloying, which is why we always look for "brut." And while vintage Champagnes are truly quite wonderful, we've found some very delightful nonvintages from France, and *methode traditionnelle* or "sparkling" wines from California, Long Island, Oregon, and Michigan that have become our everyday bubblies. These are affordable enough for us to sip whenever the mood strikes.

KINDS OF CHAMPAGNE

NONVINTAGE: Wine from a year's harvest blended with reserve wines to produce the Champagne characteristic of each house.

VINTAGE: Wine made in exceptional years only; usually not produced more than once or twice a decade.

TÊTE DE CUVÊE: A superior blend made especially for the connoisseur.

BLANC DE BLANCS: A Champagne made from exclusively white (Chardonnay) grapes rather than a mixture of black (Pinot Noir) and white grapes.

ROSÉ: Champagne tinted by leaving the skin of black grapes in for longer than the normal period.

COFFEE

Coffee has become hot in America! It all began in the late 60s in San Francisco with a tiny, hip shop called Peets, where the local intellectuals shopped, migrated north to Seattle, and then moved eastward. Serious coffee lovers have made their passion contagious, and today everyone's got their own favorite "grande" or "'accino." We feel it's because the secret of what makes good coffee is finally out. Simply put, it's about delivering quality and freshness. That's all. Easy to say, but very complex to deliver consistently in each and every cup! Thanks to very serious growers, importers, roasters, and baristas, though, who are absolutely passionate about what they do, there are some very good cups of coffee being made today.

Coffee begins with the growers in Costa Rica, Brazil, Guatemala, Peru, Ethiopia, Mexico, Rwanda, Sumatra, New Guinea, Colombia, and other countries where conditions are right for growing high-quality coffee beans and where farmers are paid enough to make it worth their while. The coffee roaster must be willing to buy only the very best green coffee beans, sparing no expense, from an importer or directly from the grower. The beans must then be roasted properly, with a slow rise in heat, so they develop their flavor from the inside out and aren't over-roasted, which results in a burned aftertaste. Finally, the roasted beans must reach the consumer within a few days for optimal freshness.

Freshness is the key to the brewing process, too. The beans should be bought freshly roasted, stored in the freezer, and ground just prior to brewing, using short cycles of the grinder so the heat of the grinder doesn't affect the beans' flavor. Then, the coffee should be brewed using cold, fresh water. Finally, you can enjoy your freshly brewed cup, with all its aroma and flavor intact.

> "Nanny likes her coffee hot hot hot."
>
> —KAY THOMPSON, *ELOISE*

MAKING COFFEE

Our choice of coffeemakers for years has been the Melitta pot. To use it, bring cold tap water to a boil and pour it over the freshly ground beans in the pot's filter cone. Having the water pass through the coffee only once is believed by most coffee lovers to make the best brew, and that has to include us.

The proportion of coffee to water is a matter of preference; we go by the following measures:

REGULAR-STRENGTH COFFEE:
2 tablespoons to 6 ounces water

EXTRA-STRENGTH COFFEE:
2 tablespoons to 4 ounces water

A second method is to use a glass "plunger" pot, which allows the water and coffee to steep together for 4 or 5 minutes, then separates them by means of a plunger disc. Some of these pots hold 10 to 12 cups and so are easier to deal with than a smaller filter-cone pot when we have guests.

Espresso, ideally, should be brewed properly in an espresso maker, and served with a twist of lemon and a sugar cube.

TYPES OF COFFEE

Select the roast best suited to your intended use. The following list may help.

COLOMBIAN: A rich, all-round flavor. Good by itself or blended with other beans.

COSTA RICAN: Excellent flavor.

FRENCH ROAST OR ITALIAN ROAST: Full espresso; beans roasted to a glossy near-black.

HAWAIIAN KONA COFFEE: Mild, sweet, full-flavored, and full-bodied.

HOUSE BLEND: Try it once and judge for yourself.

JAMAICAN BLUE MOUNTAIN AND HIGH MOUNTAIN SUPREME: Two superb, mellow, rare coffees: Blue Mountain is extremely rare and High Mountain only slightly less so; both are sweet-tasting with fine flavor and full body. If you ever see either, buy it!

MOCHA JAVA: Genuine Java coffee blended with mocha coffee.

PUERTO RICAN: An excellent coffee; very little is shipped here.

VIENNA ROAST: Mild espresso; lighter than French or Italian roast.

EUROPEAN VARIATIONS

CAFÉ AU LAIT: Equal amounts of hot, freshly brewed, strong French roast and warm milk poured into a cup simultaneously.

CAPPUCCINO: A taste of Italy that is easily made without a cappuccino machine by whipping warm milk in a blender for 1 minute to produce a bit of foam. Combine equal quantities of very strong, freshly brewed Italian-roast coffee with the frothy milk; dust with chocolate shavings and ground cinnamon and serve with sugar.

TEA, PLEASE

Chinese legends tell of the discovery of tea by Shennong, the emperor over 5,000 years ago who developed Chinese agriculture and medicine. After Shennong boiled his drinking water to purify it one day, some leaves from a bush fell into his cup. Always curious, the emperor took a sip—and enjoyed the brew. A cup of tea was born. For centuries afterward, tea was a drink only

For the Chinese nobility who celebrated the tea ceremony. Tea was introduced to Europe in the late seventeenth century by Portuguese and Dutch traders, and before long, Britain was at the center of the world tea trade. Today there are several thousand varieties of tea growing in China, Japan, Sri Lanka, Indonesia, Africa, India, and recently also Argentina.

Tea is often compared to wine in that one basic plant, *Camellia sinensis*, produces thousands of wonderfully complex flavors affected by terroir, altitude, season of harvest, the drying process, blending, and the care and handling of the leaves at every stage. Look for tea leaves that are whole and handpicked—many English teas and the tea in teabags are chips of leaves that have been machine processed. The basic categories of tea are white, green, oolong, and black, all related to the degree of oxidation the leaves have undergone after harvest. Here are some of our favorites:

CHINA

WHITE—White teas are made from young leaves (new-growth buds) that have undergone no oxidation. The tea is low in caffeine, gentle, complex, and sweet . . . best with delicate foods. Fine ones include Bai Mu Dan, Yin Zhen, and organic snow buds. White tea can be very expensive.

GREEN—Made from young leaves that have experienced little oxidation. There are many classic green teas; two excellent ones are Dragon Well (Lung Ching) and Yellow Mountain (Mao Feng). The Chinese sages believed green tea bestowed long life and wisdom.

OOLONG—For this type, the oxidation level falls between that of green and black tea. Try Wu Ti teas from 100-year-old bushes, usually rich and toasty in flavor. Ti Kuan Yi has a toasted chestnut flavor. And "the Champagne of tea," the Formosa or Taiwan oolongs called Dong Feng, Mei Ren, or Oriental Beauty have a delicate wildflower and peach taste.

BLACK—Called red tea in China, it is the result of highly oxidized leaves. The Yunnan is a full-bodied, smoky tea with a peppery finish, and the Keemun, known as "the Burgundy of China," has a complex chocolate, sugarcane, pine, and red wine note. Lapsang souchong is strong and smoky.

SCENTED TEAS—These are sometimes simply flower infusions and sometimes tea with flower petals. Jasmine is common. Avoid mass-market varieties that are made by spraying the tea with floral essence.

JAPAN

Japanese tea is predominantly green. We like Gyokuro, a mellow shade-grown tea from the first picking. Sencha is the green tea most widely consumed in Japan. Kukicha is made from early leaves and brown twigs, which give the tea a complex, toasty flavor.

INDIA

Darjeeling—Grows in high altitudes—the higher the altitude, the better the tea. It brews to a light amber, tastes like almonds and apricots, and is naturally high in tannins.

Nilgiri—Excellent teas from single estates.

Assam—One of the most prized teas in the world for its complex flavor.

BASICS

PATE BRISEE

1½ cups unbleached all-purpose flour
½ teaspoon salt
Pinch of sugar
5½ tablespoons (⅔ stick) unsalted butter, chilled
3 tablespoons solid vegetable shortening, chilled
¼ cup ice water

1. Sift the flour, salt, and sugar together into a bowl; add the butter and shortening and cut them into the dry ingredients with a pastry blender or 2 knives until the mixture is like coarse meal.

2. Sprinkle on and blend in enough of the ice water to make a workable dough, mixing the water in lightly with a fork.

3. Turn the dough out onto your work surface and, using the heel of your hand, smear the dough away from you, about ¼ cup at a time. Scrape the smeared dough into a ball, wrap, and refrigerate for at least 2 hours.

4. Unwrap the dough, place it on a floured work surface, and pound it a few times with your rolling pin to soften it. Roll it out ⅛ inch thick, or to the desired thickness.

5. Drape the dough over a quiche pan or tart pan, ease it into the pan without stretching, pat into place, trim off any excess, and crimp the edge if desired. Refrigerate for 30 minutes.

6. Preheat the oven to 400°F.

7. Remove the chilled dough from the refrigerator and prick the bottom and sides well with a fork. Line the pan with aluminum foil or wax paper; fill with beans or rice to weight the crust. Bake until the crust is just beginning to color, 10 minutes.

8. Remove from the oven, remove the weights and lining, and cool slightly. You now have a partially baked crust that can be filled and rebaked for a quiche or tart.

9. For a fully baked crust—for a fresh fruit tart, for example—remove the weights and lining from the shell after 10 minutes and continue to bake until it is golden brown and crisply flaky, about 25 minutes total. Cool completely before filling.

One 11-inch shell or 5 or 6 small tart shells

PATE A CHOUX

½ cup water
4 tablespoons (½ stick) unsalted butter, plus extra for greasing the baking sheet
½ teaspoon salt
½ cup sifted unbleached all-purpose flour
3 eggs

1. Combine the water, butter, and salt in a small saucepan and bring to a boil.

QUICHES

Quiches are classic. Nothing is quite so quick and satisfying to assemble as a quiche. Provided you have a bit of Pâte Brisée in your freezer (and since it freezes beautifully you should), some eggs, and heavy cream or half-and-half on hand, you can leave the rest up to the improvisations of the moment. A handful of mushrooms sautéed with a shallot and finished with a little sherry or Port to taste can join grated Swiss cheese in an elegant quiche. Onions and salami or pepperoni, left over from last night's pizza, can be hearty and delicious. Combine cold crabmeat with a bit of sautéed green bell pepper; pair cooked chicken with black olives and Cheddar; try scallions sautéed in butter—add grated cheese as you like, or not at all. A bit of ham or bacon, fresh herbs, even some cooked Italian sausage—all can enliven a meal by flavoring a quiche. The possibilities are endless and always fascinating.

For a 10-inch quiche crust (and we think this is the best size) you will need 2 to 3 cups of filling and 3 eggs beaten with 1½ cups of heavy cream or half-and-half. Season the egg mixture generously with salt, nutmeg, and fresh black pepper to taste. Top the assembled quiche with cheese if it seems appropriate.

"Simple cooking cannot be trusted to a simple cook."

—COUNTESS MORPHE

2. Remove the pan from the heat and pour in the flour all at once. Stir well to combine and return to medium heat. Cook, stirring constantly, until the mixture becomes sticky and pulls away in a ball from the sides of the pan.

3. Remove the pan from the heat, cool for a moment or two, and stir in 2 of the eggs, one at a time, making certain the first egg is completely incorporated before adding the second, and beating vigorously at the end.

4. Preheat the oven to 400°F. Lightly grease a baking sheet.

5. Drop the batter onto the sheet by spoonfuls of the size required by the recipe, or pipe out of a pastry bag into the desired shapes.

6. Beat the remaining egg in a small bowl. Brush only the tops of the batter portions with the beaten egg. Set the baking sheet on the center rack of the oven. Reduce the heat to 375°F and bake the batter until it has puffed and is firm and golden brown, 20 minutes.

7. Remove the puffs from the oven. Using a small knife, cut a slit in the side of each puff; this will let out steam that would otherwise make the puffs soggy. Cool the puffs completely on a rack before proceeding with filling and serving.

About 25 cocktail-size puffs or cocktail éclairs

PUFF PASTRY

4 cups unbleached all-purpose flour
2 teaspoons salt
1 to 1¼ cups ice water, as needed
1½ cups (3 sticks) unsalted butter, well chilled

1. Measure the flour by scooping a dry-measure cup into the container and sweeping off the excess with a knife. Place 3½ cups of the flour in a mixing bowl. Refrigerate the remaining ½ cup of flour.

2. Dissolve the salt in 1 cup of the ice water, and then gradually stir the ice water into the flour. When all the flour is moistened and is just beginning to hang together in a ragged dough, stop adding water. Turn the dough out onto your work surface and gather it into a ball. The dough may be crumbly; it will certainly look awful; this is as it should be. Wrap the dough in plastic or a bag, and refrigerate for 1 hour or longer.

3. Remove the dough from the refrigerator, lightly flour your work surface, and roll out the dough very evenly into a square about 12 x 12 inches.

4. Remove the butter from the refrigerator and unwrap it. Beat it with a rolling pin a few times to soften it. Sprinkle it with the chilled ½ cup flour. Mash and knead the butter further, using the rolling pin and the heel of your hand, until it is smooth and creamy and all the flour is incorporated. This should not go on so long that the butter begins to melt. (To keep your hands from becoming too warm, you can dip them in cold water for about 1 minute, then dry them, before kneading in the flour. Your goal is to get the butter and the dough as close to the same texture as possible. Form the butter into a rectangle.

5. Fold the square of dough in half. Center the rectangle of butter on the folded dough and fold the long sides of the dough over it, enclosing it completely. Pinch to seal. Gather the dough around the ends and pinch to seal. Sprinkle it very lightly with flour and turn it over, seam side down. Roll it out gently into a rectangle and fold it one third of the way over itself. Fold the other end over this, as if folding a letter.

6. Rotate the dough 90 degrees and roll it out again into a rectangle 20 x 24 inches. Again fold one end one third of the way in, and then fold the other end over that. You now have the "letter" of dough again. Gently press the ends of 2 fingers into the dough; you have made 2 of the 6 turns, and this will mark it so you don't forget. Rewrap and refrigerate it for at least 1 hour.

7. Remove the dough from the refrigerator once more and unwrap it. If it is very cold, let it stand for 10 minutes or so before rolling, otherwise the hardened butter may tear its way out of the package. Lightly flour the work surface and again roll out the dough into a rectangle 20 x 24 inches. Form the "letter," roll out again, and again fold it in thirds. Mark the dough with 4 depressions; you have completed 4 of the 6 turns. Rewrap and refrigerate the dough for at least 1 hour.

8. Repeat step 7. The dough has now been turned 6 times and is ready to be shaped and baked. It can also be rewrapped and refrigerated for a few days or frozen for up to several weeks at this point.

About 2 pounds puff pastry

PASTRY CREAM

2 cups milk
½ cup sugar
¼ cup unbleached all-purpose flour
2 egg yolks
1 tablespoon unsalted butter
2 teaspoons vanilla extract

1. Scald the milk in a heavy saucepan.

2. While the milk is heating, whisk the sugar and flour together in a stainless-steel mixing bowl.

3. When the milk is scalded, remove the top skin and slowly pour the milk into the flour and sugar, whisking constantly. Place the bowl over a saucepan of simmering water and cook, stirring, until the mixture lightly coats the back of a spoon, about 10 minutes.

4. Add the egg yolks and cook, stirring constantly, until the mixture heavily coats the back of a spoon, about 10 minutes more. Remove from the heat.

5. Add the butter and vanilla and mix well. Cover the top with a light coating of butter or cover the surface directly with plastic wrap to prevent the formation of a skin, then chill.

2½ cups pastry cream

ABOUT PUFF PASTRY

Puff pastry is one of the glorious foundations of French baking. It is nothing more than layers of butter and layers of flour-and-water dough, but such is its magic that it rises to amazing heights, as much as 5 to 10 times the height of the original dough. The result is light, crisp, and ravishingly buttery.

The classic uses of this pastry are many. It can be formed into pastry shells, large, small, or smaller, and filled with savory appetizer mixtures, or it can be used for extravagant entrées and magnificent desserts. It is the basis for napoleons. Cut into decorative shapes, it becomes *fleurons*—the haute-cuisine garniture *par excellence.* Contemporary cuisine has embraced its crisp delicacy and adapted it to newer uses. In short, it's wonderful stuff.

Unfortunately, this pastry has the reputation of being difficult to make. While it's true there are a few tricks involved, and the method at first seems unnecessarily complicated, puff pastry is really no more difficult to make than a good piecrust, and much more impressive. The careful steps outlined in the recipe reveal that for much of the time the puff pastry is relaxing in the refrigerator, while you are out playing tennis. Less than an hour of work, total, is needed and this can be stretched out over a day or even two. The result then waits in your refrigerator or freezer until you are ready for it.

Before beginning, it will help if you try to visualize what is going to happen. First, you will prepare a simple dough of flour and water. After a short rest, this will be rolled out and used to wrap up a square of kneaded, softened butter. This "package" will again be rolled out, folded triple, and then rolled and tripled 5 more times. These 6 "turns" create hundreds of alternating butter and flour layers. The pastry rises so spectacularly because moisture and handling activate the gluten, the elastic web of protein that makes bread dough stretchy, but makes pastry dough tough if it isn't outwitted. The puff pastry dough is refrigerated after every turn in order to allow the gluten to relax. The chilling also keeps the butter from melting—an occurrence that would ruin the pastry. The refrigerated resting periods should be at least an hour long, but can be much longer, and this is where you gain a measure of flexibility.

In these modern times, it is also possible to buy frozen prepared puff pastry. We feel that it's good to know how to make your own, but once you have gotten the hang of making it, this frozen pastry can be a time-saver, *if* you can find a reliable brand. (Pepperidge Farm and DuFour make excellent frozen puff pastry.) Read the list of ingredients; if it includes anything but flour, butter, salt, and water, you will probably be disappointed. (We have even seen some brands that contain no butter at all.) After you have located a reputable brand, defrost and prepare it according to the directions on the package.

PIECRUST

2½ cups unbleached all-purpose flour
2 teaspoons sugar
1 teaspoon salt
8 tablespoons (1 stick) unsalted butter, chilled
6 tablespoons solid vegetable shortening, chilled
5 to 6 tablespoons ice water, as needed

1. Sift the flour, sugar, and salt into a mixing bowl. Add the chilled butter and shortening. Working quickly and using your fingertips or a pastry blender, rub or cut the fat into the dry ingredients until the mixture resembles coarse meal.

2. Sprinkle on the ice water, 2 to 3 tablespoons at a time, and toss with a fork. Turn the dough out onto your work surface and, using the heel of your hand, smear the dough away from you, about ¼ cup at a time. Scrape it up into a ball and wrap in wax paper. Chill in the refrigerator for 2 hours.

3. Remove the dough from the refrigerator and roll it out to ¼-inch thickness on a floured work surface. For a single-crust pie, line a 9-inch pie plate with half of the dough and crimp the edges. Wrap the remaining dough and refrigerate or freeze it. For a double-crust pie, line a 9-inch pie plate with half of the dough and reserve the other half for the top of the pie.

4. To prebake, preheat the oven to 425°F.

5. Line the dough in the pie plate with aluminum foil and fill with beans or rice to weight it. Bake for 8 minutes, then remove the beans and lining. Prick the bottom of the dough with a fork and return the pie plate to the oven until the crust is golden brown, 10 to 13 minutes longer.

One 9-inch double crust, or two 9-inch single crusts

SWEET BUTTERY TART CRUST

1⅔ cups unbleached all-purpose flour
¼ cup very fine sugar
½ teaspoon salt
10 tablespoons (1¼ sticks) unsalted butter, chilled
2 egg yolks
1 teaspoon vanilla extract
2 teaspoons cold water

1. Sift the flour, sugar, and salt into a mixing bowl. Cut the chilled butter into pieces into the bowl. Using your fingertips, rapidly rub the butter and dry ingredients together until the mixture resembles coarse meal. Be careful to use only your fingertips as your palms will warm the dough.

FLAVORED MAYONNAISES

Homemade Mayonnaise, combined with other ingredients and blended in the food processor, yields variations of dressings and spreads limited only by your imagination. Some favorites:

- ♥ ANCHOVY MAYONNAISE: 1 cup Homemade Mayonnaise, 1 tablespoon anchovy paste (or more or less to taste).
- ♥ CHUTNEY MAYONNAISE: 1 cup Homemade Mayonnaise, ¼ cup mango chutney.
- ♥ CILANTRO MAYONNAISE: 1 cup Homemade Mayonnaise, prepared with lime juice instead of lemon, 1 loosely packed cup of fresh cilantro leaves, rinsed and patted dry.
- ♥ PESTO MAYONNAISE: 1 cup Homemade Mayonnaise, ½ cup Pesto (page 99) completed through the addition of the cheeses.

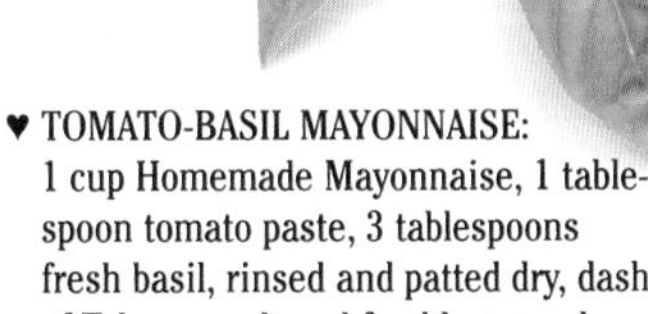

- ♥ TOMATO-BASIL MAYONNAISE: 1 cup Homemade Mayonnaise, 1 tablespoon tomato paste, 3 tablespoons fresh basil, rinsed and patted dry, dash of Tabasco, salt and freshly ground black pepper taste.
- ♥ MINT AND YOGURT MAYONNAISE: 1 cup Homemade Mayonnaise, ½ cup plain yogurt, 1 cup fresh mint leaves, rinsed, patted dry, and chopped, 1 to 2 tablespoons fresh lemon juice (stirred into the mixture after processing).
- ♥ APPLE-HORSERADISH MAYONNAISE: 1 cup Homemade Mayonnaise, ¾ medium-size tart red apple (unpeeled), cored and sliced thinly (then halve the slices), 1½ tablespoons finely minced yellow onion, ¼ cup drained prepared horseradish, 1 tablespoon fresh lemon juice, pinch of white pepper, and ¼ cup chopped fresh dill (optional).

Once cool, Sweet Buttery Tart Crust is ready to be filled.

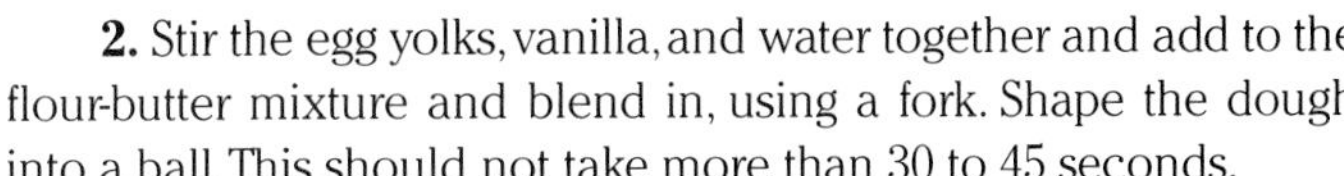

2. Stir the egg yolks, vanilla, and water together and add to the flour-butter mixture and blend in, using a fork. Shape the dough into a ball. This should not take more than 30 to 45 seconds.

3. Place the ball of dough on a pastry board. With the heel of your hand, smear about ¼ cup of the dough away from you into a 6- to 8-inch smear; repeat until all the dough has been smeared. Scrape the dough together; re-form into a ball, wrap in wax paper, and chill for 2 to 3 hours.

4. Roll out the dough between 2 sheets of wax paper (or use a floured pastry cloth and floured stockinette on your rolling pin) into a round large enough to line your pan. Work quickly, as the dough can become sticky.

5. Line an 8- or 9-inch removable-bottom tart pan with the dough, fitting it loosely into the pan and pressing to fit the sides. Trim the edges ¾ inch outside the top of the pan, fold this edge over to the inside, and press into place with your fingers. Cover and chill.

6. Preheat the oven to 425°F.

7. Line the dough in the tart pan with a piece of aluminum foil or wax paper and weight it with beans or rice. Bake for 8 minutes. Remove the foil and beans. Prick the bottom of the dough with a fork in several places. For a partially baked shell, return to the oven for 3 to 4 minutes longer. For a fully baked shell, bake until the edges are a light brown, 8 to 10 minutes longer.

One 8-inch to 9-inch tart shell

HOMEMADE MAYONNAISE

Luscious and versatile; and ready in minutes. Use very high quality, fresh eggs.

2 egg yolks
1 whole egg
1 tablespoon Dijon mustard
Pinch of salt
Freshly ground black pepper, to taste
¼ cup fresh lemon juice
2 cups corn oil or other vegetable oil, or best-quality olive oil

1. Combine the egg yolks, whole egg, mustard, salt, freshly ground black pepper, and half of the lemon juice in a food processor. Process for 1 minute.

2. With the motor running, dribble in the oil in a slow steady stream. When you have added all the oil, shut the motor off and scrape down the sides of the bowl with a spatula.

3. Taste the mayonnaise. Correct the seasoning if necessary; if you are using vegetable oil, you will probably need the remaining lemon juice. Scrape the mayonnaise into a storage container, cover, and refrigerate until ready to use. The mayonnaise will keep safely, if refrigerated, for at least 5 days. Let it return to room temperature before stirring and using.

3 cups

CREME FRAICHE

1 cup heavy cream (not ultra-pasteurized)
1 cup sour cream

1. Whisk the heavy cream and sour cream together in a bowl. Cover loosely with plastic wrap and let stand in the kitchen or other reasonably warm spot overnight, or until thickened. In cold weather this may take as long as 24 hours.

2. Cover and refrigerate for at least 4 hours, after which the crème fraîche will be quite thick. The tart flavor will continue to develop as the crème fraîche sits in the refrigerator.

2 cups

CREME FRAICHE

This cultured heavy cream thickens and develops a delicate sour taste as it sits. Spoon it over fruit desserts and fresh berries, with which its tart flavor is delicious. Use it to add body and richness to sauces. Since it can be boiled without fear of separation, it is more versatile than sour cream. Stir a few spoonfuls into butter-warmed vegetables for a simple sauce. Whisk a dollop into a salad dressing for extra thickness. Since crème fraîche keeps under refrigeration for at least two weeks, we are seldom without some in our kitchen.

HOLLANDAISE SAUCE

3 egg yolks
1 tablespoon fresh lemon juice, or to taste
Pinch of salt
1 cup (2 sticks) unsalted butter, melted
White pepper, to taste

1. Whisk the egg yolks and 1 tablespoon of the lemon juice together in a small heavy saucepan or the top of a double boiler. Add a pinch of salt and whisk until the sauce is thick and creamy.

2. Set the pan over very low heat, or over simmering water in a double boiler, and begin whisking immediately. Continue to whisk until the egg mixture just begins to thicken: The wires of the whisk will begin to leave "tracks" through which you can see the bottom of the pan.

3. Remove the pan from the heat and begin to dribble in the melted butter, whisking constantly. Incorporate all the butter, but leave the white residue behind.

4. Add white pepper and a spoonful or two of additional lemon juice if you like. The sauce will keep, covered, in a warm (not hot) place for at least 30 minutes.

About 1½ cups

BEARNAISE SAUCE

Sherry vinegar makes this hearty butter-based sauce even better. Try it on beef, lamb, or other meat.

from THE SILVER PALATE NOTEBOOK

When planning a party, don't stretch yourself too thin by inviting more guests than you honestly feel comfortable entertaining, or testing out a recipe you've never tried before.

When you invite your guests—whether by mail, phone, or e-mail—be specific about the details. Let them know when the party begins, the occasion, the dress, the type of food you'll be serving, something about the other guests invited, and how long the festivities are expected to last. Nothing is more dismaying than arriving at a party expecting a sit-down dinner and being served only cheeses and nuts. If you think of the details ahead of time and let your guests know what's in store, everyone will have more fun.

"True life is lived when tiny changes occur."

—LEO TOLSTOY

½ cup sherry vinegar or white wine vinegar
¼ cup dry white vermouth
1 tablespoon finely chopped shallot
½ teaspoon dried tarragon
Pinch of salt
3 egg yolks
1 cup (2 sticks) unsalted butter, melted

1. Combine the vinegar, vermouth, shallot, tarragon, and salt in a small heavy saucepan over medium heat. Bring to a boil, lower the heat, and simmer until reduced to a few spoonfuls. Cool to room temperature.

2. Strain the cooled mixture into another small heavy saucepan, or the top of a double boiler, and whisk in the egg yolks. Beat until thick and creamy.

3. Set the pan over very low heat, or over simmering water in a double boiler, and begin whisking immediately. Continue to whisk until the egg mixture just begins to thicken; the surest sign of this is that the wires of the whisk will begin to leave "tracks" through which you can see the bottom of the pan.

4. Remove the pan from the heat and begin to dribble in the melted butter, whisking constantly. Incorporate all the butter, but leave the milky residue behind.

5. Taste, and correct the seasoning; add a few more drops of vinegar if you like. Set the sauce aside, covered, in a warm (not hot) place. The sauce will keep for at least 30 minutes.

About 1½ cups

BECHAMEL SAUCE

4 tablespoons (½ stick) unsalted butter
6 tablespoons unbleached all-purpose flour
2 cups milk
Salt, to taste
Freshly ground black pepper, to taste
Freshly grated nutmeg, to taste

1. Melt the butter in a heavy saucepan over low heat. Sprinkle in the flour and cook gently, stirring almost constantly, for 5 minutes. Do not let the flour and butter brown at all.

2. Meanwhile, bring the milk to a boil. When the milk reaches a boil, remove the butter and flour mixture from the heat and pour in the boiling milk all at once. As the mixture boils and bubbles, beat it vigorously with a wire whisk.

3. When the bubbling stops, return the pan to medium heat and bring the béchamel to a boil, stirring constantly for 5 minutes. Season with the salt, pepper, and nutmeg. Use at once, or scrape into a bowl, cover, and refrigerate.

2 cups thick sauce

Note: For thinner sauce, use 3 tablespoons butter and ¼ cup all-purpose flour with the same amount of milk.

BEEF STOCK

4 pounds meaty beef bones (such as shank or neckbones)
1 calf's foot, cleaned and split (see Note)
⅓ cup vegetable oil
4 cups finely chopped yellow onions
2 leeks, white part only, well rinsed and sliced
3 cups chopped peeled carrots
2 small or 1 medium parsnip, peeled and chopped
1½ tablespoons dried thyme
4 bay leaves
6 whole cloves
12 black peppercorns
6 parsley sprigs
1 tablespoon salt
1 can (6 ounces) tomato paste
Water, as needed

1. Preheat the oven to 400°F.

2. Spread the beef bones and calf's foot in a baking pan just large enough to hold the meat in a single layer. Bake until the meats are very brown, 1½ hours. Turn the pieces occasionally and drain the rendered fat as necessary.

3. Heat the oil in a large pot. Add the onions, leeks, carrots, and parsnips and cook over high heat, stirring often, until well browned, about 25 minutes.

4. Add the browned bones and calf's foot to the vegetables, along with the remaining ingredients.

5. Pour 1 cup water into the pan in which the meats were browned and set over high heat. Stir and scrape up any caramelized particles from the bottom and sides. Pour the liquid into the pot. Add additional water to cover the ingredients by 2 inches, and set the pot over medium heat. When the stock reaches a boil, skim, reduce the heat so the liquid simmers, partially cover, and simmer for 4 hours. Skim occasionally.

6. Strain out and discard the solids. Refrigerate the stock, or chill and then freeze. Before using the refrigerated stock or freezing chilled stock, remove any fat that has solidified on top.

2 to 3 quarts

Note: If calf's foot is unavailable, ask your butcher for recommendations.

CHICKEN STOCK

Homemade chicken stock is an indispensable base for soups and sauces; its richness and freshness put it head and shoulders above canned. Refrigerate it if you're using it within a few days, or stash it in the freezer—frozen assets of the very best kind.

BARBECUING

Barbecue now knows no season. Cooking over coals just makes food taste great, and if time is taken for marinating or enhancing the meat, fish, or poultry with a sauce or chutney, simplicity becomes sublime.

Mastering the age-old technique of barbecuing is not complicated, but it does require some attention to detail. Remember, no rushing allowed. The slower your timing when you cook, the juicier, more tender, and tastier the results will be.

♥ Layer the charcoal wider than the size of the food that you are grilling.

♥ Coals take 30 to 45 minutes to achieve the gray ash coating and glowing red inside that is ideal for grilling. Smoking should be done during the last 15 to 20 minutes of cooking.

♥ Fruitwood (peach, apple, cherry, pear, apricot, citrus) and even oak, maple, hickory, and sprigs of pine can be used to add an exciting dimension to your grilling. For a wonderful flavor, soak the leaves and branches in water before setting them over the fire so that you will get smoke, not flames. Try this easy smoking technique also with fresh or dried juniper berries, whole sweet spices such as cinnamon, cloves, nutmeg, and orange or lemon peel. Placing a bundle of fresh herbs over the coals produces a great flavor, too.

♥ Marinating adds flavor and breaks down any toughness to make meats tender.

♥ Olive oil in a marinade ensures that the meat won't stick to the grill. If you're not marinating, brush the oil lightly over the meat before taking it to the grill.

♥ We like to precook many foods before grilling. It ensures that they will not dry out during a lengthy time over the coals but will still have the wonderful aroma and flavor that only outdoor grilling gives. This is especially true of chicken, spareribs, and whole roasts. We always allow at least 30 minutes of cooking time for basting and cooking over the coals.

"Every morning must start from scratch, with nothing on the stoves—that is cuisine."

—FERNAND POINT

¼ cup vegetable cooking oil
3 pounds (more or less) chicken necks and backs
4 cups chopped yellow onions
2 cups chopped peeled carrots
Small handful of parsley sprigs
2 cans (1 quart, 14 ounces each) chicken broth
Water, as needed
1 tablespoon dried thyme
4 bay leaves

1. Pour the oil into a large heavy pot and heat over medium-high heat until almost smoking. Pat the chicken parts dry with paper towels and drop into the hot oil. Toss and turn them until well browned, about 15 minutes.

2. Add the chopped onions and carrots and continue to cook, stirring frequently, until the vegetables are beginning to brown lightly and are losing their crunch.

3. Add the remaining ingredients, using enough water to cover the solids by 2 inches, and bring the stock to a boil. Boil vigorously for 15 minutes, skimming off all the scum. Reduce the heat, cover, and simmer briskly for 2 hours, skimming occasionally if necessary.

4. Cool the stock slightly, then pour it through a strainer set over a bowl, pressing hard on the vegetables and chicken parts with the back of a spoon to extract as much flavor as possible.

5. Cover the stock and refrigerate overnight. Skim any congealed fat from the stock before using. Transfer the defatted stock to storage containers, label, and freeze.

3 quarts

FISH STOCK

4 tablespoons (½ stick) unsalted butter
¾ cup peeled and chopped carrots
2 cups finely chopped yellow onions
1 cup chopped celery
1 cup chopped mushrooms (stems are fine to use)
10 cups water, or as needed
2 cups dry white wine
Pinch of salt (optional)
12 white peppercorns
6 parsley sprigs
1 bay leaf
1 teaspoon dried thyme
Bones and heads of 6 or 7 white-fleshed nonoily fish (such as flounder or sole), viscera and gills removed (see Note)

1. Melt the butter in a 4-quart soup pot. Add the carrots, onions, celery, and mushrooms and cook, covered, over low heat, stirring occasionally, until the vegetables are tender and lightly colored, 25 to 30 minutes.

2. Add the remaining ingredients, using enough water to cover the solids, and bring slowly to a boil. Reduce the heat and simmer, partially covered, for 30 minutes, no longer.

3. Remove the stock from the heat and cool. Pour through a cheesecloth-lined strainer set over a large bowl, and discard the solids.

4. Taste the stock. If it seems to lack intensity, return it to the pot and boil for another 15 to 20 minutes.

5. Store the stock, covered, in the refrigerator. Remove any solid fat that rises to the surface before serving or freezing.

2 to 3 quarts

Note: Order the bones from your fish dealer and tell him you are using them for stock. He will do the rest.

QUICK TOMATO SAUCE

½ cup best-quality olive oil
3 cups finely chopped yellow onions
2 medium-size carrots, peeled and finely chopped
2 cans (28 ounces each) Italian plum tomatoes in tomato purée
1 tablespoon dried basil
1 teaspoon dried thyme
1 teaspoon salt
⅛ teaspoon cayenne pepper
1 bay leaf
1 cup finely chopped fresh Italian (flat-leaf) parsley
4 garlic cloves, peeled and finely chopped
1 tablespoon balsamic or other mild vinegar (optional)

1. Heat the oil in a heavy pot over low heat. Add the onions and carrots and cook, covered, until the vegetables are tender, about 25 minutes.

2. Add the tomatoes, basil, thyme, salt, cayenne pepper, and bay leaf. Cook over medium heat, stirring occasionally, for 30 minutes.

3. Remove the bay leaf and carefully transfer the tomato mixture to a food processor, or use a food mill fitted with a medium disc, and purée.

4. Return the sauce to the pot and set the pot over medium heat. Add the parsley and garlic and cook for another 5 minutes.

5. Taste and correct the seasoning. Add the balsamic vinegar if the sauce seems to lack intensity. Serve immediately, or cool to room temperature, cover, and refrigerate or freeze.

About 2 quarts

"If there is one thing in particular that ruffles my usually smooth temper, it is that awful habit my husband has of bringing unexpected friends to lunch, breakfast, dinner, tea or supper. No one can be more happy [than I] to see my friends, but I don't like to be taken unawares. Let me know."

—*THE LADY'S HOME COMPANION*, 1851

This sauce is quick, easy, and fresh-tasting. Since it's made from canned tomatoes, it can be available year-round. Keep some on hand in the freezer for use in lasagna and eggplant Parmigiana, or for a quick dish of spaghetti. Add fresh seafood, canned tuna, or crisp-cooked vegetables (about 1 cup for every 3 cups of sauce) to improvise your own sauce; the possibilities are endless.

SPICY TOMATO SAUCE

Another tomato sauce, this one made with fresh tomatoes and long simmered to bring out the flavors of the herbs. We use lots of pepper and serve this sauce on gnocchi, or use it when making lasagna or Eggplant Parmigiana (page 204).

½ cup best-quality olive oil
2 cups finely chopped yellow onions
4 pounds ripe plum or other meaty tomatoes, skinned and seeded
1 can (6 ounces) tomato paste
2 tablespoons minced fresh basil
½ teaspoon dried oregano
1 teaspoon salt
1 tablespoon freshly ground black pepper
4 cups water
5 garlic cloves, peeled and finely minced
½ cup finely chopped fresh Italian (flat-leaf) parsley

1. Heat the olive oil in a large deep pot over low heat. Add the onions and cook, covered, until tender and lightly colored, about 25 minutes.

2. Add the tomatoes, tomato paste, basil, oregano, salt, and pepper. Simmer for 10 minutes, stirring occasionally.

3. Add the water and cook very slowly, uncovered, for 3 hours.

4. Stir in the garlic and parsley and simmer for another 5 minutes.

5. Taste and correct the seasoning. Use immediately, or cool to room temperature before covering. Refrigerate or freeze.

About 3 quarts

SAFFRON RICE

Follow the method for Parsleyed Rice, adding a few threads of saffron as you bring the water to the boil. Reduce the butter by half, and omit the parsley. Add a handful of fresh or frozen peas, if you like.

PARSLEYED RICE

We prefer untreated long-grain rice, but you can use converted rice if you like, following package directions.

4 cups water or Chicken Stock (page 416)
2 cups uncooked long-grain rice
1 tablespoon salt
8 tablespoons (1 stick) unsalted butter, cut into 8 pieces
1½ cups finely chopped fresh Italian (flat-leaf) parsley

1. Bring the water or stock to a boil in a heavy pan. Stir in the rice and salt, return to a boil, reduce the heat to low, and cover tightly. Let the rice cook, undisturbed, for 25 minutes.

2. Uncover the pan, add the butter and parsley (do not stir), and cover. Remove the pan from the heat and let stand for 5 minutes.

3. Uncover the pan, toss the rice with a fork to mix in the butter and parsley, and serve immediately.

6 cups cooked rice, 6 to 8 portions

NUTTED WILD RICE

1 cup (½ pound) raw wild rice
5½ cups defatted Chicken Stock (page 416) or water
1 cup shelled pecan halves
1 cup yellow raisins
Grated zest of 1 large orange
¼ cup chopped fresh mint
4 scallions (green onions), well rinsed and thinly sliced
¼ cup olive oil
⅓ cup fresh orange juice
1½ teaspoons salt, or to taste
Freshly ground black pepper, to taste

1. Put the rice in a strainer and run cold water over it; rinse thoroughly.

2. Place the rice in a medium-size heavy saucepan. Add the stock or water and bring to a rapid boil. Adjust the heat to a gentle simmer and cook, uncovered, for 45 minutes. After 30 minutes check for doneness; the rice should not be too soft. Place a thin towel inside a colander and turn the rice into the colander and drain. Transfer the drained rice to a bowl.

3. Add the remaining ingredients to the rice and toss gently. Adjust the seasonings and let the mixture stand for 2 hours to allow the flavors to develop. Serve at room temperature.

6 portions

HUMMUS BI TAHINI

Serve this Middle Eastern chickpea and sesame spread as a dip with torn pieces of hot pita bread or as a component of a cold lunch or appetizer plate.

WILD RICE

Wild rice is one of North America's most distinguished native foods. It grows in the shallow, muddy lakes and lowland waterways of Minnesota and Wisconsin, among other places. The Native Americans originally living in those areas called it *menomin* and gathered it into canoes piloted through still water.

Wild rice has slender ash-brown to blackish grains and a distinctive nutty taste. The best grades are usually those with the longer, darker grains. It has been said that there is nothing wilder than wild rice, and we agree. We like to use this special rice alone, though higher prices (and price increases) have challenged us to develop recipes using it with wheat and other kinds of rices.

VERSATILE VINEGAR

Some interesting uses for vinegars include these:

- Moisten and fluff a chocolate cake by adding 1 tablespoon vinegar to the baking soda.
- If something is too sweet, add 1 tablespoon cider vinegar.
- Marinate and tenderize meats in vinegar.
- Add 1 tablespoon vinegar to poaching eggs to make the whites retain their shape.
- Add vinegar to the cooking water of artichokes and red vegetables to keep them from discoloring.
- A touch of vinegar will disguise the fact that you've reduced the salt in a recipe.
- Put vinegar on sunburn to take the sting away.

"Tomorrow is the most important thing in life, comes in to us at midnight very clean. It's perfect when it arrives and puts itself in our hands and hopes we've learned something from yesterday."

—JOHN WAYNE

4 cups (about 2½ cans) garbanzos (chickpeas), drained
½ cup tahini (sesame paste) (see Note)
⅓ cup warm water
⅓ cup best-quality olive oil
Juice of 2 or 3 lemons, to taste
4 or more garlic cloves, to taste
1½ teaspoons salt, or to taste
2 teaspoons ground cumin
Freshly ground black pepper, to taste

1. Combine the garbanzos, tahini, warm water, olive oil, and juice of 1 lemon in a food processor. Process until smooth and creamy, pausing once or twice to scrape down the sides of the bowl with a spatula.

2. Add the garlic, salt, cumin, and pepper, and process to blend. Taste and correct the seasoning if necessary. Add more lemon juice to taste. Scrape into a storage container, cover, and refrigerate until ready to use.

1 quart

Note: Available at specialty food shops.

PECAN CREAM CHEESE

½ cup shelled pecans
8 ounces cream cheese, at room temperature

1. Chop the pecans coarsely in a food processor.

2. Add the cream cheese and process until smooth. Scrape out with a rubber spatula, cover, and refrigerate until ready to use.

1 cup

RED CURRANT GLAZE

3 tablespoons red currant jelly
1 tablespoon kirsch

Whisk the jelly and kirsch together in a small saucepan over medium heat until smooth. Use the glaze while warm.

About ¼ cup

METRIC CONVERSION CHARTS

TABLESPOONS AND OUNCES — GRAMS

TABLESPOONS AND OUNCES *(U.S. Customary System)*	GRAMS *(Metric System)*
1 pinch = less than ⅛ teaspoon (dry)	0.5 grams
1 dash = 3 drops to ¼ teaspoon (liquid)	1.25 grams
1 teaspoon (liquid)	5.0 grams
3 teaspoons = 1 tablespoon = ½ ounce	14.3 grams
2 tablespoons = 1 ounce	28.35 grams
4 tablespoons = 2 ounces = ¼ cup	56.7 grams
8 tablespoons = 4 ounces = ½ cup (1 stick of butter)	113.4 grams
8 tablespoons (flour) = about 2 ounces	72.0 grams
16 tablespoons = 8 ounces = 1 cup = ½ pound	226.8 grams
32 tablespoons = 16 ounces = 2 cups = 1 pound	453.6 grams or 0.4536 kilogram
64 tablespoons = 32 ounces = 1 quart = 2 pounds	907.0 grams or 0.907 kilogram
1 quart = (roughly 1 liter)	

TEMPERATURES: °FAHRENHEIT (F) TO °CELSIUS (C)

−10°F = −23.3°C (freezer storage)
0°F = −17.7°C
32°F = 0°C (water freezes)
50°F = 10°C
68°F = 20°C (room temperature)
100°F = 37.7°C
150°F = 65.5°C
205°F = 96.1°C (water simmers)
212°F = 100°C (water boils)

300°F = 148.8°C
325°F = 162.8°C
350°F = 177°C (baking)
375°F = 190.5°C
400°F = 204.4°C (hot oven)
425°F = 218.3°C
450°F = 232°C (very hot oven)
475°F = 246.1°C
500°F = 260°C (broiling)

CONVERSION FACTORS

ounces to grams: multiply ounce figure by 28.3 to get number of grams

grams to ounces: multiply gram figure by 0.0353 to get number of ounces

pounds to grams: multiply pound figure by 453.59 to get number of grams

pounds to kilograms: multiply pound figure by 0.45 to get number of kilograms

ounces to milliliters: multiply ounce figure by 30 to get number of milliliters

cups to liters: multiply cup figure by 0.24 to get number of liters

Fahrenheit to Celsius: subtract 32 from the Fahrenheit figure, multiply by 5, then divide by 9 to get Celsius figure

Celsius to Fahrenheit: multiply Celsius figure by 9, divide by 5, then add 32 to get Fahrenheit figure

inches to centimeters: multiply inch figure by 2.54 to get number of centimeters

centimeters to inches: multiply centimeter figure by 0.39 to get number of inches

INDEX

Page numbers in *italic* refer to illustrations.

A

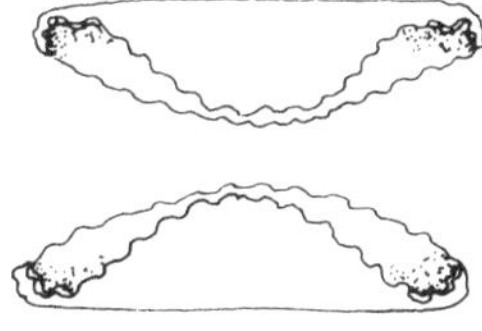

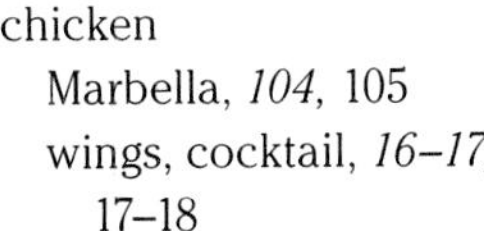

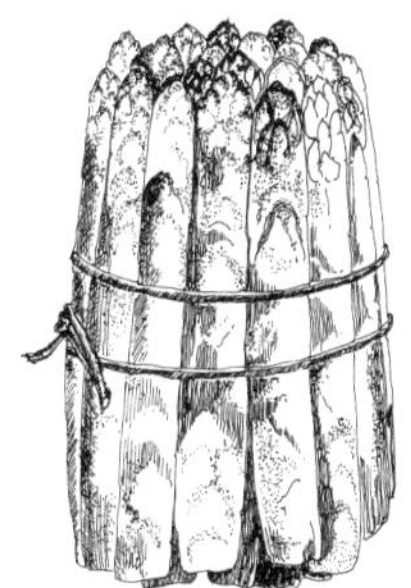

B

BRIE BRIE BRIE
BRIE

C

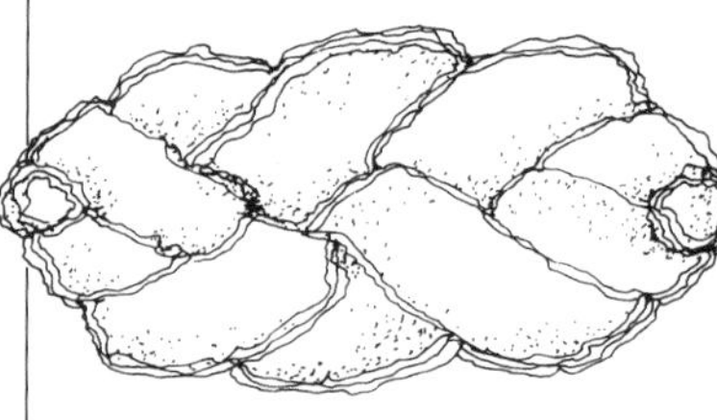

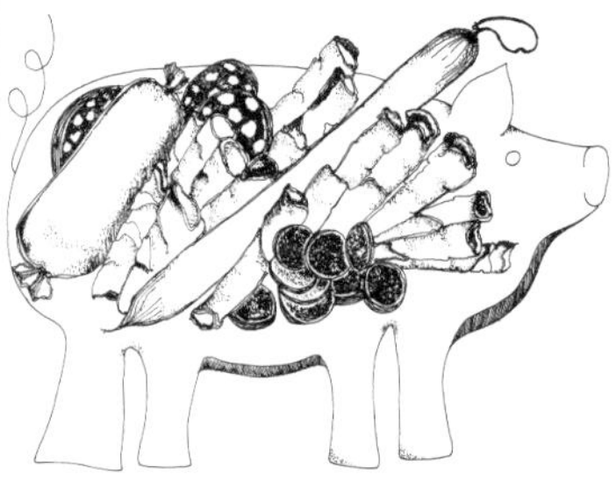

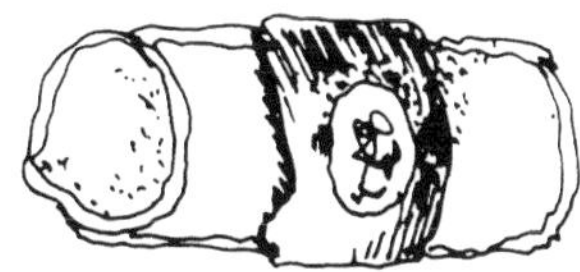

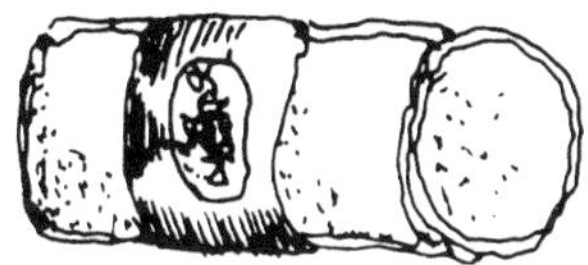

Stock

D

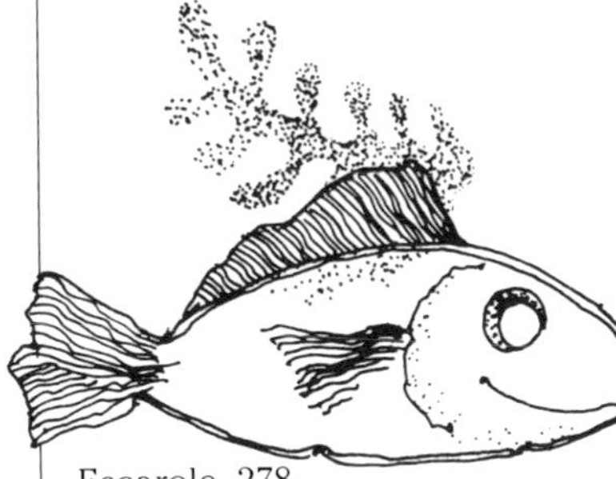

F

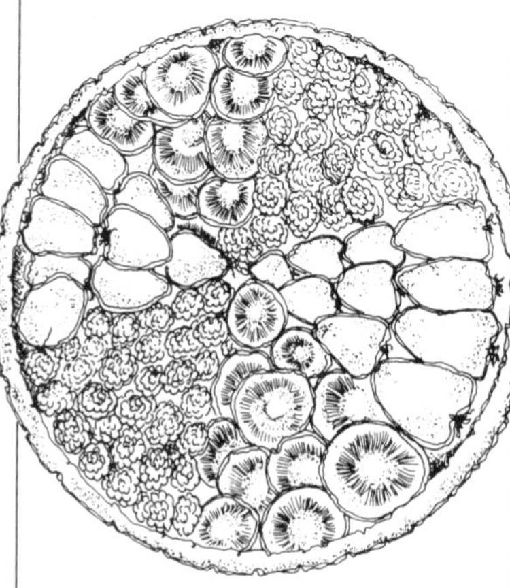

G

H

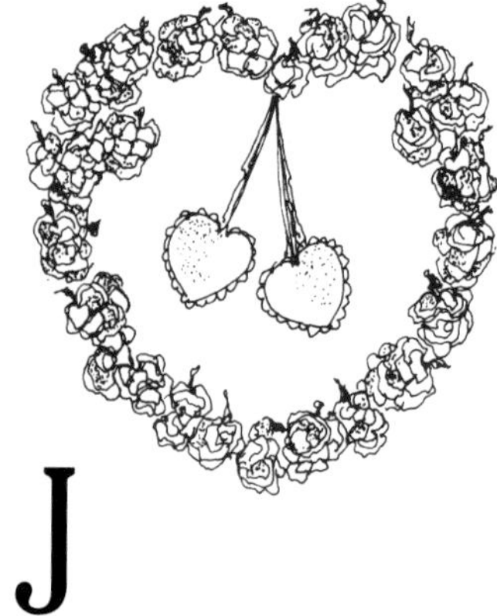

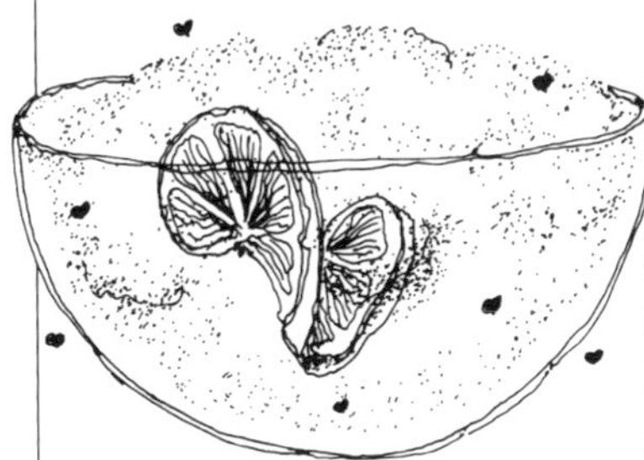

M

N

O

P

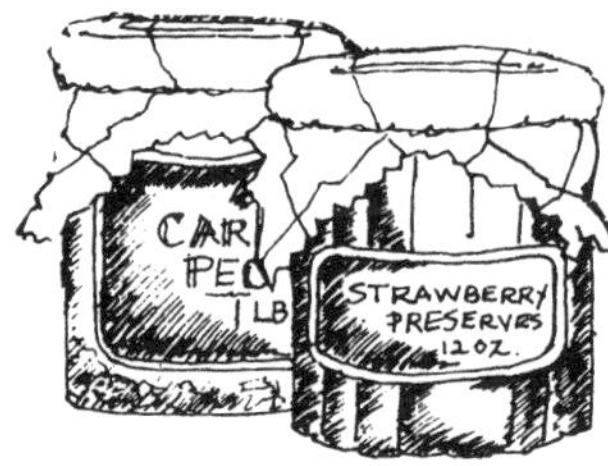

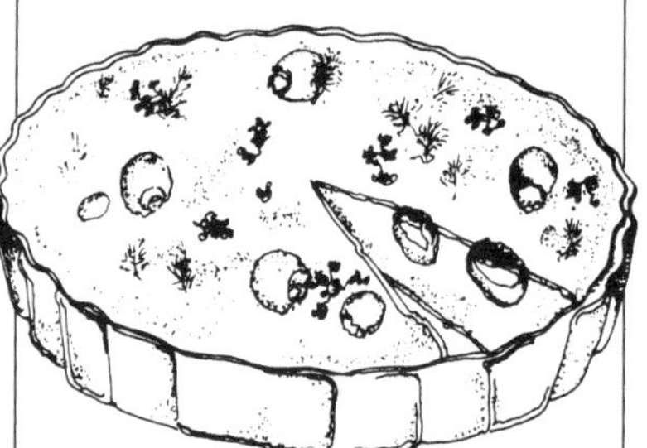

R

S

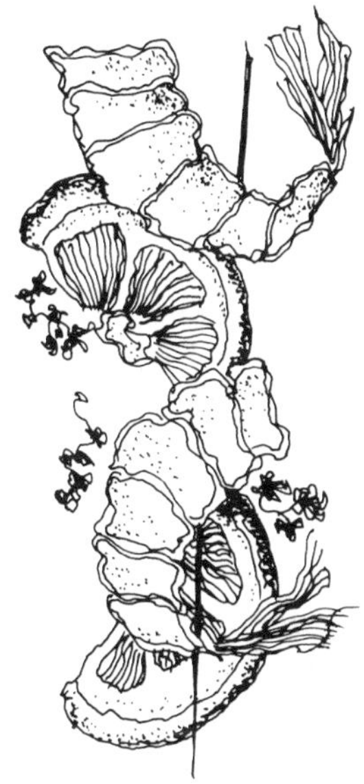

T

V

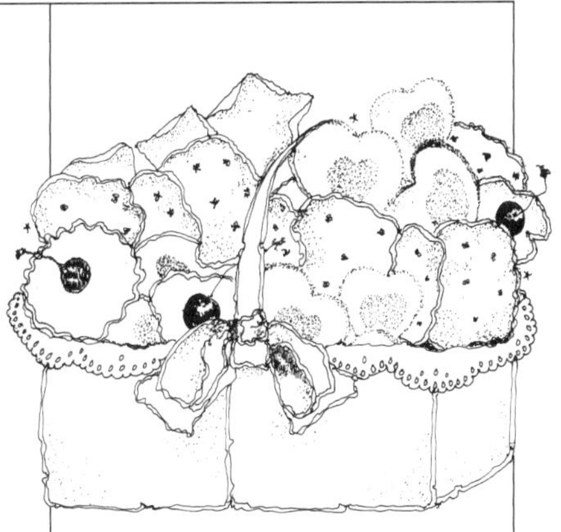

Y

Z

RECIPE NOTES

RECIPE NOTES